Ann Bessell

APPROACHES
TO PSYCHOLOGY

APPROACHES TO PSYCHOLOGY

EDITORS
John Medcof and John Roth

CONTRIBUTING AUTHORS
Gordon R. Emslie, William E. Glassman,
Paul H. Hirschorn, Judith Kelly Waalen

*The editors and contributing authors teach psychology
at Ryerson Polytechnical Institute, Toronto*

Open University Press

Milton Keynes

Open University Press
12 Cofferidge Close
Stony Stratford
Milton Keynes MK11 1BY
England

First Published in this edition 1979
Reprinted 1984, 1986, 1988, 1989

British Library Cataloguing in Publication Data

Approaches to psychology.
  1. Psychology
  I. Medcof, John W
  150   BF121

    ISBN 0–335–00265–X

Printed in Great Britain by J W Arrowsmith Ltd. Bristol

CONTENTS

PREFACE

Traditionally, a textbook designed for an introductory course presents a survey of the accumulated knowledge of its discipline. Psychology is no exception to this rule. The traditional introductory psychology work presents an overview of the science, touching on all major areas and reporting the most important research findings. This presentation is well suited to the student whose major field of study is psychology, and we, the authors of *Approaches to Psychology*, cut our own psychological teeth on such texts when we were students. However, when it came to teaching one-semester introductory psychology courses to students in business, technology, home economics, secretarial science, fashion designing, and numerous other areas at Ryerson Polytechnical Institute in Toronto, we found that the books which had served us so well as students did not meet our needs as instructors.

As we discussed the ideal book for our own introductory courses, three things became apparent.

First, traditional survey texts were too long; it was impossible to cover an appreciable portion of the material in a single semester, and students resented buying expensive, bulky tomes, whose contents went largely unread.

Second, students studying psychology as an adjunct to their professional fields, or as a liberal-arts option, were not interested in material dealing with rats and other non-human organisms. To them, psychology meant the study of human behaviour, and that is what they wished to learn.

Third, survey texts appear to the newcomer to the field to be a disjointed collection of conflicting theories and findings. They give the student the impression that psychologists cannot make up their minds.

These considerations dictated the goals of *Approaches to Psychology*: brevity; a stress on human behaviour; and coherence. To achieve brevity we decided to confine ourselves to five major viewpoints, the psychobiological approach to behaviour, behaviourism, the cognitive approach, psychoanalysis and humanism. Among them, we believe, these five approaches account for a large proportion of psychology's major insights. It turned out that the second goal, stressing human behaviour, placed very few limitations on our choice of material. Psychology is defined as a science dealing with the behaviour of living organisms, but it always has focussed primarily on human beings.

If the second goal was the easiest to achieve, the third goal, coherence, was the most difficult. Eventually we realized that if the book were to be anything more than just another psychological grab bag, we needed to step back and take a searching look at the process of arriving at knowledge about human behaviour. Social sciences involve an organism studying itself. This reflexive mode is especially characteristic of psychology, and the structure of the discipline cannot be uncovered without a conscious and deliberate effort to step back and view the process from afar. It was during this exercise that we realized how important it was to stress the basic assumptions of the different approaches. These assumptions dictate the nature of the data-gathering process, the concepts and the form of the theory, but they often are not stated explicitly by the proponents of approaches, who tend to view them as self-evident truths. It also was brought home to us that there is a strong subjective aspect to any scientific theory; it represents the scientist's perceptual space, or his personal view of the world. Like all perceptions, theories involve an organizational process, and serve to make the world understandable and predictable.

Both the structure and the contents of this book represent an attempt to communicate these insights to the reader. The first chapter, for instance, is both a discussion of perception, and an exposition of the principles that govern the structure of the book. In Chapter 1 it is pointed out that each of the five approaches to psychology represents a viewpoint or perception of behaviour. As such, the question of whether or not a particular approach is "correct" is inappropriate. The value of perception lies not in a nebulous concept of correctness, but in its value as a tool for understanding and problem-solving. Freed from the fixation of searching for a single "truth," it becomes apparent that the different approaches are not antagonistic but complementary; each offers its own unique insights into human behaviour.

Chapter 2 presents the common ground between the approaches. All are scientific attempts to grapple with human behaviour and are based on the general processes of scientific inquiry, despite wide differences in the notion of what constitutes admissible data, and in the techniques used to collect and examine that data.

Chapters 3 through 7 present the five approaches that form the core of this book. Since each approach is influenced by the time and society it sprang from, each chapter discusses the historical context of the ideas it contains. Each approach also involves self-imposed limitations, governed largely by the particular aspect of human behaviour that is the focus of interest, and by the basic assumptions that underlie the approach. Freud, for instance, developed his theory in early twentieth century Vienna, and brought to the task a medical background and clinical interests. His insights reflect the male-dominated society of the time, his assumptions about the biological basis of human drives, and his focus on psychopathology. By stressing the nature of the limitations and assumptions inherent in the approaches, the authors explain how each approach acquired its distinctive characteristics.

In Chapter 8 the use of each of the approaches in psychotherapy is discussed. The different assumptions that are made about human nature and human behaviour lead to different conceptions of normal and abnormal behaviour, and to varied therapeutic techniques. Chapter 8 demonstrates how all five viewpoints can co-exist in applications within the same field.

Like the first chapter, the final chapter of the book serves to tie together the content in a coherent and unified structure. Chapter 9 does this by reiterating the point that the approaches are perceptual frameworks. But the final chapter goes further by looking on the consequences when scientific theories become part of the ideology that guides a society. The radically different views of destructive aggression and sex-role development that result from embracing each of the five approaches are considered as examples of the way in which dominant scientific theories can shape societies. Dealing with controversial social issues is an exercise in problem solving, and the importance of flexibility and of having alternative perceptual schemes available becomes apparent once again.

Finally, we wish to thank our colleagues and the students at Ryerson. Their comments, suggestions and criticisms have done much to impress upon us the folly of fixedness, and the insights that result from using varied perceptual frames.

The Authors

1

PROBLEMS AND PROGRESS OF PSYCHOLOGY
John Roth

Editor's Preface

What does psychology have to offer us? Why study psychology? Psychology offers us ways of viewing behaviour, particularly human behaviour, that make it understandable. A better understanding of behaviour makes it easier for us to predict how people, including ourselves, will act. It also improves our chances of controlling behaviour, so that our interactions with other people can be mutually satisfying and constructive, rather than destructive.

Chapters 3 to 7 present five different ways of viewing and understanding behaviour. The student may ask, "Why so many approaches? Isn't there one single, correct way of looking at behaviour? Which one of these five approaches is right?" To answer these questions, we need to consider what it means to "look at" something. Finding a way to look at behaviour is an exercise in problem solving. We need to consider how we solve problems and form explanations.

We especially need to understand the process of perceiving a problem and forming a solution when we study human behaviour, because we are engaged in behaving while we study behaviour. The study of behaviour is, itself, a form of behaviour. The scientist who is trying to understand human beings is, himself, part of the problem he is studying. This is why we need to step back and look at the process.

The first chapter in this book examines the nature of perception—how we "look at" things—and how we problem solve. When we become aware of something, is our awareness an accurate reflection of the object, out there in the outside world? How many "correct" ways are there of perceiving things? What is the connection between the way we perceive things, and the way in which we solve problems?

1

The answers to these questions show why the authors of this book decided to present five different approaches to psychology. Each approach is an individual viewpoint. Each is, in a sense, correct. Each is, equally, inadequate. Each approach provides its own unique insights into human behaviour. When he or she has mastered this book, the student will have a variety of strategies to form a meaningful view of human behaviour. When he or she has mastered this chapter, the student will understand why such a choice of strategies is necessary.

PROBLEMS AND PROGRESS OF PSYCHOLOGY

Introductory textbooks invariably point out that psychology is a young science, not yet one hundred years old. The study of behaviour, both in human beings and in other organisms, has a much longer history, of course, but psychology is defined as the *scientific* study of the behaviour of organisms. Usually we date the birth of this science from the establishment of Wilhelm Wundt's psychological laboratory in Leipzig in 1879.

From the beginning, psychology has included a variety of approaches which concentrate on particular aspects of human and animal functioning and rest on different assumptions. Such a situation is inevitable, considering the complexity of the task confronting the psychologist. The physicist and the chemist, by comparison, are dealing with relatively simple phenomena. The possible flight patterns of a rocket or the ways in which chemical compounds may interact are extremely limited compared to the infinitely varied behaviours of people.

There is another problem which is seldom encountered in the natural sciences, but which is especially troublesome in psychology. People tend to change their behaviour when they are observed. This responsiveness to observation, called *reactance,* obliges psychologists to resort to complicated, indirect, and sometimes devious, methods of observation. This problem is discussed in more detail in the next chapter.

The study of behaviour also poses special problems, because behaviour is the result both of factors operating within the person, and of the situation in which the person finds himself. You wake up one morning with a splitting headache, and discover the alarm clock did not ring. You are late for work. Racing down the expressway, trying to make up time, squinting painfully, you rear-end a car that changes lanes unexpectedly in front of you. Internal and external factors both had a hand in the accident. If your head had been throbbing less and your sight had been less blurred, you might have avoided the other car. If you were more philosophical about arriving late for work, you would not have been driving so quickly. These are some of the internal factors involved. On the other hand, if the alarm clock hadn't let you down or if the other driver had signalled his lane change, the accident would not have happened. These are external factors. Both internal and external factors need to be considered if a piece of behaviour is to be fully understood.

Because human behaviour is so complex, psychologists have to limit their areas of study and decide at an early stage what factors they will attend to. One of the earliest schools of psychology, Structuralism, chose to concentrate on the conscious experiences of the mind. Another school which dates back to the inception of psychology, Functionalism, was less interested in the contents of the mind, and more concerned with the question of how and why the mind worked. Yet another school, spearheaded by the American psychologist John Watson, felt that the most important aspect of human functioning was behaviour.

Today, few psychologists would describe themselves as belonging to a particular school. They usually classify themselves according to the fields of human behaviour in which they specialize. Clinical psychologists concentrate on the area of abnormal behaviour, for example. They provide therapy for people unable to cope with their life situations. Social psychologists focus on the behaviour of people in groups. Cognitive psychologists are concerned with thought and memory. Educational psychologists study learning in more formal, institutional settings. Many other areas have also been opened, and each one is distinguished by a focus on a particular aspect of human behaviour. The aspect focussed on, in turn, often dictates the methods of study that are used by the psychologist.

Another way of classifying psychologists is in terms of the approaches that they use. There are certain similarities between these approaches and the schools that we discussed earlier. Five different approaches are discussed in this book, and the reader, as he progresses, will note that each approach makes its own assumptions, uses its own distinctive concepts, and often tends to focus on a particular aspect of human functioning. In some cases the approaches overlap with the fields of psychology mentioned earlier. Most psychoanalysts, for example, are clinical psychologists, though not all clinical psychologists are psychoanalysts.

When first introduced to different approaches the newcomer to the field often asks: "Well, which of these approaches is the correct one?" The question is understandable, but the answer must be that no approach embodies the entire truth—all represent, at the best, a partial truth. The ideal situation would be to have one theory capable of accounting for all types of behaviour in a few clear statements. Given the complexity of the subject, however, this is not likely to be attained in the foreseeable future. For now, the best strategy is to have available a variety of approaches, each offering its own unique insights and contributing to a larger understanding. Approaches are not competing ideologies, but complementary perspectives, each offering different insights into that complex organism—*Homo sapiens.*

As human beings who are attempting to cope with the demands of the environment, our lives may be simplistically viewed as a series of actions which we hope are suitable responses to the situations in which we find ourselves. However, we do not have direct access to these situations. Our awareness of the environment begins with physical events, such as light and sound waves, which stimulate our sense organs and are turned into messages which are sent along the nerves to the brain. These messages are subjected to processes of selection, organization and supplementation before we become aware of them; awareness is the end product of a long and complex operation. It is this end product which is our perception of our environment. Despite the impression that we are in direct and immediate contact with the world, our perception is, in fact, separated from reality by a long chain of processing.

The above description is a highly simplified version of what is still only a partially understood process. It may sound familiar to space flight buffs: i.e., the U.S. space program makes use of a computer which receives transmissions from television cameras on satellites and probes. It selects the message from extraneous electronic noise, organizes the electronic impulses into a visible picture, and supplements the transmitted information with inferred data, replacing information which was lost in passage. The result is a clear, sharp picture. It is the computer's perception of the extraterrestrial body being photographed.

The human need to select from the stream of information that bombards our senses arises from our inability to attend to too many things simultaneously. The need to supplement incoming data with inferences arises because full information is seldom available to us. We are in the unenviable position of constantly having to act on the basis of incomplete information.

Imagine that you are a passenger on one of those doomed

airliners so popular with moviemakers. The crew of the aircraft and most of the passengers have been stricken by a deadly virus. With his last breath the pilot gasps that you should engage the automatic pilot.

"Throw the switch . . . ." he mutters, as he expires.

Your difficulty is that the entire control panel of the aircraft, as well as a large portion of the roof, is covered with switches. You do not have the faintest idea which one to throw. You are being exposed to too much data. At the same time, because none of the switches are labelled, you are without vital information that would permit you to make a reasoned decision. However, you cannot avoid making a decision, as the aircraft spirals slowly towards the earth . . . .

Everyday life is seldom as dramatic as this scenario, but the same basic problem is continually confronting us. We need to ignore most of the available data and concentrate selectively on understanding the essential facets of the situation. At the same time we must make assumptions or inferences to fill the gaps in our knowledge. If you consider this for a moment, it will be clear that perceiving is not the passive process we often assume it to be. Perceiving is a highly active process, involving the selection of part of the available data, the organization of the data into a meaningful pattern, and the filling in of gaps with assumptions.

We would cope very poorly with our environment if the integration and restructuring of data into perceptions was done in a haphazard manner. Fortunately the construction of a perception is not a hit-and-miss procedure. Our past experiences have left us with a wealth of knowledge about appropriate schemes for organizing data which are constantly being applied, modified and updated. We shall use the term *schemata* to refer to those guidelines which are used to select, structure and supplement incoming data to form the perceptions of which we become aware. You may think of schemata as mental maps that contain information about the properties things are believed to have, and the relationships that are believed to exist between things. This information is applied to incoming data, guiding the selection and organization processes. Where important data appears to be missing, the blank areas may be filled in from schemata.

The particular schemata we apply to a situation will depend in part on our current needs and interests. As a result, similar situations may have different schemata applied to them, so they may be perceived in quite different ways. The infants being wheeled around the park in their carriages may be a matter of total indifference to the teenager. Several years later, as an expectant father or mother, the former teenager begins to perceive them as objects of enormous charm and fascination. A different schemata is being applied. Schemata also vary with our values and experiences. The industrialist gives a gratified sigh as he sees his pulp-and-paper mill spewing out clouds of black smoke. He perceives industry, organization and progress. But the environmentalist grits his teeth as he perceives a ravaged landscape.

In the two examples we have just cited one would be hard put to describe any of the perceptions as either correct or incorrect. Value judgments are involved. But it should be clear that the use of schemata to construct perceptions is fraught with potential for bias, distortion and error. This is especially so when the beliefs incorporated in the schemata do not accurately reflect reality. When this happens, it is quite common for information embodied in the schemata to displace factual information coming from the environment. Incoming information is distorted to fit our beliefs. The tendency to substitute information that we believe to be true for the evidence of our senses especially is prevalent when we deal with people whom we have known for a long time, and for whom we have constructed elaborate schemata. Look carefully at a photograph of a new acquaintance and then examine a recent photograph of your husband or wife. Probably you will find that the photograph of the acquaintance looks much as you visualize him or her, but you may be surprised to find how different your spouse looks in the photograph. The reason, of course, is that your perception of your spouse not only is based on things you noticed years before, but also has been distorted by all the peripheral facts you know about habits, personality traits and behaviours.

When we perceive people, it is not only their physical appearance that is liable to be distorted; behaviours, abilities and motives are even more likely to be coloured. Because the schemata that parents hold about their children are formed primarily while the children are young, parents often are unable to perceive the changes and developments that their children undergo. In the eyes of our parents, we will, to some extent, always be children. Some of our behaviours will always be perceived as immature. In turn, we may experience difficulty in seeing our own children as the competent teenagers they are, rather than as the dependent preschoolers they were. Because our perceptions are so vulnerable to distortion, it may be more accurate to say Believing is Seeing, rather than Seeing is Believing.

It would be misleading to dwell only on the distortions introduced by our schemata. Remember that without schemata there can be no perception. That is to say, we cannot become aware of our environment without filtering the information and organizing it. Problems arise only when the schemata involved are inappropriate for the task.

It should also be noted that ways of dealing with information that we have learned in the past are applied again and again to permit us to make predictions and solve problems. Our schemata permit us to go beyond hit-and-miss methods of problem solving. The next section will examine some of the ways in which the preconceptions and expectations we bring to a task may both help and hinder us.

PROBLEM SOLVING

The study of problem solving has shown that it is an activity in which the schemata discussed above play a very important role. However, much of the early thinking of psychologists about problem solving was based on the principle of parsimony. This principle suggests that we should not assume that complex mental processes are involved in problem-solving behaviour if simpler explanations are available. This principle is still widely respected by psychologists whose primary interest is in the learning and problem-solving behaviours of animals. For example, when a rat learns to run a maze to earn a food reward at the end, it is possible to see its problem-solving activities as an example of trial-and-error behaviour. Many behaviours are tried until one is rewarded. It thereupon becomes more frequent.

A group of psychologists, called Gestalt psychologists, or Gestaltists, have long maintained that most human problem solving is based on higher mental processes rather than trial and error. The Gestalt approach stresses the organization of information into a coherent whole. When a suitable perception has been achieved the solution of problems appears as a flash of insight. Achieving a suitable perception of the problem involves the same processes of selecting relevant information and discarding irrelevant data, structuring the information and supplementing it, that we have discussed. An appropriate schemata leads to suitable selection, structuring, and supplementing of data to produce a "proper" perception of the problem—one that makes the solution apparent.

Human problem solving more often appears to be of this order rather than by trial-and-error. An appropriate schemata is invoked, a suitable perception of the situation is achieved, and the solution comes quickly and surely. By the same token, a fixation on inappropriate schemata leads to inaccurate perceptions, and a failure to solve the problem.

The most obvious examples of the use of schemata to solve problems occur when the schemata are of the visual kind, incorporating information about distances and spatial configurations. When I visit a city I first sit down and study a street map. My examination of the map leads to the development of a mental map or schemata. This permits me to find my way around quickly and surely in novel surroundings. Even without a map, I would eventually build suitable schemata through my exploratory forays. In such cases there is a very simple and obvious analogue in the physical world for my mental schemata.

When we fail to perceive the elements of a problem in such a way that the solution appears, it is usually because we make unnecessary assumptions about the problem and/or the solution, or because we display "fixedness." *Fixedness* is an inability to depart from the current and inappropriate schemata which we have.

Consider, for example, this problem. In Figure 1 nine dots are arranged in a square. It is possible to connect the nine dots by drawing four continuous straight lines, without lifting the pencil from the paper. Can you do it?

Figure 1

If you could not solve the problem, turn to Figure 2 for the correct solution. Most people fail to solve this problem for the reason we stated above—they make an unnecessary assumption. In this case the assumption was that the four lines should stay within the group of dots. Only when the problem is perceived without this constraint does the solution appear.

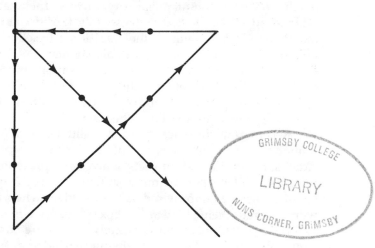

Figure 2

Where does fixedness come from? Why do we become wedded to certain schemata even though they may be inappropriate for a current problem? Schemata are formed on the basis of our previous experiences, and we become wedded to them because we have enjoyed at least partial success with them in the past. Psychologists have noticed that there seems to be a principle of "psychological inertia," in that we often demonstrate a resistance to changing an established schemata or pattern of thought or behaviour. This fixedness prevents flexibility, or the ability to see problems through fresh eyes, without preconceptions. It hinders the ability to construct new and appropriate schemata.

We should not leap to the conclusion that fixedness is altogether bad, however. The use of established schemata permits us to act quickly and decisively, as long as the problem confronting us is not too different from previous problems we have encountered. As long as conditions remain more or less stable, our established schemata provide effective problem-solving routines. It is when conditions change and new circumstances arise that fixedness interferes with our finding solutions.

In the problem with the nine dots we demonstrated how an unnecessary assumption interferes with problem solving. In that case, an assumption was made about the shape of the solution. Often, however, we demonstrate our fixedness by making unnecessary assumptions about the use of the resources available for solving a particular problem. So, when the solution requires the use of a familiar object in an unfamiliar way, our fixedness leads us to employ established schemata that suggest only traditional functions for the tool at hand. For example, the traditional function for a nail file is grooming the nails. However, a nail file may also be used as a letter opener. This is a fairly obvious improvisation, but the first time we saw a nail file as a potential letter opener we were overcoming fixedness. *Recentering* is a term employed by Gestalt psychologists to refer to abandoning an established schemata.

Recentering becomes more difficult if we have recently been reminded of the customary use of an object. One psychologist, R. E. Adamson, found that subjects who were presented with candles, matches, and boxes had more difficulty perceiving that the boxes could be used as improvised candle-holders when the other articles were given to them *placed in* the boxes, than when candles, matches, and boxes were presented separately. Boxes are customarily used as containers, not candle-holders. Being reminded of the customary use of boxes prevented subjects perceiving the boxes as potential candle-holders.

An American psychologist, Martin Scheerer, developed another task which shows that the mere sight of an object performing a traditional function evokes an established schemata and leads to fixedness. Scheerer asked his subjects to place two rings on a peg from a position six feet away from both the rings and the peg. The task could not be done without the subjects using some tool to extend their reaches. Subjects were told they could use any article in the room as a tool. The room contained two sticks, but neither, by itself, was long enough to bridge the gap; they had to be joined together in some fashion. The only suitable thing in the room for binding the sticks together was a piece of string. The solution of the problem required that the subjects use the string to tie the sticks together, then use the sticks to reach the rings and the peg.

You might think that the task is a fairly straightforward one. In fact, all subjects were successful when the string was simply left hanging on a nail on the wall of the laboratory. All subjects already possessed schemata that suggested tying things together was an appropriate use for string, and extending one's reach with a stick was an appropriate use for sticks. No recentering was required and the subjects were able to use their established schemata successfully to solve the problem. However, tying two things together with a piece of string is only one use to which string is typically put. Another schemata suggests that string may be used to suspend things. Scheerer managed to evoke the second schemata by leaving the string in plain view, hanging from the same nail, but using it to suspend a calendar. This time half the subjects failed to solve the problem. The established schemata, evoked by the sight of the string suspending a calendar, caused them to fixate on that mode of employment for the string. Fixedness prevented subjects from recentering and producing alternative schemta.

Interestingly, even the subjects who failed reported that they realized early in the experiment that a string was needed. They saw the string supporting the calendar and saw that the string could be easily untied. They did not think they were forbidden to use the string, but simply did not think of taking the string down and using it to bind the sticks together.

The inability to recenter, or to forsake established schemata and perceive novel uses for familiar resources, is a major cause of poor problem solving. It is also a prevalent cause of the inefficient use of human resources. Sometimes in a business organization an employee who has worked long and faithfully in a particular job will be over-looked for promotion simply because his superiors are employing schemata that cast him in that role and no other. This is especially likely to happen when there is no established pattern for promoting workers from the job they hold to the new post. On one newspaper the practice was for new editorial staff to begin as general assignment reporters, progress to more specialized beats such as labour relations and politics, and finally to be promoted to copy editors. Most staffers were quite happy with the arrangement until a new, elite category of investigative reporters was established. The general manager and senior editors fell victim to their established schemata that reporters should report and deskmen should edit copy. They promoted several reporters to the new investigative unit over the heads of more experi-enced deskmen. The result was a sharp drop in morale, culminating in several resignations. At least two of the copy editors who resigned joined other newspapers as investigative reporters and went on to outstanding careers.

One might expect that the more important a problem is, and the more highly motivated one is to solve it, the harder one will work at developing new schemata. Oddly, this does not seem to be the case. Very high levels of arousal or motivation may inhibit recentering and interfere with problem solving. Anxious students writing a vital examination sometimes fail *because* they have an overwhelming need to succeed. If the problems confronting them require new schemata, their high level of motivation may induce fixedness and prevent recentering, with disastrous results. Those of us who have grunted and cursed as we have tried vainly to move a sticking bolt with the wrong type of wrench on a hot day, unwilling to go out and borrow the correct tool, will sympathize with the students. Fixedness is accentuated by an unwillingness to accept any detour to reach the goal, even if a detour is the only way to reach the goal.

This suggests it might be profitable to think of problem solving in two different lights. On the one hand, being experienced and having established schemata available can result in rapid and efficient problem resolution, when the problem is not too different from the familiar problems for which the schemata were originally developed. On the other hand, when a new type of problem presents itself, especially a problem that has a superficial resemblance to a familiar variety, our experience may boomerang on us. By fixating on established schemata we inhibit recentering and the development of new schemata which could lead to problem resolution.

The first step to become more efficient problem solvers is to be aware of the role played by our schemata and to be continually alert to the possibility that recentering is required. When we are thoroughly habituated to the use of certain schemata, a period of disinvolvement may be needed before we can successfully recenter. Highly creative men like Edison and Einstein talked about solutions coming to them after a period of incubation, during which their minds "played with" the problem. This playing with problems amounts to developing tentative new schemata, trying novel uses for familiar resources, and concentrating on new relationships between the elements of the problem. Finally, a schemata is developed which is appropriate to the problem and everything falls into place. The solution appears to present itself in a flash of insight.

University professors have traditionally been given sabbaticals every few years, during which time they are relieved of their academic duties for a year and are free to travel, write and explore new problems. This is a time for recentering and is often followed by a new spurt of creative work. Some business organizations are now giving their senior executives similar sabbaticals. Other organizations tackle the problem of fixedness by hiring "new blood" and bringing in individuals who do not have preconceived schemata. It is often easier for these new employees to devise appropriate solutions than it is for established people to abandon their schemata and recenter.

PERCEIVING PEOPLE

Our relationships with people are at the root of most of our satisfactions and dissatisfactions, our successes and our failures, and our total mental adjustment, good or poor. The way we interact with people, in turn, depends on the way we perceive them and the way we understand and interpret their behaviour, especially their behaviour towards us. Any distortions that creep into our perception of people must, then, exert a profound effect upon the entire pattern of our lives.

We have already pointed out that schemata about individuals, based on our past experiences, can shape our later perceptions and cause us to be "out of date." But what happens when we meet someone for the first time? Are we free to perceive in a totally objective fashion and to draw accurate inferences about the person's personality? The answer appears to be that we are not free, but not because of past experience with *that* individual. We are constrained by our past experiences with people in general and by our assimilation of our culture's folklore about people. They provide us with schemata that lead us to expect, on the basis of our first impressions, that the person we have just met will possess certain personality traits. Believing is seeing, so our expectations, in turn, may cause us actually to perceive non-existent traits and behaviours. More insidiously still, because we expect our new acquaintance to behave in certain ways, based on our first impressions, we may behave towards him in ways that will provoke the very responses we expect.

This elicitation of expected behaviour is an example of what social psychologists call a *self-fulfilling prophecy*. In this case the result is that our faith in our schemata is confirmed and we are likely to use that schemata again.

An example should make this point clear. At a party you are introduced to an athletic-looking type whom you recognize as a former football player. Your previous experience with football players, together with impressions you have gleaned from the media and through talking to members of your own circle, has led you to believe that they tend to be rather unsubtle fellows, given to boorishness and displays of violence and aggression. You acknowledge the introduction, exchange some chit-chat which revolves around sports, and then move on to more rewarding company. Your schemata about football players is unshaken. You do not discover that the man you have just met is a prominent figure in local community activities and a passionate admirer of classical music, both of which are interests you share. You have used your schemata to extrapolate from *football player* to *uninteresting, insensitive* and *uncultured,* and behaved accordingly. Because you predicted that he would not be interested in the activities you enjoy, but would instead be interested in sports gossip, you limited your conversation. By not presenting an opening for the expression of his interests, you created a situation in which your prophecy about football players could not fail to be fulfilled. Thus, you confirmed your schemata and reinforced your distorted perception of footballers.

Stereotypes

When we have a schemata which associates a set of personality traits with members of a group, such as football players, psychologists speak about us possessing a *stereotype*. When we use our schemata to predict traits and behaviours this way we are *stereotyping*. The best known and socially most dangerous stereotypes are ethnic and racial stereotypes. These schemata lead us to predict, merely on the basis of an individual's group membership, what personality traits he is likely to have and how he is likely to behave. Stereotypes are rampant in all societies, including our own. Consider, for example, such popular gems as: "Blacks have great rhythm"; "Latins are the best lovers"; "The English are reserved."

Since Walter Lippmann first used the term "stereotype" in 1922, there has been debate about the definition of a stereotype. Much of the debate hinged around whether a set of beliefs held about a group must be unjustified or incorrect to be called a stereotype. Today it is generally accepted by psychologists that although stereotyped beliefs may be incorrect, we simply do not know in most cases whether they actually are incorrect or not. What is demonstrably incorrect about all stereotypes is not the beliefs involved, but rather that characteristics attributed to group members are attributed to *all* members of the group, with no account being taken of individual differences. One thing psychologists and other social scientists have learned through bitter experience is that there is no such thing as a homogeneous group, all of whose members have similar traits and behaviours. Individual differences invariably predominate and overshadow any group similarities that may exist.

Because negative stereotypes that ascribe negative qualities to certain groups are potent sources of injustice and inter-group friction, they have attracted most attention from researchers. Strictly speaking, however, it is quite possible to have a positive stereotype of a group. Many professional groups, such as doctors and lawyers, enjoy positive stereotypes that result in the ascription of such qualities as intelligence, diligence and altruism to all members of the group.

Another aspect of stereotyping that is worth noting is that the stereotype need not be based on personal experience with group members; it may be wholly based on vicarious or secondhand experience, such as hearsay, folklore and media reports. It is quite possible for people to hold stereotypes about groups they have never come into contact with. In their pioneering studies of stereotyping in the 1930s, Daniel Katz and Kenneth Braly found that Princeton University students held stereotypes about Turks and Chinese, even though few, if any, of the students had ever met a representative of either group. Furthermore, the individual students showed considerable agreement in ascribing such traits as intelligence, industry, cruelty, laziness and honesty to different ethnic groups. This indicates that there can be strong consensus among the members of a culture in the stereotypes they hold about others. Common schemata are often held by members of the same culture.

You might be wondering whether ethnic stereotypes still exist in an era when racial discrimination and prejudice have become unfashionable. Surely we are too enlightened these days to make sweeping generalizations about the characteristics of other groups. In fact, the original Princeton study has been repeated twice at that university, once in 1951 and again in 1967. The later studies demonstrated that stereotypes still exist, although students, and presumably the rest of us, have become less certain about the attribution of stereotyped characteristics. The actual nature of the stereotypes, however, changed surprisingly little over the three studies. In all three studies, Turks were the most negatively stereotyped of all the groups examined. Interestingly, while the 1933 students stereotyped Americans most positively of ten national groups, by 1967 Americans had dropped to fifth place, with Japanese, Germans, Jews and English (in that order) being more favourably characterized. The four traits most often ascribed to Americans in 1933 were, in order, *industrious, intelligent, materialistic* and *ambitious*. In 1967 the order and content had changed so that the top four traits were *materialistic, ambitious, pleasure loving* and *industrious*. The stereotype of the American Black underwent even more dramatic changes over the period of the studies. This suggests that changes in our perception of our own group, and of other groups, go hand-in-hand with social and political fluctuations. (Karlins, Coffman, and Walters, 1969.) It is an interesting exercise to examine some of your own stereotypes, and those of your friends.

First decide which group you wish to look at. Then compile a list of characteristics which you think might be used by yourself and others to describe the group. There should be about twenty to forty characteristics on your list, half of them positive or desirable characteristics and half negative ones. A list for a stereotype of lawyers, for example, might look like this.

Lawyers

wealthy	weak	dishonest
intelligent	conscientious	upstanding citizens
avaricious	loyal	respectful
ambitious	generous	well-mannered
pushy	bragging	serious
materialistic	jealous	quiet
lazy	talkative	socially concerned
pleasure-loving	gregarious	stubborn
conventional	self-centred	radical
brave	kind	ugly

Go through the list and underline all those characteristics which seem to you to be typical of lawyers. If you think some important characteristics have been left out, add them to the list. Now go through the list again, examining all the terms you have underlined. Choose the five terms which seem to you *most* typical of lawyers and circle them.

The terms you have circled represent the stereotype you hold of lawyers. If you want to know how other people like yourself feel about lawyers, you should have about ten acquaintances perform the same task and then list all the terms that each of your friends has circled. Undoubtedly there will be more than five terms because you will not all be in perfect agreement, but you will probably notice that some terms are circled repeatedly by different subjects. As their definition of a stereotype, Katz and Braly used the twelve terms most often mentioned by their subjects as being most typical of a group.

It is interesting to examine the characteristics ascribed to a group and to notice how much agreement there is between subjects. It is also interesting to compare the stereotypes that the same set of subjects holds towards different groups. To make comparisons you should repeat the task we have described for two or more occupational groups, such as salesmen, accountants or janitors. The differences in the stereotypes will give you some insight into the schemata governing your perception of the groups. Characteristics suggested by the schemata are more likely to be perceived when a group member is encountered, than are contradictory qualities.

Inferring Characteristics From Other Cues

In stereotyping, an ethnic label such as *Italian*, or an occupational title such as *lawyer*, acts as a cue to trigger a schemata which predisposes us to perceive stereotypical qualities in a member of the group. Often we have been exposed only briefly to the person concerned. Information about the characteristics of the person is lacking, and schemata are used to fill the gap. Ethnicity and occupation are not the only cues able to evoke schemata. Any easily accessible piece of information about a person, such as attractiveness, dress, speech, use of mannerisms, or even size, tends to evoke schemata-based assumptions about "hidden" or covert characteristics, such as intelligence, morality and honesty. Where people have similar cultural backgrounds and have been exposed to similar experiences, there is often considerable agreement about the type of covert characteristics ascribed. Recent research suggests that physical attractiveness plays a particularly important part in the impressions we form of others. In psychological studies, subjects have been shown pictures of attractive people, moderately attractive people and unattractive people, and then asked to speculate about what characteristics the people in the photographs were likely to have. Subjects consistently credit the attractive people with more desirable qualities. They are perceived to be more intelligent, more moral, better adjusted, more warm, more poised and more sexually responsive. In addition, when subjects are asked to assess such things as the future happiness and success of the people in the photographs, they invariably suggest that the more attractive people will be happier and have more successful careers. Interestingly, *extremely* attractive people are not necessarily seen as possessing only desirable properties. Although subjects tend to write glowing descriptions of attractive women, when the women are very attractive the subjects tend to perceive some undesirable qualities as well. Egotism, vanity, materialism and snobbishness are attributed, and less successful marriages are predicted. (Dermer and Thiel, 1975)

Psychologists have also used tape-recorded speeches to assess the effect of accents on the perception of characteristics. In one study conducted in Canada, two groups of students heard a tape-recorded speech delivered either by a speaker with a French-Canadian accent or by a speaker with an English-Canadian accent. Although the speeches were identical in their content, the students who heard the French-Canadian accent rated the contents of the speech, and the speaker, less highly. Studies in other parts of the world have demonstrated the same thing. The accent used by a person affects our assessment of the message he delivers, and causes us to perceive him as having more or less desirable qualities. Generally, we prefer those accents which we consider to be the standard for our particular country or region. However, some "foreign" accents sometimes evoke particularly favourable responses. The so-called mid-Atlantic accent used by John Kennedy, some other American politicians and many television personalities is highly rated, even by Americans who themselves speak with a Southern drawl or New England twang.

Physical size is a determinant of our perceptions of males. Men who are tall and have a good physique are often perceived to have more desirable personality characteristics and greater status than smaller, shorter, fatter and skinnier men. One study demonstrated that taller graduates from a business college were offered, on the average, higher starting salaries than shorter men. Is there a disproportionate number of tall executives in the organizations you are familiar with? If there is, those responsible for promotions may be allowing their schemata to distort their perceptions.

Another experiment demonstrated that the tall-status link is reversible. The same individual was introduced to three separate classes of students as an eminent professor, a junior instructor or a student. Later, after their visitor had left the room, the students were asked to estimate his height. Those students who believed they had met a high-status professor consistently over-estimated his height. Those students who thought the visitor was merely another student, tended to under-estimate how tall he was. Our tendency to associate characteristics in a regular and systematic way not only distorts our impression of fairly intangible qualities such as intelligence, but even distorts our recollection of highly visible qualities such as height and appearance. We see and we remember what we expect to see. Perceptions and memories are influenced by schemata that suggest relationships between personal characteristics. We are predisposed to perceive the qualities that should be there, according to our schemata.

Before we jump to the conclusion that all this is grossly unfair and that the only way to the top is to be born beautiful and buy elevator shoes, it is instructive to observe some scientific caution and consider how a scientist would examine the issue. First of all, although the scientist might be disposed to reject the idea that tallness is related to greater leadership qualities, he would push aside his preconceptions and go out into the field to compare tall and short men. Let us assume that he does find a relationship between height and leadership ability. Would he be satisfied? No, because then he would feel compelled to establish whether the objective differences he has found justify the premium we place on tallness. It could be that we place more emphasis on this characteristic than the "kernel of truth" warrants.

He would also be interested in determining if leadership is associated with tallness through some innate mechanism or whether this is a social phenomenon. For example, the self-fulfilling prophecy we mentioned earlier is quite capable of creating the leadership-tallness correlation. If most people assume that tall boys are likely to be better leaders, then parents and teachers are likely to thrust more leadership responsibilities on them. As qualities of leadership can be learned, tall boys would have more opportunities to practice being leaders. By the time they become adults, they might have more highly developed leadership ability, even though there might be no discernible innate differences.

When we meet a tall individual is it fair and sensible, then, to assume he has leadership qualities which his shorter counterparts lack? This is basically the same question as we faced when we considered in what sense ethnic and racial stereotypes might be unjustified and incorrect. The answer is the same. If we permit our perceptions of people to be distorted by our schemata, we will often behave inappropriately and unfairly, to our own disadvantage and to the disadvantage of others. This is because individual differences always overshadow any kernel of truth that might reside in generalizations made about groups. Obviously it would be contrary to our interests and unfair to overlook a small man for promotion because we tend to perceive tall men as having greater leadership qualities. The short individual we ignore may have outstanding leadership potential.

Does this mean that we should throw aside all preconceptions? This might be the ideal solution and we should probably avoid being influenced by our preconceptions as far as possible. Unfortunately, there is reason to believe that the inferences we make involve psychic short cuts that are so strongly ingrained in our mental processes that we probably cannot totally eradicate them. The best we can do is to become aware that we do have schemata which predispose us to make unwarranted inferences, and to guard against them.

The Halo Effect

Most of us have had the experience of meeting a new acquaintance through a mutual friend. Quite often the mutual friend will prime us, telling us before the meeting what the person is like. "You will really like Bernie; he's one of the most intelligent people I know. He can talk about any subject you care to name. A fascinating person."

Notice that all you have been told in advance, explicitly, is that Bernie is *intelligent*. Without a schemata relating personality traits you can go no further. However, there is a great deal of evidence to suggest that this is not what is done. Look through the list of personality traits provided below and circle, for each pair, that trait which you think Bernie is *most likely* to possess. Remember that all you know, definitely, is that he is intelligent. Probably you will not feel absolute certainty about your choices, but go ahead anyhow, and guess.

sincere	insincere
cold	warm
generous	miserly
unreliable	reliable
industrious	lazy

Knowing that people use schemata about personality traits, and knowing that the schemata tend to be similar for members of the same culture, I would predict that the traits you have circled are *sincere, warm, generous, reliable* and *industrious*. Furthermore, if you have several other people perform the same task you will almost certainly find that most of them will choose the same personality traits that you chose. To some people it is so obvious that an intelligent person must also be sincere rather than insincere, industrious rather than lazy, and so forth, that the task seems pointless. But, when one considers the matter, there is clearly nothing logically inconsistent about an intelligent person who is also rather a cold fish, devious and insincere, lazy, unreliable and miserly. Psychologically, however, because the one piece of information we do have is positive, it seems somehow inconsistent for Bernie to have other traits which are negative or undesirable.

Our knowledge that Bernie is intelligent has created a halo around him which incorporates other positive characteristics. This tendency for one positive quality to encourage the perception of other positive qualities, even where objective evidence is lacking, is one of the best-known psychological phenomenon of person perception and is called, for obvious reasons, the *halo effect*. Negative halo effects also exist. Given one undesirable characteristic, there is a tendency to extrapolate and perceive other undesirable qualities. What would your perception of Bernie be, do you think, if your friend warned you he was insincere?

Did you notice that you were more certain about some of the inferences you made than about others? Most people are quite certain that a person who is intelligent is also *industrious* and *reliable*, and less certain that he is *warm, sincere* and *generous*. The reason for this is that our schemata tend to be selective, with stronger relationships being perceived among traits that are similar. Most people, in fact, perceive personality traits as falling into two major groups, those which pertain to intellectual performance, such as *intelligent, reliable* and *industrious,* and those which pertain to social behaviour, such as *sincere, warm* and *generous.* Given an intellectual trait, we are more certain about inferring other intellectual traits than we are about inferring social traits. But the general halo effect will also predispose us to infer desirable social traits when we know the person possesses a desirable intellectual quality.

Here are some examples of positive and negative halo effects based on a recent study done at the Ryerson Polytechnical Institute in Toronto. Given that a person was known to be *intelligent,* Ryerson students inferred the person also was likely to be *sincere, polite, educated, clean, good-natured, musical* and inclined to *smile a lot.* On the other hand an *intelligent* person was unlikely to be *sickly, noisy, unsociable, superstitious, clumsy* or *unreliable.*

Similarly, students predicted that an unreliable person was likely to have *shifty eyes,* and be *lazy* and *quick-tempered,* while an unreliable person was unlikely to be *sincere, intelligent* or *polite.*

Mental schemata about the co-occurrence of personality traits are so prevalent and colour our perceptions of people to such an extent, that psychologists speak about people having *implicit personality theories.* An implicit personality theory is a type of schemata. It is a mental map or diagram reflecting the way we believe human personalities are structured. The word *implicit,* in implicit personality theory, underlines the fact that most of us are not consciously aware of the types of inferences we make or their underlying basis.

An implicit personality theory performs essentially the same function for the layman that the highly explicit and detailed personality theories of the psychologists perform for scientists. By representing the structure of personalities, such theories enable us to understand and to make predictions about personality traits. To distinguish the implicit personality theories of laymen from scientific theories, some psychologists speak about *lay* personality theories which all people possess even though they may not be aware of them.

EFFECTS OF PERCEIVER CHARACTERISTICS

Our mental maps or schemata can lead us to extrapolate from the knowledge we have about people and to infer other properties, about which there is little or no evidence. These expectancies may then blind us to properties which are inconsistent with our inferences, or make us prone to perceive properties which we expect to see. Our mental schemata can result in a distorted perception of reality.

There are other factors in the perceiver which can lead to a distortion of perceptions, including the perceiver's needs, motives and interests. A *need* may be thought of as a physiological or psychological deficit, such as lack of sleep or lack of human company. *Motives* generally refer to wider areas of desired experience, such as a general motive to mingle with others and be gregarious, or a motive to dominate others. *Interests,* for the purposes of this discussion, may be thought of as orientations towards certain fields, such as politics, business or art. There is a great deal of research evidence to suggest that all three of these factors can induce perceptual distortions.

We have all had experience with the effects of need on perception. The field of courting behaviour springs readily to mind. There is a popular comic strip in which one of the characters is Lyle the lion. He ardently pursues a certain lioness who does not have the slightest interest in him. Lyle is oblivious to the innumerable rebuffs he receives, adamantly perceiving the object of his love as returning his affection. Here Lyle's need for the lioness's affection has distorted his perceptions to such an extent that every rebuff is perceived as an expression of interest. Most of us have had similar experiences, or noticed other people indulging in this type of perceptual distortion. Charlie Brown presents another example from the comic strips. At the start of each football season Lucy cajoles Charlie into taking a tremendous running kick at a football she is holding. At the last moment she whips the ball away and Charlie Brown crashes to the ground. This scene is re-enacted, with variations, year after year. Here Charlie's deep need to perceive other people as trustworthy and sincere distorts his perceptions and leads to his undoing.

In their laboratories, psychologists have demonstrated another type of perceptual distortion that results from needs. One group of male subjects is sexually aroused by being given titillating, sexually oriented material to read. Another group is given a sample of more mundane reading matter. The two groups are then shown identical photographs of a woman and asked to rate her on such attributes as her attractiveness. The sexually aroused men invariably rate the woman in the picture as more sexually receptive and better looking. If the aroused men are led to believe that the woman is a possible date, their ratings are even higher. It is interesting to note that it is only the perception of those qualities which are relevant to the induced sexual needs of the subjects that are distorted. Other qualities, such as the intelligence of the woman, are rated the same by aroused and unaroused subjects.

In the same way, our motives often lead us to distort reality. If we have a very strong motivation to be successful and to achieve, we may perceive ourselves as being more successful than we actually are.

If we have a strong motivation to dominate others and wield power, or to serve in a leadership role, we are likely to distort our perceptions of the actual power we do wield, and over-estimate how influential we are. Our interests operate in a similar way, making us more sensitive and more likely to perceive things within the orbit of our interests. We are also likely to overlook things that do not interest us very much.

In one experiment subjects were classified according to their interests as being *theoretical*, interested in the discovery of truth; *economic*, interested in practical and utilitarian things; *aesthetic*, interested in beauty; *social*, with strong needs for affection and respect; *political*, interested in power; and *religious*, interested in mysticism and grand, universal designs. The subjects were then exposed to words flashed on a screen for very short times, each word being most relevant to one or the other of the above categories. It was found that the subjects most easily recognized words that were relevant to their particular category of interests and increasingly less successful at identifying the words related to categories of lesser interest. (Postman, Bruner, and McGinnies, 1948)

Psychologists have called this tendency to be more aware of those things which are relevant to our needs, motives and interests *perceptual-accentuation*. Perceptual-accentuation may result in us perceiving relevant things as being larger, more valuable and more attractive, and makes us more likely to notice those things. There is a corresponding phenomenon called *perceptual-defence* which results in us perceiving things which are less relevant to us as being smaller, less valuable and less attractive. Perceptual defence may also cause us to overlook things which are disagreeable, humiliating or upsetting to us.

In its simplest form, psychologists have demonstrated perceptual-defence in the laboratory by flashing obscene words, mixed with neutral words that would give offence to nobody, on a screen for very short periods of time. Subjects typically have more difficulty in identifying the offensive words. In real life, examples of perceptual-defence abound. Parents who refuse to recognize the consistently anti-social behaviour of their offspring, lovers who are blind to the faults of their loved ones, and executives who are unable to perceive their mistakes, are all victims of perceptual-defence.

Another factor that affects the accuracy of our perception of others is called *projection*. The theory of projection is that if we have a conspicuous trait in ourselves, we are likely to perceive that trait in other people, whether it exists, in fact, or not. Thus, an extremely hostile person may constantly perceive that other people are hostile and aggressive towards him; he projects the hostility that he feels on to others. At the other extreme, a loving and compassionate person may perceive the world to be filled with loving and compassionate people.

Temporary moods influence our perception just as enduring personality traits do. If you are persuaded to attend a party at a time when you are not feeling particularly social, you might well be bored and feel alienated from the other party goers. Looking around the room, you are likely to perceive many other people who also appear to be bored and alienated. Now, if you enter into the swing of things and begin to enjoy yourself, you are likely to perceive other people as also having a good time. It is possible that it was a boring party to begin with, of course, and that the party later picked up, but projection alone is quite capable of producing the impression.

Who Perceives Others Accurately?

Our discussion of perceptual-accentuation and perceptual-defence demonstrates that our accuracy may vary from time to time and from situation to situation. When we are strongly involved emotionally and motivated either to see or not to see certain personality traits or behaviours, all of us are vulnerable to perceptual distortions. If we use our mental schemata blindly, and let our expectations over-rule more objective observation, we may get a distorted view of other people.

There are several factors which may lead to distortion of our perceptions of other people and make us poor judges of character. But are some people less susceptible to perceptual distortion, and therefore consistently better judges of others? Psychologists have studied this question by having subjects watch extensive filmed interviews, then assess the personality characteristics of the interviewee. The assessments may be graded for accuracy by comparing them with the results of a battery of personality tests and assessments made off-camera by trained psychologists and friends of the interviewee. The studies indicate that some subjects are consistently better than others at "summing up" the interviewees seen on the films, and are usually better despite wide variations in the background of the interviewees. (Cline and Richards, 1960) It seems that there is a person-perception skill, and that some people are more accurate in summing up people than the rest of us. Obviously such a skill would be a valuable one to have. What are the characteristics of a good judge of people? Gordon Allport has listed six attributes which he considers of major importance:

1. A good judge has wide experience with many people of diverse backgrounds.

2. We are more accurate in assessing the characteristics of people who are similar to ourselves than we are in judging people who are dissimilar.

3. More intelligent people tend to be better judges.

4. To be a good judge of other people, one needs insight and understanding of oneself.

5. Good judges tend to be well-adjusted people who are emotionally stable, with well-developed social skills.

6. A certain degree of detachment is required to be a good judge of others.

These six attributes, coupled with the factors already discussed, suggest that accurate perception of other people can be developed and that we can learn to identify those situations in which our judgments are likely to be suspect. In summary, we should widen our circle of acquaintances to include as many disparate types of people as possible; we should develop our social skills, the ability to detach ourselves from a situation and our insight into ourselves; and we should not place too much reliance on our judgment in situations where we are dealing with unfamiliar types, or in situations where we are strongly emotionally involved.

THE PERCEPTIONS OF PSYCHOLOGISTS

Psychologists, like all scientists, are in the business of trying to explain the things that they perceive to be happening. The major focus of their interest is in the behaviour of human beings. But psychologists are in essentially the same position as anyone else. They are bombarded with data which must be selectively attended to. They must organize it in some way that will facilitate understanding of the causes of the behaviour. In addition, they must make predictions about behaviours.

To cope with this problem psychologists use elaborate schemata. The schemata involve selectively attending to part of the overwhelming amount of information available and ignoring the rest. The schemata provide methods of organizing data into a coherent, easily grasped whole. And, finally, the schemata include inferences and assumptions that are required to fill the gaps left by the data at hand.

Individuals may hold different schemata that lead them to perceive the same phenomena in various ways. Similarly, psychologists may apply different schemata to human behaviour and come up with widely differing perceptions. The question to be asked is not which of these perceptions is correct, but, rather, which perception leads to the most full and complete understanding of the particular problem being examined.

In their most elaborate and explicit form, the schemata used by psychologists constitute the different approaches we mentioned at the beginning of this chapter. You will recall that the approaches involve selective attention to different fields of human behaviour and to different types of data; they involve different methods of organizing the selected information with the use of suitable terms and concepts; and each approach involves certain basic assumptions made necessary by the absence of data.

The five approaches presented in later chapters of this book may be viewed as five separate, highly sophisticated and explicit schemata. Each one leads to a unique perception of human behaviour and each approach offers its own special insights. At the same time, each approach, if used inappropriately, may lead to misconceptions about the nature and behaviour of human beings.

What is the final goal? The final goal is a schemata so complete that it can embrace all available data about human behaviour and organize it into an understandable picture. Then, and only then, will we be able to perceive all aspects of the human condition. Such a goal involves ultimate knowledge and will always be unattainable, not only in psychology but in all the sciences. Nevertheless, it provides the ideal towards which all sciences strive, and provides a direction for scientific inquiry.

SUMMARY

This chapter has underlined the role that our perception of people, situations and events plays in shaping our behaviour. Perception is not a passive process of recording things that are happening around us. It is an active process of constructing a meaningful version of reality which typically ignores many visible facets and supplies other, invisible ones. We are not free to perceive things as they actually are because we employ mental maps or schemata developed on the basis of our past experiences. They fill in the gaps when information is not available, permit predictions about future occurrences and indicate appropriate behaviours.

In the general area of problem solving we employ schemata which incorporate preconceived notions about the relationships among the elements of a problem and ideas about the use of resources. Fixedness, or an inflexible attachment to inappropriate schemata, may prevent us from successfully tackling new problems, especially when those problems bear a superficial resemblance to familiar ones. So we continue to apply inappropriate methods and avoid recentering, or constructing new and more suitable schemata. The result is inefficient problem solving and an inability to use resources to the best advantage.

In the field of person-perception, our schemata include preconceptions about the co-occurrence of characteristics or properties of people. Given incomplete information we extrapolate and infer other properties. Sometimes the cues we use are far removed from the properties that we infer, as for example when we infer personality characteristics such as intelligence or honesty on the basis of physical attractiveness. When the cues are occupational or ethnic labels, the inferred properties form a stereotype.

When they are used prudently, our schemata for perceiving people permit us to act decisively and appropriately on the basis of minimum information. However, when too much reliance is placed on schemata, sometimes to the extent that available information that is inconsistent with our expectations is ignored, our schemata may lead to inappropriate actions, self-defeating behaviour and injustices. Our behaviour, based on expectations derived from our schemata, may also lead to self-fulfilling prophecies where people eventually come to behave as we expect them to because our actions prevent other forms of behaviour.

The development of flexibility, exposing oneself to a wide range of experiences, insight into one's perceptual processes and problem-solving behaviours, and the preservation of a certain detachment encourages recentering, better interpersonal relationships and more effective problem solving.

Further Reading

An important social and legal result of the distortion of perception is the conflicting evidence often given by eyewitnesses to crimes. Robert Buckhout published a detailed discussion of eyewitness testimony in the December, 1974 edition of *Scientific American*.

Robert Rosenthal and Lenore Jacobson have written a fascinating and somewhat alarming account of the effect of teacher expectations on the performance of their pupils. The book is called *Pygmalion in the Classroom* and should be required reading for all those of us who are in the position of evaluating and judging others.

Processes of person-perception have been dealt with in detail by Peter Warr and C. Knapper in their book, *The Perception of People and Events*. Another detailed but fairly technical book is *Person Perception*, by Albert Hastorf, David Schneider and Judith Polefka.

Problem solving and recentering are discussed in three eminently readable books by Edward de Bono, called *The Use of Lateral Thinking*, *The Mechanism of the Mind* and *Think Tank*.

2

THE RULES OF THE CRAFT
John Roth

Editor's Preface

It was pointed out in the first chapter that psychologists, scientists in other fields, and laymen confront the same problems in their attempts to understand the world. Successful coping behaviour requires appropriate perceptions, the creation of which involves selection of information, organization and supplementation of existing data with inferences. The idea of schemata was introduced to stress the regular way in which these processes operate. In this chapter the differences between the scientist's approach and the approach of the layman will be considered. Whereas the layman's schemata are developed in an unsystematic fashion and are seldom completely conscious, the scientist follows established conventions. As a result, both the schemata of the scientist and the development of those schemata are explicit and open to examination.

This chapter reflects the author's belief that the scientific method is the best route for understanding human behaviour. Students of psychology sometimes become impatient with scientific method. The prime focus of interest is, after all, human behaviour. As members of the species, we are insiders with privileged information, at least about our own behaviour. Because of our insider status it is very tempting to let intuition outstrip facts. These intuitive insights are not always wrong; quite often they are correct. The trouble is that without the systematic scientific approach, we can never *know* whether our intuitive understanding is right or wrong.

The purpose of this chapter is to provide an outline of the scientific method, especially as it is used in psychology. Armed with an understanding of how scientists systematically sift their data and build their theories, the student will be better able to assess and understand the five approaches to psychology that follow in the next chapters.

THE RULES OF THE CRAFT

The American psychologist George Kelly was fond of saying that all people are scientists. By that he did not mean that we spend our lives in an environment dominated by white coats and bunsen burners; he was suggesting that to succeed in our complex world, and sometimes simply to survive, we are constantly obliged to gather information, understand it, and then attempt to predict future events. These predictions form the basis of our attempts to *control* our lives, steering a course that, we hope, will permit us to achieve our goals and avoid harm.

It is perfectly true that successful human behaviour and successful science involve the same attempts to understand, predict and control. But scientists differ from the public because they are more aware of the enquiry process and consciously attempt to abide by the accepted methods of scientific investigation. This is the major difference between the psychologist and the layman. Although both share an abiding interest in human behaviour and both use approximately the same types of processes, the layman often is not as aware of the methods he uses. The psychologist works systematically and according to explicit rules of procedure.

It is this adherence to standard procedures that distinguishes scientific conclusions from those arrived at in a less systematic fashion. The use of accepted procedures for gathering information and for arriving at and testing conclusions is implied in the definition of psychology as the *scientific* study of the behaviour of organisms.

The explosive growth of psychology since its emergence as a separate discipline reflects the strong need that people feel to understand more about behaviour in a world that is changing at an ever accelerating pace, with an inexhaustible variety of new stresses and problems, opportunities and challenges. Because of the rapid changes that confront us we cannot afford the luxury of inefficient methods of understanding people. Our grandparents could fall back on insights handed down through generations, and apply them with some success because social and technological conditions were relatively constant. The human environment, the people they associated with, and their beliefs and attitudes were comparatively stable and homogeneous. By contrast, our social and technological environment will change beyond recognition within our lifetimes, and we are exposed to a vast array of people with different customs, different beliefs, different attitudes and different behaviours. In such circumstances our understanding of people needs to be far more complete, more open to new information and based on an explicit, systematic set of procedures. In other words, it should be more scientific.

SCIENCE AND COMMON SENSE

Much of the time we rely on common sense to guide us in our dealings with other people and with the rest of the world. However, "common sense" has become a cult with some people. They challenge the assertions of the social sciences because they are contrary to common sense, or, when a scientifically based prediction does agree with their preconceptions, disparage science by saying, "Everyone knows that; it's only common sense." The question we must consider is, what constitutes common sense, and can it serve as a substitute for scientific enquiries?

Common sense, broadly defined, is simply our understanding of the processes of the environment around us. It is our perception of cause and effect. This understanding is achieved partly through personal experience and partly vicariously through experiences that, we believe, others have been exposed to. The latter experiences are transmitted to us sometimes by word of mouth and sometimes through radio, television and the print media. These vicarious experiences may be in the form of anecdotes about actual incidents, or they may be in the form of conclusions that others have drawn about relations between events. In the former case we are free to draw our own conclusions about the nature of the relationships that the anecdotes illustrate; in the latter case we may adopt conclusions without knowledge of the evidence, if any, that they were based upon.

We should not play down the important role that common sense beliefs play. We rely on common sense in most of our dealings with the rest of the world. Nor are the courses of action suggested by common sense always wrong; obviously, if too many of the decisions based on common sense were faulty, we would not be capable of coping with our environment. The trouble with common sense is that it is so often vague and frequently ambiguous that the courses of action open to us cannot be clearly evaluated. Common sense theories frequently come to us in the form of sayings which represent folk wisdom. Very often there are two totally contradictory sayings which are both accepted by uncritical minds. Consider for example these two sayings: "Birds of a feather flock together," and "Opposites attract." Both are drawn from the store of common sense. Yet if we tried to use them as a basis for choosing a spouse, we would be torn between looking for someone as much like ourselves as possible on the one hand, and someone totally different from ourselves on the other.

Fortunately, the question of interpersonal attraction has been studied scientifically by psychologists. We are now able to add the all-important qualifications and modifications that permit us to make sense of these two common sense statements. We know that similarity of attitudes and backgrounds does result in interpersonal attraction. Other things being equal, this supports the truth of the first bit of folk wisdom. We also know that another ingredient of a successful relationship may be *complementary* (not opposite) personality traits, so that a stable relationship may be formed between a person who likes to dominate and a person who likes to be dominated, or between a person who likes to play the parental role and a person who prefers to play the childlike, dependent role.

The difference between scientific statements and the guidelines provided by common sense is that the former clearly and precisely delineate the conditions under which certain rules hold, and provide guidelines that are not contradictory. The latter provide contradictory guidelines, which may or may not contain a kernel of truth under particular, but usually unspecified, conditions. Common sense truths are probably derived, originally, by some quasi-scientific process. The distortions occur because the people who derive these truths are not particularly conscious of the methods they are using, nor are they constrained to follow scientific principles of investigation. As a result, apart from their ambiguous nature and the failure to specify the conditions under which they hold true, common sense truths are also particularly susceptible to biases and prejudices. Sometimes these biases are unconscious. Sometimes they are introduced quite deliberately, as in propaganda during times of war or international tension.

If people who relied on common sense were willing to treat their beliefs as possibly fallible, and were prepared to test them against reality, the cult of common sense would not be nearly as destructive as it frequently is. Unfortunately, those people who cling most strongly to common sense tenets usually close their minds to contradictory evidence and thus are not open to correction of faulty beliefs. Worse, too strong an adherence to common sense sometimes leads to the attitude that investigation and critical scientific scrutiny of the facts are unnecessary and doomed to be a waste of time, because the truth is "self-evident."

Here is a list of self-evident truths or common sense propositions. You may subscribe to some or all of them yourself.

1. Women, by their innate natures, are more emotional than men.

2. People who learn slowly remember more of what they learn than do fast learners.

3. In terms of the number of people affected, marijuana is the most abused drug in Canada.

4. Watching a violent sport when we are angry releases tensions and makes it less likely that we will behave aggressively.

5. Sport builds character.

6. The mentally retarded usually are also insane.

These self-evident truths are some of the many common sense beliefs that have been scientifically investigated by psychologists. We have strong evidence that suggests all of them are false. If scientists accepted common sense as truth, these fallacies would never have been challenged and our actions would continue to be based on false premises. The aim of science is not to negate common sense; still less is the aim of science to confirm the common wisdom. The aim is to make accurate and unambiguous statements. Whether these statements confirm, qualify or totally contradict popular beliefs should not be a consideration. Common sense adages are unreliable guides to behaviour because of the suspect process used in forming them. The distinction between scientific and non-scientific conclusions rests on the methodology used to test the conclusions, a distinction which will become increasingly apparent as we proceed to examine scientific methods in detail.

THE SCIENTIFIC METHOD

Discussions of scientific method invariably begin by stressing that scientific method is *empirical*. This is a statement about the type of evidence or data that is examined, and it means the data must be the product of direct experience or observation. If this seems an obvious requirement, remember that for much of our history empirical evidence had no special status. In fact, it was often scorned in favour of quotations from earlier "authorities" or religious writings, or took second place to intuition and mystical insights. Where direct observation is not demanded, one person's opinion is as good as another's, and debates rage endlessly. No reliable structure of knowledge, each piece resting on earlier work, can be built under such circumstances. Directly observable evidence is accessible to more than one observer. That is, it is open to public scrutiny. There may be disagreements about the interpretation or meaning of the evidence, but there should be agreement about its nature.

It is permissible to use the findings of other researchers without personally repeating their observations, and scientists often cite earlier work. At first glance this may smack of the philosopher quoting an authority, such as Plato or Aristotle, but there is an important difference. A scientific report, unlike a philosophical treatise, clearly describes the way in which observations were made. Another researcher can replicate the procedures and check the findings, and a great deal of research does involve replication of earlier studies. Nevertheless, the individual scientist who uses the findings of another researcher is demonstrating trust, and the betrayal of this trust by falsifying data and reporting faked observations is regarded as the most heinous crime in the scientific community.

The type of psychological evidence that most clearly meets the empirical criteria is the data used by psychobiologists and behaviourists, whose approaches are discussed in Chapters 3 and 4 of this text. The psychobiologist examines physiological structures and biochemical processes. The behaviourist focusses on the directly observable behaviour of organisms. However, when you proceed to Chapter 5 and examine the cognitive approach, you will find that many of the concepts employed, such as coding and organization of information, are processes that must be inferred to some extent from observed behaviours.

The humanist approach (Chapter 7) uses data such as a person's perception of himself or herself, and here too one might wonder whether this data meets the empirical criteria. A self-perception is directly observable only by the person who is perceiving himself and is not directly accessible to the observations of others. Nevertheless, such evidence is widely used and many psychologists are willing to accept it as legitimate data. Usually, however, there is a requirement that personal experiences, such as a self-perception, be made accessible to public scrutiny in some way. One technique used is the Q-sort, where a subject picks out adjectives, written on cards, that he feels are descriptive of himself. With this technique the primary data that the psychologist uses in gauging the perception of the subject is a piece of behaviour—the subject's choice of adjectives—and this piece of behaviour is verifiable by other observers.

The psychoanalyst, whose approach is described in Chapter 6, has the most difficulty in clearly meeting empirical standards, because his focus is on the unconscious contents and processes of the mind. Not only can these not be directly observed by an outsider, they are not even accessible to the subject concerned, as they are not part of his conscious awareness. Once again, however, techniques are available to make these phenomena more accessible. Among the data used by psychoanalysts are the subject's dreams and interpretations of ambiguous pictures and ink blots. The subject's actual behaviour in recounting the dreams or interpreting the ambiguous pictures is a piece of raw data that is directly observable and accessible to outsiders.

Although a case may be made that basic elements of the evidence used in all the approaches discussed in this book do meet empiricai standards, psychologists have disagreed whether approaches such as humanism and psychoanalysis are truly empirical. The authors of this book take the position that all the approaches discussed can potentially meet the rigid data requirements of an empirical science, at least as far as the raw data are concerned. However, some of the theoretical structures that are inferred from the raw data are more easily tested than others. In the critical discussions of the approaches that are presented later, the reader will discover that this is often a more pertinent factor in assessing the value of an approach than is the nature of the basic data.

The gathering of facts or data is merely the first step of the scientific process. Science also involves the ordering of facts and the identification and discovery of lawful relations between facts. This step involves *induction,* or the deriving of abstract, general rules from the observations. A systematic and organized set of such hypotheses is called a *theory.*

Let us suppose that a researcher has noticed that people who were the first-born child in their families have a greater tendency than later-born children to be relatively conservative in their views, anxious, and dependent on the social support of others. In addition, later-born children tend to be freer thinkers, less anxious and more independent of other people. The researcher proceeds systematically to gather evidence about the behavioural styles of first- and later-born children. He takes care to define precisely what he means by such terms as "conservative" and "anxious," and he ensures that he is observing a representative sample of men and women of varied backgrounds and ages.

Studying his data the researcher observes that there is a reliable tendency for first-born and later-born people to differ in their behaviours. By induction he proceeds from the data he has, which refers to only a sample of people, to the general hypothesis that first-born children have different patterns of behaviour in later life than do later-born children. The first-born tend to be more conservative, anxious and dependent. As we suggested earlier, the process of induction has involved proceeding from a limited set of observations to an abstract and general rule.

However, the researcher is not yet finished. He has a theory based on empirical observation and induction, but the theory has not been tested. The next step involves a process of *deduction,* or the derivation of new hypotheses or predictions from the theory. If the predictions are not confirmed, when tested, the theory must be reconsidered. But what happens if the predictions are confirmed?

Does this prove that the theory is correct? The answer is No. The fact that some predictions based on the theory are confirmed does not imply that all future predictions will be confirmed. In a sense the dice are loaded against the researcher. A hundred accurate predictions cannot prove that his theory is true, but one inaccurate prediction disconfirms the theory, at least in part. It is this aspect of scientific procedure that is most strikingly different from the informal theorizing that people often indulge in. Too often we consider our informal theories to have been proven if one or two predictions based on the theories are confirmed. We regard the matter as closed. The scientist's theory, on the other hand, is an open system that is constantly being exposed to further tests. The scientist is always prepared to modify or even abandon a theory if new data suggests the theory is inadequate.

In the example we cited, the researcher can proceed from his general proposition about the nature of first- and later-born people to any number of specific predictions. For example, he may deduce that first-borns will function more effectively in stressful situations if they have company, and that they will seek out other people when they are anxious or frightened. In this form, these hypotheses do not immediately suggest ways of confirming or disconfirming themselves, because they are still too general in their nature. So the researcher goes further and may predict that in a particular situation, such as a wartime air force, first-borns will be more successful bomber pilots than fighter pilots. Furthermore, if later-borns prefer to face stress by themselves, they should be more successful as fighter pilots than as bomber pilots, because the fighter pilot meets dangerous situations individually, while the bomber pilot is a member of a closely knit team. (These predictions were tested during the Second World War, and both were confirmed.)

The second hypothesis that was deduced suggests that first-borns, more than later-borns, will seek out the company of other people when they are anxious. Making a testable prediction out of this hypothesis involves creating a specific situation in which people are made nervous, and then observing whether they opt to be with others or by themselves. Stanley Schachter led subjects to believe they would be receiving a painful electric shock, and then gave them the option of waiting by themselves or with others. First-borns usually chose to wait with others while later-borns indicated no preference, supporting the second hypothesis.

You will notice that the theory, as we phrased it, is a sparse one scarcely worthy of the name "theory." Many other questions immediately present themselves, such as what causes first-borns and later-borns to differ in their behavioural styles? And other hypotheses might be added as well. It could be predicted that parents have different ways of interacting with their first- and later-born offspring. They may be more protective and supportive of first-born children who, for a time, have the status of only children. Obviously this hypothesis may also be tested and it, in turn, leads to other hypotheses. For instance, only children, and later-born children who are much younger than their elder siblings, also are likely to be over-protected and receive an unusual amount of social support; they may be similar to first-borns. Thus the theory tends to grow and develop into a detailed set of hypotheses and statements about the effects of birth order on behaviour. This is another noticeable characteristic of the scientific procedure—theories are dynamic and tend to grow, as well as being constantly subject to modification and qualification as more and more evidence is collected.

Earlier we mentioned that to collect rigorous data about such qualities as "anxiety" or "conservative attitude," the researcher must define precisely what he means by these terms. This precision of definition is another way in which scientists differ from lay people. The problem is more urgent in psychology than in many other sciences because so many of the quantities dealt with in psychology are familiar to lay people and have vague colloquial meanings. This is not a problem shared by the physicist, for example, because the quantities he deals with, such as entropy, radiation or energy quanta, are not part of the common language and have only a single, precisely defined scientific meaning.

Compare the physicist's terms with terms such as "anxiety" or "conservatism." Most of us could present some sort of definition for these terms, but almost certainly we would not be in total agreement with each other. Similarly, psychologists, if they relied upon vague colloquial understandings of such terms, would not be able to agree with each other as to what the terms meant. To overcome this problem psychologists and other scientists use what are termed *operational definitions*. Operational definitions are precisely worded in terms of the operations necessary to measure a particular concept. By stipulating the *method of measuring* things such as anxiety and conservatism, psychologists can agree about what constitutes an anxious or a conservative person. Two psychologists, using the same operational definition, can agree precisely how anxious or how conservative any given person is.

What operational definitions gain in precision, they inevitably lose in richness and in the connotations of the lay language. Thus, when one describes a person as being "anxious," in layman's terms, much more is conveyed than if one describes him as having an anxiety score of 36 on a questionnaire designed to measure anxiety. The latter score may be derived from the number of times the subject answers "Yes" to questions such as: "Do you often feel as though you have butterflies in your stomach?" or "Do you worry a great deal about what the future holds for you?" Because of the specificity of the items that are used to measure the level of anxiety in an anxiety questionnaire, the resulting score has a very precise meaning, but it lacks the fullness of connotation of the word "anxiety" used by the layman.

In summary, the scientific method involves:

1. The precise definition of terms in the form of *operational definitions* that stipulate the methods of measurement to be used.

2. The collection of data by *empirical, first-hand observation*.

3. The *induction* of general principles.

4. The building of *theories*, consisting of organized sets of hypotheses.

5. The *deduction* of new hypotheses that can be tested from the theories.

COLLECTING THE DATA

We have stressed that the basis of any scientific investigation is the collection of data by first-hand observation. Psychologists use many different techniques to collect their data; the technique usually is dictated by the nature of the subject studied. In this section we will discuss six important methods of data collection: surveys, naturalistic observations, experimentation, correlational studies, case studies and psychological tests.

Surveys

Surveys are frequently used by social psychologists seeking to discover the attitudes of large populations of people. The opinion polls conducted by governments, newspapers, and radio and television stations are examples of surveys. Most surveys are conducted by mailing questionnaires which the respondents are supposed to answer and return to the researcher. Although it is cheap and quick, this is not the preferred method because the proportion of questionnaires returned is usually low. In addition, a written set of questions is an inflexible instrument, likely to be interpreted slightly differently by each respondent. Most of us have been in the position of having to answer a question with a "Yes" or a "No," when what we would prefer to answer with was a qualified Yes, stating the conditions under which our answer holds.

More elaborate surveys use interviewers who visit the respondents at their homes or places of employment, and present the questions orally. A good interviewer can help the respondents interpret the questions, and formulate answers that reflect opinions more accurately than do the answers to written questionnaires. When a government ministry launches a survey using interviewers, a commercial company which specializes in surveys is frequently hired to conduct the door-to-door interview. It is usually stipulated that a definite percentage of the predetermined sample, for example 75 per cent, must be located and interviewed. Often this necessitates four or five attempts by the interviewers to catch the respondents at home—a costly technique.

You might wonder why researchers are so concerned about getting a high proportion of replies. The first reason is that if we are trying to determine the attitudes of a large population, as the federal government wished when it surveyed the attitude of Canadians to capital punishment, it is necessary to obtain a relatively large sample if results are to be trustworthy. If we were content to stop the first six people who passed a certain street corner in Vancouver, their responses might be totally unrepresentative of the attitudes of Canadians in general. By sheer chance we might stop six diehard abolitionists and come away with the conclusion that 100 per cent of Canadians are strongly opposed to capital punishment. Obviously our chances of getting a representative sample with opinions reflecting the opinions of Canadians in general would be better if we stopped 100 people, and even better if we interviewed 1,000 people.

But there is more to it than this. Suppose we decide in advance that the sample of the population being surveyed should contain at least 1,000 respondents. It is easier to start off with an initial sample of 2,000 and settle for a 50 per cent response rate, which would give us our 1,000 respondents, rather than to start with a sample of 1,330, and insist on a 75 per cent contact rate. However, the latter method is the preferred one. The reason is that we know from past experience that opinions about such things as capital punishment tend to change with the level of education, the social class and sex of the respondent, as well as other factors. If our survey is to produce information about the attitudes of Canadians in general, it is essential that the sample we use have a makeup similar to the makeup of the total Canadian population. Thus, it should contain roughly the same proportion of people with university degrees as the general population, the same proportion of men and women, the same proportion of people of various ages, proportionate numbers of people from different geographical regions, and so on. Only by choosing a sample that corresponds to the general population in important characteristics such as those mentioned, can we extrapolate from our sample to the opinions of Canadians in general. A sample whose composition corresponds to the composition of the population from which it is drawn is called a *representative sample*. It should now be clear why researchers try to achieve a high contact rate: it is futile to plan a carefully balanced and selected sample if the sample that actually responds is only a small, possibly biased, version of the original.

Say, for example, that the interviewers were visiting the chosen respondents at home. If all visits were made during normal office hours on weekdays, most of the respondents contacted would be housewives, although we might have painstakingly balanced our sample for sex and occupation. Only by insisting on a high contact rate, which would require the interviewers to return in the evenings and/or during weekends, can we be sure that the representative nature of the original sample is maintained.

Generally, when one plans a survey, detailed information about all the potential respondents is not available. What researchers often do in cases like this is to choose a *random sample* from the general population. If the sample is truly random, in that any member of the population has an equal chance of being sampled and the sample is sufficiently large, there is an excellent statistical chance that the sample will be a truly representative one. It will contain the same proportions of different types of people as the general population from which the sample was drawn. Reliable data from surveys, then, depend on surveying an appropriate sample of the population. This sample may be obtained by ensuring that it is sufficiently large and truly representative of the population, either because it was chosen to represent the population fairly, or because it was drawn at random from the population.

Naturalistic Observations and Unobtrusive Measures

Surveys are often the only feasible instruments to use when one is investigating the attitudes of large populations. However, all forms of questionnaires and interviews suffer from the fact that people often do not behave in perfect accordance with their reported attitudes. In a classical study of racial discrimination in the United States carried out in the 1930s, Richard LaPiere found that although a very large number of restaurant owners indicated on a questionnaire that they would not serve Asian patrons, those restaurants usually did admit Asians when they presented themselves. The point is that whatever our attitudes and intentions may be, the situational imperatives present at any given moment are often more influential in dictating our actions. In the study mentioned it is likely that the restaurateurs simply did not want to make a scene in front of their other customers, so the situation produced actions that one could not predict from a simple knowledge of their stated attitudes.

Another common problem with attitude measures, surveys and questionnaires is that the subjects are often concerned about presenting a certain image to the researcher. Usually this takes the form of presenting themselves as having attitudes similar to the researcher's. If two interviewers, one strongly in favour of capital punishment and one strongly opposed to capital punishment, interviewed the same sample of subjects, it is very likely that subtle cues given off by the interviewers, whether they intended to cue the subjects or not, would influence the results. So the abolitionist would get many more abolitionist-type responses and the retentionist would find many supporters of capital punishment.

This is not to suggest that the interviewers would be trying deliberately to bias the subject responses in any way. Despite the best efforts of interviewers and experimenters, human subjects are extremely responsive to subtle cues. They are very willing to present suitable attitudes or to act in a fashion that they perceive as being cooperative. This is known as responding to the *demand characteristics* of the study.

Apart from the discrepancy between attitudes and actions, it has often been pointed out that subjects answering questionnaires or taking part in a study in a laboratory are in unfamiliar and unnatural situations. Therefore their behaviour is not necessarily truly representative of their behaviour in the real world. But it is real world behaviour that is usually of most interest to social scientists. The ideal way to collect data, therefore, is by *naturalistic observation,* or observing the way people normally behave in their usual environments. One problem that presents itself in this kind of study, however, is that when an observer is present people cease to behave naturally. Heisenberg, a German physicist, stated a Principle of Indeterminacy in 1927, suggesting that it is theoretically impossible to observe *both* the position and the speed of an electron, because the act of observing one of these variables immediately alters the other. In the same way, when psychologists try to observe human subjects in natural surroundings, their observations may change the phenomena they are trying to investigate. Subjects react to the simple presence of an observer. To minimize this effect, psychologists have devoted a great deal of time and ingenuity to developing *unobtrusive* or *non-reactive measures*. The ideal is to become the proverbial fly-on-the-wall. It observes everything without in any way influencing the behaviour of the subjects being observed.

One of the most obvious ways of making unobtrusive observations is by means of hidden hardware such as movie cameras, tape recorders and one-way mirrors. Apart from the unethical nature of such practices, and their illegality in many cases, hidden hardware is generally clumsy and not well adapted to real life observation. Some of the more ingenious methods developed by psychologists and others interested in unobtrusive measurement are suggested by detective stories and real life police practices. Sherlock Holmes was adept at drawing inferences about behaviour from physical traces. By observing that the stairs leading to Dr. Watson's newly purchased practice were well-worn, he was able to infer that the previous physician had had a steady stream of patients. Watson had, therefore, made a wise choice. The list of unobtrusive measures available is too long to catalogue here. Interested readers are referred to the excellent book by Webb, Campbell, Schwartz and Sechrest mentioned at the end of this chapter. Here is a small sample of the techniques that have been successfully used:

1. Wear and tear on library books have been used as an index of the interests of a population.

2. The dial settings on the radios of cars brought in for servicing have been used to compare the popularity of different radio stations.

3. A comparison of the number of male and female tombstones in ancient Rome was used to decide whether male or female Romans lived longest. Although the dates of birth and death were not on the stones, the assumption was made that the first spouse to die was more likely to be commemorated by a tombstone erected by the survivor.

4. The number of life insurance policies sold by automatic vending machines at airports immediately after a major air disaster has been used to estimate the increased apprehension of air travellers.

5. Letters addressed to different organizations or people with obviously ethnic names have been left on the sidewalk. The number of letters picked up and mailed by passers-by serves as an index of the favour or disfavour with which the organizations or ethnic groups are viewed.

6. Many other invaluable sources of information about the behaviour of people are a matter of public record, for example marriage records, births and deaths, and census information stored in government archives. Archival information of this kind was used by sociologist Emile Durkheim to relate the incidence of suicide to sex, race, marital status, time of day, season of year, education and religion.

It is not always necessary to go to these elaborate lengths to make naturalistic observations unobtrusively. Sometimes the behaviour social scientists wish to observe is public behaviour, such as driving habits, behaviour on subways, or behaviour towards beggars. However, when unobtrusive measures are required, there is a vast array of non-reactive methods available to provide information about the behaviour of that most fascinating of animals—man.

Experiments

Despite their desirability, naturalistic observations suffer from one major defect—lack of control. One irrefutable fact which psychologists are constantly confronted with is that human behaviour is multi-determined. There are almost always a number of factors affecting it. To determine the effect of a single factor, it is essential that all other influences on a particular behaviour be held constant. Within a naturalistic situation it is usually impossible to achieve this kind of control. It is the need to limit the number of possible influences, or at least to hold all of them but the one being examined constant, that drives psychologists away from naturalistic observation into the more manageable environment of the laboratory. There, controlled experiments can be carried out. It is from laboratory experimentation that much of our knowledge about human behaviour is derived.

Strictly speaking, an experiment does not have to be carried out in a laboratory to be an experiment. If a suitable degree of control can be achieved in a real world environment, it is perfectly possibly to carry out a true experiment there. These experiments are called field experiments. It is not the venue that determines whether or not an investigation can be called experimentation—it is the existence of the necessary degree of control. To illustrate the experimental process, and to stress that a perfectly rigorous experiment can be conducted in the field, we will examine a social psychology experiment performed by Anthony Doob and Alan Gross. (1968)

Psychologists have spent a great deal of time investigating aggressive behaviour in human beings. One of the best-supported hypotheses about aggressive behaviour is that we tend to aggress when we are frustrated or when something prevents us reaching a desired goal. Frustration leads to aggression which very often takes the form of making a hostile move against the person or object who frustrates us. A three-year-old who cannot play with a toy because another child has taken it attacks the other child physically; an adult who has lost money to a recalcitrant cigarette-vending machine kicks the machine; while an employee who has been passed over for promotion makes scathing comments about the supervisor.

Doob and Gross hypothesized that the status of the frustrating agent determines the probability of us actually making an overt, aggressive move against that person. The frustrated three-year-old is more likely to attack another child who takes his toy than an adult who does the same thing. The employee who has been frustrated by missing promotion is unlikely to verbally attack his supervisor to his face. The supervisor's status, with its attendant power, inhibits direct aggressive action because the employee fears retaliation. Doob and Gross theorized that even in situations where a high-status frustrator is unlikely to retaliate, our previous experience with the powers wielded by high-status people will probably inhibit aggression. In a general form their hypothesis may be stated: the high-status of a frustrating person inhibits aggression against that person.

Notice that in this form there is no clear indication of how the hypothesis might be tested. Notice too that key terms such as *frustration* and *aggression* have not been precisely defined. One might say the hypothesis is couched in pre-scientific or colloquial language. To test the hypothesis, Doob and Gross had to proceed from the general statement to a specific hypothesis, and provide operational definitions of the key terms.

Instead of a laboratory experiment they decided to conduct a field experiment within a context that often provides for frustrating situations—driving a car in city traffic. Their specific hypothesis was that *a frustrated driver would be more likely to behave aggressively towards a frustrating driver when the frustrator appeared to have low, rather than high status. Frustration* was operationally defined as the experience of being held up by a car stopped at a green light. *Aggression* was defined as horn honking. *High status* was defined as being well-dressed and driving a late-model Chrysler Imperial. *Low status* was defined as being sloppily dressed and driving an old, rusty Ford station wagon or Rambler (two cars were used in the low-status condition). You will notice that the operational definitions of the key terms lack the generality and richness of connotation of the terms used in everyday language; however, what is lost in richness has been gained in precision. It is now perfectly clear what is meant by the key terms.

The experiment went as follows: high-status and low-status drivers, appropriately attired and driving appropriate cars, timed their arrivals at an intersection controlled by a traffic light. They arrived just as the light turned red. If a single car stopped behind them, a trial was counted, and when the light turned green, the experimenter's car remained stationary until twelve seconds had elapsed, or until the driver of the car behind honked twice.

The involuntary subjects of the experiment, the eighty-two men and women who were blocked behind the experimenters' cars, were considered to have taken aggressive action if they honked at least once within the twelve seconds.

Doob and Gross' hypothesis was well supported; 84 per cent of the frustrated victims honked at the poorly dressed drivers in the old cars, but only 50 per cent of the victims honked at the high-status drivers. Considering only those who did honk, the victims waited longer before they honked at the high-status drivers. Doob and Gross also noted that two drivers rammed the low-status cars, while no drivers attempted to ram the high-status vehicle.

So far we have mentioned a general statement of the hypothesis being investigated and a specific statement with attendant operational definitions. These are characteristic of all experiments. Another important characteristic is the existence of a variable which is manipulated and a variable which, it is predicted, will change as a result of the manipulations. (A variable is any measurable quantity.) In the Doob and Gross study, the variable that was manipulated was the status of the frustrating drivers. The variables that, it was predicted, would be affected by the manipulation were whether the frustrated driver would honk at all and, if he did, how long he would wait before honking.

All true experiments have one or more variables which are manipulated called the *independent variable*(s) and one or more variables which, according to the hypothesis, will change as a result of the manipulation called the *dependent variable*(s). In the Doob and Gross experiment, the independent variable was the status of the frustrator; the dependent variables were honking, and elapsed time before honking when honking did occur.

An experiment has at least two conditions distinguished by manipulations of the independent variable. Because it is the effects of the independent variable that we are interested in, we seek to control any other variables which might also affect the dependent variable. In the Doob and Gross experiment, two other variables which might have had an effect were the location of the traffic light (conceivably one would be more likely to honk downtown than in a sedate residential neighbourhood or in front of a hospital) and the day of the week. The experimenters controlled for these variables by ensuring that approximately equal numbers of high- and low-status trials were run at each intersection used, and by conducting all trials between 10:30 A.M. and 5:30 P.M. on a Sunday.

Other important extraneous variables which often affect the dependent variable in an experiment are subject characteristics. In a typical laboratory experiment we try to ensure that the groups of subjects used in each condition are similar by allocating subjects in a way that will ensure similarity of sex, background and personality factors across the groups. This was not possible in the Doob and Gross study because there was no way of vetting the subjects beforehand. It was quite fortuitous *who* stopped behind the experimenters. In this case, however, similarity of the subject groups in the high- and low-status conditions could be assumed, because, of the total driver population being sampled, any driver had an equal chance of being stuck behind the low- or high-status driver. The subject selection meets the criterion of *random sampling* which we discussed when we considered the choice of samples for surveys.

In the Doob and Gross study the independent variable was manipulated to achieve high-status and low-status conditions. In a sense both experimental drivers had status, though of different kinds. In some experiments though, the manipulation of the independent variable involves the presence of the variable in one condition and its absence in the other. If, for example, we were conducting an experiment to test the hypothesis that the consumption of alcohol results in a greater number of errors in a driver-simulation task, the manipulation might involve drivers who had imbibed no alcohol at all, and drivers who had consumed a stipulated amount of alcohol— such as four shots of whisky in a period of one hour. In this case the teetotal group is being used essentially to establish a baseline, or to find out how many errors are normally made by sober drivers. When we conduct this type of experiment, where the one value of the independent variable is zero (the teetotal condition), we often speak of an *experimental* group and a *control* group (the drinkers and the non-drinkers respectively).

In the drinking-driving experiment we have outlined we could ensure similarity of subject characteristics in the experimental and control groups by carefully allocating the same number of males and females, younger people and older people and so on, to each group. As an alternative we might use random selection by assigning subjects at random to either the experimental or the control condition. In the drinking-driver case we have another option which is highly desirable when it is possible. Each subject can serve as his own control. To achieve this we would have all subjects attempt the simulation task twice, once when they had been drinking and once when they had not been imbibing. To prevent practice of the task from introducing unwanted effects, we would have half the subjects first attempt the task in the teetotal condition and, later, perform the task in the drinking condition. The other half of the subjects would reverse the procedure. They first attempt the task after consuming their four whiskies. Later, when the alcohol had been eliminated from their systems, they attempt the task teetotal.

Correlational Studies

In an experiment the hypothesis postulates or implies a cause-effect relationship between the independent and the dependent variables. We employ some manipulation of the independent variable to test the hypothesis. But it is not always possible to perform such manipulations. We might, for example, postulate that adults who possess a personality style marked by an extreme respect for authority, conservative economic thinking and exaggerated patriotism (sometimes called "authoritarian personalities") are, as a result, more prone to racial prejudice.

If personality characteristics of this type could be created by experimental manipulation, which they cannot, and if it were considered ethical and proper to perform such manipulations, which it is not, one could conceivably design an experiment to test the hypothesis. We could create different levels of authoritarianism (the independent variable) and measure the extent of racial prejudice shown by our subjects (the dependent variable). However, the experimental manipulation cannot be performed. In cases like these, it is common to proceed with a *correlational* study. This involves examining the extent to which two variables are *correlated* or covary. In the case cited, we might proceed to define authoritarianism and racial prejudice operationally by developing questionnaires designed to measure these two variables. The operational definition of authoritarianism is, then, the score on the authoritarian measure. The operational definition of prejudice is the score on the prejudice measure. We sample the population, giving all subjects both measures. If high authoritarian scores consistently co-occur with high prejudice scores, while low authoritarian scores occur in conjunction with low prejudice scores, we could state that authoritarianism and prejudice are highly correlated. Unlike a true experiment, however, such a correlational study does *not* permit us to claim that a cause-effect relationship exists between authoritarianism and prejudice.

A simple example should make this point clear. A scientist observes that the number of popsicles sold in the city of Vancouver correlates with the softness of the tarmac on the roads, i.e., high popsicle sales coincide with soft tar, while low popsicle sales co-occur with hard tar. Obviously the softening of the tar is not the cause of the increased consumption of popsicles. Nor is the consumption of popsicles the cause of the softening. Both variables are, in fact, dependent variables influenced by a third variable, the heat of the sun. On hot days tar melts, and people rush to buy cooling popsicles. On cool days the tar hardens, and thoughts of popsicles are replaced by thoughts of hot cocoa or rum toddies. In the social sciences it is not always clear what the third, common factor that is influencing two correlated variables may be, if one does exist. So, with scientific caution, psychologists do not claim cause-effect relationships when only a correlation between two variables has been observed. To claim that a cause-effect relationship has been demonstrated one must have performed a true experiment with a manipulation of the independent variable.

Although correlations cannot demonstrate cause and effect, they do have the valuable property of permitting us to make predictions about the state of one variable on the basis of knowledge about the other one. In the example we cited, one might predict from a knowledge of the softness of the tar on the roads the approximate consumption of popsicles. The accuracy of such predictions depends on the extent to which the variables are correlated; a high correlation permits more accurate predictions.

Educational psychologists have repeatedly noted a high correlation between intelligence, as measured by intelligence tests, and success at school and college. However, the correlation is not perfect because intelligence is not the only factor related to academic success. Motivation, availability of time and financial means, to name only three other factors, are also involved. Because the correlation between intelligence and academic success is not perfect, one cannot predict with absolute certainty whether or not a given individual will succeed academically when all that is known is the intelligence score.

A high correlation permits you to make predictions with a greater accuracy than a random estimate possesses. It is an informed guess, and the guess becomes progressively more informed with higher correlations.

Case Studies

Most psychological studies and experiments are conducted on groups of subjects rather than on individuals. This is not because the psychologist is unconcerned about the behaviour of the individual human being, but because scientists aim at producing statements or propositions that are generally true. It is fascinating, and often useful, to be able to make a prediction about an individual, but it is more useful and more informative to be able to make predictions that are true for large numbers of people. Such predictions are probabilistic in their nature, and they may not be perfectly accurate for any given individual. For instance, it is generally true that people tend to conform and behave in the same way as the people around them, but that does not mean that you will always follow the pack.

At this point two important concepts dealing with the nature of experiments and the nature of the sample of subjects involved in an experiment are needed: the concepts of *internal* and *external* validity. When we speak of the internal validity of an experiment, we are considering whether or not the experiment was carried out in such a way that external factors that could effect the outcome were controlled. If the changes noted in the dependent variable could have been brought about *only* by manipulations of the independent variable, and not by any other factor, then we are entitled to say that the experiment possesses internal validity and demonstrates a cause-effect relationship. In the Doob and Gross study, external factors that might have affected the aggressive behaviour of the subjects, such as the day of the week and the location of the traffic light, were similar in both high- and low-status conditions. Therefore the experimenters were entitled to claim that their study possessed internal validity, i.e., only the differences in status of the frustrating motorists (the experimenters) could have caused the differences in behaviour of the subjects. Because the experiment was properly controlled it had internal validity and the experimenters were able to demonstrate a cause-effect relationship.

External validity is another question: it refers to the extent to which we may justifiably generalize from experimental results obtained from a limited sample of subjects to a larger population of people. The essential condition for being able to generalize from a sample to a larger population is that the sample must be truly representative of the population. If you refer back to our discussion of sampling in surveys, you will remember that there are two ways to ensure that a sample is representative of a population. Either the sample must be drawn in such a way that all important qualities of the population, such as age, education and income, are proportionately represented, or the sample must be drawn from the population randomly. Random sampling means that every member of the population has an equal chance of being selected for the sample. In the Doob and Gross study, the representativeness of the sample was ensured by random selection, and this is the usual experimental practice. The Doob and Gross study, therefore, not only possessed internal validity, it also possessed external validity. The experimenters were not only entitled to draw conclusions about cause and effect, but also to extrapolate from the sample and make a general statement about the population of car drivers.

Therefore the majority of psychological experiments involve groups of subjects rather than a single subject, because psychologists are seeking external validity, with the intention of making statements that will be generally true about a population of people. However, working with a single subject does permit detailed observations and experiments that simply cannot be conducted on a group. Clinical psychologists, especially, whose major involvement is with individuals need this kind of detailed information. To provide it they carry out a *case study* or a study on a single subject. Such case studies are typically extremely rich in detail and make for fascinating reading. Often case studies also are extremely suggestive, and some major psychological theories have been developed by workers such as Sigmund Freud and Jean Piaget, who derived their data from detailed case studies.

Case studies are a legitimate means of psychological investigation, as are experiments involving only one subject. The limitation is that an experiment involving a single person may have internal validity if it is properly carried out, and therefore may be used as the basis for a conclusion about cause and effect. It cannot have external validity. A single individual cannot satisfactorily represent a group, and results obtained with a single person cannot be used to make statements about a population. How then did Freud and Piaget justify theories that purport to describe the functioning of people in general? The justification rests on repeated case studies, carried out on many individuals, one at a time. If the final sample can be considered representative of a population, then extrapolation to the population is warranted. Conclusions based on case study methods should be examined with this criterion in mind before external validity is assumed.

Psychological Tests

Research psychologists and psychologists in the clinical, counselling and personality areas, frequently wish to obtain information about a particular aspect of a person's mental functioning, such as their verbal ability. They obtain this information by sampling the subject's performance, using a psychological test. Often, though not always, these tests are pencil-and-paper affairs, such as the familiar intelligence tests. Some of the more important tests are: achievement tests, which measure the extent to which one has mastered a particular skill (the examinations you took at school were achievement tests); aptitude tests, which measure one's potential for learning various skills; interest inventories designed to reveal where one's interests lie; and personality tests designed to probe different aspects of personality. Psychological tests have become part and parcel of the repertoire of personnel and placement officers in recent years, so many people have been exposed to them when being assessed for promotion or a new job.

Whatever the natures of different psychological tests, they all have this much in common: tests deal with a relatively small sample of behaviours and their results are used to throw light on a much larger population of possible behaviours. In this respect, psychological tests function rather like surveys, except that when we use tests we are looking at a sample of the *behaviours* of one person in an attempt to draw conclusions about a larger *behavioural picture*. A survey looks at a sample of people in an attempt to draw conclusions about a larger population of people.

To give results that are useful a test must possess two characteristics: it must be *reliable* and it must be *valid*. In its simplest form, reliability refers to the ability of a test to give the same result consistently. If you stepped on your bathroom scales and noted that the scales read 160 pounds, stepped off, and then immediately stepped back on and noticed that the reading was now 175 pounds, you would be likely to conclude that the scales were malfunctioning and were unreliable. In the same way, one of the most important considerations for a psychological test is whether or not test and re-test results are similar. If we test the same individual several times at weekly intervals and find that she obtains different scores each time, we would seriously doubt whether the test was reliable enough to provide dependable and useful information.

The second consideration, validity, concerns the fact that a test must necessarily rely on only a small sample of behaviour. An aptitude test designed to indicate whether an applicant has the potential to learn a clerical job may take less than one hour and involve a number of paper and pencil tasks which are related to the functions of a clerk. We cannot expose the examinee to all the real life activities of a clerk in the time available. Nor can the paper and pencil test items fully reflect all the different real life tasks a clerk might have to perform on the job. The question of validity then becomes the question of whether or not our aptitude test really is measuring clerical potential. The validity of a test is analogous to the external validity of an experiment. In both cases the question is whether we may generalize from our limited sample of behaviours or people, respectively, to a larger population of behaviours or people.

There are different kinds of test validity, but all are concerned with the basic question: "*What* is it that this test is measuring?" (The equivalent question when we are considering the reliability of a test is: "*How accurately* does this test measure whatever it is that it is measuring?") To determine whether or not a test is valid, test results must be compared with some standard. The different kinds of validity that tests may possess are differentiated by the kind of standard used to evaluate the tests.

The simplest type of validity that a test may possess, and the least satisfactory, is *face validity*. This usually takes the form of having a panel of informed judges scan the items on the test, deciding whether or not the items look as if they measure the property they are supposed to be measuring. The difficulty with this approach is that the criterion being used by the judges is subjective. Consider, for example, a teacher-education questionnaire designed to evaluate the effectiveness of college instructors. If the panel of judges feel that a sense of humour is an important requirement for effective teaching, they may consider that an item such as "Does this instructor make jokes?" has face validity and measures teaching effectiveness. However, without objective evidence the beliefs of the judges cannot be assessed, and the subjective criteria they use must be taken on faith. Psychologists sometimes scathingly refer to this type of validity as "faith validity."

A more satisfactory type of validity is *convergent validity*. Here the scores that subjects obtain on a new test are compared with the scores the same subjects obtain on an established test that measures the same thing. The new test has convergent validity if the two sets of test scores have a high correlation, allocating the same ranks to the subjects, and reflecting the same differences between the performances of subjects.

A third type of validity is *known-groups validity*. Say that we know that one group of instructors, the *A* group, are exceptional teachers. Their students always do well in common examinations, persevere with their studies and demonstrate a high level of interest. A second group, the Z instructors, regularly turn out students who fail common examinations, drop out of school, and show no interest or enthusiasm. If we accept the difference in student performance as the criterion, we can compare the scores obtained by A and Z teachers on the teacher-evaluation questionnaire. For the questionnaire to have known-groups validity, A teachers should do substantially better than Z teachers.

The final type of validity to be considered is *predictive validity*. A test has predictive validity if the test results are good predictors of some later performance. If we had apprentice mechanics write a test of mechanical aptitude before beginning their apprenticeships, the level of expertise attained by the mechanics after their training should correlate with their aptitude scores. If the correlation is low the aptitude test has poor predictive validity. The usefulness of the aptitude tests used by counsellors when they help their clients decide on careers hinges on the tests having predictive validity.

INTELLIGENCE TESTS

Tests of intelligence are of particular interest because almost all of us have written intelligence tests and been allotted "IQ scores," or intelligence quotients. In some cases these scores may have had major impacts on our career choices. There is a great deal of mythology about IQ, so a brief note about the background of intelligence tests and their uses is in order.

A French psychologist, Alfred Binet, is generally credited with originating intelligence tests at the turn of the century. At the time Binet was attempting to develop a method for identifying retarded school children for the French ministry of education. In collaboration with psychiatrist Theodore Simon, Binet devised a short test comprising items arranged in order of increasing difficulty. The items were chosen so that older children, in general, successfully answered more items than younger children. Binet considered that the most appropriate measure of intelligence was one based on the ability of a child to perform relative to his age level. Thus, if a ten-year-old performed at the average level of eleven-year-olds, that child was presumed to be more intelligent than the average ten-year-old. Similarly, children who performed at a level below the average level for their age group could be considered less intelligent. It thus became possible to speak of the *mental age* of a child, the age appropriate to his performance on the Binet test. *Chronological* age is the actual age of the children. If the mental age exceeded the chronological age, the child was considered more intelligent than average. If the mental age lagged behind the chronological age, the child was considered less intelligent. This procedure was soon improved by using as the measure of intelligence the intelligence quotient, the *ratio* of mental to chronological age.

An example will help make the procedure clear. Consider the case we cited of a ten-year-old performing at the average level of eleven-year-olds. The child has a mental age of eleven, but a chronological age of ten. The child's intelligence quotient is the ratio of mental to chronological age, or 11/10, multiplied by 100 to remove decimal points. Thus the child in this example has an IQ of 110. Similarly, a ten-year-old performing at an eight-year-old level would have an IQ of 80, a six-year-old with a mental age of nine would have an IQ of 150, and so on.

With some refinements most of the intelligence tests in use today use a similar principle to estimate intelligence scores.

Intelligence tests come in forms suitable for administration to groups, as well as for use with single individuals. In general, the individual tests show greater reliability and validity and are to be preferred. The reason for this is not so much in the makeup of the test as in the testing procedure. An administrator working with one examinee is in a position to notice whether or not the examinee is feeling physically up to par, exhibits symptoms of test anxiety or stress, and is taking the test seriously. In a group situation such factors may be overlooked, resulting in misleading scores. Unfortunately, lack of funds and lack of skilled personnel often mean that schoolchildren are tested in a group situation rather than individually. For this reason it is probably unwise to place tremendous stock on the results of a single IQ score. It is not unheard of for IQ's to change by as much as twenty points over two group testings.

There are correct and incorrect uses of intelligence tests. A general rule of thumb is that no psychological test result should be used in a way that may be detrimental to a subject. To exclude a person from admission to college or from a job solely on the basis of an IQ, especially if the IQ comes from a group-administered test, is both unfair and unwise. Intelligence tests do not reflect such factors as application and motivation which contribute substantially to the success of individuals in the academic and business world. Furthermore, intelligence tests have an inevitable cultural bias. The tests used in North America have been compiled largely by white, middle-class psychologists for use with upper- and middle-class children. Their ability to measure the intelligence of children from different social and cultural backgrounds has frequently been challenged.

It should also be noted that most intelligence tests have a large verbal component, and a large component that measures ability to deal with numerical problems. That is to say, in general only two aptitudes are being fully measured. Human beings have many other aptitudes which may not be correctly reflected by an IQ. Creativity, for example, or the ability to produce fresh, inventive and innovative thinking does not correlate very highly with IQ, although it is indisputably a major asset to people in a number of fields. It is because of the limited applicability of intelligence test scores that vocational guidance counsellors prefer to use batteries of aptitude tests. These measure qualities such as mechanical and spatial reasoning, as well as verbal fluency and numerical ability. Thus counsellors obtain a profile or set of separate scores about different abilities a person may possess.

By this time you may be wondering what the relevance of IQ is. The major role of intelligence tests and the area in which these tests possess fairly good predictive ability is in assessing potential for success in academic fields. It is for this reason that educational systems use intelligence tests widely. Taken by themselves, IQ's are not especially good predictors of success in non-academic fields, so it is unwise to base career decisions solely or largely on an IQ.

Much of the criticism of IQ has resulted from the neglect of this principle. Teachers, especially, have been accused of placing undue stress on IQ and not having a proper understanding of the limitations of intelligence tests. A study by Robert Rosenthal and Lenore Jacobson which demonstrates the dangers of this is often quoted. In the study, teachers were fed false information about students' "IQ's." It was suggested that certain children were "late bloomers" and could be expected to begin to make exceptional academic progress. Sure enough, the children singled out (who were chosen purely at random by the experimenters) did show marked improvement. This is, of course, simply another example of a self-fulfilling prophecy. The teachers, on the basis of the misinformation provided by the experimenters, subtly encouraged the children whom they thought were late bloomers, with the results that we have mentioned. For ethical reasons, other children could not be singled out as unlikely to make progress. However, the implication is that if teachers can effect improvement simply by having certain expectations, they also may influence children to perform below their potential level if they believe the children lack ability.

SUMMARY

In this section we have tried to throw some light on the factors that are involved in the scientific method of enquiry. These principles are general to all scientific disciplines and not the exclusive bailiwick of psychology and psychologists. The rigorous and highly conscious application of scientific method in psychology is especially important because most of us are already amateur psychologists and bring to the study of human behaviour stores of common-sense beliefs. These are frequently misleading, vague, ambiguous or factually incorrect. Physicists, astronomers and chemists are not plagued by the same problem because the phenomena they deal with do not have the same immediacy for the general population. Psychologists are faced with another special problem that makes the study of human behaviour one of the most difficult: atoms, stars and elements do not usually react and change their behaviour when they are observed, while human beings are highly reactive. For this reason much ingenuity has gone into developing non-reactive or unobtrusive methods of studying human behaviour.

While the preferred method of gaining information about behaviour is the experiment, surveys, correlational studies and case histories also play an important part. It is important to be able to distinguish a true experiment, from which cause-effect relationships can justifiably be deduced, from quasi-experimental investigations.

True experiments involve precisely worded hypotheses to be tested, with key terms operationally defined. They involve one or more independent variables which are manipulated, and one or more dependent variables which, it is hypothesized, will change as a result of the manipulations. A true experiment is also characterized by the control of extraneous variables that might effect the dependent measures, one of the most important forms of control being the appropriate allocation of subjects to experimental and control conditions.

Finally, the role of psychological tests was considered. It was pointed out that psychological tests sample only a small range of behaviours, so their validity must always be carefully examined. Too much emphasis on test results alone is unwise and may lead to unfair treatment of individuals. Ideally, the correct use of psychological tests is to help an individual gain insights into his own abilities, aptitudes and psychological makeup. Use of psychological tests by others to exclude individuals from jobs or study programs is considered unethical by many counselling psychologists.

Further Readings

Readers looking for a more detailed introduction to psychological research will find *Psychological Research* by Arthur Bachrach readable and informative. Thomas Kuhn has written a book called the *Structure of Scientific Revolutions,* which provides more general insights into the nature of the scientific process.

Focussing on psychology, H. J. Eysenck has provided a sort of consumer guide to psychology and psychologists in the *Uses and Abuses of Psychology*. In his book he tries to separate well-founded psychological findings from tentative results.

Finally, the most comprehensive work on unobtrusive measures is probably a paperback by Webb, Campbell, Schwartz and Sechrest, entitled *Unobtrusive Measures: Nonreactive Research in the Social Sciences*. Well-written, the book is a compendium of human ingenuity, as well as a valuable source of techniques for social scientists.

3

THE BIOLOGICAL APPROACH
William E. Glassman

Editor's Preface

In the first chapter we pointed out that one of the complicating factors in understanding behaviour is that behaviour is affected both by internal and external factors. The most stable of citizens changes his behaviour after downing several quick whiskies. But whether he attacks us or pledges eternal friendship depends on whether we insult him or buy a round of drinks.

A basic decision that must be made by a theorist trying to understand behaviour is whether to concentrate on internal or external factors. The psychobiologists largely choose to ignore external factors in favour of the internal, biological nature of the organisms whose behaviour they seek to understand. The focus of this chapter is on two internal components of human beings: their genetic inheritance and their makeup. By concentrating on these aspects, the psychobiologists have scored some notable successes in modifying behaviour through drug therapy. They have also provided us with invaluable insights into the effects that biological mechanisms have on our cognition, our moods and our actions.

THE BIOLOGICAL APPROACH

The biological approach to psychology, as its name implies, views man as a biological organism. What we do, and even what we think, is seen as having its basis in our physiological structure. The approach focusses on two major concerns: the relationship between mind and body, and the influence of heredity on behaviour. Each is a reflection of our biological nature, but the two aspects have separate histories.

Today, physiological researchers tend to view behaviour as being purely physical. As a doctor commented about possible chemical influences causing schizophrenia, *"Of course* it has to be physical. There isn't anything else up there." By "up there," he was referring to the brain. His starting assumption was that the brain determines behaviour. Although you may not find that surprising, in earlier times it would have been seen as very radical. In the seventeenth century, most people believed the body was controlled by an intangible soul. René Descartes (known for "I think, therefore I am") grappled with such questions of philosophy and human nature. ("Psychology" did not exist as a discipline yet.) A keen observer, but also deeply religious, Descartes tried to reconcile the apparent physical nature of the body with the intangible nature of the soul. The human body, he felt, was constructed like that of an animal—both were basically *machines.* However, he believed a person also had a soul which interacted with the physical body through a small gland in the brain called the pineal gland.

At one level, Descartes was a "materialist," seeing behaviour as having a physical basis. At the same time, his interactionist view (based on interaction of body and soul) was a compromise. Although it was a step forward, the conflict remained until the next century. In 1745, a French priest-turned-physician named Julien de La Mettrie contracted a fever, and noticed that this physical condition affected his mental powers as well as his physical ones. After his recovery, he published a book, *L'histoire naturelle de l'âme* (The Natural History of the Soul) in which he argued that the soul is no different from the mind, and that the body is but a machine. Further, he said the mind was part of the body. This caused a great outcry, but he held fast to his views, although he had to leave France. By the time of the French Revolution, a physician named Cabanis was able to argue that guillotine victims were not conscious after beheading, because consciousness was the function of the brain, just as digestion was the function of the stomach. Then, in 1861, a doctor at the insane asylum at Bicêtre, Paul Broca, was able to demonstrate, by post-mortem autopsy, that the cause of a man's inability to speak lay in a defect in a specific point in the brain. The proof of this "localization of function" was the final step in the progression of ideas. The acceptance of this finding completed the gradual change in attitude, from seeing behaviour as governed by an intangible soul, to the modern view of behaviour as having a physical basis. Many other workers in different countries also contributed to the accumulation of knowledge. The milestones mentioned here were chosen to demonstrate the gradual evolution of the approach.

The other main aspect of the biological approach, the role of heredity in behaviour, also had a gradual development. In the eighteenth century, people believed that each species of plant and animal had been independently created: as the Bible says, "every living creature after his kind." Still, there were indications that this might not be true. The great biologist Linneaus had published a catalogue of over 4,000 plant and animal species in 1735, and his orderly categories suggested connections among the species. Then, in 1809, a French naturalist named Lamarck presented the first widely known theory of evolution. Lamarck believed that variations developed through inheritance of acquired characteristics. For instance, giraffes acquired long necks because each generation strained a little further to get food, slightly stretching their necks, and passed this difference on to their offspring. Today Lamarckian evolution is generally discredited, but it was a significant step forward in suggesting a hereditary basis for characteristics.

The real revolution in thought came with the work of Charles Darwin. Darwin's theory, published in *The Origin of Species* (1859), was that variations among individuals of a species would occur by chance, but could in turn be passed on. His doctrine of "survival of the fittest" meant that only those variations which helped the individuals survive long enough to breed would be passed on. Darwin was not only advocating the inheritance of characteristics, but also an evolutionary link between man and all other species. In 1872 he made this even clearer by writing *The Expression of the Emotions in Man and Animals*. (Actually, it remained for the re-discovery of the work of the Austrian monk, Gregor Mendel, for a specific mechanism of heredity to be suggested.)

As with La Mettrie, Darwin came into conflict with religious doctrine, this time with the view that man was created "in God's image." The controversy raged for many years, but ultimately the evolutionary viewpoint expressed by Darwin became dominant. It formed the basis for the study of hereditary influences on behaviour.

Today, these two ideas—materialism and heredity—are the basic foundation of the biological approach to psychology. Compared to other approaches, the biological approach emphasizes getting "inside the black box"—that is, looking at the internal structure of the organism. Broca showed that a specific defect in the brain could destroy speech in an otherwise normal person. Darwin showed that what we are is at least partly due to what our parents are. In this chapter, we will look at how these ideas have been applied to provide current insights in psychology.

THE NATURE OF THE PHYSIOLOGICAL SYSTEM

The biological approach emphasizes the physical (or physiological) basis of behaviour, and the interactions between mind and body. The interactions work both ways: body can affect mind (as when coffee makes you tense); and mind can affect body (as when executives get ulcers). In the course of our discussion, we will try to deal with these questions in terms of what is currently known about the physiological bases of behaviour, and also consider some of the problems psychologists face in trying to develop answers.

Mind, Brain and the CNS

In order to understand the interaction of physical and mental states, it is necessary to have some understanding of the structure of the body. One of the first difficulties faced is dealing with common terms. For instance where is "the mind," physiologically? Where is the "self"? Terms like these, while fairly clear in their ordinary usage, are not so clear when one tries to connect them to physiology.

Most people would equate "mind" with "brain," and this is partially correct. But in more precise terms, the word "mind" was created to refer to a psychological concept, not a physiological one. The *mind* is usually regarded as the seat of consciousness or awareness, not as a physiological structure. Contemporary knowledge indicates that the brain is, indeed, involved in our experience of consciousness, but no one is currently certain just how, or if consciousness involves only the brain. About seventy-five years ago a psychologist named William James said, "The explanation of consciousness is the ultimate question for psychology." It still is. So, in discussing interactions of the physical (brain) and mental (mind), one is restricted to saying that somehow the two must be connected, or even the same, but it is not clear how. (The alternative, that consciousness is non-physical, perhaps a soul, would take us back before Descartes, and would make scientific study impossible.) No pretense will be made here to answer William James's question, but we will examine what is known about the structure of the physiological system and its effects on behaviour.

The human body is comprised of billions of individual cells of many specialized types. Certain cells in the stomach lining, for instance, do nothing but produce digestive secretions; and those which make up the nervous system are called nerve cells. Coordinating the activity of all these cells requires communication, and this is one of the key functions of the nervous system. Nerve cells, or neurons, are like wires in that they carry an electro-chemical message from one point to another. Each time a neuron connects to another neuron, it is possible for a message to be switched to other sites. The brain forms part of what is called the *central nervous system*(CNS), composed of nerves in the spinal cord, and various structures in the brain. *Sensory nerves* carry messages to the CNS from the outside world via the sense receptors, such as those located in the eyes and ears, while *motor nerves* are responsible for initiating muscle activity at the order of the CNS. Although the brain is responsible for integrating incoming information and directing activity, the spinal cord is a vital relay station. For protection the spinal cord passes within the bones (vertebre) of the spinal column, like wires in a casing. Nevertheless, a back injury can result in disruption of the spinal cord, which can cause loss of all feeling (sensory) and movement (motor) below the point of injury (see Figure 1.A).

The brain itself is subdivided into many areas, each serving one or more specialized functions. The outer portion, with many ridges and valleys, is called the *cortex* (Greek for "bark," as on a tree). (See Fig. 1.B.) The cortex is made up of two distinct hemispheres, left and right, each of which basically controls the opposite side of the body (e.g., your right hand is controlled by your left hemisphere). The cortex itself can be broken down into smaller regions called *lobes*, which are identified by the valleys or "fissures" on the surface. The two major fissures are the central fissure, which divides each hemisphere roughly in half, in a front-to-back orientation, and the lateral fissure, which runs along the side of each hemisphere. (It will help to refer to Figure 1.B in understanding these terms.) The *frontal lobe* is associated with subtle colourings of emotional response or "affect." For this reason, operations were once done which cut off or removed portions of the frontal lobe, in cases of manic depression or chronic pain. The operation, popular in the 1940s and '50s, ultimately was shown to be a poor treatment and such frontal lobotomies have been abandoned. The area of the frontal lobe just before the central fissure is called the *frontal motor area*, because it controls voluntary motor activity. Interestingly, the body areas capable of very subtle motor control (e.g., hands, lips) show a greater representation in the frontal motor area. Information about touch is relayed to a region of the *parietal lobe* just behind the central fissure. Hearing is located just below the lateral fissure, in the *temporal lobe*. Our memory for past experiences also seems to be located in the temporal lobe. Vision has a whole region, the *occipital lobe*, to itself. This suggests that vision is either very complex, or very important, or both.

Below the cortex are the subcortical layers connecting the cortex to other regions, notably the *limbic system* and *midbrain*. These regions are sometimes referred to as the "primitive brain." (See Figure 1.C.) As the name implies, these structures control fundamental aspects of behaviour that we share with many lower organisms. The hypothalamus, for example, is important in regulating hunger, thirst, sex, and other basic drive behaviours. Other regions of the limbic system

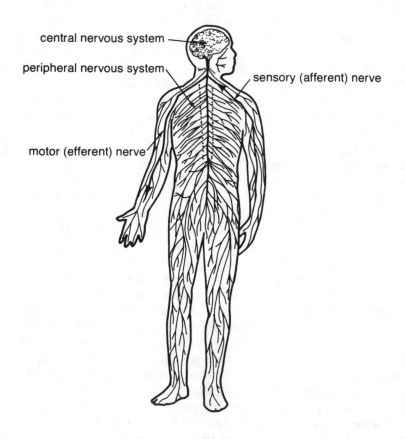

Figure 1.A
Peripheral and Central Nervous Systems
Peripheral sensory and motor nerves travel similar routes, but carry messages in opposite directions.

have been associated with the primitive emotions of fear and rage, and possibly with maternal behaviour. The *reticular formation* (reticular means "finely interwoven") is a set of non-localized nerve fibres which run from the midbrain up through the limbic system. The reticular formation appears to act as a relay network, controlling sensory inputs. It plays a key role in modulating our arousal level, controlling alertness and sleep. Thus, the brain is made up of a number of specific structures, which ultimately must function as an integrated system to regulate our behaviour. The description given here should not be taken as complete, but merely as an introduction to this incredible system.

Our understanding of the brain has long been dependent on observation. At one time, researchers had to rely on clinical cases to study the various structures. This type of *clinical observation* has its drawbacks, particularly in terms of lack of control. For example, a person may receive a severe blow to the back of the head and complain of numbness in one arm. Unfortunately, one cannot easily

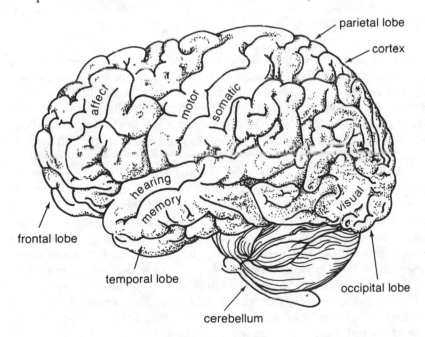

Figure 1.B
Exterior View of the Left Hemisphere
Each region (lobe) of the cortex seems to serve a particular function, as noted on this drawing by the early French anatomist, Louis Pierre Gratiolet (1815-1865).

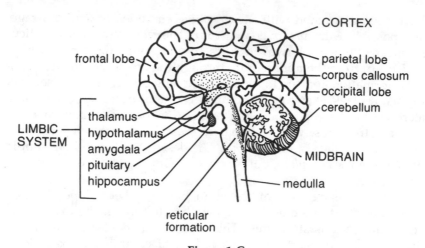

frontal lobe

CORTEX

parietal lobe
corpus callosum
occipital lobe
cerebellum

LIMBIC
SYSTEM

thalamus
hypothalamus
amygdala
pituitary
hippocampus

MIDBRAIN

medulla

reticular
formation

Figure 1.C
A Schematic Diagram of a Side View of the Human Brain
This internal view shows the structures of the "primitive" brain, as well as
the corpus callosum fibres which serve to connect the two hemispheres.
(Adapted from Sagan, 1977.)

connect the blow and the symptom, because the impact would have
been transmitted throughout the skull. Occasionally, though, the
clinical method can lead to important breakthroughs. In the case of
Broca's discovery of the speech centre, the patient had been carefully
studied, since his problem had existed for many years. When he died,
an autopsy clearly showed a lesion (tissue injury) in the left frontal
lobe.

Today, researchers use more refined techniques which seek to
pinpoint the effects of activity in small areas of the brain. Electrical
stimulation of nerve cells is one such method. Small clusters of cells
are activated by inserting a fine wire carrying a tiny electrical current.
Often use of this technique must proceed by analogy, looking at
effects in animals and extrapolating to humans, but in some cases
researchers have observed people directly. One example is the work
of Wilder Penfield, a Montreal neurosurgeon. In treating epileptics
suffering from severe seizures, Penfield would sometimes operate to
destroy cells in the area where the seizure originated. To do this, he
would first stimulate various areas of the cortex and observe effects
reported by the patient (who was conscious throughout the operation). From this he could produce a "map" of the cortex and its functions. Thus, in some cases, both our search for knowledge and the
alleviation of suffering can be served. (More will be said about electrical stimulation at a later point.)

One of the main points to be noted in our understanding of the nervous system is that activity is highly integrated. While various portions serve specialized functions, no one part can really be considered without the others. (An analogy might be an assembly line: each worker has a set task, but the finished product depends on all.) It is through the working of the whole that psychological processes are best seen.

Chemistry and Behaviour

As discussed in the preceding section, the CNS plays an essential role in coordinating behaviour. Neurons transmit sensory messages and allow motor responses nearly instantaneously; the process of touching a hot stove and quickly removing one's hand is a good example. (Nerve conduction is not truly instantaneous—the fastest speed for impulses is about 150 metres/sec. in large sensory nerves, slowing to a mere tenth of a metre per second in the mid-brain. "Reaction time" is a reflection of the limits of this communication system. For example, it takes three-quarters of a second to lift your foot off the gas, from the moment of seeing something you should stop for, in a car.) At eighty kph, you cover almost seventeen metres in that time. Nerves only communicate while they are active, and while changes in activity can take place over fractions of a second, a nerve cannot remain active indefinitely. This makes it difficult to understand the regulation of slower-changing processes like metabolism, growth, and reproduction.

The answer lies not with nerve conduction as such, but with chemical processes. One such process is the activity of the glandular cells. These cells "communicate" by means of chemical secretions. The most significant glands, from a "communication" standpoint, are the endocrine glands. These are a number of glands which secrete chemicals called hormones directly into the bloodstream, where they are carried to all parts of the body. The effects of these "chemical messengers" are not as swift as neural transmission—often it can be minutes, hours, weeks, or longer before the response is shown—but are longer lasting than those under direct neural control. Thus, neural (electrical) and hormonal (chemical) processes are not competitive, but complementary.

Hormones operate to regulate, or in some cases alter, the functioning of the physiological system. Many of these processes do not control specific behaviours, but rather act indirectly, making certain behaviours more (or less) likely. Some scientists have argued that certain actions—for example, maternal protection of an infant—are directly controlled by hormones, but the general issue of how hormones relate to behaviour is far from resolved.

As chemical messengers, the hormones interact with various specialized cells in the body. Adrenaline, for example, is produced by the adrenal glands during stress, and can affect dilation of blood vessels and carbohydrate metabolism. In addition, adrenaline can be secreted by certain nerve cells to aid transmission from one cell to another. This brings us to another aspect of chemical processes—their role in transmission in the nervous system.

As noted earlier, nerve cells are specialized for the purpose of communication. In a sense, a nerve cell is like a wire through which an electrical impulse passes. The length of the axon or "wire" of the nerve cell may range from about one mm to about one metre, depending on location and function of the cell. The electrical impulse, however, only travels within a single neuron (nerve cell). At the junction of any two neurons, there is a small physical gap, called a *synapse*. Communication across this synapse depends on an exchange of chemicals called *neurotransmitters*. Adrenaline is one such neurotransmitter. Chemicals which prevent communication across the synapse are called *neuroinhibitors*. Thus, proper communication through the body depends not only on an intact network of nerve cells, but also on proper chemical interactions at the synapses between neurons. Most drugs which affect behaviour seem to do so by altering the ongoing neural activity.

Both neural and chemical processes are important to our understanding of the relation between the brain and behaviour. In this chapter, we cannot cover all that is known about these processes. Rather, the intent is to give a basic description of how these physiological processes fit into the biological approach. Man may be a "machine" in the materialist sense, but he is an exceedingly complex one, as a study of the interactions of mind and body shows.

INTERACTIONS OF MIND AND BODY IN BEHAVIOUR

As already noted, it is impossible to identify the "mind" with one particular brain structure or portion of the body. In some senses the entire body is the receptacle of the mind. Consciousness may depend on a normally functioning cortex, but other aspects of behaviour depend on other elements of the system. If we cannot identify the mind as a portion of the body, how is it possible to study interactions of the two? Precisely because they are separate conceptually and require different types of description, one can seek parallels. It is almost like trying to translate between two different languages—the words may not always be easy to match up, but in the end the ideas can be communicated. We seek to translate between physiologically based "body," and psychologically based "mind" terms.

THE EFFECTS OF BODY ON MIND

When we speak of effects of the body on the mind, we are referring to the effects of physically identifiable events (e.g., changes within the body) on psychological functioning. Nearly all of the identifiable events can be described in terms of neural and/or chemical processes. Obviously, this can include a wide range of effects, both transitory (e.g., a cup of coffee as a drug) and enduring (e.g., spinal injury or alcohol-induced memory dysfunction). In this section, we will focus on some problems which have significance because of what they tell us about the bases of behaviour. These include drugs, the electrical nature of brain activity, and specialization in the brain.

Drugs

Technically, a drug is any substance which has an effect on living cells. Since this could include virtually any substance, including water, we will take a more restricted meaning of the term "drug." *Drugs* are chemical substances which are foreign to the body, either totally or in the form introduced. (For example, adrenaline is a hormone, but may also be *injected* as a drug.) It is worth noting that not all drugs have discernible effects on behaviour. For example, penicillin reduces infections, but does not noticeably affect behaviour. Nor need drugs always be medically prescribed: a morning cup of coffee is an example of drug use (or abuse), as is the illegal use of marijuana. The study of psychoactive ("mind-affecting") drugs is a concern in both psychology and medicine, and has given rise to a hybrid field called psychopharmacology.

Psychoactive drugs are probably as old as recorded history. Nearly every culture has used some type of fermented grain or vegetable to produce an alcoholic drink. Some South American tribes have long traditions of eating plants to produce hallucinations for religious rites. But it is only recently that doctors have considered the use of drugs as a therapeutic tool, or that researchers have had effective methods to study drug effects.

The use of drugs as therapy is very closely tied to the medical orientation to disorders. Prior to about 1800, mental disorders or insanity were regarded as the product of demons, and the insane were beaten or cast in chains into dungeons. Then, reformers like

Philippe Pinel in France and Benjamin Rush in the United States, began advocating a different view. Pinel, working as head of the hospital at Bicêtre (where Broca was later to make his discovery), argued that insanity was the result of disease, not demonic possession. Therefore, its victims should be handled like any other patients, and treated by medical means. This point of view—that mental disorders are based on disease or organic disfunction—came to be known as the *medical model*.

In Pinel's time the medical model was just a theory, for knowledge of physiology was limited. (Recall that Pinel was a contemporary of Cabanis.) Gradually, discoveries in physiology and pharmacology began to change this picture. Nitrous oxide, a gas now used for anesthetic purposes, was investigated by Sir Humphrey Davy in 1799, who reported, "I lost all connections with external things; trains of vivid images rapidly passed through my mind." Ether, although discovered in 1543, was first used as an anesthetic in the 1840s. The nineteenth century also saw the introduction and increasing popularity of bromides as sedatives. (They also caused side-effects, and although still an ingredient in some headache remedies, "bromide" has come to mean a commonplace idea.)

As the number of known psychoactive drugs increased, the medical model had a growing impact on the treatment of mental disorders. Today, a wide variety of drugs, mostly synthetic compounds, are used in dealing with behavioural problems, ranging from hypertension to depression and psychosis. No attempt will be made to review all such uses. Rather, we shall focus on three aspects: methods of drug research, the use of the medical model today, and some aspects of use and abuse of popular drugs.

Psychopharmacology has become a complex field. In the early days of drug research, research methods were more informal, and hence simpler. Many psychoactive agents were first isolated from plants which had already been used as folk remedies. For example, reserpine, one of the first tranquilizers, was originally isolated from Indian snakeroot. In other cases, researchers even experimented on themselves. Heinrich Kluver, a man known for his contributions in other areas of physiological research, wrote a paper on his experiences with mescaline, attempting to assess its effects. Today, research techniques have become much more sophisticated.

The usual methods of research on psychoactive drugs today are much like those for other types of drugs. Experimental animals are used to assess toxicity, strength and basis of effects. This may involve intricate techniques and chemical analyses, such as injecting tiny amounts of the drug directly into specific regions of the brain and then examining concentrations of neurotransmitters at nearby synapses. These methods often yield important information which is necessary as preliminary screening. Unfortunately, they are not adequate by themselves.

Ultimately, psychoactive drugs must still be assessed by use on human subjects. There are several reasons for this. First, even the use of closely related species like rhesus monkeys and chimpanzees does not always yield the same results as with people. Second, even if the effects are the same, assessing them can be difficult. By definition, the key aspect of psychoactive drugs is their effect on behaviour, which can include changes in alertness, responsiveness, mood and even perceptions. Obviously, it is difficult to assess these effects in animals. This leads to the most fundamental problem, and one which is again tied up with the medical model: how to categorize the effects of drugs.

By their nature, drugs operate on the physical system, yet the behavioural changes are basically psychological. This leads back to the problem of linking mind and body. Consider some of the possibilities: (1) Some drugs will affect only certain clinical groups, and not normal individuals or other types of patients. (2) Some drugs affect sensory capacities in ways that are not directly expressed in behaviour. Even with verbal reports, it can be difficult to determine what is happening. Hallucinogens like LSD present problems of this nature. (3) It is convenient to categorize drugs, but discrete categories do not always fit well with the subtle shadings of behavioural effects. There is also the temptation to focus on one major effect, ignoring various side effects. These problems are not insurmountable, as the increasing sophistication of psychopharmacology shows, but they do present continual challenges to researchers.

The expansion of psychopharmacology has had an impact on the acceptance of the medical model. The discovery of psychoactive drugs has led to changes in the methods of treating mental disorders, and particularly in the ways of handling patients. Tranquilizers are used to reduce anxiety, anti-depressants help relieve depression, and sedatives often take the place of physical restraints, such as strait-jackets. In the sense of altering behaviour by chemical means, these methods are consistent with the view that mental disorders have a physical basis. However, they do not address the basic question, which is determining the original reason for the problems. Consequently, many other researchers are involved in the hunt for chemical causes of disorders.

This aspect of the medical model—that finding a cure depends on finding the cause—seemed to gain momentum with work in the

1950s on model psychoses. Since its discovery in 1943, the mind-altering aspects of LSD (lysergic acid diethylamide) had been described by researchers. Noting the behavioural effects, doctors felt that LSD was very much like psychosis, which is characterized by lack of contact with reality, often with hallucinations and other sensory distortions. LSD produced a "model psychosis" which, it was hoped, could aid in understanding natural psychoses. Ultimately treatment using LSD proved of little clinical value, but it *did* show the powerful changes that could be caused by even slight alterations of brain chemistry. This strengthened belief in the medical model.

Advances in psychopharmacology offer great promise. Unlike alternative forms of therapy (e.g., psychoanalysis or behaviour therapy), drug therapy is relatively low cost, fast-acting, and efficient, requiring comparatively little of the doctor's time. Critics, however, have raised several doubts. First, it is not clear that most current use of drugs is anything more than a way of keeping patients docile, particularly in institutions. Second, it is not proven that all mental disorders have an organic basis (as the medical model assumes). Early experiences and learned behaviours may also be causes. At present there is no resolution of this debate. Whatever the final outcome, psychoactive drugs now play, and likely will continue to play, an important role in medicine.

Advances in psychopharmacology have led to more widespread use of various psychoactive drugs. At the same time, the frequency of their use has led to a change in social attitudes, so that drugs are more widely accepted, and in fact may be actively sought. A recent spot survey of Toronto pharmacists revealed that approximately 25 per cent of all prescriptions filled were for some form of tranquilizer. As well, there are a number of drugs which have behavioural effects, but because of their non-prescriptive nature they are often overlooked. Let us briefly examine some commonly encountered drugs and their effects.

Psychoactive drugs may be divided into various categories, according to the general nature of their effects on behaviour. One category often overlooked in our daily experiences is the *stimulants*. Stimulants act on the autonomic nervous system (a portion of the CNS that controls such functions as heart-rate and breathing, as well as general arousal level) to increase activity. These drugs tend to decrease fatigue, increase physical activity and alertness, diminish hunger, and produce a temporary elevation in mood (including euphoria). Both caffeine and nicotine are stimulants, although not as powerful as the prescription-regulated family of stimulants called amphetamines.

Because stimulants tend to diminish hunger, amphetamines are sometimes prescribed as "diet pills." Smokers often experience a related effect when they reduce their smoking: the reduced nicotine level tends to cause an increase in hunger. Amphetamines are also used for treating hyperactive children who show abnormally high activity levels and an inability to concentrate. Amphetamine paradoxically acts to calm down hyperactive children for reasons which are not clear.

Beyond these two uses, stimulants have very few legitimate applications. They do not usually reduce depression, nor are they an indefinite substitute for sleep when fatigued. Yet their use (and misuse) is widespread in our society.

Caffeine is found not only in coffee, but also in tea, cola, and even chocolate bars. Children exposed to average amounts of cola and candy may be accustomed to caffeine long before they ever taste coffee. Stopping intake of caffeine after long periods of use does not lead to the physical withdrawn symptoms of drug *addiction*, which can include vomiting, muscle and heart tremors, and CNS seizures. However, use can lead to *tolerance*, which means one needs higher and higher doses to maintain the effect. Although caffeine and nicotine are treated casually in our culture, they nonetheless can cause adverse effects such as sleeplessness, and it is unwise to regard the "pick-me-up" as a free ride.

Abuse of amphetamines is more serious, whether it be by truck drivers, students, or others seeking to combat fatigue, or by users who inject the drug to experience euphoria. Chronic high doses of amphetamines (Benzedrine, Dexedrine and Methamphetamine are common trade names, "Bennies," "Dexies," "Meth," and "speed" are common "street" names) can lead to marked side effects, including hallucinations, delusions, and even a psychosis very similar to paranoid schizophrenia.

One drug that is commonly confused with stimulants is *alcohol*. In reality, alcohol is a physiological *depressant*, which reduces CNS activity, and in large doses can cause coma and even death. People often regard it as a stimulant, because in small doses it reduces inhibitions and increases talkativeness. Actually, these effects are due to differential sensitivity to the depressant effects by different parts of the brain. The "higher" functions of the cortex are the first to be affected, which can lead to less self-consciousness and a reduction in learned social inhibitions. In large enough quantities, alcohol is a general anaesthetic, producing loss of consciousness. Over time, large doses can also cause severe physiological effects, including memory deficits and liver damage.

Abuse of alcohol may well be endemic in our culture: it has been estimated that 5 per cent of the population in both the United States and Canada have a serious drinking problem, and alcoholism is a problem in virtually all Western countries. In France it is the cause of one of every ten chronic hospital cases. No one is certain whether alcoholism is based on a physiological malfunction (in keeping with the medical model), or is based on learned drinking patterns. There is evidence that it runs in families, but this may mean either that there is a genetic cause, or that the children learn patterns from their parents. In either case, most treatments show only limited rates of success. Alcohol is probably our largest drug problem.

The chronic, casual use of drugs can be a danger in many ways. One example is the use of barbiturates. Barbiturates are most frequently used as sedatives; because they depress activity in the CNS, they are used to treat anxiety and/or insomnia. Unfortunately, barbiturates sometimes serve to aggravate the problem they were intended to solve. They are a poor long-term cure for insomnia, because they radically alter normal brain wave patterns during sleep, including suppressing the REM activity associated with dreaming. Thus, they may produce a rebound when use is terminated, including nightmares and other sleep disturbances.

Another potential problem can arise due to the interaction of a drug with other drugs or even certain foods. Such interactions can be fatal. Barbiturates, for example, tend to interact with alcohol in a *synergistic* manner—that is, the effect of the two together is greater than for either alone. Some cheeses, such as Blue or Roquefort, can also be dangerous or even lethal if consumed while taking certain drugs. Our knowledge of synergistic effects is limited at present, and undiscovered combinations may exist. Wisdom would suggest a more conservative policy than the prevailing social attitude: never take a drug without cause, and then only under a doctor's supervision. Always tell a doctor about medicines being taken which may have been prescribed by another doctor. If you take a drug, watch for drowsiness or other side-effects that may affect your ability to deal with your surroundings.

Mood-altering drugs are not new, nor are the circumstances that lead people to seek relief from anxiety. However, our understanding of the mechanisms of such drugs is growing. More and more, we must look to the psychopharmacologist for answers to questions of drug use and abuse. The methods of research are becoming more sophisticated, and with them our ability to use drugs as a therapeutic tool. No amount of research can ever determine social attitudes, but ideally such attitudes are based on knowledge. To this end, the next few years offer hope of great strides in our ability to understand the role of drugs in mind-body interactions.

Electrical Stimulation of the Brain

While chemical processes in the brain are important, brain activity is also electrical. This aspect of the brain is emphasized by research on *electrical stimulation of the brain (ESB)*. ESB refers to artificial stimulation of neurons by means of a current applied through an implanted electrode. As has been noted, the CNS functions by means of electro-chemical conduction through neurons. By applying minute currents to brain tissue, one can force the neurons to conduct. Although the details are complex, the basic concept is quite simple.

It has long been known that the brain somehow involved electrical activity. In ancient Rome, Pliny the Elder recommended the shock of an electric fish, applied to the forehead, to ease the pain of child-birth. Without knowing why, Pliny recognized that the shock stunned the patient, reducing conscious awareness. The electrical nature of nerve activity was first recognized by Luigi Galvani in 1791, when he observed that a frog's leg could be made to twitch at the touch of dissimilar metals, which created a battery. Galvani thought, wrongly, that the frog's leg generated the impulse, rather than being activated by the metal probe. Still, it was not long before the true nature of the process was recognized. Despite this awareness of the electrical nature of neural activity, it was only about fifty years ago that researchers began to focus on the brain.

In the 1920s, the first recordings of brain-wave activity were made using the electroencephalograph (EEG—"writing of electricity of the brain"), but it was not until the 1950s that techniques permitted more direct intervention. In 1954, W. W. Roberts discovered that stimulation of certain regions of the limbic system and midbrain in animals seemed to produce pain. This was not too surprising: since an electrical shock to the fingertip can be painful, why not in the brain? However, in the same year, James Olds, working independently of Roberts, discovered that stimulation of regions in the midbrain could *also* produce pleasure. Roberts and Olds were studying areas of the "primitive brain" in animals, and the effects they discovered seemed to reflect primitive emotions and drives. At the same time, however, Wilder Penfield at the Montreal Neurological Institute was working with epileptic patients. As part of the surgical method of treatment, he discovered effects of stimulation of the cortex in conscious individuals, as noted earlier.

These discoveries set the stage for more sophisticated approaches. In the early 1960s, two doctors, Heath and Mickle, reported pleasurable/painful effects from midbrain stimulation in conscious patients. Other researchers found that ESB could be used to control particular behaviours. The potential of ESB was demonstrated in headline-making form by Dr. José Delgado of Yale when he went into an arena with a full-grown, electrode-implanted bull, and used ESB to stop the bull in mid-charge! Michael Crichton has probed the topic in vivid, but not entirely accurate, form in *Terminal Man*.

ESB is presently only in its infancy, but it raises basic questions about the brain and the mind. One of the most basic issues concerns the localization of functions. The materialist view argues that all functions of the mind are based on activity in the body. The simplest form of this view is to say that each aspect of behaviour is produced by a specific location in the brain—that is, that functions are localized. Broca offered support for this position by pinpointing speech function within the third convolution of the left cortical hemisphere. Similarly, Penfield's work indicated that specific regions of the cortex control particular movements, sensations, and even memories. (See Figure 2 for a description of his findings.) Thus, it would seem that ESB may enable us to identify—and ultimately control—all aspects of behaviour.

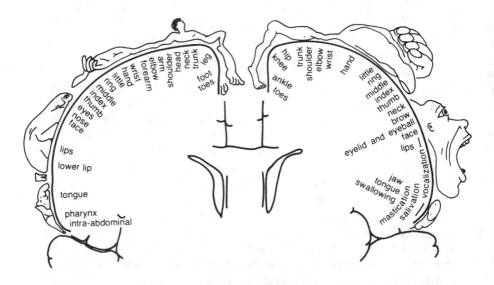

Figure 2
Sensory and Motor Representation in the Cortex
Penfield's research with ESB was instrumental in describing sensory and motor functions in the cortex. The right side of the diagram shows the frontal motor area; the left side shows the sensory representation for touch, located in the parietal lobe immediately behind the frontal motor area. In both cases the relative size of the body parts shown describes the relative representation in the cortex. (Adapted from Penfield and Rasmussen, 1957.)

   This line of thought gives rise to all sorts of scenarios. Consider the following examples, which might seem plausible based on current research and the assumption of localization of function. First, imagine you're at the office, and you feel a mood of depression coming on. You reach for a small box in your desk, set a timer for ten seconds, and press the button. A signal is transmitted to a small unit previously implanted in your scalp, and a message flashes to your brain. There is a moment of blankness, a feeling of well-being—and the depression is gone. Or consider this scene. You are driving your car, hurrying to make an appointment. The traffic frustrates you, and you gun the accelerator. As the car reaches the speed limit, and exceeds it, you feel a flash of exruciating pain. The speedometer has sensed that you were exceeding the limit, and has signalled a punishing shock to your brain. Almost involuntarily, you slow down.
   These scenarios seem frighteningly Orwellian, and critics of ESB research have been quick to raise questions. If electrodes were implanted in the pleasure/pain centres of all people, then law enforcement might be given over to computer-controlled monitoring systems. What makes this vision even more plausible, and therefore more scary, is a possible transition stage. People might voluntarily seek electrode implants in their pleasure centres as a new form of escapism. Since the precise nature and duration of effects could be controlled (unlike drugs, which have a fixed time-course of action), it could be an attractive concept. As one researcher has suggested, "The ultimate turn-on might well be electrical."
   When this type of scenario is presented, the critics typically focus on the moral aspect: that is, who is to control the computers that control behaviour, and what sort of behaviours are to be rewarded or punished. But before accepting this as a purely moral crisis, one should look more carefully at the scientific basis of the issue.
   Problems do exist with ESB, and in some sense they are all connected with the issue of localization of function. If one accepts it in the simplest form, then there exists a specific centre for any type of behaviour. At present, there is inadequate evidence for this view. Lower animals show a great degree of physiological pre-determination of their behaviour (often called "instincts"). In humans, however, there appear to be relatively few such patterns, even for comparable behaviour. For example, while male stickleback fish show stereotyped courtship rituals, human males do so only to the extent that their culture dictates. If true localization of function does not exist, one must question whether complete control of every action would ever be possible.
   Although ESB has greatly aided our understanding of the brain,

it does have limitations as a tool. First of all, ESB is an artificial process Inserting an electrode destroys a few hundred cells in the immediate vicinity, and the effects of the stimulation itself are not the same as normal neural activity. The current applied is either some type of alternating current, or a series of brief, direct-current pulses. The effect in either case is to artificially stimulate all the neurons in the immediate area, perhaps a few thousand cells. They then fire in *synchrony*, which is hardly typical of "normal" neural function over such a large number of cells. Current techniques of ESB do initiate brain activity, but they do *not* duplicate the normal workings of the brain. Given the approximately seven *billion* neurons in the brain, no ESB technique is ever likely to mimic the brain's patterns over any significant area. Still, the record to date has been impressive, and one can speculate that precise mimicry may not be necessary.

A secondary issue is the practicality of "plug-in" ESB, as the futuristic scenarios propose. While research has indicated that electrodes may remain implanted for months with no apparent ill effects, it is also true that sometimes the effects will "drift": the electrode may no longer elicit the same effect, or the same current may not always have the same degree of effect. This raises questions about the advisability of long-term implants in humans. There is also an ethical issue. Heath and Mickle have been criticized for their use of patients to explore effects of ESB, since the nature of the disorders (most patients were schizophrenics) made informed consent impossible. On the other hand, clinical work like Penfield's may lead to better, simpler methods of treating disorders ranging from epilepsy to depression. The issue is unsettled and one can only paraphrase José Delgado. "The technology exists, and if society does not choose, the decisions may be made arbitrarily." Whatever the resolution of these dilemmas, the study of electrical stimulation effects has considerably advanced our understanding of the brain.

The Split-Brain and the Whole Mind

The study of ESB has indicated that a remarkable number of behaviours can be produced by direct stimulation of brain areas. But as yet, this has not led to a direct understanding of consciousness. According to the materialist view, consciousness *must* have a physical basis, and most probably it should be associated with the brain itself. The problem is to find a way of identifying it.

Normally, our experience of the world, our inner thoughts and feelings, seems unitary—that is, we have only a single consciousness. Yet the structure of the brain, especially the cortex, is basically two symmetrical halves. Connecting the two cerebral[1] hemispheres is a wide band of nerve fibres called the *corpus callosum*. Researchers have long known that each hemisphere is basically responsible for the opposite side of the body (e.g., your left hemisphere receives sensations from, and gives motor commands to, the right side of your body). Now, if consciousness is associated with the cortex, it suggests that the unitary nature of our experience is based on the integration of the two hemispheres. This led Gustav Fechner to speculate, more than one hundred years ago, that if the two hemispheres could somehow be separated we would have *two* separate consciousnesses. Fechner never thought that this could be tested, but time has proven differently. Research in the 1950s by Roger Sperry, working with monkeys, suggested that cutting the fibres of the corpus callosum (separating the cerebral hemispheres) had no grave effects on behaviour—certainly less than procedures like frontal lobotomies. Still, this gave no indication of what might happen in humans. One obvious difference between primates and people is that monkeys do not speak, and Broca had shown that speech was *one* function that was not symmetrical.

The answer to the question came as a result of medical needs. In the 1960s a Los Angeles surgeon named Philip Vogel was trying to treat patients with a long history of epilepsy. While in many cases epileptics can be treated with drugs, these patients could not, and consequently had major seizures on the average of twice a week. Epilepsy is a condition in which random neural activity starts at a point in one hemisphere and spreads outward, creating seizures and convulsions. In cases of *grand mal* attacks, the seizure activity spreads from one hemisphere to the other across the fibres of the corpus collosum. In such cases, the recurring seizures can disrupt normal life, and even present a life-threatening situation. When all other treatments failed, Vogel tried a new and radical approach. By cutting the fibres of the corpus callosum, he hoped to restrict the seizures to one hemisphere, and thus prevent *grand mal* attacks. He knew of Sperry's work, and there had been occasional clinical reports of accidental damage to the corpus callosum, but no one had ever purposely separated the hemispheres before.

Medically, the treatment worked. Not only did it prevent further *grand mal* attacks but, for reasons still unclear, more limited seizures also became less frequent. At the same time, it was desirable to know what negative effects, if any, the surgery had caused. Knowing of

---

[1] Cerebral—referring to the cortex together with its underlying "white matter," or subcortical tissue.

Sperry's research, Vogel asked him to collaborate on evaluating the patients. The results were a surprise to all concerned.

Initial observations suggested that the patients were remarkably normal. However, by a series of ingenious procedures, Sperry, Vogel and their co-workers discovered that, in fact, these individuals had an unusual mental syndrome. As Sperry reported in 1968, "instead of the normally unified single stream of consciousness, these patients behave in many ways as if they have two independent streams of conscious awareness, one in each hemisphere, each of which is cut off from and out of contact with the mental experience of the other." In other words, *two* minds, each functioning separately from the other!

To assess the effects of the surgery, the researchers had to use techniques whereby information was presented to only one hemisphere. The simplest case involved touch: if the split-brain person were given an object in their left hand while blindfolded, the left hand could pick it out again, by touch, from a selection of several articles. However, if the *right* hand were asked to pick out the article previously held by the left hand, it did no better than chance. In the case of vision, the situation is a bit more complicated, because each eye is connected to both hemispheres. However, the visual world of each eye is split in two, so that objects on the left *side* of the visual field are seen by the right hemisphere, and objects on the right side are seen by the left hemisphere, regardless of which eye is used. (See Figure 3.) Thus, if a person looks straight ahead and an image briefly appears to the left, only the right hemisphere receives the information. This led to an interesting discovery. Because only the *left* hemisphere had language, a person presented with a word or picture on the left side (and thus the right hemisphere) could not say what they had seen! Only the left hemisphere seems able to talk, while the right hemisphere is silent. This has led researchers to refer to the left hemisphere as dominant.

As it turns out, the differences are not quite what they first seemed. The right hemisphere, while unable to speak, is not completely illiterate. If presented with a word or picture, it can *point* to a corresponding picture or word. Thus, seeing the word "key," the left hand can correctly choose a key. At the same time, the right hemisphere has musical and spatial skills which seem to be lacking in the dominant left hemisphere. If given geometric figures to copy (such as a circle overlapping a square), the left hand (right hemisphere) does a better job of copying it than does the right hand (left hemisphere). This is particularly striking, since the patients thus far have all been right-handed, so in principle one would expect the right hand to be

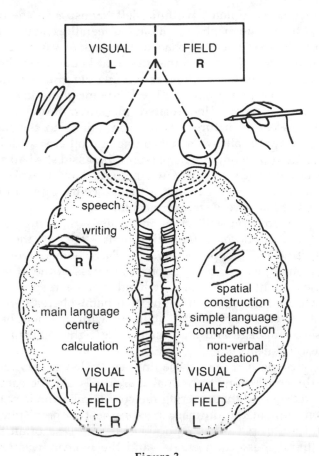

Figure 3
A schematic diagram showing lateralization of functions in persons with a
severed corpus callosum. (Adapted from Sperry, 1966.)

more manually skilled. For handwriting, the right hand *is* better; for
drawing, it is not. (This raises a fascinating problem: since lettering is
a type of artistic skill, why is it that the left hand, so superior for other
spatial tasks, cannot reproduce letters and words? It seems this aspect
of the split-brain phenomenon has never been fully explored.)

Despite the apparent handicap and dual-consciousness they
possess, split-brain individuals learn to cope very well. Even tasks
requiring motor coordination of the two hemispheres, such as riding
a bicycle, can be mastered. Sometimes, the means of communicating
between sides are quite interesting. In one experiment, Sperry
flashed either a red or green card to the right hemisphere, and then

asked the person to name (with the left hemisphere) the colour. As expected, the left hemisphere,not having seen the colour, did poorly. However, if given a second chance, the person was always correct. What seemed to happen was that the right hemisphere, hearing the spoken response of the left hemisphere, would grimace and shrug if the answer was wrong. This let the left hemisphere know its error, which it then corrected! In a related, more humourous case, Sperry showed a series of pictures of common objects to the right hemisphere of a split-brain woman. Among the otherwise dull pictures was one of a nude woman. The person at first said she had seen nothing, but began to blush. Finally, when pressed for an explanation, the left hemisphere (which had not actually seen the picture) said the experimenter had a very strange machine!

The research on split-brain individuals thus suggests several things: (1) If the normal connecting tissues are cut, the two hemispheres function independently. (2) Each hemisphere seems to possess consciousness, but without awareness of the other. (In one case, one patient, seeing her left hand make a response, said, "It wasn't me that did that!") (3) The two hemispheres seem to show different types of specialized abilities, with the left hemisphere possessing language and math skills, the right hemisphere spatial and musical skills.

The striking nature of these findings makes it very tempting to extend the conclusions to normal individuals. At the same time, it must be recognized that severing the corpus callosum is not a normal condition, and in the ordinary person the two hemispheres freely communicate. (Sperry has reported only one case of an individual born without these connections—and the woman was twenty-one before it was discovered!) Still, research does indicate that the two hemispheres tend to become specialized in ways similar to what Sperry has observed in split-brain individuals. For example, damage to the left hemisphere, whether by disease or by accident, will normally impair speech.[2] Only in very young children (before speech is normally well-developed) is recovery from such damage ever completely compensated for. In the same vein, a tentative study by Sperry of right- and left-handed people on verbal and spatial aptitudes, found that right-handers tended to do better verbally than spatially, while left-handers were better spatially than verbally. While this suggests that the language hemisphere may not always be the dominant one, Sperry cautioned that the results were based on group

---

[2] It should be noted that in a small number of people, probably fewer than 1 per cent, specialization is apparently reversed, with speech located in the *right* hemisphere.

averages, and did not necessarily fit every person in each group.

The development of specialization and cerebral dominance has caused much speculation among researchers. There is some indication that dominance, and the associated preferences for one side, is already developing at birth. (In most individuals, one hand, foot, ear, and eye are usually preferred, or dominant—for instance, if standing, we begin walking with the dominant foot. If using a camera or telescope, we focus with the dominant eye.) As yet, no one is certain what causes one hemisphere to be dominant, although one Canadian psychologist, David Bakan, has suggested that left-handedness is associated with minor congenital brain damage. Whatever the cause, most authorities today suggest one should not interfere with preferences shown by a young child.

The research on the split-brain and cerebral dominance brings us back to our initial questions: is localization of function correct, and does consciousness reside in the brain? The answer seems to be, no and yes. The research on split-brain individuals seems to indicate that consciousness involves the cortex, for splitting the cerebral hemispheres seems to split consciousness as well. However, since it involves such a large-scale division, it offers us very little in terms of determining *where* consciousness resides. After all, the hemispheres each involve cortex, underlying sub-cortical tissue, limbic system structures, and so on, down into the spinal cord and beyond. To say that the two sides of the body can each have their own consciousness does not tell us what sort of structure *produces* consciousness. The extreme materialist position would say we should be able to find some particular neural circuit that represents conscious awareness. Yet, as Penfield has noted, no study of ESB has yet found such a circuit. This dilemma has led different researchers to take different points of view. Sperry, for example is a materialist, but he says that consciousness is the product of complex interactions, and no study of individual parts will ever enable us to pin it down. In this sense, the mind *is* connected to the body—but the terms may forever remain separate in our descriptions.

THE EFFECTS OF MIND ON BODY

"Mind over matter." The phrase has been used to describe many things, from accomplishing a difficult task to levitation. But the most common meaning is in describing how physical reactions are seemingly altered by mental processes. A common example is reaction to painful stimuli. To one person a trip to the dentist may be terrifying, whereas to another it is no more painful than scratching an itch. In our culture, childbirth is usually regarded as a painful experience, yet advocates of natural childbirth, and members of some other cultures, do not regard it as such. Thus, response to painful stimuli seems to show considerable variation. Pain researcher Ronald Melzack believes that such variations in response are due to differing cognitive expectations. Since cognitive processes (including expectations and beliefs) are viewed as functions of the cortex, Melzack's theory says expectations are mediated by cortical influences on pain experience. Such cognitive effects on physical state truly represent what is meant by "mind over matter," or the effect of mental states on physical functioning and behaviour.

Stress

Equally as common as pain, in human experience, is stress. We are all familiar with those moments: the boss wants to see you *now* about the last quarter's sales figures; or you're in a hurry and you gulp lunch; or you go to bed only to hear the neighbour's stereo blasting away. The pulse-pounding, gut-wrenching sensations that result from such moments are common to modern life. When we recognize the feelings, we may experience a desire to run away to a desert island. Unfortunately, even this may not solve the problem of stress.

According to Dr. Hans Selye, pioneer in stress research, *stress* is the non-specific response of the body to any demand on it. Simply being alive is "stressful"; in this sense, there is no escape from stress. But not all stress situations are alike, nor are all reactions harmful. To understand this, first consider what happens when one experiences stress.

Biologically, stress reactions are an emergency response intended to prepare one for "fight or flight." A significant link in the body's chain of responses is the release of hormones by the adrenal glands. The *adrenal glands*, located just above the kidneys, are made up of two portions, the cortex or outer covering, and the medulla or inner core. (See Figure 4.) When stimulated, the adrenal medulla secretes two hormones, epinephrine and nor-epinephrine (also called adrenaline and noradrenaline). Each of these plays a role in stress reactions. The release of epinephrine shuts off digestion, increases heart rate, and raises blood pressure. Because it alters arousal level by affecting midbrain activity, the stress reaction produced by epinephrine is prolonged. Anyone who has been startled or otherwise experienced a stress reaction knows that the racing heartbeat and other signs may linger beyond the moment of stress.

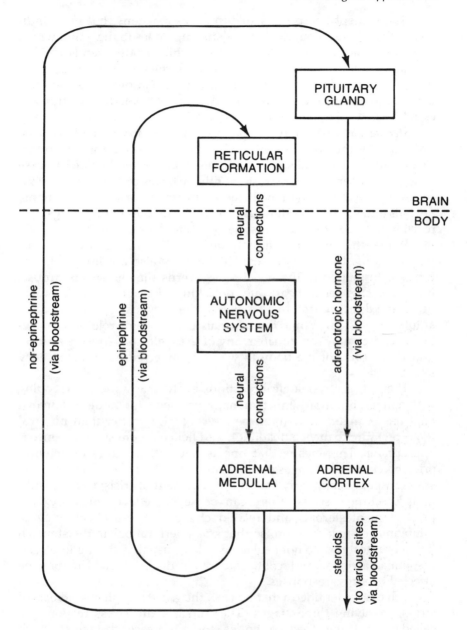

Figure 4

A schematic diagram of basic physiological responses to stress. Note that epinephrine production is part of a "closed loop" process that can be self-perpetuating.

Nor-epinephrine plays a role in stress reactions, but more indirectly. Travelling through the bloodstream, it goes to the brain, where it activates another gland, the *pituitary*, which in turn sends another hormone back to the adrenals, causing the release of steroids. (Note that this is an *indirect* process. Given what we know of the steroids, one might speculate about the disadvantages created if the adrenals could directly stimulate themselves.)

Steroids, as distinct from epinephrine and nor-epinephrine, are produced by the adrenal cortex. The steroids play a role in normal regulation of water and sugar metabolism, including the quick release of sugar for energy under stress. Synthetic forms of the steroids (e.g., cortisone) are also used in medicine for treatment of allergic reactions, arthritis and shock. The steroids can also be mood-altering drugs: one reaction to large doses of cortisone is severe depression.

While this description emphasizes the role of the adrenal hormones in stress, other parts of the body also are involved. The reticular formation in the mid-brain governs the changes in arousal level. The changes in heart rate, breathing, digestion, and so on are under the direct control of a portion of the nervous system called the autonomic system. While the adrenals play a major role (e.g., injections of adrenaline can initiate many of these effects), stress is an integrated response of the body to what is perceived as an emergency situation.

This set of physiological reactions evolved as a means of coping with danger, but it presents two major problems for modern humans. First the "danger" may often be psychological rather than physical (e.g., pressure to meet a deadline), and hence no physical response is appropriate. This means that one is left with a surge of activity-oriented chemical changes, and no outlet for the energy. Second, the stress response may carry beyond the moment of crisis; under conditions of chronic stress, there can be severe effects due to excess production of steroids and related changes. These effects include inhibiting cell regeneration, so that small perforations in the stomach lining or intestines do not heal as readily as usual, resulting in ulcers. Insomnia, asthma, and colitis are other disorders which may be affected by stress responses.

Selye has identified what he calls the *general adaption syndrome* of stress, involving three stages. The initial, acute stress response is called *alarm*. If the stress continues, there is a second stage at which the organism seems to be coping with the stress and outward signs of arousal disappear (*resistance* stage). But if the situation continues, this is followed by *exhaustion*, which results in sickness or death, at least in experimental studies with animals. Autopsies on these animals reveal enlarged adrenal glands, severe ulcers of the stomach, and shrinkage of the thymus gland and lymph nodes, which are both involved in the body's immunity systems.

Interestingly, what first led Selye to the study of stress was an observation he made as a second-year medical student in 1926. As part of their clinical training, the students were shown patients suffering from a variety of disorders. Despite the wide range of symptoms, Selye noted that "they all looked sick." His professors and fellow students laughed at his suggestion that disease, no matter what its nature, could produce certain consistent reactions. Some ten years later, Selye was led back to this question, and he named the syndrome "stress" (the term, borrowed from physics, was meant to refer to the effects of resisting an outside force). Since then, his basic description of the general adaptation syndrome has been accepted as an important contribution.

Research by two psychiatrists suggests that chronic stress may be as dangerous to people as to animals. In the late 1940s Dr. Thomas Holmes became interested in the effects of major life-changes on the health of his patients. For this purpose, he examined the case histories of more than 5,000 patients, and developed a "stress barometer" of life-changes. (See Box.) Later, Dr. Richard Rahe used Holmes's work as the basis for a study of 2,500 men in the U.S. Navy. Using the stress scale as a predictor of illness over a twelve month period, he found that those who underwent the highest number of life-changes suffered nearly twice as many ailments as those in the lowest category. While this research is correlational (as is most of the research on stress), taken with other data it suggests stress is a powerful factor in determining health.

One may ask if this relationship is inevitable, or whether one should (or could) escape to the proverbial desert isle. Research suggests that, in fact, options exist. While stress can be created by living situations, one's perception of the situation and one's typical mode of reaction can make an important difference. Psychologists David Glass and Jerome Singer have explored how our perceptions affect our response to stress. Their work, which concerns sources of urban stress, arose out of the observation that it is very hard to get agreement about what is a *stressor* (source of stress). They have found that, for most stressors in modern life, the social and emotional aspects are as important as the physical nature of the stressor. For instance, the noise of a lawnmower on Sunday morning may be less stressful if it is *your* lawn being mowed than if it is your neighbour's. Similarly, being pushed into cold water may sound stressful, yet every New Year's Day members of "polar bear clubs" willingly jump

A Barometer of Stress

Stressful experiences can have great impact on a person's ability to function. But what are stressful circumstances, and what types of experience typically cause the greatest stress? A long-term study by Rahe, referred to in the text, attempted to answer these questions by looking at the effects of various events on probability of becoming ill. Generally, the effects were found to be additive: people who went through more life changes were more likely to get sick. In Selye's terms, the high stress levels produce exhaustion of the organism.

A look at the table below will tell you the estimated stress-value of various life changes. The original researcher suggested that if your stress total went above 150 for any twelve-month period, you were in a high-risk group, and should heed the storm warnings of this stress barometer.

Rank	Life event	Mean value
1	Death of spouse	100
2	Divorce	73
3	Marital separation	65
4	Jail term	63
5	Death of close family member	63
6	Personal injury or illness	53
7	Marriage	50
8	Fired at work	47
9	Marital reconciliation	45
10	Retirement	45
14	Gain of new family member	39
18	Change to different line of work	36
25	Outstanding personal achievement	28
27	Begin or end school	26
30	Trouble with boss	23
32	Change in residence	20
37	Mortgage or loan less than $10,000	17
40	Change in eating habits	13
41	Vacation	13
42	Christmas	12
43	Minor violations of the law	11

(This list has been abridged from the original in Rahe, R.H., "Subjects' recent life changes and their near-future illness susceptibility." *Advances in Psychosomatic Medicine*, 1972, *8*, 2-19.)

into icy lakes and the sea. Thus control (or even the *feeling* that you have control) of the situation can reduce the effects of a stressor. Another factor in reducing effects of stressors is predictability. People who live near subways or railroad tracks often show no discomfort from the sounds, which occur at fixed times. Visitors, however, may be greatly stressed by the (for them) "unpredictable" noise. Thus, the way we perceive the situation may be an important factor in reducing our susceptibility to stress.

Hans Seyle has also suggested that the way one reacts to a stressor is an important factor. Basically, he distinguishes between those responses intended to resist the situation *(catatoxic reactions)* and those intended to let one adapt to the situation *(syntoxic reactions)*. If someone cuts in front of you on the highway, you may get angry and upset (an aggressive, or catatoxic, response), or you can accept that the other driver is not your worry (a passive, or syntoxic, response). According to Selye, the syntoxic response would often be the better one. However, sometimes people are caught in a double-bind. When they are passive they wish they could be aggressive, and when they are aggressive they feel guilty. Selye argues that suppressing anger may be itself stressful—we occasionally need the safety valve of a catatoxic reaction. Unfortunately, Selye offers very little in terms of defining which situations merit which response, causing critics to say his theory is either circular or platitudinous. Selye's basic message comes down to recognizing when you are stressed, and what level of stress you best cope with. Individuals differ in their response to everyday pressures.

The individual's perception of the situation, and whether they react catatoxically or syntoxically, may be the most important determinants of the effects of "stressful" situations. Perhaps the best illustration of this is Selye himself. At the time of writing his last book, he used to get up at dawn to bicycle five miles to his office and work till eight at night—and this from a sixty-eight-year-old man with two artificial hips!

Altered States of Consciousness

Our reactions to painful or stressful events show that our mental state can affect our physical state. As such, they show the influence of the mind on the body. One of the questions raised by these influences concerns our definitions of reality. Usually, we think of reality as being objective—for example, the results of a physics experiment are repeatable and independent of the particular observer. However, when it comes to studying behaviour, we are forced to acknowledge that reality is subjective, for the same external stimulus does not always produce the same response by the person. While the materialist view asserts that such variations must be due to *internal* physical changes, the nature of these changes often is impossible to pinpoint. It is this aspect of the mind/body relation that has fascinated thinkers, and has led to speculations about the nature of mental states. Traditionally, such questions have been left to mystics and philosophers because psychologists have had no techniques to get at the problem. In the past ten years, however, researchers have been able to examine seriously the nature of mental states. Usually, this is referred to in terms of altered states of consciousness.

Today, when people hear the term "altered state of consciousness," it conjures up images of drugs and/or mysticism. However, this is too limited a view. Basically, an *altered state of consciousness* represents any (subjective) state of awareness different from that normally experienced. As such, the term could apply to psychosis and meditation, as well as drugs and mysticism. Even fever can induce an altered state of consciousness, as Julien de La Mettrie noted. Because the questions raised by these states are basically the same, we will focus on only one—meditation.

Meditation, until very recently, was primarily found in Eastern cultures. Now, for many reasons (including a concern with stress and dissatisfaction with Western life-styles), North Americans have begun to explore various meditative disciplines. In a broad sense, *meditation* refers to a variety of techniques that seek to achieve mental and physical relaxation, a more passive, receptive awareness, and harmony of mind and nature. Often practitioners will use metaphors like "existing in the here and now" or "becoming part of the circle of being." To those who have not experienced such states, these statements often sound like the claims for Dr. John's Snakebite Oil. For the researcher, it becomes a challenge to define meditation in a measureable way, that is, in terms of its effects on physical functioning.

The nature of meditation as a subjective experience is difficult to define, because in many respects it is non-verbal. Instead, one tends to talk about the process or technique involved. Most forms involve focussing awareness on some stable source of stimulation for a given period of time. This may involve sitting and focussing on nothing, as in Za-Zen (sitting Zen), or chanting, as in TM (Transcendental Meditation), or focussing one's full concentration on a task, as in Do-Zen (moving Zen). It is claimed that such practices result in relaxation, greater awareness of one's surroundings, and renewed energy. The difficulty with these claims is determining a way to assess them.

Research on meditation has focussed on two aspects: (1) seeking changes in brain activity that might define the mental state; and (2) seeking effects of meditation on other aspects of physiology. In terms of brain activity, the typical method has been to look at changes in brain-wave patterns by means of an EEG. It has long been known that brain waves change with level of alertness (e.g., actively thinking vs. relaxation vs. sleep), and the brain waves found during relaxation have been labelled the *alpha* rhythm. Most studies of meditation, of whatever form, have found that advanced practitioners produce more alpha waves during meditation. Of particular interest are the results of a study of advanced Zen states. One of the metaphors used in describing satori, or Zen enlightenment, is a sense of "freshness" to all events; each moment exists for itself. Studies of human physiological response to sudden noise usually indicate a startle response, measurable in the brain waves, which gradually fades if the sound occurs repeatedly. In a study done with three Zen masters, they did not show this fading of response but rather reacted to each repetition of the sound as if it truly were a "fresh" event.

Another area of study has been to look for other types of changes in physical functioning. For example, studies on physiological effects associated with TM have reported a general reduction of sympathetic nervous activity. The sympathetic nervous system, as previously noted, reacts to stress by increasing its activity. Thus, meditation may in fact counter the effects of stress.

One area of dispute until recently was the claim that meditators can alter vital body functions like heart rate and breathing. One of the first studies to evaluate this scientifically was done by psychologist Neal Miller. Using an airtight chamber and sophisticated recording equipment, he found that a yogi he tested was able to control heart rate, breathing, and other processes to a degree previously assumed to be impossible. Practitioners of TM and Zen masters also have shown changes in heart rate, breathing, and metabolic rate. In unusual cases, advanced practitioners also have exhibited no pain, nor have they bled when their skin was pierced. Such demonstrations indicate that meditation can have physical effects.

Before assuming meditation is the way to bliss, one should be aware of several limitations of the available evidence. First, not all claims made are likely to be true. Legitimate, long-term practitioners do seem to show effects, but there are also cases of fraud, particularly where schools are opened for financial gain. In all the studies in which verifiable physiological changes have been noted, the persons tested were experienced practitioners. In most cases, they had devoted their lives to meditation as a part of their religious training. (TM may be an exception, since proponents claim effects after only a few months of training when practised for twenty minutes twice a day. However, recent critics have suggested these claims require more study.) Second, no studies have yet attempted to separate the effects of meditation in these practitioners from other factors such as diet and general life-style. It may be that these play an important role. Again, TM claims no other changes are necessary. Third, no study has systematically explored individual differences in susceptibility. Again, TM is a case in point: while it does appear that those who regularly use TM benefit from it, it is not clear who "drops out" of TM or why, and the approach does not seem successful with all who attempt it.

The evidence, then, suggests that states of awareness can be influenced by conscious effort, and that the effects of these states can be measured physically. Until recently, most Western researchers would have been unwilling to consider these phenomena. One reason for this was the lack of adequate technology. A second reason, though, had more to do with the theories in fashion at the time, which said such effects were impossible. The problem was that a sharp distinction was made between "voluntary" and "involuntary" responses, and processes like heart rate and metabolism were assumed to be involuntary. Thus, scientists were unwilling to consider claims that seemed, on the surface, absurd. Not until Neal Miller began work on biofeedback in the late 1960s was there a theoretical framework that could offer insight into the effects of meditation.

Biofeedback

Consider the following demonstrations: a person raises the temperature in one hand, but not the other. A person wiggles their ears—in fact, each ear independently. Or a person twitches a single muscle fibre in the bicep, while all the fibres around it stay relaxed.

While these may sound like feats of yoga, requiring years to perfect, they have all been accomplished recently by individuals with no more than a few hours training on the specific task. In each case, the response involved is one which once would have seemed impossible to bring under conscious, voluntary control. This has changed, however, with the advent of biofeedback techniques.

Biofeedback refers to techniques which allow a person to become directly aware *(feedback)* of physiological processes *(bio)* which are normally not observable. For all voluntary muscle movements, our brain receives information, called *proprioceptive feedback*, about the execution of the movement. It is proprioceptive feedback which tells you the position of your arm even when your eyes are closed, for example. But for the involuntary functions (involving the autonomic nervous system), there is little or no proprioceptive feedback. To compensate, biofeedback techniques make use of sophisticated electronic equipment which can record and render observable these hidden processes. While the recording of physiological activity is not new (dating back to the 1930s) the idea of altering the activity by being aware of it was not considered until the late 1960s. Since then biofeedback has become a booming field, with tremendous potential for application.

The earliest studies of biofeedback were done with animals, and included successful attempts to change heart rate, brain-wave patterns, and even blood flow. Since then, problems have been encountered, both in repeating the early animal tests, and in extending them to people. Despite this, extravagant claims have been made (especially by companies seeking to sell biofeedback devices to the public). In order to understand the future potential of biofeedback, it is worth considering both the techniques and their present accomplishments.

Basically, use of any biofeedback procedure requires equipment to monitor the response one is interested in, and a means of conveying information to the subject about changes in their response. For example, if interested in muscle relaxation, one would use a device called an EMG, which measures the activity of the motor neurons which activate the muscles. If interested in the heart, one would use an ECG (electrocardiograph), and so on. The means of informing the person might be a buzzer or a light which flashes when the desired response is occurring. (See Figure 5.)

Currently, clinical researchers are evaluating a number of applications. For example, biofeedback has proven very effective for relaxation of voluntary muscles (e.g., arms, legs, neck). It has been applied to tension control, relief of lower back pain, and other problems. The involuntary activity of the muscles of the inner organs is also being studied, although the techniques become more complex. A group at St. Michael's Hospital in Toronto is attempting to use biofeedback to relieve spastic colitis and other intestinal disorders. Biofeedback has also proven moderately effective for reducing blood pressure and regulating the rhythm of the heart (but not very effective for reducing overall heart rate). Although its clinical value is debated, biofeedback of brain-wave patterns can be useful in increasing alpha wave production, a pattern which seems to be associated with a relaxed state of awareness.

One of the most promising uses of biofeedback thus far has been

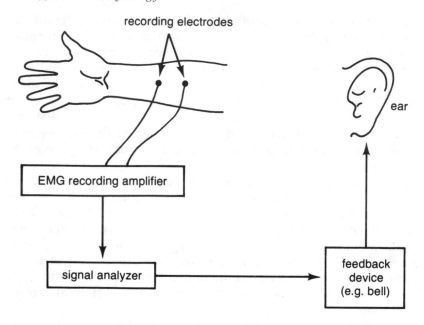

Figure 5
A Schematic Diagram of Biofeedback for Muscle (EMG) Relaxation
Electrodes on skin of forearms (other muscles could also be used) pick up
electrical activity in motor neurons that control muscles. EMG recorder am-
plifies signals, sending out continuous output to signal analyzer, which determines the threshold level. When activity reaches threshold, feedback device is activated, alerting subject that tension has increased. Eventually,
subject can learn to relax, keeping bell from ringing.

in the treatment of epilepsy. As discussed earlier, epilepsy can be
very disabling if the seizures cannot be controlled by drugs. In such
cases, treatment in the past has often meant surgery, ranging from
removing a small area of brain tissue (as in Penfield's work) to
separating the two hemispheres (as in the cases Sperry studied).
Now, research by M. B. Sterman and his colleagues at UCLA and
Sepulveda VA Hospital have suggested an alternative.

One of the indications of epilepsy is an abnormal pattern of brain
waves which shows up on an EEG, particularly during sleep. By
contrast, Sterman found that animals trained to produce what he
called sensorimotor rhythm (a bit faster than alpha waves, but still
indicative of a relaxed state) were resistant to seizures. Typically,
epileptics show an almost complete absence of sensorimotor rhythm
patterns.

Sterman began working with epileptics for whom other treatments had failed, attempting to use biofeedback instead. By use of an EEG, the researchers could monitor the brain activity of the patient, and try to encourage increased production of sensorimotor rhythm. As of 1977, they had worked with about twenty patients, using an average of three half-hour sessions per week. In one typical case, a twenty-three-year-old woman, who had been suffering grand mal seizures since the age of sixteen, was trained intensively for two years, with the training gradually tapering off. After five years, she had gone for over fourteen months without an attack. In about 75 per cent of the cases studied so far, the results have been equally encouraging. If Sterman's approach can be extended to other cases, it may offer a new era of hope for those epileptics for whom conventional treatment fails. At the same time, it offers a concrete example of the relationship between mind and body.

Biofeedback, then, may herald a new era. Outside the clinic, it often invites comparison with meditation, since many of the changes possible with biofeedback are also found in meditation states (e.g., the relaxing of muscles, slowing of breathing, and production of alpha waves). While biofeedback might seem a short cut to these states, at present it is not clear that the methods are fully equivalent. For one thing, not all of the effects found in meditation by "masters" have been reliably produced by means of biofeedback (e.g., lowering of heart rate). Further, it is not easy to compare the significance of the procedures in terms of the accompanying mental state. For example, many people do report feeling relaxed-yet-alert when producing alpha waves, but some don't, and a few people never show alpha patterns, no matter what their mental state. So is alpha production really the same as meditation? It's hard to say, but conservative researchers are reluctant to hail alpha-wave training as a short cut to Nirvana.

Another problem is that the changes associated with meditation are holistic, involving simultaneous alterations in many physiological functions, while biofeedback focuses on single functions, like brain waves. The question has yet to be explored fully, but present biofeedback procedures seem effective in changing only one or two functions at one time.

Easterners might say that Western researchers have once again mistaken two trees for a forest, but any final judgment about the potential of biofeedback is premature at this time. It is already proving useful in medical treatment, and it may eventually lead to consciousness expansion—but don't go shopping for a home machine just yet. (In fact, changes proposed in U.S. federal laws would make the sale of biofeedback devices to non-medical personnel illegal. The issue has not yet been raised in Canada.)

The study of biofeedback brings us full circle in the study of mind and body. We have seen how processes in the body affect our mental state, and in turn how conscious mental processes can affect our body. Obviously, questions remain, but the basic assumption of the materialists—that "mind" and "body" are different ways of talking about the same thing—seems relatively secure. As such, it has led to exciting discoveries about the way we function. However, looking at physiological processes in an adult obscures another basic question, which is how did we come to be what we are? To understand that, we must look at another aspect of the biological approach—the study of heredity.

THE HEREDITARY BASIS OF BEHAVIOUR

About ten years ago, some researchers announced that they had found a genetic pattern associated with criminal behaviour. Men born with the XYY chromosome pattern, it was argued, were born with the tendency to be criminals. This led to great controversy both among researchers and the public. If someone could be identified at birth as a potential criminal, advocates argued, they could be watched, or even locked up before they did harm. However, it was discovered that many XYY men were walking the streets without any apparent past record of criminal actions. Eventually the evidence for an XYY syndrome was cast into doubt, and the controversy died down. Still, it is significant that throughout, no one ever questioned the basic concept that behaviour *could* be inherited.

Today, the concept of inherited traits is so widely known that it is difficult for us to recognize its impact on our thinking. Yet it is scarcely more than a hundred years since Darwin suggested that variations could be passed on from one generation to another. "Like father, like son," we say. But how *much* like, we scarcely realize. Even Darwin, although he believed in the phenomenon, had no clue as to how heredity actually functioned.

Linked to the concept of inheritance between generations is the concept of evolution. The same process which produces variations within a species, biologists believe, also produces the variations which ultimately are labelled as different species. Thus, the comparison of human behaviour and physiology to that of other species becomes important as a way of improving our understanding. This is not to say that chimpanzee studies, for example, are a substitute for research on humans, but that comparisons of similarities and differences can lead us to new questions. At the same time, anthropologists like Richard Leakey are engaged in trying to understand the ancestors of humanity. In the end, the goal is to better understand and appreciate who and what we are.

These concepts—heredity and evolution—have both been significant in improving our knowledge of human behaviour. Before we consider the results of research, however, it is worth considering the basics of what geneticist George Beadle has called "the language of life."

Basic Mechanisms of Heredity

The word "genetics" was coined by the English biologist William Bateson. In a journal article in 1902 he urged his fellow researchers to look at the causes of inherited resemblances and differences, to understand "the essential process by which the likeness of the parent is transmitted to the offspring." At first, Bateson drew little response. For many years, the study of genetics was considered a bit eccentric, being based on taking inventories, raising generations of fruit flies, keeping animal pedigrees, and talking about concepts like "dominance," "unit characters," and "ratios." At the same time, chemists were working on the chemical structure of enzymes and other organic products. While it took many years before they realized it, the two groups were working on the same problem. Ultimately, the result was our breaking of "the code of life." The *gene* came to be recognized as the basic unit of heredity.

What is perhaps most fascinating about the development of genetics is that the early population geneticists (those involved in taking inventories) came to a clear understanding of the basic properties of genetic transmission *without* any knowledge of the underlying biochemistry. In fact, although the structure of DNA, which holds the basic structure of chromosomes of which genes are a part, was deciphered by Watson and Crick in 1953, it is only within the last ten years that anyone ever isolated a gene! Clearly, the key to heredity is the gene; clearly, too, the principles involved can be largely understood without direct reference to the biochemical processes.

In the 1860s, Gregor Mendel was living as a monk in an Augustinian monastery. The son of a farmer, he became interested in problems of plant hybridization, or the crossing of different species to produce new varieties. Working with garden peas, he set up an experimental plot to see if he could determine some orderly principles underlying the results of hybridization. As it turns out, he was wrong on many details, but correct in the general outline. Mendel discovered that an inherited characteristic is determined by a (chemical) code passed from parent to offspring. (Mendel, of course, did not know it was *chemical*, but knew there must be a mechanism.) In any individual, this code is made up of two genes, forming a pair. When reproduction takes place, the gene pair is split, so that one parent contributes only one gene to the offspring, the other member of the offspring's gene-pair coming from the *other* parent.

As time went on, it was discovered that the mechanism of splitting and recombining depends on the *chromosomes*, the larger structure of which the genes are a part. Thus, in humans, we have twenty-three pairs of chromosomes, each having hundreds or more genes, like so many bumps-on-logs. Because each of the twenty-three pairs splits and recombines independently of the others in reproduction, there are 2^{23} possible chromosome combinations from each parent, meaning that genetic recombination provides for almost limitless variety (over 8.4 million possible combinations from a single set of parents). The result is that genetic mechanisms provide a basis for variability, as well as similarity, from parent to offspring. The genetic code which an individual carries is called his *genotype*.

Genes for a particular characteristic (e.g., blood type, eye colour) can come in several variations, called *alleles*. Each allele represents the chemical code for a single variation. For example, blood types in people are based on three alleles, representing A, B, and O. Normally, for a characteristic based on a single gene (Mendelian inheritance), one allele, called the dominant allele, will be expressed whenever it occurs in the genotype. Other alleles will only be expressed (observable in the individual) if both members of the gene pair are the same. Because they are not as influential as the dominant form, these genes are called recessive alleles. For eye colour, brown is the dominant form, while blue is recessive. (See Figure 6.) Thus, the observed form of the characteristic depends on what pairing of dominant and/or recessive alleles of the gene is present.

One must distinguish between the genotype and the observed characteristics of the individual, called the *phenotype*. One reason for this has already been noted: a person may possess a recessive gene for blue eyes, but it will not be expressed if they also have a dominant gene for brown eyes. In terms of appearance, they would seem no different than a person with two brown genes. More importantly, genes only determine a *potential* for a characteristic, which must then be realized through a long sequence of biochemical processes. Along the way, other factors, including environmental influences, may intervene. For example, an individual may be born with PKU (phenylketonuria), a metabolic disorder based on a recessive gene allele. If

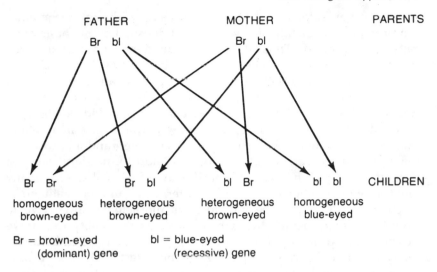

FATHER   MOTHER   PARENTS

Br bl   Br bl

Br Br	Br bl	bl Br	bl bl	CHILDREN
homogeneous brown-eyed	heterogeneous brown-eyed	heterogeneous brown-eyed	homogeneous blue-eyed	

Br = brown-eyed   bl = blue-eyed
(dominant) gene   (recessive) gene

Figure 6
Mendelian (Unigenic) Inheritance Applied to Eye Colour
In this case, both parents are brown-eyed in appearance (phenotype) but
both parents carry a recessive gene for blue eyes (heterogenous genotypes).
Statistically, the chances are three out of four that their children will have
brown eyes (phenotype), though based on either a homogeneous or hetero-
geneous genotype. In one case in four it would be possible for the children to
be blue-eyed.

untreated, it can result in severe mental retardation. However,
appropriate medical treatment and dietary restrictions can compensate if the disorder is detected early, and the individual need never
suffer the effects. Depending on the particular characteristic, the
amount of influence the environment has differs. The genetic code for
most aspects of our physical structure is relatively rigid—the eyes will
never occur other than in their normal place, for example. For traits
related to behaviour, such as intelligence, the reverse may be true—
environment may play a decisive role. Thus, the phenotypic or
observed characteristics of an individual are said to be based on the
combination of genotype and environmental influences. For psychologists, this is one of the most important aspects of heredity.

To summarize thus far, we now know that inheritance is based
on a chemical code carried by genes. Genes function in pairs, and
various forms (alleles) of the gene for a characteristic exist. The
recombination of genes from parents to offspring provides the basis
for genetic variability. The characteristics of an individual, however,
depend on the interaction of genetic and environmental factors.

One other factor must be mentioned here. Although recombination provides for considerable variation, it does not allow for any *new* traits to be created. Thus, if heredity functioned only in the way described above, there would be no possibility of evolution. Darwin recognized this, even without knowing anything about the basis of hereditary mechanisms. Along with the normal sequence of biochemical processes, it is possible for new gene forms, called *mutations*, to occur. Mutations are very rare, happening perhaps once in a million times. However, when they do occur, by whatever random process, a new trait may appear. Again, Darwin was alert to the significance of such events, which he expressed in the law of natural selection: any new trait which offers an advantage in terms of survival will tend to be passed on (because the individual is more likely to survive to reproduce), whereas any trait which weakens the ability to survive will normally disappear (due to the early death of the individual). Today this is often called "survival of the fittest." Over long time spans, the gradual introduction of new traits by mutation can lead to the genetic "drift" which we refer to as evolution. From a psychological point of view, this is significant, because it indicates that the development of human characteristics has a long history. The structure of our brain is linked to the structure of the brains of other species. Legs are related to flippers and wings. Darwin recognized this, but knew also that his contemporaries would not be likely to accept it. So, in his first book, *Origin of Species*, he carefully avoided any mention of *human* evolution. Only later did he become more explicit.

Heredity, then, is an important key to understanding behaviour. To the extent that it provides the organizational code for the developing embryo, it underlines all that we have talked about in terms of physiological processes. Through evolution, man has achieved significant gains over other species. Our cortex, which in many respects seems more highly developed than that of any other species, has played an important part in those gains. At the same time, the environment, through experience, has a significant impact on our cortex. What we are depends on both our genotype and our environment. Therefore, before leaving the biological approach, it is worth examining how heredity and environment interact.

Nature and Nurture in Behaviour

One of the most basic disputes in psychology concerns the importance of heredity vs. experience. Long before Mendel's genetic theory, people had an intuitive belief that something like hereditary factors existed. Plato, for example, talked about knowledge being inborn or "native" to the person, rather than being acquired through experience. This led to the view of knowledge and behaviour called *nativism*; the belief that characteristics are innate.

However, not everyone accepted this view. Other writers maintained that all newborn babies were basically alike, and only developed unique characteristics as a result of differing experiences. John Locke, an English philosopher, expressed it by saying the mind at birth is like a blank paper, on which experience is gradually written. This view, which emphasizes the importance of environmental influences, is often called *empiricism*. "One rotten apple can spoil the barrel," suggests the importance of external (environmental) factors.

The split between nativism and empiricism has led to arguments about the relative importance of hereditary and environmental factors in specific aspects of human functioning. One such aspect is intelligence, where the relative contributions of nature and nurture are still being assessed. Similarly, the mental disorder called schizophrenia, characterized by hallucinations, loss of contact with reality and displays of inappropriate emotion, may have both genetic and environmental roots. Recent advances in genetics have made systematic studies of the nature-nurture issue feasible.

Ideally, one would like to have a total control of both genetic and environmental factors, so that they might be manipulated experimentally. Technically and ethically this is impossible, but the ideal can be approached through *concordance* studies (roughly, concordance means "agreement"), where the behaviour of individuals whose genetic relationship is known can be examined. In concordance studies, identical twins are preferred subjects because they come from the same fertilized egg and have exactly the same genetic makeup. Where heredity is the decisive influence, identical twins should develop similarly, whether they are raised in the same family, or separately. Where environmental influence is the major determinant, however, identical twins raised in the same family should be no more similar than other siblings, while identical twins raised in different families should be more like the other members of their adopted families than like each other.

Unfortunately the methodology is not as clear-cut as it sounds. First, it is quite difficult to find identical twins who, because of family breakups, have been reared separately. One researcher, for instance, resorted to comparing identical twins, one of whom was raised by a maiden aunt and one by the parents, living fifty yards apart. In cases such as this, it cannot be claimed that the environments are truly different. A second problem arises from the fact that even when identical twins are separated at birth and raised separately, they still share the same prenatal environment in the mother's womb. It is, therefore, a practical impossibility to find identical twins who have been exposed to completely different environments.

The other side of the question, finding two individuals who have grown up in identical environments, is equally tricky. Identical twins reared in the same family appear, superficially, to meet this criterion because both prenatal and postnatal experiences are shared. Fraternal twins, conceived at the same time but developing from separate eggs, also would appear to share a common environment. However, even when two children grow up in the same family there is no guarantee that they will have identical experiences, or be treated in exactly the same way. This becomes especially clear when one considers fraternal twins of different sexes. The socialization practices of our culture are bound to result in different treatment.

Despite the difficulties of conducting rigorous experiments, concordance studies have added to our knowledge of the nature vs. nurture controversy. Modern psychologists largely lean towards an interactionist view, which suggests that genetic and environmental factors interact to determine the final shape of personality and behaviour.

Biological Constraints on Behaviour

In some species, most behaviour is determined by heredity, expressed through the physiological structure of the organism. In this sense, behaviour is "pre-wired," rather than learned. At one time, such behaviours were called "instincts." Today, because the term instinct has become over-used and vague, most researchers prefer the term "species-specific behaviour." This denotes behaviours which occur in all members of the species in the same way, and which do not seem to depend on any specific environmental experience. Unlike simple reflexes (like a knee-jerk), species-specific behaviour can involve fairly complex sequences, such as the ritual fighting in some species of tropical fish.

While species-specific behaviours occur in lower animals, it is questionable to what extent they exist in people. Despite this, our physiology is not infinitely flexible, and some behaviours are easier to acquire than others. (For example, clapping your hands is easier than rubbing your stomach and tapping your head simultaneously.) Also, some behaviours seem to be best learned at certain times during growth. A child who is not exposed to language prior to six years of age will have difficulty learning to speak later. This variability has led psychologists to seek a way to describe the interaction of heredity and experience in the learning of behaviour.

One such description is the preparedness dimension developed by Martin Seligman. *Preparedness* refers to the degree to which physiological structure influences the acquisition of behaviour. Some behaviours seem to develop with little or no specific experience. Seligman refers to these as "prepared" behaviours, because the physiological structure seems oriented to producing the behaviour. The species-specific behaviours referred to above would belong to this category. Most of our behaviour, however, does not stem from such "pre-wired" origins. For example, while we are capable of the balance and coordination required to ride a bicycle, the specific behaviours involved are not inborn. This type of behaviour has to be learned, because we have no hereditary pattern for it. Seligman refers to such behaviours as "unprepared," for this reason. At the other extreme, there are some types of complex patterns that we find very difficult, if not impossible, to acquire. In these cases, it seems that the physiological structure is not intended to cope with these situations. Because the difficulty seems to be inborn, Seligman says we are "contraprepared" to acquire such behaviour patterns. For instance, cats are "prepared" to lick themselves after eating, but they are "contraprepared" to use licking as a signal that they are hungry. Their physiology is oriented towards a "food, then lick" sequence, not "lick, then food."

Both prepared and contraprepared behaviours suggest that our evolutionary development has contributed significantly to what we are today. For example, man is basically a daytime creature. To our ancestors, who depended (as we still do) more on vision than smell or hearing, the night world of darkness was a place of invisible dangers. Thus, we may be "prepared" to be afraid of the dark. Similarly, some researchers have suggested that the "startle" behaviour we show to loud noises may stem from when the ancestors of mankind lived in trees, and had to be ready to grasp a branch at any moment. (Notice next time someone is startled that they not only jump, but their hands clutch, as if grasping at something.) There may also be reasons why we seem contraprepared for some behaviours. (For a detailed discussion of this aspect, see Chapter 4, "The Behavioural Approach".)

Seligman sees "preparedness" as a continuous dimension along which types of behaviour lie. Unlearned species-specific behaviours are prepared, but there are some behaviours which, though learned, are learned so quickly as also to seem prepared. One of the first people to recognize such behaviours was psychologist John Garcia. While doing research on the effects of x-ray radiation, Garcia noticed an interesting thing: the lab animals, when given large doses of x-rays, would get sick to their stomachs several hours later. If they had eaten previously, they would subsequently avoid whatever the food had been. They associated getting sick with the food, not the x-rays. This would be like a person who, coming down with the flu, happens to go out for dinner and eats something out of the ordinary, such as curried chicken. Later, they become nauseated because of the flu— but the next time they consider curried chicken, the reaction reoccurs. Garcia called this behaviour "bait-shyness" (based on fishermens' belief that a fish nearly hooked on a particular lure won't strike it again).

Further exploration of this phenomenon led Garcia to the conclusion that many species, including man, have developed in such a way that getting sick is very readily associated with the taste of the last-eaten food. Several things pointed to this being an evolutionary trait. First, it made no difference what actually caused the sickness (x-rays, drugs, etc.). Second, *only* the taste was associated with sickness, not the colour or appearance of the food or the place where it was eaten. Third, taste was not readily associated with other aversive events, such as being given electric shocks. Fourth, the link between food and sickness often occurred after a single experience, despite the long delay between eating and getting sick. Garcia suggested that this behaviour evolved because it was adaptive: an animal which ate something harmful would do well to avoid it in the future. Thus, a neural circuit may have been created (through mutation and natural selection) to link taste with stomach upset. Seligman goes further, suggesting that this is only one of a number of such circuits which may exist in our nervous system, all representing prepared tendencies.

Not everyone agrees with the interpretation of these results. At least one noted researcher has referred to Garcia's bait-shyness explanation as "neuromythology," not neurophysiology. However, the concept does not seem impossible, given an understanding of the nature of evolution. If heredity can play a role in behaviour patterns such as schizophrenia (as it appears to), then it is not unlikely that our capabilities are, in some ways, biologically determined. Indeed, the whole focus of the biological approach to psychology is based on recognizing and understanding the ways in which mind and behaviour are based on our physical nature.

SUMMARY

The biological approach is oriented towards understanding the physiological and genetic basis of our behaviour. As an approach within psychology, it is unique both in the level at which it seeks explanations, and in the range of factors it tries to consider. The biological approach is the only one in psychology which tries to explain behaviour in terms of the workings of the physical system. By contrast consider psychoanalysis (see Chapter 6). Though Freud was medically trained, and believed that ultimately the system was biologically based, psychoanalysis uses concepts which are purely psychological, not physiological.

Each person comprises a unique combination of genetic factors *(heredity)* and life experiences *(environment)*. The biological approach, by its nature, focusses on the internal factors associated with physiology and genetics. While it allows for the role of environmental factors such as stressors, it does not emphasize these factors, or the impact they can have on behaviour. Rather, the study of environmental influences has become the focus of other approaches to psychology, such as behaviourism.

Within the biological approach, the basic assumption advanced by Julien de La Mettrie over two hundred years ago seems to be paying off. As our understanding of physiological processes increases, it becomes more and more evident that mind and body *are* integrally related. Our knowledge is constantly expanding, and the insights are being applied—in the clinic, in business, and in everyday activities. For example, between 1955 and 1971 the number of psychotic patients in state mental hospitals in the United States was halved thanks to the use of psychoactive drugs. Advances such as biofeedback may offer new benefits as yet undreamed of.

Still, problems remain. One of the greatest challenges concerns the complexity of the physiological system. We know there are over six *billion* neurons in the brain alone. In addition, there are countless chemical interactions, and environmental influences. This complexity makes it difficult to predict a person's behaviour. Further, the ways in which factors interact make it difficult to make specific statements about one factor (e.g., stress as a cause of heart attacks) in the absence of knowledge about other factors (e.g., exercise and family history). These restrictions lead us to recognize that the picture is not yet complete. The parts still to be seen can hardly be less exciting than those already known.

Further Readings

For a very readable, well-illustrated view of the physiological system, Colin Blakemore's *Mechanics of the Mind* is a good choice. Based on a BBC series, it presents many sidelights in a vivid, non-technical manner.

Carl Sagan's *The Dragons of Eden* is a recent best-seller dealing with the evolutionary basis of intelligence. For Sagan, the book is a venture into unfamiliar territory—he is an astronomer whose interest in intelligence stems from considering the problems of finding extra-terrestrial intelligence.

Penfield's *The Mystery of the Mind* presents an interesting and often personal view of the problems of relating mind and brain, by a distinguished neurosurgeon.

Stress pioneer Hans Selye has written several books for popular audiences; *The Stress of Life* is one of his most recent.

The puzzles of phenomena like meditation are well-presented by Robert Ornstein in *The Psychology of Consciousness*. Unlike many, Ornstein is a Western psychologist who is also comfortable with Eastern sources.

For those interested in biofeedback, free-lance science writer Gerald Jonas has presented a vivid but accurate account in *Visceral Learning*.

4

THE BEHAVIOURIST APPROACH
Paul Hirschorn

Editor's Preface

For our next approach we have moved to the far end of the internal-external dimension. Where psychobiologists concentrate on genetics and man's biochemical nature, the behaviourists focus on the environment. What are the conditions associated with a certain behaviour? What happens after the behaviour? How do the antecedents and the consequences of behaviour influence that behaviour? These are the questions that the behaviourists seek to answer. It is as though they are regarding man as the proverbial, inscrutable black box. Instead of attempting to open the box, to see what may be inside, the behaviourists poke at it, prod it, and observe how it responds to the external situations they contrive. In the process they give no more than a brief, polite nod to psychobiologists, who are wallowing in the box's contents.

The behaviourists, as the name suggests, focus on the behaviour of living organisms and how those organisms respond to events. The internal mechanisms of the organisms are largely ignored, and abstract concepts, such as "mind" and "emotions," are eschewed as (barely) polite fictions. This hard-nosed approach has been surprisingly successful. Behaviourists have made a substantial contribution to our understanding of behaviour, and their behavioural principles are widely used in such diverse areas as animal training, child psychology and therapy.

THE BEHAVIOURIST APPROACH

As with any single psychological model, the case for "man-as-a-biological-entity" is limited. Like the physician in search of a set of symptoms, the biologically oriented psychologist adopts an *internal* frame of reference in seeking the principles underlying patterns of behaviour. The psychobiological model chooses to exclude considerations of the *external* context in which behaviour must always occur: *the environment*. At some point should the physician who is treating his chronically anxious patient with minor tranquilizers pay attention to possible environmental agents, which might be contributing to the patient's distress? Any number of external stressors—a winning lottery ticket, problems at work, or an extended visit from in-laws— might be triggering the patient's symptoms.

In attempting to understand human behaviour, its external context is a basic consideration: when, or under what conditions, does a given behaviour occur? What events precede the behaviour? What events are produced or changed by the behaviour? Such issues belong to the domain of *Learning Theory* or *Behaviourism*, an approach which focusses on how the developing human organism is shaped through its constant interactions with the environment. You enter the world with a genetic potential that contributes to your ultimate patterns of adjustment. But learning and experience also determine the kind of person you become.

This shift in emphasis from internal to external factors dates back to the early 1900s, a time when a growing number of psychologists— in particular, American investigators like Edward L. Thorndike and John B. Watson—were becoming disenchanted with traditional methods. These early approaches were concerned with attempts to study thoughts, experiences, emotions, motives—the so-called "inner states of mind"—using methods of introspection, verbal reporting and intuitive common sense. But mentalistic phenomena are subjective and often vague, and therefore difficult to study systematically. Science must be empirical, the behaviourists argued, based on *observable* events which could be precisely specified and measured. If psychology was to become a genuine scientific enterprise, it had to limit itself to observable behaviour, and how behaviour was influenced by the environment.

J. B. Watson expressed his faith in the predictive power of this psychological approach in his famous proclamation: "Give me a dozen healthy infants, well-informed, and my own specified world to bring them up in, and I'll guarantee to take any one at random and train him to become any type of specialist I might select—doctor, lawyer, artist, merchant, chief, and yes, even beggarman and thief—regardless of his talents, penchants, tendencies, vocations and race of his ancestors." (1926)

Although Watson and his behaviourist successors have been criticized, sixty odd years of pure and applied research has yielded a well-established body of scientific knowledge based on the premise that, to a very great extent, we are what we learn.

This chapter will present the basic principles and findings which derive from the behaviouristic approach to psychology, with emphasis on applications of behavioural *analysis* to familiar situations.

CLASSICAL CONDITIONING

Environment begins to affect us not at birth, but at the moment of conception. It requires no great stretch of the imagination to appreciate the effects which the prenatal environment might have on the unborn child. Expectant mothers who smoke, for example, tend to have smaller babies than those who don't smoke. Expectant mothers who are heroin addicts give birth to heroin-dependent neonates, who must undergo systematic withdrawl treatments if they are to survive. Here, the developing human embryo has been exposed to a chemical environment which is radically different from the norm, and the result is a radically altered newborn infant.

More generally, the term "environment" is usually taken to mean the world we are born into—our physical and social surroundings. Consider how this world might appear to a two-week-old child. How does the infant perceive its new surroundings? Does he or she think, feel or perceive at all? For many years people thought that newborns weren't capable of too much beyond gurgling, feeding, sleeping, eliminating, crying, and being generally cuddly and adorable. The actual evidence, however, doesn't lend much support to this notion of the human infant as little more than a passive blob. Rather, the results of extensive experimentation with infants paint quite a different picture. Even at a very early age, infants are tuned in to their surroundings and perfectly capable of exerting active control over the environment. When a pacifier is hooked up to an overhead mobile, so that the mobile rotates as the infant sucks, newborns suck on the pacifier more often than when sucking is unrelated to movement of the mobile. One has only to witness the flurry of activity and the delight of the infant who suddenly "understands" the operation of that universal first toy, the rattle, to appreciate that the infant can, and does, act upon and respond to the environment.

Now admittedly, playing with rattles and pacifier mobile

contraptions are not major achievements. To answer our original questions about infant perceptions one would want to probe more deeply into the newborn's psyche. But this, of course, raises a problem, since infants do not possess the requisite skills for communicating their feelings, and wants. Or do they?

Let us imagine that we could verbalize the "train of thought" (assuming, of course, there is one) of the infant who has just been brought into his new home and placed in his crib. Would it run something like: *"Well, here I am and this must be my new room and I'm glad to see that my parents have chosen blue for the walls because I am a baby boy and blue is considered most appropriate, oh, and that loud noise I'm hearing must be Mr. Jones, our neighbour, mowing the lawn next door . . . and now I'm getting hungry so I think I'll try to get the attention of Mom in the next room so she'll bring me my bottle . . ."*? I think you would agree that this is not likely to be the experience of our hypothetical infant. Almost certainly we are not equipped at birth for this sort of complex information processing. The world of the newborn infant must be a confusing, perhaps frightening, place to be. When not asleep, the neonate is continually bombarded by an assortment of unfamiliar events—sights, sounds, tactile stimulations, and internal sensations like pain, hunger, and so on. These environmental events are referred to as *stimuli*. A stimulus (abbreviated as *S*) refers to *any internal or external event, situation, object or factor that is measurable and which may affect behaviour.* Just as the chemist attempts to study the chemical units that make up the substances, so the learning psychologist examines the effects of the environment on the behaving organism with respect to its analyzable units, namely stimuli. Stimuli may be as complex and exciting as a good film or a successful encounter with a business client, or may be as simple as the ticking of a watch, a pin prick or a brief pang of hunger. Each represents an internal or external stimulus.

Back to where we left our infant, we may begin to examine his surroundings more systematically by referring to the specific stimuli he is likely to encounter. The infant's mother or caretaker is bound to become a reliable stimulus feature of the infant's surroundings. The mother may be thought of as a single stimulus, or may be seen as comprising several discrete stimulus units: her appearance, smell, voice and the manner in which she holds the infant are all stimuli which are central features of the infant's experience. The sound of Mr. Jones's lawnmower is yet another stimulus event, as is the soiled diaper which causes the infant discomfort. It is how organisms respond to stimuli in a systematic and predictable manner that is the main interest of environmentally oriented behavioural analysis.

The Classical Conditioning Paradigm

The learning psychologist observes that if the human organism is to survive in the world of boggling complexity in which it finds itself, it must begin attending to, and sorting out, those stimuli which reliably occur together. It is only as the newborn comes to *anticipate relationships among stimuli* that its world gradually becomes one which seems more orderly and secure. At first consideration, this might seem like a fairly major order of business for a mere infant. It isn't. Even the lowly planaria (flatworm) and cockroach have been shown to be capable of this achievement. It is considered to be the most basic form of learning and is termed *Classical Conditioning* (or *Respondent Conditioning*). The phenomenon was discovered by the famous Russian physiologist Ivan Pavlov in the early 1900s. Once again, the classical conditioning process involves the organism becoming sensitive to the fact that certain stimuli reliably occur together.

But classical conditioning entails more than stimuli. It also involves *responses*[1] to stimuli. Much of the behaviour of organisms involves a general category of responses termed *unconditioned responses* (URs). What identifies this class of responses is that they tend to crop up without any prior experience on the part of the behaving organism. "Automatic" or "reflexive" in nature and appearance, such responses are among the "biological givens" referred to earlier, which the organism possesses at birth. Shine a light in someone's eyes or have them bite into a fresh lemon and highly predictable unconditioned responses will result; pupillary contraction in the first instance, and salivation in the second case. The point here is that the individual doesn't have to *learn* these responses, any more than an infant has to learn to feel pain and to cry when hurt. Such reactions are built into the human nervous system.

The environmental events which reliably produce URs have been termed *unconditioned stimuli*. An unconditioned stimulus is *an environmental event which precedes and reflexively triggers an unconditioned response*. Pin pricks, sudden loud noises, a speck of dirt in the eye, are all examples of unconditioned stimuli. The URs which they trigger are pain, startlement, and tear gland secretion, respectively.

Now there is certainly nothing unusual about the fact that unconditioned stimuli will reliably produce unconditioned responses. It's only "natural," you might say, and you'd be right. (How often would you hear a proud parent boast, "Oh, my little

---

[1] Responses are usually simple acts, or physiological reactions. Just as the environment is examined by looking at small components or stimuli, so behaviour is studied by examining the responses (Rs) that comprise behaviour.

Myrtle is progressing brilliantly; why just the other day she actually *sneezed* while filling the pepper shaker!") But unconditioned stimuli have the ability to affect responding in another way: under certain conditions they will result in the organism responding to stimuli which don't "naturally" produce a response. When a *neutral* stimulus (i.e., one which has no effect on responding) occurs repeatedly and slightly in advance of, or simultaneously with, an unconditioned stimulus, the neutral stimulus soon elicits a response that is almost identical to the unconditioned response—the response normally produced by the US. When this happens, when the organism begins responding to a (previously) neutral stimulus *as though it were the unconditioned stimulus* with which it has been repeatedly paired, classical conditioning is said to have occurred.

This phenomenon attracted the attention and interest of Ivan Pavlov through a somewhat curious set of circumstances: as a renowned physiologist, Pavlov's original interests involved the study of the various digestive secretions of dogs. He had devised a surgical technique (for which he was awarded the Nobel prize) where the insertion of tubes into the digestive glands permitted the direct observation of digestive processes in living subjects. His research procedure was simple and straightforward: present meat powder to a hungry, surgically prepared animal and observe its salivary or other secretions. But the procedure ran into serious difficulty as, one after another, Pavlov's dogs began salivating freely before they had been readied for measurement, let alone fed. The mere sight of Pavlov or an assistant would cause the dogs to begin slavering uncontrollably. This "psychic activity," which seemingly defied scientific explanation, was both a source of frustration and fascination for Pavlov and his colleagues. Curiosity won, and he decided to shift his scientific interest from physiology to the systematic investigation of this unexpected phenomenon.

In his basic demonstration of classical conditioning, one of Pavlov's experimental dogs was presented with a brief musical tone, immediately followed by the insertion of meat powder into the hungry animal's mouth, which produced extensive salivation. After several such stimulus pairings of the tone (a "neutral stimulus") with the food (an "unconditioned stimulus"), which produced salivation (the "unconditioned response"), the tone was presented once again, without the food. Reliably, each dog tested would begin to salivate, now termed a *conditioned response* (or CR) to the tone (a conditioned stimulus of CS), just as it had previously responded to the food. (See Figure 1.) Thus through this process of association, an entirely novel feature of the experimental animals' environment, a brief tone came to control their behaviour by acquiring the capacity to *elicit* salvation.

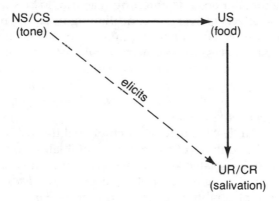

Figure 1
The Basic Classical Conditioning Paradigm

It was suggested earlier that if the human infant is to survive and begin to impart some semblance of order into its confusing surroundings, it must begin to anticipate which environmental stimuli reliably occur together. It is through the classical conditioning process that this task is achieved. For example, the repetition of the word "bottle" (or the sounds associated with its preparation) by the parent at feeding time is reliably paired with the pleasurable sensations of hunger satisfaction. Gradually, this stimulus ("bottle") becomes sufficient in itself to elicit a measure of comfort. After a while the hungry infant may stop crying when it merely hears the word "bottle" (the CS). Via classical conditioning, the word has become a reliable predictor of good things to come.

However, conditioning is just as often the result of stimuli that become associated with painful or unpleasant unconditioned stimuli. Such "aversive conditioning" enables the individual to anticipate, and perhaps avoid, these unpleasant or threatening events. In *Brave New World*, Aldous Huxley describes a nightmarish scene in the state-controlled nursery, where, each day, infants are seated in a room decorated to simulate an outdoor, park-like setting—a green expanse with trees, flowers and the like. In the presence of these cues (NS), the infants are administered a series of painful electric shocks (US). The infants react violently: they scream, they eliminate, some are sick (URs). For several consecutive days the young citizens are exposed to this same sequence of events; green settings—electric shock. We learn that the purpose of this procedure is to establish in these children a powerful aversion to outdoor settings (CR) which are no longer available to the inhabitants of Huxley's brave new world. What these children of the state don't like to begin with, they will hardly long for later on. A frightening scenario, to be sure! But, as we shall see, the effects of aversive conditioning in our own lives should not be underestimated, nor undervalued, for aversive conditioning teaches us many necessary and helpful rules of survival.

Classical conditioning then, is a basic *learning phenomenon in which reflexive, involuntary and/or emotional behaviour comes under the control of a stimulus which has reliably occurred more-or-less simultaneously with an unconditioned stimulus.*

At this point, lest the reader conclude that this learning process is restricted to the confines of the experimental laboratory, the infant's crib, or to certain isolated and implausible human situations, a few everyday examples are in order. The recent movie *Jaws* employed an aversive classical conditioning technique to enhance audience reaction to a specific suspenseful element in the film, namely, the shark. While viewing *Jaws*, this author became aware of the film's systematic presentation of an audible signal (US)—a high-pitched, inhuman, and somewhat unnerving sound—whenever underwater footage of the shark (CS) appeared on screen. Here, the intent was to increase the fear-arousing properties of the ravaging killer shark; and indeed the overall effect was chilling. One can only speculate as to what emotional response this creature might have elicited had its appearance been consistently paired with a pleasant and lively jingle instead of an eerie and gut-rending unconditioned stimulus. In a typical Walt Disney animal epic this latter technique is used to create just the opposite emotional atmosphere!

Reliance on the effects of classical conditioning is far more widespread in the media advertising industry than in the film industry. Vance Packard's best seller, *The Hidden Persuaders* (1957), describes how learning principles are applied to various marketing situations. One has only to encounter Anne Murray discoursing about the merits of term banking deposits or Joe Namath modelling a new line of panty hose to realize that the promoters must have something in mind other than enhancing the credibility or expertise of their communicators. Ms. Murray did not achieve her success and public exposure as a banking executive. And Broadway Joe is not (at least in the literal sense) an authority on women's hosiery. If he were he would, hopefully, not wish to advertise the fact! The behavioural principle underlying the "star endorsement" is basic respondent conditioning. The advertiser banks on the glamorous qualities of the star becoming associated with the promoted product, so that when the product alone is encountered (a conditioned stimulus), our emotional reaction to it will be more favourable. Moreover, presenting powerful unconditioned stimuli, such as beautiful models in aesthetically pleasing surroundings, enhances the effect. As one psychologist wryly observed, "You'll never see a whining brat or a swarm of mosquitos at a Pepsi Cola picnic!"

CLASSICAL CONDITIONING PHENOMENA

Stimulus Generalization

Consider the following situation: little Myrtle, an active, inquisitive three-year-old is attracted to the glowing circular area atop the kitchen stove. Although her mother has previously warned Myrtle about this particular feature of her environment, she is still curious, and besides, Mom is not around to curb her fascination with the red-hot element. She approaches the stove, reaches out to touch the element and is burned. Very rapidly (with perhaps just one such experience) there will be established a conditioned aversion to the red-hot element. This ensures that Myrtle will likely avoid repeating the same mistake in the future. But does this mean that if she should find herself in a totally different situation, confronted with a *different* red-hot glowing object which captures her attention, Myrtle will be burned once again to learn about this new and potentially dangerous situation? Definitely not. Via a phenomenon which is related to basic classical conditioning, and termed *stimulus generalization*, the effects of conditioning tend to extend into new learning situations.

In what has become a classical research example, two psychologists, Watson and Rayner, set out to establish that Pavlovian conditioning could be demonstrated with a human subject. Their subject was an eleven-month old institutionalized infant called Little Albert. On different occasions the experimenters presented Albert with a variety of stimulus objects, including blocks, a ball of cotton, a white rat, some furry material and some masks. The infant readily approached these novel objects and began playing with them, Little Albert being no different in this respect from any curious and outgoing infant of his age.

The investigators then began a systematic aversive conditioning procedure, selecting the white rat as the to-be-conditioned stimulus object. On the first conditioning trial, the white rat was presented to Albert who, as before, eagerly approached the animal. At this point, the unconditioned stimulus was presented—a loud, unexpected noise delivered from behind the infant's crib by striking a large steel bar with a hammer. Albert was startled by the sound and began to cry. This basic procedure was repeated, one trial per day, for the following six days. Then the rat was presented alone, without the loud noise. Albert saw the rat, began to cry and drew away. A fear reaction had been classically conditioned to a previously attractive stimulus object. But Little Albert's problems were far from over. About a week later, the experimenters returned to Albert with some of the neutral objects he had been shown prior to the conditioning— the blocks, masks, fur, ball of cotton, and so on. Albert still showed his original playful interest in the blocks and all but one of the masks. However, when confronted with the cotton, or the fur, or a Santa Claus mask with white fluff on it, Albert grew frightened and avoided these objects, even though none of them had been employed in the actual aversive conditioning procedure! His conditioned fear response had *generalized* to those stimuli which were furry, like the white rat. Once a conditioned response has been established to a given conditioned stimulus, stimulus generalization refers to *the ability of stimuli different from (though similar to) the original conditioned stimulus to elicit the same conditioned response.*

Extensive experimentation on a variety of animal species has shown that generalization is basic to the process of conditioning, and that a response becomes conditioned not just to a specific stimulus (the CS), but to a *whole class of stimuli* which can elicit the same conditioned response. Thus, a child who has learned to duck when a volleyball flies at his face (because he has been hurt before for not doing this) will tend to avoid any stimulus which shares with the original CS (the volleyball) the property of being a rapidly approaching visual stimulus. In the future, the child will exhibit rapid avoidance of a wide range of generalized stimuli of this type, be they tennis balls, golf balls, or attempted slaps in the face! Similarly, the child who utters its first garbled "da-da" might be hailed a prodigy by the delighted father, until it is discovered that the appearance of an uncle, grandfather, deliveryman, or other similar "male" stimulus elicits this identical greeting from the child.

Why should stimulus generalization be such a reliable feature of respondent behaviour? The most likely answer lies in the biological process of natural selection. In the course of their species' development, organisms displaying generalization from conditioned stimuli to stimuli which they identified as similar would have a better chance of surviving than those that didn't.

Generalization results in a classically conditioned response acquired in one situation reliably transfering to numerous unfamiliar situations and untried activities. It means that little Myrtle, in our first example, learned an extremely important lesson in her mother's kitchen, one which will work to her benefit in the future.

Response Generalization

We have seen that any stimulus which bears a physical resemblance to a conditioned stimulus will reliably elicit a conditioned response.

This is stimulus generalization. A related phenomenon, termed *response generalization,* refers to the fact that a CS elicits *not just one, but a whole class of conditioned responses.* Pavlov's dogs did not just salivate (CR) when confronted with the conditioned tone, but exhibited a spectrum of responses which, along with salivation, became conditioned to the sounding of the tone. Such generalized responses include vocal behaviour (barking, whining) and general autonomic arousal (increased heart rate, respiration, muscular activation, etc.). Response generalization is said to occur *when a conditioned stimulus elicits a response that is different from (though similar to) the original conditioned response.*

We have yet to consider the ultimate fate of classically conditioned responses. How long do they persist following their establishment and continue to exert an influence on the behaving organism? The possibility of long-term and highly adverse effects of response generalization has been proposed by psychobiologist W. H. Gantt, who offers the following hypothesis:

> "The fact that [conditioned responses] are so difficult to eradicate, once formed, makes the individual a museum of antiquities as he grows older. . . . He is encumbered with many reactions no longer useful or even . . . detrimental to life. This is especially true for the cardiovascular function, and it is these [conditioned responses] that are most enduring. A person may be reacting to some old injury or situation which no longer exists, and he is usually unconscious of what it is that is causing an increase in heart rate or blood pressure. The result may be chronic hypertension. This may be the cause of many cardiac deaths." (1966)

Gantt has termed this condition "schizokinesis," but whether its effects are as exaggerated or as common as this excerpt suggests has not been determined. However, response generalization might well lead to the individual carrying about varying amounts of excess "conditioned emotional baggage" throughout his life. An athlete who once suffered a leg injury might believe she has completely recovered from the injury yet unconsciously continues to respond on certain occasions as she did to the injury. She may reinstate a tendency to limp, or wince internally in situations reminiscent of the original injury.

Likewise, a person who believes he has long since forgotten his very first love affair, inexplicably finds his hands trembling and heart palpitating when he accidentally runs into the woman in question (or even one who bears a strong resemblance!). He, too, is experiencing the effects of response generalization. A *part* of this person's repertoire of original conditioned emotional/autonomic responses continues to be elicited by the original conditioned stimulus, or a generalized version of it.

Both stimulus and response generalization are important features of classically conditioned behaviour insofar as *these phenomena allow for the extension of conditioned responding beyond the actual situations in which they were originally acquired. They extend our capacity to respond emotionally or physiologically to novel situations.* Sometimes generalization impairs subsequent learning and experience (as in the case of Little Albert who acquired a generalized fear of all furry objects); but more often, generalization serves to facilitate the organism's subsequent interactions with the environment.

Stimulus Discrimination

Even when the effects of generalization result in inappropriate or "surplus" conditioned responding, this doesn't mean that such maladaptive behaviour must persist unchanged. Through the process of *stimulus discrimination,* the behaving organism may learn to *limit and refine* the range of stimuli that are capable of eliciting conditioned responding. As we shall see, this process is valuable, and often essential, in our adjustments to and complex dealings with the environment. But before examining some of its more general implications for human behaviour, let us look briefly at the detailed mechanics of stimulus discrimination.

As with most classical-conditioning phenomena, Ivan Pavlov is credited with pioneering the early experimental investigation of stimulus discrimination. Pavlov began by conditioning his canine subjects to salivate when they saw a circle was presented, by repeatedly pairing the circle with the presentation of food. Once this conditioned responding to circles was fairly well established, Pavlov began presenting similar (but different) configurations: when *ellipses* were displayed, his non-discriminating subjects salivated freely. In other words, they exhibited the tendency to *generalize* conditioned responding to these roughly circular stimuli. However, through continued training in which *only* the presentation of a circle was consistently followed by food, and where other stimulus configurations were *never* paired with food, the dogs gradually stopped salivating when confronted with non-circular stimuli. They showed this conditioned response only in the presence of circles—often demonstrating remarkably fine visual discriminations.

Stimulus discrimination, then, is *the tendency to exhibit differential conditioned responding to only those stimuli which are consistently associated with unconditioned stimuli.*

Because conditioning phenomena occur spontaneously, and

often without our being conscious of them, it is easy to overlook parallels between such laboratory demonstrations and our everyday actions and experiences. But we have all acquired innumerable conditioned discriminations in the course of our lives, and will acquire countless others. It is a process which is basic to just about any area of human experience or endeavour. Consider: to the uninitiated (i.e., the non-discriminating or "generalizing") person, wine—be it imported or domestic, vintage or "do-it-yourself"—is just wine. "It all tastes the same to me," such a person might say. But to the wine connoisseur, there are differences which are detectable only to his discriminating palate, because he has learned how to differentiate among subtle characteristics. Similarly, by studying the visual details of various precious stones, the gemologist comes to appreciate distinctions in quality among them: some of his initial responses (e.g., "Now this is a fine diamond.") have met with positive reactions or results (e.g., "That's right—you're learning!"), some with negative ones ("No, you idiot—this one's fake!"). Gradually, through experience, we learn to limit our tendencies to generalize (e.g., "Wine is just wine," or "One novel is pretty much the same as any other.") and to our conditioned responses accordingly.

As a final example, consider the extremely difficult social discriminations we are faced with daily in our dealings with other people: "Is this person being aggressive toward me because of something *I* did or said, or is it their problem—and besides, why do I care? Why *should* I care?" Or: "I consider myself an honest individual—yet should I tell this person what I *really* think, or perhaps consider their feelings, show a little diplomacy, bend the truth a bit? Or is this a time to keep my opinions to myself?" Such dilemmas are only too common. Learning *when* it is appropriate to exhibit certain tendencies and when it is not, can be a demanding task, one involving complex and fine discriminations. Yet it is a skill to master if we are to learn to interact effectively with those around us.

Higher-Order Conditioning

A conditioning phenomenon of considerable practical importance is termed *higher-order conditioning*. Pavlov investigated this phenomenon using the following experimental procedure: initially, he established a strong conditioned response in his dogs by repeatedly pairing the sound of a metronome with food (US) until the metronome (CS) assumed control over the salivary response (CR). He then began pairing yet another (initially) neutral stimulus, a black square, with the sound of the metronome which, in turn, elicited salivation. Pavlov found that after repeated pairings of the black square with the sound of the metronome, the black square presented alone (and termed a "first-order" or "higher-order" conditioned stimulus (CS)) would produce salivation, although the responding was somewhat weaker than that elicited by the metronome, the original CS.

Higher-order conditioning involves *having a well-established CS function as if it were a US in bringing the conditioned response under the control of a novel and physically dissimilar stimulus.* Such CS_1—CS pairings permit stimuli which bear little or no physical similarity to the original CS, to gain control over respondent behaviour.[2] Say a parent who punishes little Willie for misbehaving tends to shout "Bad boy!" immediately prior to spanking. Soon, this verbalization ("Bad boy!") will assume control over the child's emotional responding. In public, where the parent might not wish to be seen as a potential child abuser, I have seen such conditioned stimuli (e.g., "Bad boy!") cause a child to literally freeze in his tracks and wince, almost as though he had been physically punished. Straightforward classical conditioning. But suppose one day little Willie carelessly tracks mud all over the clean kitchen floor. His mother might shout something like, "Willie, just look at all that *dirt*, you *bad boy!*" It is not difficult to appreciate how the word "dirt" might soon come to acquire unpleasant connotations through being repeatedly paired with a well-established conditioned stimulus. In fact, it is through the process of higher-order conditioning that words in general come to generate an emotional impact. It should now be apparent why your trips to the family doctor are able to elicit fear and discomfort, even though we may be far removed from the medical examining room. Through experience, we come to associate stimuli that consistently lead to or eventually result in pain with this unpleasantness. This is why the smell of certain antiseptic solutions or the sight of bleak corridors reminiscent of hospital wards are sufficient to induce severe discomfort and emotional stress in certain individuals. Such environmental cues serve as higher-order conditioned stimuli and may exert a powerful influence on our emotional reactions.

Classical Extinction

Up till now, we have not considered a rather crucial point regarding conditioned stimuli and the conditioned responses they reliably

---

[2] In laboratory settings, higher-order conditioning does not ordinarily "take" beyond the second order (i.e. CS_2-CS_1-CS). However, in everyday settings, it is not uncommon for stimuli far removed from the original conditioned stimulus to gain control over responding.

produce. The question, "How long do the effects of classical conditioning last?" may have already occurred to you. For instance, are we to believe that Little Albert grew up with an irrational, life-long fear of furry objects? Once conditioned associations have been established between an actor and a particular role, say William Shatner as commander James T. Kirk of the U.S.S. *Enterprise*, does this mean that if we should see Mr. Shatner in a serious dramatic part we will be overcome with fantasies about intergalactic travel and adventure? Are we like the proverbial "elephant who never forgets," retaining each and every classically conditioned response we ever acquired?

The answers to these questions depend on an understanding of the phenomenon termed *classical extinction*. We have seen that the basic conditioning process and its attendant phenomena serve a generally adaptive function; they allow the behaving organism to make adjustments to a complex and often dangerous environment by learning to react with responses (emotional, reflexive and autonomic) which anticipate the occurrence of pleasant or harmful events. But since the environment is continually changing, just as the behaving organism is constantly developing and/or changing, it would be disadvantageous, and even debilitating, for the individual to continue to exhibit all the conditioned reactions he ever possessed.

This is where extinction enters the picture. Extinction is the scientific term that refers to *the weakening of a conditioned response, as a result of the repeated presentation of the conditioned stimulus which elicits it, in the absence of the unconditioned stimulus.*

Thus, with reference to speculations about William Shatner and Little Albert, conditioning theorists would conclude the following: that if we see Mr. Shatner in enough contexts other than in his "Star Trek" role, he will lose his capacity to evoke conditioned associations with this role. (If the initial associations are strong, however, it may be difficult to break this so-called "type-casting," which is why serious actors attempt to avoid it in the first place.) In other words, extinction will occur. And what of Little Albert? Unfortunately, we would have to predict (as did the original investigators) that Albert would, as an adult, harbour an irrational fear of furry objects, with the magnitude of his fear response being proportional to the objects' similarity to the original white rat.[3]

Irrational fears elicited by objects or situations, that are in reality harmless, are termed *phobic reactions*. Phobic reactions are highly

---

[3] Current rigidly enforced codes of ethics for psychological research involving human subjects preclude experiments such as the one conducted by Watson *et al.* No one knows what eventually became of Little Albert, as he was removed from the institution, before follow-up observations could be made.

common and range from fear of the dark to fears about snakes, heights, or public speaking. In fact, the range of phobias appears to be as limitless as the number of objects or situations to which fear may be conditioned. Moreover, such reactions tend to be highly resistant to the effects of classical extinction, for an indirect reason. For example, the fear conditioned in Little Albert* would likely tend to persist because, as he grew older, Albert would try to actively *escape from or avoid* situations where he encountered fear-eliciting stimuli such as small furry animals. For classical extinction to occur, Albert would have to experience the CS on several occasions in the absence of the original US (the loud noise). However, Albert would probably never tolerate a small cat or dog long enough for his anxiety to undergo extinction.

The individual who finds himself seriously handicapped by such inappropriate fear reactions might eventually seek some form of professional assistance. Phobias are among the most common disorders treated by clinical psychologists and psychiatrists. Depending on the clinician's particular orientation, the type of treatment recommended for the individual will vary widely. A traditional psychoanalyst would wish to delve into the early childhood experiences of the phobic to look for sources of the individual's "repressed conflicts." However, a recent movement in clinical practice known as *behaviour therapy* or *behaviour modification* derives its approach directly from the principles of Learning Theory. This approach tends to be neutral and objective, so that the behaviour therapist tends not to distinguish between behaviour that is "normal" versus "abnormal." Rather, he believes that all behaviour is learned according to the same basic principles, with some being simply less adaptive than others. These therapists also tend to avoid the traditional clinical classifications (neurotic, psychotic, obsessional, manic, etc.) and refer only to behaviour that is "maladaptive." Such a therapist would no more want to delve into the early life history of his client than would a garage mechanic want to find out where your car has been for the past 20,000 miles. If your car's alignment needed adjusting, the mechanic would make the necessary adjustment rather than try to discover the original cause of the faulty alignment! Similarly, the behaviour therapist deals with his clients in the here-and-now and invokes the principles of classical and operant conditioning in altering problematic behaviour, as is evidenced in the following case study involving the treatment of a somewhat uncommon phobic reaction:

*"Stardust" and the Extinction of a Music Phobia**
"A few years ago a young man was incapacitated because of the very intense misery he experienced whenever he heard the tune "Stardust." His life was further complicated by the fact that

music in general made him distraught and uncomfortable. This phobia was so upsetting that it began to interfere with many of his daily activities. If he was in a restaurant, he had to leave if someone played the jukebox. If he was at a gathering where music was part of the entertainment, the overwhelming anxiety elicited by the music led him to escape from the situation in order to reduce his discomfort. Since music was part of nearly all his pre-phobic routine, this unfortunate individual soon found himself withdrawing from all social activity. In desperation, he sought professional help. . . .

". . . Beginning with the second interview, the patient was seated in a room, and a taped version of "Stardust" and tunes the patient identified as similar to "Stardust" were played over and over again. During this session, the patient evidenced all the responses characteristic of acute fear and anxiety, such as hyper-ventilation, sweating, and vocalizations, suggesting excessive discomfort. In the third and fourth sessions, the anxiety responses were still manifest, but they were diminishing in both frequency and intensity.

"After a few more sessions, all of the patient's unsettling emotional reactions to music disappeared, and he appeared calm and relaxed. Tests were conducted to determine whether extinction had generalized to music unrelated to "Stardust" and to extra-therapeutic situations. According to the tests and the verbal report of the patient, this extinction procedure proved successful in the elimination of his music phobia, and he was able to resume normal activity."
(Wenrich, 1970. pp. 14)

Notice that in this case study, the therapist made only the assumption that at some time the feared stimulus (i.e., music) had been paired with an unusually aversive experience, and that the music phobia reflected the persistent effects of original classical conditioning. By repeatedly presenting the music (the assumed CS) to this individual, the fear response (CR) began to weaken and eventually underwent complete extinction.

Spontaneous Recovery

Once conditioned responding has undergone classical extinction, it is tempting to conclude that these learned responses have left the organism's behavioural repertoire for good—as though extinction some-how "erases" learned associations from the brain and nervous

* From *A Primer of Behavior Modification*, by W. W. Wenrich. Copyright© 1970 by Wadsworth, Inc. Reprinted by permission of the publisher, Brooks/Cole Publishing Company, Monterey, California 93940.

system. A reliable phenomenon known as *spontaneous recovery* makes this a questionable hypothesis. Spontaneous recovery refers to *the spontaneous re-emergence of the CR after a rest interval, subsequent to its extinction and at the first presentation of the CS.*

Thus, Pavlov's experimental animals would cease salivating entirely after repeated exposures to the tone in the absence of food, but would exhibit the tendency to salivate at some later time, when the tone (CS) was encountered once again. These "recovered" responses, however, were not as strong as they were prior to experimental extinction and would *re-extinguish* quite rapidly in the continued absence of the US (food).

Independent investigations have observed spontaneous recovery in such diverse species as rats, sheep, and pigeons after a post-extinction rest interval which lasted up to two-thirds of the lifespan(s) of these animal subjects! Since the extinction process is considered as the experimental counterpart to human forgetting, it might well be the case that well-established conditioned responses never really leave the individual. Rather, the phenomenon of spontaneous recovery suggests that previously acquired associations might merely be *interfered with* by subsequent conditioned responses.

The spontaneous reappearance of bad habits like nail biting, smoking, childish displays of temper and the like, which we may have thought we had overcome long ago, are common occurrences involving spontaneous recovery. Its effects are also apparent in situations that suddenly bring to mind long-forgotten items of information, such as the words to a poem or song or a melody learned as a child. Who is to say? It may be that we are more like "the elephant who never forgets" than we might have suspected.

OPERANT CONDITIONING

Classical conditioning deals mainly with the way in which emotional behaviour and our autonomic "gut reactions" are brought under the control of conditioned stimuli. We encounter a conditioned stimulus and react to it with an appropriate response which anticipates the occurrence of another environmental event. This basic learning process is extremely important to our everyday behaviour and, in certain circumstances, to our continued survival.

But these learned "anticipatory" responses cannot account for the rich variety and complexity of human activities and endeavours. Much of our daily behaviour involves *doing* and not simply "reacting to." We are able to react to the demands of the environment with our battery of conditioned responses only where we encounter the conditioned stimuli which trigger the responses. Yet we don't seem to spend much of our time simply waiting around for stimuli to prompt our brief reactions. Such may be true for the simplest forms of life, but we wouldn't fare very well were this the case.

Classically conditioned reactions represent only one of two general classes of behaviour, the second class being *operant behaviour*. Presenting a monthly report, having an argument, enjoying a hobby, opening the back door, solving a problem, or cooking breakfast are examples of such operant behaviour—activities that are *emitted* (i.e., originating *from* the individual), as opposed to *elicited* by conditioned stimuli.

Behaviourists assert that the individual's continual adjustments to the environment, not to mention his ultimate skills, preferences, choice of lifestyle, and even his personality, are the result of a lifelong learning process which involves discovering relationships between actions and their immediate effects on the environment. In infancy, at the same time as classically conditioned associations are being established, our *operant* responses (they serve to *operate* on the environment) are also being conditioned according to how they affect our physical and social surroundings. It is almost as though we were constantly posing the questions: "What changes or events in the environment can I postpone or prevent?"

Stated differently, much of our behaviour is dependent upon its immediate *consequences*. (See right portion of Figure 2.) The principles which specify precisely how these diverse operant activities are acquired, modified, and maintained belong to the area of behaviourist theory termed *operant conditioning*.

Reinforcers and the Principle of Reinforcement

Reinforcers all around us exert a powerful influence on our behaviour, though we are often unaware of their presence and their effects. *A reinforcer (Sr⁺) is an stimulus event which follows an operant response and increases its probability of recurrence.* To reinforce means to strengthen. When an environmental event makes an operant response more likely to occur again in the future, it has effectively strengthened this bit of behaviour. The "principle of reinforcement" is simply the occurrence of a reinforcer. The popular term "reward" is sometimes (but not always) what is meant by a reinforcer. The problem is that "reward" is an overworked term, one which lacks the precision of meaning required by the behaviourist.

Food is probably the most basic, and one of the first reinforcers we encounter. A baby cries because he or she is hungry, and is fed. As a result, the food serves to strengthen the crying response. (Notice that when food is involved in classical conditioning, its occurrence is *before* the response, while in operant conditioning it occurs *after* the response.) Food, water, physical comfort, plus many commonly used drugs, such as nicotine, caffeine and alcohol, belong to a class of reinforcers termed *primary reinforcers*, which are directly related to the organism's biological needs. But these primary reinforcers are far from being the only behavioural consequences that strengthen operant behaviour. The principle known as *conditioned reinforcement* vastly expands the number of environmental events which may come to act as reinforcers.

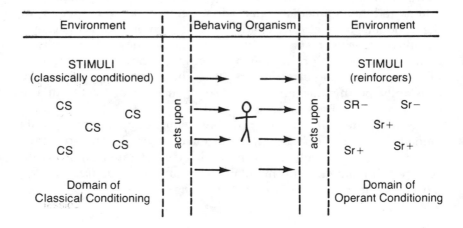

Figure 2
Representation of Classical and Operant
Environmental Influence on Behaviour

A conditioned reinforcer is a stimulus which has reliably occurred in the presence of a primary reinforcer and has gradually assumed reinforcing properties (through the process of classical conditioning). Recall for a moment how you used to swell with pride when your public school teacher presented you with a red, blue, silver, or gold star. Think of the persistent effort we expend in order to win the praise and approval of others. Observe the influence that money can have on our lives. Such stimuli, gold stars, medals, diplomas, praise, approval, the smell of food, national flags, and, of course, money, are all conditioned reinforcers which shape and maintain many human endeavours.

Two points should be stressed about reinforcers and the reinforcement principle. First, their effects are often badly underestimated. We have all used reinforcers such as approval, praise or gifts, but may have questioned their effectiveness in strengthening the desirable behaviour for which they were offered. Some parents, for example, make the claim that they "gave their children everything" and cannot understand why their offspring are obnoxious, anti-social adults. Operant theory suggests that the "rewards" were either not administered immediately after the desired behaviours or were employed in an unsystematic or inconsistent manner. Reinforcers do not, in-and-of-themselves, guarantee "good" behaviour or "bad" behaviour—or any type of behaviour at all. Rather, it is *when and how regularly* reinforcers occur with respect to ongoing behaviour that determines their effects and effectiveness. A second point regarding the reinforcement principle is that it is an excellent descriptive tool which may be invoked to provide precise explanations of behavioural phenomena, while avoiding what are known as "explanatory fictions"—vague and unobservable factors which supposedly govern behaviour.

Ask someone who smokes excessively why they do, and you may hear any number of vague explanations: "It's just a bad habit," they might tell you, or, "I guess I must lack will power." Neither explanation would suffice for the behavioural analyst. However, if this person had told you, "I smoke because I enjoy smoking," he would be providing you with a far more meaningful explanation, one that is compatible with reinforcement theory.

> Question: How does the principle of reinforcement explain excessive smoking?

> Answer: The smoking response is immediately reinforced by the intake of nicotine. In some cases other reinforcers may be at work as well, such as tactile stimulation, or peer approval.

> Question: But isn't there also another potential reinforcer operating here, one which should strengthen the smoker's desire to quit? Namely, the likelihood of a longer, healthier life, which is surely more powerful than these other reinforcers?

> Answer: There is. But this latter source of reinforcement loses out to the more *immediate* effects of the nicotine.

The problem is that habitual smokers are victims of immediate reinforcement. Typically, our operant behaviour is more easily influenced by small but immediate reinforcers, than by more powerful but distant and uncertain reinforcers. (See Figure 3.) The smoker who tries unsuccessfully to quit never experiences the beneficial changes that would result if he refrained for the necessary adjustment interval. More often than not, such persons (including, alas, myself) succumb to the immediately available cigarette and its briefly reinforcing effects. Similarly, the immediacy of reinforcement provided by snacking precludes the overeater experiencing the more remote benefits of being slimmer and feeling better. The reinforcing effects of food are immediate, while those of dieting are longer-term.

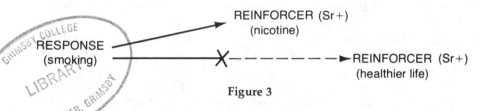

Figure 3

Notice that such explanations make no reference to explanatory fictions like "will-power" or "lack of control." Too often such descriptions direct attention away from observable variables contributing to behaviour. Using them to account for questionable habits or actions sheds little light on what the person can do to acquire these (presumably lacking) qualities, and may leave him feeling that there is no practical way his behaviour can be changed. It is not unlike telling a friend who is having trouble sleeping, "You have *insomnia*—all you need is a good night's sleep." As we shall see, a reinforcement analysis affords the individual, or therapist, an opportunity to identify and restructure the environmental stimuli maintaining undesirable habits or tendencies.

The Shaping of Operant Behaviour

The argument that our everyday behaviour patterns are being continually influenced by powerful reinforcers might be a hard pill to swallow. You may well be asking yourself how the reinforcement principle applies to complex behaviour. How does reinforcement cause a child to learn how to read, enable a teenager to master the skills necessary to operate an automobile, or a fledgling manager to acquire the capacities and skills of the middle or upper level manager?

Are we to believe that all we have to do is wait for these activities to occur, and to be followed by reinforcers for them to become well-established patterns of behaviour? The problem is that most of our complex operant behaviour does not occur "full-blown," but must be gradually acquired, with mastery of simpler aspects leading to mastery of more complex components. It is only *after* such complex patterns of operant behaviour have been established as a part of the individual's behavioural repertoire that simple reinforcement will serve to maintain them (e.g., offering a child praise for reading well, or a proportionately larger pay cheque for the upper-level manager).

The process of *shaping* allows for the eventual emergence of operants not yet in the person's existing behavioural storehouse. Shaping refers to *the reinforcement of successive approximations of the desired operant response*. Harvard University's B.F. Skinner, the foremost authority on behaviourism, compares the process of behaviour shaping to the way clay is moulded by the sculptor to assume its final form.

An acquaintance once recounted how he and a small group of graduate students attending a seminar in advanced Learning Theory used shaping to introduce a novel pattern of behaviour in their unsuspecting professor. The behaviour selected for shaping was chalk-throwing. This instructor would occasionally begin tossing his chalk lightly in one hand as he lectured to the group. The reinforcer for this activity was selective attention. The students, by mutual and secret agreement, would assume enraptured expressions and commence feverish note-taking *contingent on* the occurrence of chalk-tossing (i.e., *only after* this response occurred). At all other times, the students engaged in head-scratching, yawning, and other activities suggesting acute, if not terminal, boredom. In a very short time, the professor had acquired a fairly high rate of chalk-tossing, whereupon shaping was initiated. Reinforcement was, at this point, administered only for successively more vigourous chalk-tossing. In other words, to keep the attention of his class, the professor had to toss his chalk higher and higher. My friend informs me that by the end of the semester the poor unwitting prof had regularly taken to the habit of tossing his chalk so high as he lectured on the principles of conditioning, that on a few occasions he actually hit the ceiling! At this point, the students informed him of their shaping strategy. Their prank was accepted in good spirits and the professor even thanked the group— for not having selected a more embarrassing operant to be shaped, such as a stammer or facial tic!

In a more serious vein, operant shaping has been employed successfully with children having language and/or learning disabilities. It is basic to the educational technique known as *programmed instruction* in which teaching machines allow the learner to progress at his own pace, with mastery of simpler material leading to programs of increasing difficulty and comprehensiveness.

It is only recently that operant principles have been systematically applied in industrial and organizational settings. For example, a major air-freight forwarder, Emery Air Freight, uses freight containers extensively. Owing to constraints of time and space, Emery loses vast sums of money if their containers are not fully packed. Company executives were convinced that their containers were being used to 90 per cent capacity. However, a performance audit showed that the figure was actually 45 per cent efficiency. An operant shaping technique combining self-monitoring and positive reinforcement was applied. Self-monitoring took the form of providing the warehousemen with continuous feedback regarding their packing performance; positive reinforcement took the form of words of approval and solicitations of advice by the supervisor whenever packaging behaviour matched predesignated performance levels.

This deceptively simple set of procedures proved highly effective: container utilization jumped tremendously, and Emery benefited to the extend of $650,000 savings in the first year, and $2,000,000 in three years!

Schedules of Reinforcement

Given the information presented thus far, students may harbour a healthy skepticism regarding the importance of reinforcement in maintaining operant responding. A typical (not to mention insightful) question might be, "If reinforcers are so important, how does Learning Theory account for the fact that I'm bound to work hard and persistently as a student for up to three or four years until I receive my ultimate reinforcer—a university degree? Is this not a glaring exception to the principle of reinforcement which, as I understand it, says that each and every operant response must be followed by a reinforcer to maintain its strength and persist?"

It is true that certain of our *simple* operant acts, especially those which operate directly on the physical environment, meet with reinforcement each and every time they are emitted. Flicking a light switch, turning a door knob and pushing, or sequentially raising your legs to climb a flight of stairs, are operant acts that are generally *continuously reinforced;* normally the light goes on, the door opens, and we successfully ascend the stairs. However, in the contest of our myriad daily activities, continuous reinforcement appears to be the exception to the rule of reinforcement, rather than the rule itself. This becomes increasingly apparent as we turn to more complex operant behaviour and/or operants involving social, rather than physical consequences. Here, as it turns out, nature is very stingy with her reinforcers. Your own experience may confirm that it often requires *several* attempts at humour or wisdom in social settings, before such attempts are met with social reinforcement. Even the most competent and skilled among us commonly fail to achieve continuous reinforcement, despite our best efforts.

The phrase "schedule of reinforcement" refers to the pattern according to which reinforcement occurs. If we *did* meet with uproarious laughter each and every time we attempted humour (an unlikely prospect), such behaviour would be maintained on a *schedule of continuous reinforcement*. When reinforcement for operant responding occurs only intermittently (as is true for most operant behaviour), such behaviour is said to be governed by a *partial schedule of reinforcement*. The reason for such classifications is that there are reliable and, therefore, highly predictable differences in operant behaviour, depending on the schedule of reinforcement maintaining it. *The salient feature of partial reinforcement is that the behaviour it maintains is far more persistent (i.e., shows greater resistance to extinction) than behaviour maintained according to continuous reinforcement.* For example, an experiment was conducted in which college students were allowed to try their luck at one of two slot machines. Unknown to them, the experimenter had rigged one of these devices to pay off each and every time it was tried, according to a schedule of continuous reinforcement. The control group were given a set number of tries at a machine which paid off only part of the time (i.e., according to partial reinforcement) as do regular slot machines. The experimental group (continuous reinforcement) tried the rigged machine the same number of times. The final phase of the demonstration involved both groups of students returning at a later time to play machines that had now been rigged never to pay off. The result of this simple experiment was that the control group, which had experienced partial reinforcement of their gambling responses, continued playing the non-delivering apparatus long after the experimental group had stopped trying. The group experiencing partial reinforcement earlier had learned to respond in the absence of reinforcement, while the group who had operated the machines under continuous reinforcement hadn't. As a result, the partially reinforced gamblers were more persistent in the complete absence of reinforcement.

Similarly, suppose Sam has been accustomed to presenting his projects to two supervisors: supervisor X has *always* complimented

Sam on a job well done, while Supervisor Y has *sometimes* complimented him. Which supervisor would Sam continue bringing his
work to if, for some reason, both supervisors stopped offering reinforcement altogether? While the reasons might differ in this situation,
the *behaviour* emitted by Sam would parallel that of the partially reinforced group in the previous example; that is, he would be more
likely to continue bringing his work to Supervisor Y who had partially
reinforced Sam's behaviour.

Partial reinforcement may appear as two different forms of reinforcement schedules, each generating predictable patterns of
behaviour.

Interval Schedules of Reinforcement

An interval schedule of reinforcement is said to be in effect when
(partial) reinforcement occurs according to the *passage of some interval
of time*. The line-worker whose supervisor comes around to inspect
his performance at *regular intervals* is said to be operating under a
fixed-interval (FI) reinforcement schedule. The child practising her
piano lessons in the basement who hears her mother call down to
her, "That sounds just lovely dear!" *at regular intervals* is also being
reinforced according to a fixed-interval schedule. If the regular interval in this case is, say fifteen minutes, then this particular schedule is
abbreviated, Fl-15.

Behaviour that is maintained under Fl schedules will, typically,
assume a predictable pattern, with the number of operant responses
emitted increasing sharply as the reinforcement interval elapses. The
line-worker or child in these examples will soon learn to gauge the
length of the fixed interval, and will increase their rates of responding
toward the end of the interval in anticipation of reinforcement.
Although the overall amount of responding under such a reinforcement schedule will increase as the interval is reduced (so that the
worker or the child will work harder if reinforcements occur more
frequently), that actual *pattern* of responding will remain unchanged.
Teachers who administer tests to their students at regular intervals
may not be aware that their students' studying will not remain
constant from day to day; rather, the rate will vary, with the most
studious behaviour occurring just prior to any given test. Typically,
the least amount of studying will be done immediately following a
test. In fact, practically none should occur, because FI schedules yield
what is termed a *post-reinforcement pause*. This is a period following
the occurrence of (Fl) reinforcement during which no responding

occurs, after which the rate of emission gradually increases through the next interval.

But suppose in the preceding examples that the schedule of reinforcement is altered so that reinforcers now occur at *varying* as opposed to fixed intervals. Behaviour would now be maintained according to a *variable-interval schedule*(VI) in which the occurrence of reinforcement varies about an average length of time. The effect of VI schedules will be *a more constant rate of responding.* For instance, under a "VI-20" minute schedule of reinforcement, our line-worker's supervisor will come around for his inspection on the average of once every twenty minutes; but sometimes an hour might elapse before he reappears, sometimes only fifteen minutes. If he does not want to be caught loafing, this worker will begin to perform more uniformly under variable-interval reinforcement.

When reinforcers occur after such random temporal intervals, the operant behaviour produced becomes *remarkably uniform and persistent,* as the behaving organism is never certain when its next reinforcer will occur. Consider: Jane is anxiously awaiting the arrival of her dinner companion who said he would show up some time between seven and eight. She begins tidying the living room and goes over to the window, goes into the kitchen and a moment later returns to the window, goes back to tidying, only to be drawn like a magnet to the window once again. Constant, highly repetitive acts like "window-watching," checking the mailbox or a pot of water on the stove, may appear bizarre or unsettling to the observer. They shouldn't. Such seemingly compulsive acts are typical behavioural products of variable-interval reinforcement.

Ratio Schedules of Reinforcement

The distinguishing feature of the ratio schedules is that here reinforcement depends not upon the passage of time but on fixed or varying amounts of *behaviour.* Take the previous hypothetical example of Jane waiting for the arrival of her date. If she knew this individual to be highly punctual, and if he had indicated that he would be by at eight o'clock sharp, then Jane would have to have gone to the window only once to receive reinforcement. Similarly, under a fixed-interval reinforcement schedule, our assembly-line workers might not have had to actually *do* too much to leave his supervisor with the impression that he was a persistent and diligent worker; provided only that he was working whenever the supervisor made his appearance. With interval schedules, time determines the frequency of reinforcement.

But because ratio schedules make reinforcement dependent upon behaviour, they typically generate more activity than do the interval schedules (all other things being equal). *Fixed-ratio* (FR) schedules are said to be in effect when a reinforcer occurs after a fixed number of emitted responses. (The "ratio" refers to the quantity of non-reinforced-to-reinforced responses.) In factory "piece-work," the worker is paid a given amount for a predetermined and fixed number of units produced. If, for instance, fifty "pieces" of some commodity must be produced by the individual for every dollar earned, the reinforcement schedule in effect is termed "FR-50." By working at an accelerated pace, this individual will receive more than if his rate of work were less. Students, writers, and commissioned salespersons often work under FR schedules of reinforcement.

As is the case with fixed-interval schedules, behaviour maintained under FR schedules is *patterned* such that there is a surge in ongoing activity as the ratio requirement nears completion. (Consider how easily you are distracted when *beginning* a project as opposed to when you are near its completion!) Also, there will be a brief post-reinforcement pause or "letdown" immediately following reinforcement under such schedules. If the fixed-ratio in effect is extremely large, this pause may be quite lengthy. (What writer would want to immediately embark on a new project after having just completed a lengthy novel?)

When the occurrence of reinforcement varies about some average number of responses, a *variable-ratio* (VR) reinforcement schedule is operating. For example, if, on the average, Fred sells a life insurance policy to one out of every twenty potential clients he sees, his selling behaviour is being maintained on a "VR-20" schedule of reinforcement. VR schedules usually *yield the strongest (i.e., the most persistent) operant behaviour of any reinforcement schedule.* In behavioural labs, using animal subjects, VR schedules have sustained fantastically high rates of responding over considerable lengths of time. Most perseverant human activities are maintained on a variable-ratio basis: watching TV, attempting to make new acquaintances, playing golf, or going fishing represent activities that are reinforced *some of the time.* Just when that great round of golf, or especially satisfying outing or friendship, will occur, is never known. The result is that we plug away and continue to engage in these activities again and again, year-in, year-out, because the probability is always there (though never guaranteed) that such activities will provide reinforcement. All forms of gambling rely on the persistent quality of variable-ratio responding. The individual who places a bet on a given horse race, pass at roulette, or throw of the dice, is never certain whether that particular bet will pay off or not. And how could it be otherwise? Take a moment to imagine the house losses, not to mention the confusion, chaos and worse that would result if slot machines were programmed to pay off on a fixed rather than variable-ratio basis!

Under variable-ratio schedules, the probability of reinforcement for any given response is usually low and constant, resulting in conditioned responding which is uniform and extremely persistent. Thus, the chronic gambler becomes locked into a predictable pattern of behaviour. Such a person learns over time that if he just keeps at it long enough, reinforcement ("winning") will occur sooner or later. The problem is that the wins seldom match the compulsive gambler's accrued losses. The chronic gambler is an unfortunate victim of the variable-ratio reinforcement schedule.

Negative Reinforcement and the Aversive Control of Operant Behaviour

It may have occurred to you that something has been lacking in the discussion of how reinforcers come to establish, modify, and maintain operant responding via operant conditioning, shaping, and scheduling, respectively. Previous examples, plus your own experience, should have suggested that the positive consequences of our actions are not the only outcomes which affect behaviour.

Reinforcement, like most natural phenomena, is double-edged; it has its negative aspects as well. Our previous definition of reinforcement is sometimes labelled *positive reinforcement* to distinguish it from the principle of *negative reinforcement*. This involves the occurrence of a negative reinforcer (Sr −), which is defined as *any stimulus event, the termination (escape from) or avoidance of which, increases the probability of recurrence of an operant response.* In positive reinforcement, a behaviour is conditioned and gains strength because it is immediately followed by the *presentation* of a positive reinforcer (Sr +). In the case of negative reinforcement, operant responses are also strengthened (i.e., conditioned), but they serve to *remove or avoid* unpleasant or painful events (Sr −) which have, or might have occurred. (See Figure 2.)

Negative reinforcement results in two classes of operant behaviour: *escape* and *avoidance.* Escape conditioning is said to occur when an operant response consistently terminates an aversive stimulus. Take as an example the phobic reactions discussed earlier. These were identified as fear responses that are acquired through the process of classical conditioning. However, their continuing effect on the individual is often a result of negative reinforcement, as phobic reactions lead to escape and/or avoidance responses that are continually reinforced: as an adolescent, Little Albert would often encounter stimuli (perhaps small dogs or cats) which elicited fear. What would he be likely to do in such situations? He would attempt to *escape* from the situations, and in doing so, this operant would receive negative reinforcement by removing him from the fear-arousing stimulus. This would not only increase the probability of his removing himself from future encounters with such stimuli; it would also lead to his *avoiding* such encounters wherever possible. If he were invited to a dog show, his refusal to attend (an avoidance response) would be strengthened by effectively preventing a potential anxiety-producing situation. As was mentioned earlier, one of the reasons phobias persist is that the individual continues to *actively avoid* the fear-producing CS, preventing it from undergoing classical extinction.

Skinner makes the observation that many circumstances appear to involve positive reinforcement when, in fact, negative reinforcement is a major contributor. The person who is paid on a bi-monthly basis comes to work on a Monday not because he will be reinforced (i.e., paid) two weeks hence, but in order to avoid the aversive consequences of *not* coming into work. In other words, he continues to work, not for his pay (which in many cases has already been budgeted away), but to avoid sanctions from his superiors and possible unemployment. Similarly, many relationships endure not only because of the tenderness and affection they afford the persons involved, but also because remaining in a relationship serves to avoid the loneliness, uncertainty, and other aversive consequences of *not* remaining together. Almost all social institutions—governments, churches, schools, business organizations—employ methods of *aversive control* to influence the behaviour of citizens, congregations, students, and employees, respectively. Acceptable behaviour results from people trying to avoid aversive consequences such as imprisonment, excommunication, failure, unemployment and the like. Thus, many human activities are the result of avoidance-learning in conjunction with positive reinforcement.

Punishment is an instance of aversive conditioning that deserves attention, if for no other reason than it is probably the most widely abused form of aversive control of behaviour. Punishment entails *any stimulus event which immediately follows an operant response and decreases its probability of recurrence.*

There is a little-known anecdote about a psychologist/farmer who was having dog problems. Almost every day, his loyal pet would appear at the back porch proudly bearing a newly killed prize—one of the neighbour's chickens. After repeated scoldings, and having noticed his disgruntled neighbour polishing his shotgun, the psychologist decided it was time to employ more drastic measures. The next time his dog appeared with a stolen chicken, he proceeded to give it a severe beating in the hope that this more powerful aversive stimulus would remove the unacceptable behaviour once and for all. Afterward, the psychologist believed that the method had proven successful, as his dog never again returned home with stolen chickens. It was only later that he learned his dog had not stopped poaching the neighbour's chickens! What had gone wrong? Had the punishment been ineffective in altering this animal's behaviour pattern? Definitely not, for the dog *had* stopped bringing dead chickens around. . . . The point is that when an aversive stimulus is administered (i.e., when punishment occurs), the behaviour which is suppressed is that which occurs *immediately prior* to the punishing event. In this principle lies the solution to our psychologist's dilemma: when the dog was severely punished, it learned a definite lesson; it did not learn to stop poaching chickens, but rather to stop bringing them back to its unappreciative master!

Punishment is highly effective in *suppressing* ongoing behaviour. It does not necessarily eliminate responding entirely, but drastically reduces the probability of the behaviour recurring, especially in the situation where the punishment has occurred. But *it is usually only the behaviour immediately preceding the occurrence of punishment* which is suppressed. When a concerned parent spanks a child for carelessly running onto the street, the spanking is usually administered immediately after the child is called back and returns from the road to the waiting parent. Later, when the child repeats this undesirable activity and is called back by the angered parent, he or she will, as likely as not, make a bee-line *away from the parent*. The child has been taught not to avoid running blindly into the road, but to avoid *returning* from the street to the waiting parent. Returning is the behaviour which immediately precedes punishment and which is suppressed! Imagine how confusing it must be for a child when he or she misbehaves and is told, "Just wait till your father gets home!" Later that day, the child, who has long since forgotten the earlier admonition and is playing quietly, receives a spanking or some other delayed punishment.

Apart from the fact that the principle of immediacy of punishment is seldom invoked or understood by persons who feel that the use of punishment is absolutely necessary, its use has another undesirable aspect. In addition to behavioural suppression, punishment often results in a classically conditioned aversion to the punisher, and to the situation where punishment has repeatedly occurred. The child who experiences excessive and, especially, inconsistent punishment at home, will learn to fear its parents and feel anxious in the general home environment—a highly undesirable state of affairs. For this reason, many psychologists strongly advise against the use of punishment, suggesting that simple non-reinforcement (for example, *ignoring* misbehaviour rather than reacting with a scolding, or the like, which might act as a disguised reinforcer for attention-seeking) is an effective method for eliminating troublesome behaviour. This is an especially effective method when applied consistently, and in conjunction with positive reinforcers like attention and approval for more desirable behaviour. It is unfortunate that so many parents seem to feel that where children are concerned "no news is good news." The result is that many of a child's cooperative and desirable behaviour patterns never meet with reinforcement from the parent.

OPERANT CONDITIONING PHENOMENA

Stimulus Generalization

Just as classically conditioned responses may generalize to stimuli that are physically similar to the original CS, so an operant response which has been acquired in a given situation will also tend to be emitted in environments that are similar, in some respect, to the original learning environment. The young child whose boisterous and over-enthusiastic table manners are tolerated at home will tend to show this same pattern of behaviour in any mealtime situation, including formal dining places. Likewise, a person who has acquired the habit of singing in the morning shower will likely find that this pastime readily generalizes to whatever shower he finds himself in. The phenomenon referred to as *positive transfer*—where skills demonstrated in a certain activity lead to enhanced performance of other activities—may be regarded as a form of stimulus generalization. A competent squash player, for instance, will find it easier to learn tennis than someone who has never played squash. This is because there are enough similar features in tennis for the squash player's skills to generalize to the novel situation. But generalization can and does result in impairment in acquiring new skills. This *negative transfer* of learning occurs when generalized responses are inappropriate to the new learning situation and work to the learner's disadvantage. Trying to adjust to the practices and expectations of a different culture, where one's previous cultural conditioning suddenly is seen as inappropriate and out-of-place exemplifies this phenomenon.

The Discriminative Stimulus, Discrimination Learning and Stimulus Control

No two learning situations are identical. There will almost always be something distinctive about the stimuli that are present when something is learned. These distinctive stimuli come to be associated with the learning itself, so the organism shows a tendency to exhibit these learned responses whenever such distinctive stimuli are recognized. These situation-specific stimuli are called *discriminative stimuli*— defined as *any situations or stimuli which set the occasion for operant responding*.

In the above examples, the shower and the dining room would be discriminative stimuli, in the presence of which established operant responses (namely, singing and boisterous activity) are likely to occur. A rat in an operant-conditioning apparatus, or Skinner Box[4] whose lever-pressing has led to reinforcement only when a stimulus light, positioned above the lever is on—will learn to attend to this feature of the environment. The rat will show a considerable amount of operant responding when the light is on, but the observed rate of lever-pressing will drop to almost nil as soon as the stimulus light is switched off. The specific and immediate effects of green, amber and red traffic lights on our driving provides an instance in which our own behaviour is similarly influenced by discriminative stimuli.

When organisms have learned to differentiate among various features of their stimulus surroundings, and to respond accordingly, *discrimination learning* is said to have occurred. The process of discrimination is the exact opposite of stimulus generalization. For instance, the child who has begun responding in a generalized manner by saying "da-da" to any and all adult males will gradually begin to learn that reinforcement, in the form of approval, will result from emitting this verbal response in the presence of only one stimulus, namely, the child's father. Because reinforcement will seldom result from saying "da-da" to any other person, such attempted responding will soon be extinguished, forcing the child to attend carefully to the features that distinguish the father from other similar stimuli. A discrimination will have resulted when the reliably reinforced

---

[4] Much of the empirical research from which operant principles derive has been conducted in the totally controlled environment of the *operant conditioning apparatus* or *Skinner Box*. (Skinner, who developed this apparatus, prefers the former description.) This apparatus is equipped with a stimulus light or tone, food, or an electric shock delivery system. Responses are recorded automatically to minimize human interference and bias. The salient feature of this device is a protruding lever or wall-mounted panel which the animal subject operates by pressing or pecking (for rats and pigeons, respectively).

response is controlled by the appearance of the father, and no one else.

In experiments, remarkably fine perceptual discriminations have been achieved by animal subjects, including pigeons (which possess highly sensitive vision). An impressive demonstration of this bird's discriminatory ability (not to mention the skill of the experimenters) involved the training of pigeons to act as "quality-control inspectors" on an actual pharmaceutical assembly line. Their previous training had involved continuous food reinforcement (which was gradually shifted to a VR schedule) for pecking at a disc whenever a defective capsule appeared on a belt which moved across the bird's visual field. Errors met with delay of reinforcement. After extensive training, these pigeons could spot defective products to an accuracy figure of 99 per cent—well above the level expected from human inspectors! Moreover, the VR schedule eventually employed could maintain this level of performance, *non-stop,* for up to nine hours at a time!

Discriminative stimuli exert control over the occurrence of our operant behaviour by cueing us when reinforcement for responding is likely to be available. Although this type of control is not always as reliable as the control which classically conditioned stimuli exert over our respondent behaviour, it has found its way into the applied area of Behaviour Therapy. The technique is illustrated in the following case study*:

> "This case involved a couple who did a great deal of bickering and arguing in their bedroom. Such behaviour, of course, is often at odds with "lovemaking," and in this case it impeded the progress of these more tender emotions. The problem was to rearrange the bedroom stimuli so that new stimuli might set the occasion for amorous activity and decrease the probability of the occurrence of other incompatible activities. With this in view, the couple was instructed to purchase a yellow light and place it in the bedroom. Then, whenever each of the parties evidenced obvious sexual interest, they were to turn the yellow light on and give full vent to their desires. At all other times the yellow light was to remain off. In other words . . . sexual reinforcement was made contingent upon the occurrence of behaviour only in the presence of the yellow light." (Wenrich, 1970; pp. 66)

Now it is doubtful that, having adhered to these instructions, this couple would merely have to turn on their yellow light to solve their marital disputes. Nor does it mean they would be likely to

---

* From *A Primer of Behavior Modification,* by W. W. Wenrich. Copyright © 1970 by Wadsworth, Inc. Reprinted by permission of the publisher, Brooks/Cole Publishing Company, Monterey, California 93940.

engage in an indecent scene upon entering the "Amber Room" for dinner! Discriminative stimuli (in this case, a yellow light) do not guarantee operant responding, they merely increase the probability of its occurrence, with some stimuli being more reliable than others.

Operant Extinction and Spontaneous Recovery

The reader should already be familiar with the concepts of extinction and spontaneous recovery from the earlier discussion of how classically conditioned responses are eliminated. These phenomena remain essentially the same whether we are dealing with classical or with operant responding. A conditioned operant response will gradually diminish in strength and disappear entirely, though not necessarily permanently, from the individual's repertoire *when it is emitted repeatedly in the absence of reinforcement.* In discussing the persistent effects of partial reinforcement schedules, it was observed that such schedules result in operant activities (e.g., gambling) which are quite difficult to extinguish. You should note that in such schedules, reinforcers still occur, if only sporadically. For extinction to effectively eliminate this sort of persistent operant responding, reinforcement must never occur.

It is not uncommon for parents to attempt the extinction of problem behaviour, such as bedtime crying episodes. "This time we'll just have to let Myrtle cry herself to sleep," the frustrated parents decide. It is just as common to hear these parents explain later on that this technique is useless and fails to eliminate bed-time tantrums. But what actually happens in such cases is that parents let the child cry until *they* can no longer bear it! "Well, I guess Myrtle has had enough," they decide, and proceed to minister to her wants. What has happened here is that the child has effectively modified or conditioned her parents' behaviour by creating an aversive situation from which the parents finally escape. In addition, the parents have actually strengthened the very behaviour they set out to eliminate by increasing the ratio schedule of reinforcement maintaining their child's tantrums. They have inadvertently taught Myrtle that if she just keeps on crying she will, sooner or later, be reinforced by her parents' attention. Documented research cases where children were ill and required special care at bedtime until their recovery have verified that extinction will reliably occur in such situations if reinforcement is withheld entirely.

Sometimes the everyday application of operant principles fails, not because the principles themselves are faulty, but because of difficulties encountered in their application.

BIOLOGICAL LIMITATIONS OF LEARNING

If it is true that the exception proves the rule, then having completed our examination of the basic laws of classical and operant learning, certain general exceptions to these rules of behaviour warrant consideration. Quite recently there has been a merging between behaviourist theory and an area of zoology devoted to the naturalistic study of animal behaviour, termed, *Ethology* (or Behavioural Biology). Prior to this recent trend, the behavioural biologist and the learning psychologist pursued their separate scientific paths, each relying exclusively on the orientations, assumptions and terminology of their respective disciplines.

Briefly, the ethologist is concerned with behaviour that is *species-specific* (or "instinctive"—although scientists tend to reject this description). Behaviour patterns that are identical in appearance are commonly shared by all members of a given species, and are triggered by some identifiable aspect of the stimulus environment. The feature of such behaviour which distinguishes it from classical and operant behaviour is that species-specific behaviour appears to be *unlearned* in the traditional sense. The tendency of recently hatched aquatic birds to follow a moving object ("imprinting"), the migratory tendencies of birds, and the ritualistic fighting and mating patterns of some mammals exemplify patterns of behaviour which emerge full-blown, and with little or no prior experience on the part of the creatures which display them. For example, whether raised in experimental laboratories or in the wild, rats exhibit mating and defensive behaviour patterns that are virtually indistinguishable.

Species-specific behaviour is controlled not by the environment, but by the organism's genetic and biological characteristics. The ethologist might question the importance of animal research conducted in artifical learning situations such as those employed by Pavlov or Skinner, asking, "What does salivating to the sound of a tone, or pressing a lever to obtain food in an operant apparatus have to do with behaviour as it occurs in real-life settings? Such acts are arbitrarily selected by the experimenter and cast little light on the factors operating in freely occurring, naturalistic contexts." To this, the behaviourist might respond, "But that is just the point! Behaviour as it is studied in the laboratory is no less 'real' than behaviour which occurs in less controlled environments. The fact that we *can arbitrarily* select any bit of behaviour, can maintain or modify it across any-and-all learning situations, suggests that the principles of learning are extremely reliable."

This implicit faith in the general applicability of learning principles has been referred to as the *equipotentiality premise*. Some behaviourists wholeheartedly endorse it, while others do not, recognizing that many animal species (especially those lower on the phylogenetic scale) bring with them into new learning situations certain genetic dispositions which will determine the ease or difficulty with which conditioned responses will be acquired. When organisms exhibit genetic or biological tendencies which interfere with conditioned associations, behaviour is said to be *contraprepared*. In such instances, learning is very difficult to establish, as the organism tends to respond according to its predetermined species-specific behaviour patterns. For example, it would be extremely difficult, if not altogether impossible, to teach a dog to scratch itself or to yawn to obtain food reinforcement. The animal is predisposed by its nature to associate these responses with internal stimuli—in this case, "itchiness" or "fatigue," respectively, and the association of such responses with external reinforcement (e.g., food) will be contrary to what the dog is prepared to do.

It is difficult to assess the extent to which human behaviour provides such exceptions to the laws of learning. Nevertheless, one could speculate as to when species-specific inclinations would be likely to interfere with human learning: angry threats or physical punishment are successful in eliminating unacceptable behaviour in most instances. But would this method prove effective in suppressing the tendencies of the hyperactive child? Probably not. Punishment, or threat of punishment, produces general autonomic *arousal* which is at odds with relaxation. Similarly, the employment of physical punishment would meet with little success were it intended to stop a child from crying, or from feeling frightened—although, in principle, it should. Species-specific reactions commonly occur in situations that are extremely stressful, eliciting tendencies toward flight or panic. Under such conditions, calm and decisive behaviour, which might be the most appropriate or rational way of coping with the situation, based on previous learning, is not always the behaviour produced in critical circumstances.

As was mentioned at the outset of the chapter, humans undoubtedly bring with them certain genetic and biological dispositions into the world, which may influence their ongoing adjustments to it. However, such factors do not affect human behaviour to the extent that they do the behaviour of lower animal species. Human behaviour is flexible, adaptable, and highly complex. While many animal species are quite literally off-and-running shortly after birth, the human baby remains helpless and dependent after its entry into the world longer than any other species. Perhaps this serves to ensure that the human organism will acquire its high degree of flexibility and adaptability to its environment. *Learning* to interact with the complex demands of the environment requires considerable time, and *homo sapiens* is biologically endowed with more time to devote to this task than is any other species.

SUMMARY

Behaviouristic theory limits itself to the assumption that behaviour is a product of acquired reactions and acts which have immediate effects on the stimulus environment. It tends to deemphasize or overlook entirely the realm of consciousness and internal subjective experiences. As a result, the approach has been criticized as being overly mechanistic, depicting the human organism as being no more than a wind-up automaton, a bundle of conditioned reflexes and habits—totally at the mercy of its particular history of reinforcement, or prevailing stimulus conditions.

Opponents of the model point out that behaviourism leaves no room for such things as free will or self-determination and must, therefore, post a threat to our personal values and even our sense of dignity. It is unfortunate that such stereotyped assessments exist for, as with any stereotype, they are incomplete and frequently inaccurate. The fact is that, depending on how you perceive it, the behaviourist doctrine may be seen as *enhancing* personal freedom rather than detracting from it. As Skinner notes in *Beyond Freedom and Dignity*, understanding the environmental determinants of behaviour places the individual in a unique position: it affords him or her the opportunity of changing various aspects of their behaviour by modifying elements of their environment which influence it. This in itself may be seen as a form of personal freedom.

An undeniable attribute of this approach is that it lends itself extremely well to the rigorous demands of experimental science, and can be viewed as one of the hard-core approaches to psychology. The behaviourist model, despite its limitations, has flourished since its inception seventy-odd years ago, and represents a dominant orientation in North American psychology.

Further Readings

B. F. Skinner, the foremost proponent of behaviourism, has written several books. In *Beyond Freedom and Dignity* he states the philosophy of behaviourism, and in *Walden Two*, a utopian novel, he portrays the perfect society, based of course, on behaviourist principles.

Aldous Huxley's *Island* is one of his more popular utopian novels depicting a society structured on behavioural principles.

5
THE COGNITIVE APPROACH
William E. Glassman

Editor's Preface

The behaviourists concentrate on events and behaviours, and doggedly refuse to speculate about intervening processes that might be taking place within the organisms they observe. This hard-nosed approach has not met with universal acclaim from psychologists. In the 1920s a reaction against radical behaviourism developed that forms the basis of what has now become the cognitive approach. Cognitive theorists not only refused to accept that internal processes intervening between the environmental stimulus and the response of the organism were irrelevant, but they made these "mediational processes" the major focus of their studies. By so doing, they have been able to fill in many of the gaps left by the behaviourists. They also have been able to move into new areas, such as memory and the human use of symbols, and cast light upon emotional experiences.

Unlike behaviourism, the cognitive approach has not led to a single body of theory; the areas in which the cognitive approach is applied are simply too widespread. What unites cognitive theorists is not a single, integrated body of theory, but a common approach, which stresses the importance and role of mediational processes. Implicit in much of the work of the cognitive theorists is a view of man as a basically rational, reasoning being. This view, as you will see when you read Chapter 6, is in sharp contrast to the outlook of the psychoanalysts.

THE COGNITIVE APPROACH

At the turn of the century a young physicist was working as a clerk in the Swiss patent office. In his spare time he continued his studies in theoretical physics. Like many other physicists of the day, he was puzzled by discoveries which seemed to challenge many long-held notions about matter and energy. For one thing, the speed of light appeared to be constant throughout the universe, but nobody knew how to explain it. Then, the young patent clerk tried reversing the problem, saying one could *assume* the speed of light was constant, not try to explain it. Having decided this, many aspects of the problem fell into place. His older colleagues were outraged, and said the proposal was absurd, because it was inconsistent with their own training. In the end, he was proven correct and his solution ushered in a new era for mankind. The theory is now called the special theory of relativity, and the young patent clerk was Albert Einstein.

Today, all college physics students, and many others, have a basic grasp of Einstein's insights, expressed as $E = mc^2$. It is one of the marvels of such great ideas that, once formulated, they can be readily understood by many. Yet the first formulation of such solutions is very elusive; Einstein's colleagues had difficulty seeing the solution. What leads to such creative insights? Where do new solutions to old problems come from?

To the behaviourists, all actions can be described in terms of responses to environmental cues. Motor responses, or "behaviour," are described by conditioned reflexes, shaping, and other simple processes. By its nature, this approach tends to deny that anything happening within the person is significant, and consequently that any original or creative response is possible. Viewed in this way, Einstein's insights become virtually impossible to understand.

Much of what we learn is represented not by actions, but by thinking processes involving memory, problem solving, and language. The study of these thinking processes is often called *cognitive psychology*. To the cognitive psychologist, events within the person are at least as important as environmental stimuli for understanding behaviour. These events within the person are referred to as mediational processes or *mediators*, because they come between external stimulus and the response. Memory, problem solving and language are all based on mediators. Cognitive psychologists believe one cannot explain behaviours without reference to something more than stimulus-response connections.

The development of the cognitive approach is closely related to the behavioural approach, since in part it developed as a reaction against the "radical empiricism" (placing great emphasis on external events, or experience) of the behaviourists. By 1930 the behaviourists felt they were gaining ground against the "armchair psychology" of the earlier introspectionists, but the seeds of a new alternative to behaviourism had already been sown. In 1925, a book by a young German researcher named Wolfgang Kohler appeared, called *The Mentality of Apes*. In this book he provided observations that suggested animals could be inventive, or "insightful," and he rejected behaviourism in favour of what is called Gestalt psychology. In 1932, E. C. Tolman's *Purposive Behaviour in Animals and Man* was published. His use of the term "cognitive maps" foreshadowed a whole approach within psychology.

While early behaviourists saw learning as basically a matter of trial-and-error, Kohler argued that we tend to organize our experiences in particular ways, not randomly.[1] He explained "insight" into problems as being a change in the way one organizes a problem. The impact of Kohler's work was to create a shift away from seeing behaviour as merely trial-and-error, towards a concern with the internal organizing processes which mediate behaviour.

Tolman regarded himself as a behaviourist, in that his data were strictly based on observations of stimuli and responses. But the problems he examined were very embarrassing to the traditional behaviourists of his day. For instance, behaviourists argued that unless there was a change in behaviour (performance of a new response), no learning had taken place. Tolman demonstrated that animals may learn the pattern of a maze, forming a "cognitive map," but not perform correctly until a reward is given. This "latent learning" suggested that learning is distinct from performance of a behaviour. In another example, it was observed that animals running mazes showed systematic tendencies, such as always turning left; these suggested the animals had "hypotheses" about the solution to the maze. Thus, Tolman's theory ultimately emphasized mediational processes.

Both Kohler and Tolman were influential in laying the foundations of the cognitive approach. Yet despite their early role, neither Kohler nor Tolman have many direct followers today. This does not mean that the cognitive approach is not important (if anything, the past ten or fifteen years have seen a spreading influence). Rather, it means its impact is diffused, and sometimes not directly recognized. To a greater extent than other approaches in psychology, the impor-

---

[1] Kohler's work has already been referred to in Chapter 1 of this book. The reader may wish to go back to review some of the concepts and examples given there.

tant aspects of the cognitive approach have been transformed or used piecemeal by researchers of various outlooks. One might almost say, "Kohler is alive and well, but living under an assumed name."

Since no single theorist has dominated the cognitive approach the way Skinner and Freud dominated operant conditioning and psychoanalysis, respectively, there has been greater exchange with other approaches, both within and outside psychology. Thus, today one talks about a cognitive theory of emotion, or even cognitive behaviour modification. At the same time, cognitive psychologists have borrowed from other fields, including computer technology and biology.

One reason for this broad interchange is the tendency of psychologists to seek new models. Many psychologists use metaphors and analogies to describe problems in new ways. In the seventeenth century, Descartes compared body movements to the operation of hydraulically controlled statues in the Tuileries Gardens of Paris. At the turn of this century, psychologists compared the brain (in stimulus-response terms) to a telephone switchboard. Today, computers play a large role in our lives, and psychologists have borrowed the language of computer technology, referred to as "information-processing."

Consciously or not, those who use information-processing descriptions fall within the tradition of Kohler and Tolman. "Information-processing" refers to the intervening events (mediators) which come between input (stimulus) and output (response) of the system (person). One cannot predict the output from the input without knowing something about what is going on within the computer. In this sense, the computer program is like the organizing principles and expectancies Kohler and Tolman discuss. There is a further parallel in that the computer model emphasizes the processing of information. By *processing*, we mean the output represents a qualitative change in the input, such as combination, analysis or comparison of pieces of input data. This active element is also seen in Kohler's emphasis on insight as creative, and Tolman's emphasis on cognitive maps as going beyond mere repetition of previous responses. Information-processing models fit very comfortably within the cognitive approach.

In this chapter, we will be looking at several aspects of behaviour from the cognitive viewpoint. The most general concern is simply understanding how we behave. In concrete terms, cognitive researchers are interested in how we remember, why we forget, what leads to effective solutions to problems, and related questions. This emphasis on thinking processes (memory, problem solving, language) is natural, given that the word "cognitive" refers to thinking. At the same time, the scope of the cognitive approach has broadened in recent years, and even includes such "irrational" aspects of behaviour as what causes joy or anger. Whatever the topic, the key elements of the cognitive approach remain the same:

(1) The processes within the person are considered to be as significant as the external stimuli; (2) These mediating processes operate in an organized and systematic way, not by trial-and-error.

LEARNING AND MEMORY

Learning As Information-Gathering

When we are born, we go from a dark, quiet, protected environment into a world which is bright, noisy, and often threatening. Coping with this world requires the infant to learn many things, from the simple danger of a hot stove to the complexities of language.

The learning of infants is motivated by their curiosity, but as we get older, we seem to get less curious. It may be that this change is only apparent, not real. (Have you ever stifled the impulse to stare at a wildly dressed stranger on the street? Why?) On the other hand, it may be that we outgrow curiosity as we get older. Curiosity serves as a motivation to aid our early learning when we must gather the information needed for survival. As we grow older, there is less need to know more, or be curious.

However it may change, curiosity emphasizes an important aspect of cognitive learning: learning may be considered as information-gathering. We gather, and store for later use, everything from names of new business contacts to the location of the washroom in our favourite restaurant. (No one ever said that what we store has to be "significant.") In the process, we all accumulate vast amounts of seemingly useless information. For instance, who was the Lone Ranger's faithful Indian companion? What does A-OK refer to? What did you have for breakfast today?

At first glance, the gathering and storage of information may seem less efficient as a learning system than the connection of stimuli and responses. But learning through information-gathering has one great advantage: flexibility. Tolman's work on cognitive maps shows this clearly. If, for example, your route to work is represented by a map of the city, not a fixed series of responses, then you can detour to the cleaner's, take an alternate route when traffic is bad, and so on. Information which was previously unused thus becomes significant (for example, that Barton St. is one-way affects the route you take in a traffic jam). Tolman would call this "latent learning."

For the cognitive psychologist, *learning* represents the gathering of information. The emphasis is on the mediating processes that lead from stimulus to response. Consider again the example of the traffic jam: the stimuli include your present location, the time of day, the traffic situation, and awareness of your goal. Making a detour involves several types of mediators: your knowledge of the street layout (a cognitive map), information from past experiences about where traffic is likely to be lighter, and motivational preferences (e.g., do you prefer a short route through slow-moving traffic, or a longer route by an expressway?). From all of this, you choose a detour route (your response). This raises several questions: how did you develop a cognitive map of the city? How do you recall past experiences about traffic patterns, especially if it didn't seem important earlier? And how did you decide the best route, given all of this? Let us consider first the question of how we remember things.

Memory As the Retention of Learning

Behaviour often depends on remembering information at the right time. *Memory* can be defined as retention and use of prior learning. In this sense, memory is a mediator of our behaviour because past experience affects what we do now. However, there are several ways in which this information may be used.

Usually, we simply remember the information as we need it. This is called *recall*, the active retrieval of information. Answering any of the "trivia" questions in the previous section would involve recall. Sometimes, however, we can't recall something, but are able to recognize it as correct if it is presented. For instance, does A-OK refer to Roy Rogers' ranch, beatnik slang, or astronaut's jargon? This process of correctly identifying presented information is called *recognition*.

Multiple-choice tests of memory are based on testing recognition, not recall. (What sort of examination would test recall?) There are still other circumstances in which we may be unable to recognize something, yet on reviewing it, it quickly becomes familiar. For example, a person skating for the first time in ten years adapts more quickly than a first-time skater. This type of improvement by reviewing is referred to as *relearning*.

To review these terms, consider the example of a cognitive map of your city. Identify what type of memory is involved in each of these cases: (1) Naming the street the city hall is on. (2) Remembering the name in (1) when someone suggests several possibilities.

(3) Quickly becoming familiar again with the roads in an area, when you've been away for a while.[2]

Remembering, then, can take many forms. Although it is easy to say memory is storage of information, those words do not tell us very much. To understand how memory functions, we must look more closely at the capabilities of our memories. First, try to answer the following questions: Where was the house you grew up in? Was your first teacher a man or a woman? Can you recall his or her name? These questions may sound like further trivia examples, but with a difference. Virtually everyone could answer the first two. Yet for most readers, those events occurred at least twenty years ago. Such recall is not unusual; many people have recalled personal experiences happening sixty or eighty years before. So, we might say memory is permanent (or at least potentially permanent, since we do forget some things, it seems).

Before you ask why we forget, since we are so good at remembering, let's take another example. Have you ever looked up a phone number, found it busy on dialing, and then had to look it up again to dial a minute later? Or have you ever been introduced to someone and then not been able to remember their name at the end of the conversation? Often we forget information almost immediately after we learn it. Yet, as we noted earlier, people also can remember things for their whole life. The problem is to understand these extreme variations in our remembering.

To understand these variations, one has to make a distinction between long-term memory and short-term memory. *Long-term memory*, or LTM, refers to retention over relatively long intervals, of hours, days, weeks or longer. *Short-term memory*, or STM, refers to retention over brief intervals—usually seconds, but possibly up to a few minutes. The assumption is that the two types of retention involve different processes. Several types of evidence support this assumption.

One type of evidence has already been noted: *duration*. LTM is potentially permanent. STM, on the other hand, appears to be very limited in duration; information stored in this system will normally be lost after several seconds unless it is transferred to LTM (how this might happen will be discussed later) or rehearsed. *Rehearsal* consists of repeating information over and over, usually silently. (Have you ever caught yourself rehearsing a phone number as you dial?)

It may help to understand how STM works if we draw an analogy to a leaky bucket. Normally water poured into the bucket will

---

[2] Answers to quiz above: (1) Recall (2) Recognition (3) Relearning

gradually dribble away. This is like the loss over time from STM. If you pour the contents into a good container, it will be retained (like LTM). If you use a cup below the leak to catch the drips, and periodically pour the cup back into the leaky bucket, this would be like rehearsal. It is worth noting that this is an imperfect process, because the bucket will still be leaking while you are moving the cup. Rehearsal is also imperfect and can lead to gradual loss of information.

The bucket analogy brings up another distinction between STM and LTM, that of capacity. STM is very limited in the amount of information it can retain. In order to see this, try the following test: in Figure 1 you will find a string of letters. Read through them once, then turn the page and immediately try to recall them in correct order. Then, check your accuracy. Only those letters which are correct, and in the correct location, should be scored as correct. If you remembered about seven letters, you are average. Nine or more would be very unusual. Now, how long did you have to retain the letters before writing them down? Perhaps three seconds? Yet, on the average, people forget about one-third of the letters (assuming ten to begin with). Actually, increasing the number of letters present would only lower your percentage, for the number seven, not 67 per cent, appears to be the best description in this case. The capacity of STM is often characterized as 7 ± 2. That is, STM appears to be limited to between five and nine independent items, such as random letters or random numbers. (Phone numbers, because they have familiar three-digit exchanges, are not really seven independent numbers.) Similarly, letters that spell a word are neither independent nor random, and are therefore easier to remember. Attempts to remember longer sequences of items usually result in greater forgetting of the earlier items. In terms of our bucket analogy, trying to remember a longer sequence of items is like trying to overfill the bucket—the surplus spills over the rim.

Figure 1
A Test of Short-Term Memory
To test your STM capacity, read through the list of letters below. Read the list slowly, but only once. Immediately after reading the last letter, try to write down the entire sequence in correct order. In scoring, give yourself credit only for letters in the correct order, not counting reversals, omissions, or other errors. Typical performance would be about seven correct.

L   R   X   D   V   C   M   Q   B   N

LTM, on the other hand, appears to be practically unlimited in capacity. At least no documented case of someone "running out of memory space" has ever occurred. (There *is* a story of an Oxford zoology professor, an expert on fish, who tried to remember his students' names, but found that each time he learned another student's name, he forgot the name of a species of fish. Since he preferred fish to students, he gave up trying to remember students' names!) You may have read at some point an estimate of man's brain capacity, and statements such as, "Einstein only used 40 per cent of his brain capacity." While provocative, such statements must be taken lightly, since at best they are crude estimates. The problem is that no one really knows how information is stored, so any estimate is purely guesswork.

The characteristic differences between STM and LTM have led to several theories of memory. Most share similar basic features, and owe a debt to computer theory (see Figure 2). In this view of memory as a computer system, STM is like the input buffer which can handle only limited information at one time. If the buffer is overloaded, information is lost. Once it has processed the information, the buffer has no record of it. Either case would be analogous to STM forgetting. Once processed through this input buffer or STM, the information is stored in the memory core or LTM. Information in this part of the system will remain permanently, unless there is damage to the system, or (in the case of the computer) a command to erase the information. As you may know, in the computer's memory core, information is "coded" and can only be retrieved by the proper commands. So, too, storage in human memory involves codes.

The nature of coding represents a third difference between STM and LTM. As already noted, material in STM must be actively repeated or rehearsed to be retained for very long. Usually we are subjectively aware of this as a form of repeating things to ourselves. This observation has led to the view that coding in STM is *acoustic,* or based on sounds. Even when rehearsal is silent, it is like speaking: speech muscles in the larynx are active, and errors made are typically related to the sound of the items, or what are called "acoustic confusions." An analogy to this process is the old game of passing a sentence around a group, whereby "Diane, be quiet" may become "I am on a diet"!

The coding, or way that information is represented, in LTM appears more flexible than in STM. A basic feature of all LTM coding, however, seems to be that the code must somehow "make sense" to the person. Whereas STM might respond to rhymes, the *meaning* of words or experiences is significant in LTM. There are two basic ways in which meaning is considered significant for storage.

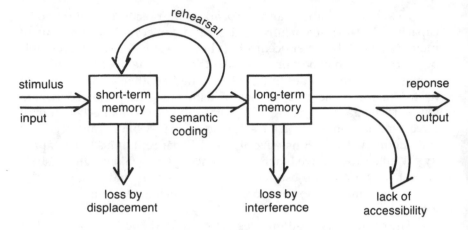

Figure 2
A Schematic Model of Memory
In computer terms, STM is the input buffer, having limited capacity, and
LTM is the information storage system. As noted in the text, there is
disagreement as to whether information in LTM can ever be truly lost (as
by interference), or whether forgetting is simply failure to recall (lack of
accessibility).

The traditional view of LTM storage is based on association. Just
as learning can be seen as forming ties between a stimulus and a
response, so memory is seen as forming ties between prior knowledge and new experiences. These ties are called *associations*. Often we
base such associations on features that have meaning. For instance, to
remember the name of someone you meet, you may associate it with
some feature of their appearance (*B*ob has a *b*eard, *S*usan is *s*hort).

Sigmund Freud recognized the significance of associations as a
tool in psychoanalysis: by asking the person to "free associate," that
is, to simply say whatever words floated into their mind, he looked
for patterns that revealed their inner conflicts. For example, a teaching colleague separated from his wife, named Barbara. A few weeks
later he met a former student on the street. He remembered having
taught this girl, her class, even her grades, but not her name. When
he asked her, it was, of course, Barbara! Freud would call this repression. The association of names reminded my colleague of an unpleasant event.

However, one need not turn to psychoanalysis to recognize that
associations are often seemingly remote, yet always based on some
internal consistency. Conversations at a party wander over many

topics, yet if you trace back carefully, you can always find the links between them. As another example, try the following: write down a list of ten words, each of which has *no* connections (in your awareness) to any of the other words. (Most people find it impossible, or nearly so!) Hence, one basis of retention, or code, in LTM may be the formation of associations.

Although it is easy to see how associations can be useful, nothing has been said about how they are formed. The usual explanation is rote *repetition*. By repeated practice, information re-enters STM, and each entry into STM makes it more probable that it will be permanently stored in LTM. To go back to our bucket analogy, suppose our bucket has *two* holes: one above a large permanent container, the other above our cup, as already discussed. Now, any drop of water might leave the bucket by either hole. If it goes into the large container, it would be going into LTM. If it goes into the cup, it would eventually be poured back into the bucket, and so have another chance to leak out by the *other* hole, into the permanent container.

One problem with this view is that the formation of associations is seen as being random. Just as it is impossible to predict which hole of the bucket a drop will go through, it is impossible to predict what type of association, if any, will be formed to mediate between stimulus and response. In fact, the early behaviourists insisted the process *was* random, based simply on trial-and-error. Unfortunately, this does not fit well with the cognitive view of mediating processes as being purposeful or systematic, nor does it seem to reflect our experience—most sequences of thought are far from random.

An alternative to the associational view exists, and it may be both closer to reality and easier to apply in improving memory. According to the concept of *context-dependent coding*, all information is stored in memory as a set of relationships which are called the context. Remembering occurs not by random associations but by restoring the context of the original event. When meeting someone on the street who seems familiar, you may try to recall *where* you met them, or who you were *with*, or *when* it was. These are all parts of the context of the previous encounter. Similarly, hearing an old song may bring back a flood of memories—the context in which you originally listened to the song. An athlete, recalling a performance, may make movements of the same muscles originally used. (Try thinking of how to do a parallel turn in skiing, for example, or use some other sport you are familiar with. If you're like most people, you'll find you tend to "think with your muscles.")

Those who support the concept of context-dependent coding as the basis of retention sometimes use different terms than STM and

LTM: they speak of *episodic* and *semantic* memory. Episodic memory consists of unconnected events or episodes, and is roughly equivalent to STM in the sense that information is easily lost. Semantic memory is considered *always permanent,* and is based on preserving meaningful aspects of the context. The context, it should be noted, is not *always* situational as it is in episodic memory. You may also remember something by relating it to some past context. For example, a "geometry theorem" may be related to "other math information." In many ways, this description of memory does not differ greatly from the associational view. Part of the difference lies in how one deals with forgetting.

Forgetting, and Ways to Avoid It

Thus far, we've seen that simply being exposed to something may not guarantee we remember it later, since STM is so limited. Yet information which does enter LTM (or semantic memory) may be available for the rest of our lives. The failure to remember, or forgetting, is an important issue. When we can't remember, we get irritated, frustrated, and curious about how to improve the situation. There are two approaches to the problem of aiding memory: one focuses on initial learning (coding); and the other on memory techniques (retrieval).

First consider STM. As already noted, STM has limited duration and limited capacity. Information enters and leaves in a chaotic way, with little or no organization. At best, material is classified by sound, which is a very crude type of code. Information passing through leaves no impression on the system itself, just as the passage of water leaves the bucket unchanged. Forgetting seems to be related to STM's limited capacity; new incoming information tends to push out previous contents. This *displacement* is the basic cause of forgetting in STM.

There are few prospects for improving STM. Since capacity is fixed, one cannot really reduce displacement. On the other hand, it *does* mean that for important material one should avoid distractions. How often have you been talking about something, been interrupted, and then been unable to recall the point where you left off? The earlier example of looking up a phone number is another case.

One way in which we can improve the use of STM is by means of coding information. As noted earlier, the capacity of STM is about 7 ± 2 meaningful items, or "chunks." A chunk may be a letter in a random series (as in the earlier test), a grocery item or other word, or a whole concept (as in the key points of a speech). A chunk represents the minimum meaningful unit. For instance, in a test of random words, the chunks are the words, not the individual letters. In a book, a chunk might be a sentence or phrase, not the individual words. This means that one can increase the effective capacity of STM by recoding into larger chunks whenever possible. Consider a grocery list. By grouping items in categories (e.g., fruits, meats, canned goods), you can focus on remembering the categories. Then, each time you think of a category, the individual items in it will be easier to recall. Another example is telephone numbers. At one time, everyone learned the initial numbers of the name of the exchange (for instance Cherry was CH, or 24). Today, the telephone company officially avoids these names, because of automation, but they can still be helpful. For instance, an all-night drugstore in Toronto has a phone number corresponding to its name, TAMBLYN. You may be able to make similar codes for the numbers you need to remember. Such number codes are one example of a memory aid or a mnemonic device.

The use of chunking compensates for the limited capacity of STM. However, it would be wrong to believe that chunking occurs independently of LTM. Clearly, the use of any coding method involves drawing on past experience which is stored in LTM. In fact, it can be argued that the *real* function of chunking or other coding is simply to increase the transfer into and out of LTM. To understand this, let us consider forgetting in LTM.

We have several times stated that LTM appears to be unlimited in capacity, so clearly forgetting cannot be a matter of displacement. Furthermore, information in LTM may remain for our whole life. Given this picture of a permanent system, unlimited in capacity, it is puzzling to understand why we ever fail to remember.

The basic explanation seems to be *interference*, or competition between various items of information. As with books in a large library, often the problem is not storage space, but finding what you want. The larger the collection of books, or information, the more difficult it can be to retrieve a particular item. The concept of interference states that as our store of information grows, it becomes harder and harder to uniquely identify a piece of information. From the viewpoint of associations, the associations for a particular item will tend to overlap those for similar items. ("Was it *last* summer I met Harry in Algonquin Park, or when I was there two years ago?") As time goes on, we experience a running together of past experience, and a consequent loss of details, due to interference. If there are too many interfering associations, you may simply not remember the desired information. (The theory of semantic memory leads to the same prediction, except one would refer to contextual cues, rather than associations.)

According to some theorists, this build-up of interference can lead to wiping out of memories; amidst all the tangles of associations, some are broken. Unfortunately there is no way to know for certain if forgotten material is truly gone forever. In fact, it may be more sensible to assume the opposite—all memories are permanent. Consider the following case: suppose someone tries to recall something, and, despite every conceivable attempt, cannot remember it. Then, a short time after they give up, the desired information mysteriously floats into consciousness. How does interference theory account for this? Clearly, the information was not permanently lost. While one could conceive of changes in associations, such a spontaneous change in a short interval would seem little short of miraculous. Hence, the idea of permanent loss, and even interference, has been seriously challenged.

As described previously, an alternative to the concept of associations in LTM is the notion of context-dependent coding. The *theory of semantic memory* states that all information is permanently stored, and remembering depends on restoring the appropriate context. If you do not remember at a particular moment, it does not mean that the information is destroyed (a lack of availability), but rather that it is not retrievable, given the search method (it is not accessible). This type of failure to retrieve desired information is called *context-dependent forgetting*. We fail to remember because the cues we use to aid our recall are inappropriate. For example, a friend once told me of having met a Nobel laureate in physics at a party the previous night. When I asked his name, my friend could not recall, except to say the last name began with P. He strove to remember, but it was not until a few days later that he could tell me the name: Dirac. "Dirac?" I said "But you said it began with P!" "Yes, I know," he replied. "But you see, his name is Paul Dirac, and on his name badge it said P. Dirac. All I could think of was seeing that letter P, until it came to me this morning!" Similarly, if in trying to remember someone's name, you place a previous encounter in the wrong physical context (e.g., at work, rather than at a party), you may block recall of the name. By relaxing, one may drop an inappropriate retrieval context, and allow the true context to be generated.

Context-dependent forgetting can be very frustrating. Normally, we think of "context" as being the physical surroundings. But part of the context is actually internal—the thoughts, feelings and state of mind that are part of our moment-to-moment experience. The changes in context associated with physical and mental state are often referred to as *state-dependent forgetting*, to distinguish these cues from external, environmental, contextual cues. Thus, if one is relaxed when studying, but anxious during the test, the change in mental state makes recall difficult. After the test, anxiety is reduced—and the answer pops into mind. As everyone knows, testing under circumstances of extreme anxiety can lead to a false impression of what is known. To reduce this state-dependent forgetting, one must make the study and test circumstances more alike—either by learning to relax during tests, or possibly creating anxiety while studying! (Since anxiety can adversely affect performance in other ways, the former is the preferred solution.) Another example of state-dependent forgetting occurs with drugs. Often users of drugs, be it alcohol, marijuana, or some other agent, show poor transfer of information between drug and normal states. The person who is "stoned" may not be able to remember something read while normal, a drinker may wake in the morning without recall of his behaviour while drunk the night before, and so on. Such effects have been found in many studies with animals, and they appear to exist to varying degrees in people, depending on dosage and other factors.

The evidence for context-dependent forgetting suggests that most memory failures are simply retrieval failures, and are potentially avoidable. Still, one cannot retrieve information that was never stored to begin with. (Failing a test because you didn't read the textbook is not context-dependent forgetting!) Hence, we must consider how coding affects initial learning, as well as subsequent retrieval.

According to the traditional view, there are two approaches to learning: by rote (repetition) and by insight (making use of context or associations). Rote learning usually occurs when information is non-meaningful and/or difficult to place in a familiar context. Such repetition is often slow and painful. To improve learning, it is desirable to change to an insightful process, using some type of coding. As noted earlier, all coding makes use of prior experience. Hence, in seeking to improve coding, it is necessary to find ways of linking the new information to previous knowledge. Whether this can be done depends on the task and one's prior knowledge, but research has given us ways of predicting the outcome. Such predictions are based on the study of transfer.

Transfer of learning refers to the relationship between one's previous knowledge and the current learning task. *Positive transfer* means that previous experience aids the new learning. Positive transfer will usually occur when there is similarity between the current situation and past experience. For example, knowing French will aid the learning of Italian, Spanish, or other Romance languages, because the Romance languages are all derived from a common origin, Latin. It should be noted that in considering transfer, one can only speak of the effects of prior learning compared to a case where the person does not have prior learning. To demonstrate this, let us compare the performance of two people, one who knows language A and one who does not, in learning language B. (See Figure 3.A.) Then, compare their performance on a test of language B after the same amount of study time. If Person 1 does better, we would say his knowledge of language A was helpful in learning language B (assuming, of course, that other factors such as intelligence were equal). To make this a proper study, one would have to repeat the comparison with many pairs of people to see if it occurred consistently. For our purposes, the basic idea will hold. Other cases where one would expect positive transfer would be going from a bicycle to a motorcycle (same sense of balance), or between ballet and gymnastics (grace and coordination).

Not all prior experiences provide for positive transfer, however. Suppose, in Figure 3.A, that Person 2 performed better on the test of language B. This would indicate negative *transfer*, where previous experience interferes with new learning. This might occur in learning German after knowing French, or learning English after knowing Chinese. Differences in words, grammar, and even conceptual structure, make learning difficult. In general, where learning involves making different responses to the same situation or stimulus, we expect negative transfer. (In the case of languages, the same object may have very different names.)

Another example might be a tennis player attempting to play badminton—both have a net, racquet, and object to be volleyed, but many of the movements and reflex reactions are quite different, and could interfere. Snow-skiing and water-skiing might be another case where knowing one makes learning the other more difficult.

It is possible to discuss transfer effects in terms of context dependence. Whenever we encounter something new, we attach meaning to it in terms of past experience. The owner of a new car compares it to other cars he's driven. Seeing "Star Wars," one may be reminded of "2001." Events which fit into a context of past experiences are easier to understand and easier to remember. Many people find higher math difficult because it seems too abstract, too remote from experience. Similarly, learning dates in history courses can seem difficult, because the events are unrelated to our direct experience. On the other hand, we are each a walking history book for the major events of our own lifetimes. Unlike the history course, these events are easy to remember, because they are part of the fabric of our own lives. Thus, any new experience which easily fits into our accumulated conception of the world will show positive transfer. Experiences which seem isolated, like math or history, may show no transfer effects (*zero transfer*). And those which contradict our past experience,

EXPERIMENTAL   LEARN A ⟶   LEARN B ⟶   TEST B

CONTROL   (REST) ⟶   LEARN B ⟶   TEST B

Figure 3.A
Paradigm for Testing Transfer
In transfer situations, one is always concerned with whether previous experience (learning task A) will affect new learning. If the experimental group does better, we would call it positive transfer. If they do worse than the control group, it would be negative transfer. If there is no difference, zero transfer.

EXPERIMENTAL   LEARN A ⟶ LEARN B ⟶   RECALL B

CONTROL   (REST) ⟶   LEARN B ⟶   RECALL B

Figure 3.B
Paradigm for Testing Proactive Interference
In interference tests, one is concerned with how well people can recall material previously learned. If the experimental group does worse than the control group, we would say there has been proactive interference by task A. Note the parallel to the test for transfer (Fig. 3.A).

EXPERIMENTAL   LEARN A ⟶ LEARN B ⟶   RECALL A

CONTROL   LEARN A ⟶   (REST) ⟶   RECALL A

Figure 3.C
Paradigm for Testing Retroactive Interference
When looking at retroactive interference, one is concerned with whether recent experiences can interfere with the ability to recall earlier learning. If the experimental group does poorer than the control group, we would call it retroactive interference.

like a tennis player learning badminton, will show negative transfer.

In terms of practical application, the concept of transfer can best be applied as a type of orienting technique. In any situation one should look for similarities to prior experience. Often this is a matter of translating from the given terms into other terms that are personally meaningful. A physicist caught in rush hour traffic once noticed that the ebb and flow of cars was like waves in a ripple tank, and went on to develop a theory of traffic flow. Similarities abound, if we seek them.

In cases where negative transfer is a problem—where seemingly similar situations actually require different responses—one would do well to emphasize the differences between the situations themselves. Driving in England is frequently hazardous for North Americans, since one must keep left instead of right. In this case, the changed position of the steering wheel could—or should—serve as a reminder that responses must differ!

Negative transfer may also be regarded as a form of interference. In this case, because *prior* experience makes learning difficult (interferes), we speak of *proactive* ("acting forward") *interference*. It also is possible for recent experiences to make recall of earlier information more difficult. This is called *retroactive* ("acting backwards") *interference*. (See Figures 3.B and 3.C.) Students often experience retroactive interference when they find this semester's physics has wiped out last semester's chemistry, which in turn rendered inaccessible last year's history course. This can happen at work whenever we change job responsibilities, or even locations. The salesman promoted to manager may lose touch with customer concerns. The programmer who becomes supervisor may get rusty at programming. And being moved from Toronto to New York may make it difficult later to renew contacts, if one is transferred back. In terms of context-dependent coding, we would say successive changes in context make it more difficult to reinstate the earlier context. Attempts at relearning, such as refresher courses, often will quickly restore the context, and hence accessibility to the information. Probably such courses should be required of all managerial staff.

The effects of variations in context should not be underestimated. Proactive and retroactive interference mean that variations can make restoring a particular mental context difficult. A further example concerns budgeting study time, or spacing of practice of any task. A common student strategy is to "cram," leaving most of the material to be studied shortly before the exam. In psychology, this is called *massed practice*. Teachers, on the other hand, usually recommend doing small amounts of material throughout the course, which is called *distributed practice.* Deciding which is better depends partly on one's goal and partly on the situation.

Clearly, for any physical task, fatigue becomes an important factor—playing tennis for ten hours a day for three days will not have the same effect as two hours a day spread over two weeks. For verbal material such as school work, the situation is a bit different. In tests of recall done shortly after the last study session, with no other task intervening, massed practice is actually slightly better. But if another task intervenes between study and testing, or if one tests several days or longer after study, the result is clear: distributed practice yields much better performance. Any intervening activity serves to increase interference, making retrieval of the original context more difficult, and hence increasing forgetting.

In fact, it has been found that recall is best if one is tested in the same room where studying takes place (so preparing for a speech, you might try rehearsing in the auditorium!). Possibly because distributed practice is likely to take place at different times of day, in different locations, etc., it makes recall less context-sensitive, and therefore reduces forgetting. As noted earlier, context can also include internal factors (state-dependent forgetting), so the more variations in context one introduces, the more likely it will be that one can avoid these problems.

The implication of these studies of massed and distributed practice is clear. In cases of short-term testing, massed practice may prove as effective as, or even better than, distributed practice. The likelihood is, however, that long term recall will be poor. Generations of students who have crammed—and later forgotten—exam material will testify to both facts. Distributed practice is superior in the long run, and often as good in the short-term (particularly with a brief review before the exam). Given that total study time is the same, logic says distributed practice is better.

Mnemonics

However good or poor our memory, there are techniques to make remembering more effective. The study and use of such memory aids is called *mnemonics.* The origin of mnemonics is credited to a Greek poet named Simonides. By a strange sequence of events, Simonides was the only survivor of a disaster when the roof of a banquet hall fell in. The bodies were so mangled that the mourning relatives could not identify them for burial. However, Simonides, by remembering the seating arrangement, was able to identify each body. Impressed with his own feat, Simonides began a systematic study of mnemonics.[3]

Today, a number of mnemonic devices, or memory aids, are known. One of the simplest is *concentration*. By focussing on the information, one may improve recall considerably. For example, many people report difficulty in learning names. When a person is introduced they are not attending to the name, but worrying about the impression they're making, what to talk about, or some other concern. The result is that the name, never having been processed, is not available (not in memory) later on. By focussing on the name during the introduction, you facilitate recall. One memory expert used to advise: "Look at the person, listen to the name, repeat it in your mind, and say their name when you shake hands."

Professional mnemonists often use some type of organizational structure, called a key-word system. In this technique, a rhyme or other mental scheme can serve as a peg on which to hang new items. Thus, if asked to remember a shopping list of milk, eggs, butter, and so on, one might use the nursery rhyme, "one is a bun, two is a shoe, three is a tree" as follows: one becomes a large hot dog bun with a bottle of milk instead of a hot dog in it; two becomes a mental image of a shoe stepping on eggs; three becomes a tree with pounds of butter instead of leaves. The result is a distinctive set of associations with a key code which is easily remembered. Such schemes do work, but they must be based on a well-practised key-list, and they work best when the associations of items to key-words are vivid and unique.

A variation on the key-word system is called the *method of loci*, or places. This technique was used by Simonides, and later recommended by Cicero. Roman orators, like Cicero, would mentally "place" key concepts in various locations around the assembly hall. By looking around the room in sequence, they would recall the key points of their speech. The exercise in Figure 4 is another example of this. This technique can also be applied to remember tasks for the next day. By vividly associating the task with some routine action, such as taking off your coat at work, you are reminded of the task when you reach the office. By appropriate choice of key action, you can jog your memory at almost any point in the day's routine. Such mnemonic codes work both by creating meaningful associations between new information and prior knowledge—a form of transfer— and by using contextual cues to aid recall, as in the method of loci.

Mnemonic devices can be helpful by providing prearranged cues for recall. But for non-meaningful material, such as long lists of items, *coding* into a meaningful form may be more effective. Generations of

---

[3] Yates tells this story in detail in *The Art of Memory*.

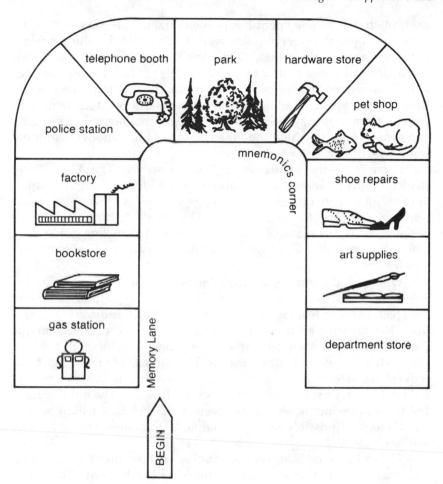

Figure 4
A Walk Down Memory Lane

The use of the method of loci can be easily demonstrated by use of the above diagram. Have someone copy the list of words below, and read them to you at the rate of about one every five seconds, while you look at the map. As you hear each word, try to associate it with the place you are at, moving around one stop each time. "Travel" the route twice to learn the twenty-two words. Then, to recall them, retrace the route, and try to recall the two words you have associated with each place. Ninety per cent recall (nineteen to twenty words) is typical. .

Word list: voice, study, dollar, lake, soldier, library, plant, train, symphony, game, desert, hat, turtle, sofa, motion, wasp, yellow, home, eat, navy, pillow, legal medical students have spent hours memorizing the body parts. The names of the cranial nerve tracts were made easier by the nameless wit who recoded them into, "On old Olympus's tallest top, a fat-assed German vaults and hops." The purpose of the low humour lies in the first letter of each word, which is also the first letter for a nerve tract. (This type of coding is called the narrative technique.) In another form, one may refer to Roy G. Biv, or that famous device, the "vibgyor"—both of which code the colours of the rainbow, using the same type of first-letter code.

Such made-up words are called acronyms. The U.S. Army (which seems to adore such creations) has added "snafu" (situation normal: all fouled up) to our language as well as "jeep" (General Purpose vehicle). Rhymes can also be used. "Thirty days hath September" is one example. Another, useful as a spelling guide, is "I before E except after C, or when sounded as ay as in neighbour and weigh."

Whatever the form, such techniques function by creating meaningful associations for information which has no natural structure. This has several advantages: stronger associations, indirectly increasing STM capacity by making links to LTM, and creating a unique context for recall. As noted earlier, the problem in memory (at least for LTM) is not storage, but retrieval. The success of mnemonic techniques illustrates this, for most function by *adding* to the information to be retained. Despite this, they make recall easier. The only limits to the use of mnemonic techniques seem to lie in one's willingness to use them, and possibly in one's imaginative abilities. (For a review, see Box.)

Given our increasing understanding of how memory operates, you may ask whether an infallible memory can be acquired. A few observations are relevant here. First, forgetting is universal, despite reports of people with so-called "photographic memories." Although differences in recall exist, experiments have usually indicated that these can be accounted for by what happens at time of learning (if activity between learning and recall is kept constant). Whether you can retrieve the information depends on whether you formed appropriate associations and contextual cues at the time of coding. Despite this, it is not clear just why some people acquire more information (and hence recall more). Where such differences exists, they may be either inborn, or due to acquisition (consciously or unconsciously) of very efficient coding strategies. Memory is not a muscle, and trying to exercise it by learning will not improve future learning. In fact it *may* create proactive interference! William James, an eminent psychologist at the turn of the century, once personally tested the exercise notion.

MAXIMIZING USE OF MEMORY

Most of us experience memory failures at one time or another—sometimes, it seems, the probability of forgetting increases with the importance of remembering. What can one do? The following represents a brief guide to some techniques for improving memory. For more detailed information, refer to the accompanying text.

Names—concentrate when introduced; don't let your mind be half elsewhere when the name is given. Repeat it silently. If there are couples, mentally link their names. Note the face—often you can link the name to physical features—e.g., "Tom is tall."

Phone numbers—the trick is to make it meaningful, or at least familiar. Is there a sequence (e.g., 1357) or other cue (e.g., 1275 is "Dec. 75")? Failing that, repeat the number several times, each time saying the person's name.

Aids to learning

1. Distribute learning time—cramming is not effective (*unless* you *only* want to know it for an hour or two after learning).
2. Make the connection—look for links between the current task and prior experiences. This may involve *transfer* (e.g., how is management of department staff like dealing with customers?) or forming *unique associations* ("This is John Smith, whose wife's name is the same as my mother's.").

Aids to remembering

1. Use context cues—this can be helpful both in organizing information ("What does this *relate* to?") and for remembering key information (e.g., using method of loci when speaking in a meeting).
2. Use mnemonic devices—any familiar scheme that will enable you to go through a sequence of tasks, names, etc., by linking them to a rhyme or other device is useful. It both aids the initial learning, and minimizes the chance of omitting items on recall.
3. Relax—it is hard to over-estimate the importance of this. Anxiety tends to create state-dependent forgetting ("blanking"), and increase the chances of fixating on the wrong context. When you start on the wrong track, it is literally true that the more you try, the less likely you are to remember.

None of these aids represents a sure fire solution to all situations. It is still true that our memories are imperfect, and there is no "pill" or other easy panacea imminent. But memory is an ability that benefits from proper practice. If all attempts fail, write it down—but then remember to look at the note!

After a month and a half of memorizing vast quantities of poetry each day he found it took him *longer* to learn that same amount. This is not to say that practice of *mnemonics* will not aid memory, but simply that random memorizing will be of little use. Newspapers often carry reports of a "memory pill" being just around the corner. At present, no such pill exists, nor is there any clear sign that one is likely in the forseeable future. Hence, we must all muddle along, forgetting at least *some* of what we'd like to remember.

Lest one consider this disappointing, it might be worth considering the consequences of never forgetting: all of life's traumas would remain vividly intact, as would every bit of trivial information, such as shopping lists from ten years previous. Given that most of the information we need ready access to is frequently used, a context-dependent system seems eminently practical: we are more likely to encounter a next-door neighbour than a high school acquaintance, and it is desirable that a neighbour's name have easier accessibility. In any case, it is often not how much information one has that matters, but what one does with it.

PROBLEM SOLVING

In many situations the utility of retaining information lies simply in being able to recall it when needed—phone numbers, for example, provide a tool for communication. In other situations, information stored in our memory is used instead to aid problem solving. For example, a person planning a trip from Toronto to Montreal will be aided by knowing the distance, route numbers, plane schedules, relative cost by car and plane, and so on. Each piece of information serves no end in itself, but is simply an input to the process of choosing the best travel arrangements.

In this sense, memory is the basis of the cognitive maps Tolman described. The information in memory mediates decisions about what response is most appropriate for a given stimulus situation. At different times one may need to make different responses. In fact, those situations that we call "problems" nearly always require a response we haven't tried before. In these cases the "cognitive maps" we have will influence how well we cope with the problem.

Apart from the specific information we have stored in memory, effective problem solving often depends on how we approach the problem. That is, problem solving is a type of skill, and like all skills it can benefit from training and practice. Unfortunately, the teaching of such skills has been sadly neglected in our society, although cognitive psychologists have been actively studying problem solving since the time of Kohler and Tolman.

To begin with, we should outline the stages involved in problem solving. Although different researchers have used slightly different labels, basically the stages are:

1. Defining the problem;
2. Developing possible solutions;
3. Selecting and evaluating the best solution.

Occasionally, researchers have talked about a process of incubation, where one temporarily abandons conscious attempts to solve the problem. Since this does not always occur, we will focus on the three major stages.

Defining the problem has several aspects. First, one must recognize that a problem exists in order to solve it. Second, the *way* one defines the problem can influence attempts to solve it. Overly broad statements can hinder by their vagueness. For instance, asking "How can we improve life for everyone?" does not lead to any specific solutions. On the other hand, overly specific definitions can hinder problem solving by inhibiting creative new solutions. For example, asking "What is the best way to get sulphur dioxide out of the air?" may inhibit the idea that one reduce the amount going *into* the air (since it is mainly a product of auto exhaust fumes). As Edward de Bono, a well-known researcher on problem solving, has said, a definition is sufficient "as soon as it allows one to do something about a situation."

The second stage of problem solving is generating solutions. The process of developing *possible* solutions often gives people trouble. First, one must try to list as many solutions as can be thought of. Sometimes this is done in groups, with each person trying to contribute ideas. (This technique, called "brainstorming," is less effective for creative tasks than for ones where a single ideal solution exists.) One should merely *list* possible solutions before worrying about selecting the best solution (that is, keep stage 2 separate from stage 3). In this section, we will discuss a variety of techniques that can improve the process of developing solutions.

The third stage, selecting and evaluating the best solution, has different characteristics than does generating ideas. First, choosing the best solution depends on what criteria one selects. For example, in 1960 many people saw nuclear reactors as a means to cheap energy production, but today there is concern over how to deal with the fuel wastes. Thus, the best solution from one point of view (or at one time) may not be the best from another. Second, some problems may not have a single ideal solution. In these cases, the selection criteria one adopts will be even more influential. Among the factors to consider might be, what the relative advantages of different solutions are, which aspects of the problem it is most important to solve, and what problems are created by the proposed solution. As in the example of nuclear energy, it is possible that people will prefer different solutions because they give different weights to these factors.

Convergent Problems

Most of the problems we face in everyday life are "convergent"—that is, they have a single solution—and everything leads towards that one goal. Sometimes, these problems are called "one-shot" or "closed-end" problems, because the problem is done when we find the solution. Because it is easy to evaluate such problems, they are often used in studies of problem solving.

The Gestalt psychologists developed a number of intriguing convergent problems, some of which have already been mentioned. (At this point, the reader should review the section on problem solving in Chapter 1.) In general, their concern was with the organizational characteristics that influence how we perceive, and therefore solve, a problem. Finding a solution requires organizing the available information in an appropriate way.

The way that we organize the elements is shaped by what the Gestalt psychologists called a "mental set." In most cases, developing a set is very useful. Consider for example the problems in Figure 5. Once you have figured out the first problem, the next four are easy. However, you will find the sixth problem impossible to do in the same way. In this case, your mental set is no longer appropriate and interferes with solving the problem. The interference caused by an inappropriate set is called *functional fixedness.*

PROBLEM	GIVEN: THE FOLLOWING EMPTY JARS AS MEASURES			OBTAIN: THE FOLLOWING AMOUNT OF WATER
	A	B	C	
SAMPLE	29	3		20
1	21	127	3	100
2	14	163	25	99
3	18	43	10	5
4	9	42	6	21
5	20	59	4	31
6	24	49	4	20

Figure 5
Functional Fixedness in Problem Solving
All of the problems above involve the same goal, with slightly different stimuli. If you work through them, you will quickly develop a schemata (or "set"). What happens in problem number 6? (Adapted from Luchins, 1942.)

Clearly, it is desirable to avoid functional fixedness. For the Gestalt psychologists, the answer was *recentering*, developing an alternate set to deal with a problem. Being aware of the danger of fixedness is the first step to avoiding it. Further, it sometimes helps to get away from the problem. Often, overfamiliarity inhibits original thinking and recentering. The development of the theory of relativity is an example: classical Newtonian theory worked pretty well for most problems, and the established physicists were reluctant to abandon it. Einstein, as a young researcher, felt no such commitment to the old theory, and so could come up with a new approach.

Unfortunately, Gestalt theory is more descriptive than prescriptive—that is, it does not offer many *concrete* suggestions to improve problem solving. Modern researchers have attempted to do so. Edward de Bono is one such person. De Bono has noted that being wrong, or functional fixedness, can take several forms, from arrogant attachment to an outmoded idea, to failure to recognize that an old solution is no longer the best. Beyond that, he has advocated the value of humour, provocativeness (or "PO"), and imagination in problem solving. His work tends to be based on demonstration experiments (like the Gestaltists) and humourous sayings. (e.g., "If you cannot imagine any alternative explanations, then it is easy to be convinced that the only one you have is absolutely right.") In this sense, his approach is still rather general, but it does point the way towards more specific methods.

People tend to adopt various strategies in dealing with problems. Some such strategies can be very effective, but others are inefficient and/or ineffective. Jerome Bruner has characterized strategies as falling into two broad categories—*wholist* and *scanning*. A wholist strategy is based on adopting a tentative solution which deals with the available information, and then modifying this basic idea only to the extent that new input requires. Such strategies tend to be logical and systematic. (Sherlock Holmes's use of deduction is an example.) Wholist strategies tend to be efficient as well as effective.

Scanning strategies are based on adopting a series of possible solutions, each unconnected to the last. One version of this is the "shotgun" approach: "if I try enough things, something *has* to work." In its most inefficient form, a scanning strategy can even lead to resampling a previously rejected idea. (Young children often make this mistake in games like "20 questions"; adults may revert to it when they feel frustrated or overwhelmed by a problem.) Apart from the inefficiency caused by repeating rejected possibilities, scanning strategies may also prove ineffective. Since solutions are chosen at random, there is no guarantee that a new one is better than previous

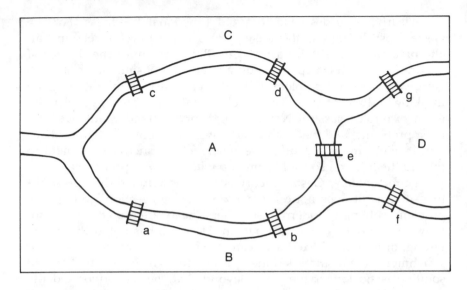

EXHAUSTIVE ALGORITHM: PATHS BEGINNING WITH A

abcdef	abcdeg	abcged	abcgf	abdcef	abdceg	abdgec	abdgf
acdbfe	acdbfg	acdefb	acdeg	acgebf	acged	acgfbd	acgfbe
adceg	adgebf	adgec	adgfbc	adgfbe	aefbcd	aefbcg	aefbdc
aegdbf	aegdc	abegcd	abegdc	abef	adcbfe	adcbfg	adcefb
aefbdg	aegcbf	aegcd					

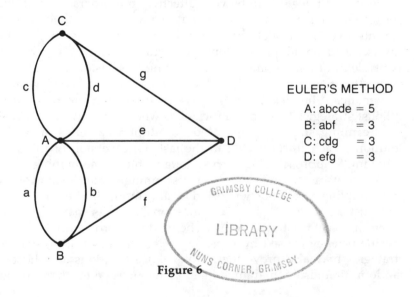

EULER'S METHOD

A: abcde = 5
B: abf   = 3
C: cdg   = 3
D: efg   = 3

Figure 6

ones. Also, this randomness means there is no assurance one will *ever* find the solution. Only if one is lucky will scanning lead to a solution more quickly than a systematic-but-plodding wholist strategy.

The need for systematic methods of solving problems is very apparent in logic and in computer applications. Computers, by their design, are not well-suited to the "get lucky" approach of scanning strategies. At the same time, their speed enables them to carry out systematic procedures very quickly. These characteristics of computers have led to increased interest in an area of logic called *algorithms*. Basically, an algorithm is any set of procedures which always enables one to solve a particular type of problem. For example, children learn algorithms for subtraction and division in school. In this sense, an algorithm is a formalized "mental set" for dealing with convergent problems, and can be very effective.

An example of the use of algorithms is seen in the Konigsborg bridges problem, described in Figure 6. Basically, the problem asks if there is a route around the city such that one crosses all the bridges, but each one only once. A scanning strategy would randomly select paths, trying to find a route. An algorithm, however, will guarantee the solution, if there is one. (It's *possible* no route exists for a given set of bridges and roads.) As noted in Figure 6, one algorithm is simply to list all possible combinations of paths, checking each one. The problem with this algorithm is that it expands greatly as one adds more bridges and/or paths; even with the given problem, it is very slow.

←———

Figure 6 (opposite):
EULER'S PROBLEM asks whether there is a path through a graph that traverses each line exactly once. In this context a graph is defined as any collection of points with lines connecting them.

The problem was first stated in terms of a walking tour through a park in the thirteenth century German city of Konigsberg (top); the path sought was required to cross each of the seven bridges in the park exactly once. The park can also be represented as a graph, as shown.

One approach to the problem is to list all the paths through the graph that continue as far as they can without repeating a line. Even for a small graph, however, there are many such paths; the sample listing shown includes only those paths that begin with line A.

A more efficient algorithm was discovered by Leonhard Euler. A graph has a path that traverses each line once, he showed, if every point of the graph (with two possible exceptions) is at the junction of an even number of lines. Such a path is now called an Eulerian path. Counting the lines meeting at each point shows that the graph of the Konigsberg park has no Eulerian path. (Adapted from Lewis and Papadimitriou, 19:8.)

Fortunately, a mathematician named Leonhard Euler developed a more efficient algorithm to see if a route exists. (See Figure 6.) Unlike the algorithm which lists all combinations, Euler's algorithm remains workable no matter how large the problem.

Algorithms, then, always enable one to reach the solution. Some algorithms, however, are more efficient than others. Another example may further this point: suppose there is a tennis tournament, with 101 players competing. What is the minimum number of matches necessary? One algorithm is to list all the necessary rounds, providing for "bys" when there is an odd number of players. A shorter algorithm is possible, however: by definition, every player except one (the winner) must lose once and only once. Thus, the minimum number of matches equals 101 − 1, or 100 matches! Unfortunately, for some problems only inefficient algorithms exist (like listing all combinations of bridge paths), and for large problems their use would tax even a computer. For still other types of problems, no algorithms at all have been discovered and, in some cases, theorists doubt if any are possible. For these situations where no efficient algorithms exist, other strategies must be used.

One approach is *heuristics,* or guides to thinking. Like algorithms, heuristics save us from the randomness of scanning strategies. Unlike algorithms, they are not rigidly formal, and can make use of metaphors, intuition, and other creative techniques. (For this reason, heuristics cannot be used by computers.) One example is known as the salesman's map problem: a salesman must visit several cities, and then return to his home city. In what order should he visit them for the shortest route? Although the problem seems simple, there is no known efficient algorithm. A heuristic that could be applied to give a *reasonable* answer (if not always the optimum) is to always go to the nearest city next. Similarly, a mechanic once told me a heuristic for fixing a stalled car: "a car needs gas, and it needs a spark. If one is OK, check the other." Other kinds of heuristics include (1) working backwards from the solution to one's current situation (e.g., "To go to Florida next winter, I need $1000. How can I get that extra money by January?), (2) using metaphors (e.g., asking how a camera could be like the eye, has led to automatic exposure and, recently, automatic focussing systems), and (3) breaking the problem down into subgoals (e.g., "How can we end pollution?" can be broken down into types of pollution, sources of pollution, etc.).

In the end, no single technique will prove useful in all cases. The Gestaltists were correct in noting that the organizing capacities which help us form sets also lead to functional fixedness. Despite this, the techniques discussed here can be useful in limiting the frequency with which we get fixated, and in increasing our ability to recenter.

Divergent Problems

Convergent problems have a single best solution, and all the information ultimately points towards this. Divergent problems, on the other hand, do not have a single solution, except according to the criteria one may adopt. For example, asking "How can I design the perfect car?" depends on what one means by "perfect." For that reason, divergent problems are often called "creative" problems.

The term "creativity" is one that is often abused. Basically, it implies two characteristics: uniqueness and goodness. Uniqueness is significant, because an idea which occurs to everyone is not regarded as creative, no matter how useful it is for solving a problem. (For example, making auto tires round, instead of square, is not creative.) On the other hand, unique ideas are seldom called creative, unless they contribute effectively to solving a problem. (For example, wearing clothes made out of spaghetti would be unique, but not very practical.) As de Bono has said, "A creative idea is just a new idea that works."

In this sense, the difference between convergent and divergent problems lies not in the means of developing solutions (stage 2), but only in the means of evaluating them (stage 3). Depending on the criteria used, a solution to a divergent problem may be judged effective or not. For convergent problems, there is seldom this room for value judgments. The distinction is one of evaluation, not production, of ideas. Unfortunately, social attitudes towards creativity have tended to blur this distinction, and to emphasize the *number* of ideas as reflecting creativity. We tend to value more highly the person who states five ideas, all of which are ineffective, than the person who describes only one, because he has already recognized that his first four were no good. Part of problem solving, of course, is recognizing when something *isn't* a solution as well as when it *is*.

Formation of Problem Solving Skills

How we develop the skills needed to solve problems is a complex issue. Kohler's concept of insight really only describes the end result, and other researchers have added to our understanding of the process. In the late 1940s, a researcher named Harry Harlow discovered a phenomenon which he called "learning to learn." Working with primates, he found that problem solving behaviour (such as choosing which of three symbols marked the location of a food reward) was initially trial and error. However, given experience with many problems of the same type, the monkeys would develop a "set" which enabled them to deal with new problems in an "insightful" way. Later research has shown that young children, and even adults, use experience to form "learning sets." (In essence, Harlow's term has the same meaning as the Gestalt term "mental set," except it emphasizes that the set develops as a result of experience.) The implication is clear: effective and efficient problem solving depends on appropriate past experience—not to know the answer, but to know how to *get* the answer. As Harlow put it, we learn how to learn.

Learning to learn provides the basis for an important aspect of problem solving skills—the formation of concepts. Most of what we experience is organized in memory, not randomly stored. Similarities among objects, or events, provide the basis for this organization in terms of concepts. A concept is a principle for organizing objects or events into categories of some kind. For example, we have a concept of what a "door" is in terms of function, shape, etc. Usually, our experiences lead us to perceive certain consistencies in the environment, and these consistencies provide the basis of our concepts.

Concept formation is an important aspect of problem solving behaviour, because defining the problem (stage 1) requires forming a concept. Further, generating possible solutions (stage 2) in an efficient way requires recognizing what is important and what is unimportant in the situation. (For example, what colour a car is has nothing to do with how it runs. Its age, however, may influence what types of malfunctions are likely.) In terms of concept learning, this is called recognizing relevant vs. irrelevant cues. The more complex the problem, the more difficult it can be to recognize the relevant cues, and ignore the irrelevant ones. Research has also shown that factors like time pressure and trying to retain information in STM can reduce efficiency.

Because complexity makes concept formation and problem solving more difficult, it also emphasizes the need for systematic strategies. Under pressure, people tend to ignore relevant information and/or fixate on irrelevant cues. The end result is a failure to solve the problem. In studies of simple problem solving by Marvin Levine, college students over-looked the simple solution to a choice task (the stimulus presented on the left was always correct) because they expected a more complex solution. In essence, the failure to examine *all* the cues led to ignoring the relevant aspect. A wholist strategy, because it is systematic, would avoid this error.

Experience, then, enables us to develop concepts, which in turn may be used as the basis of more complex mental operations. While adult behaviour is usually insightful, it is based on a foundation of early trial-and-error experience. In this sense, Kohler's emphasis on insight as *distinct* from trial and error is wrong. Trial and error and insight are related, for insight is based on concepts acquired through trial and error.

LANGUAGE

Language is a paradox: as a means of communication, we learn to use it with no difficulty. At the same time, we have great trouble understanding how it is that we manage to understand language! Psychologists, linguists, and others have raised many unresolved questions in the acquisition and use of language.

To start with, not everyone agrees on what language *is*. It clearly serves as a communication method and as a symbol system. However, not everything which communicates is regarded as language. For example, the innately determined threat gestures used by baboons to warn away rivals are signals, but not language. In order to qualify as a language, the symbols or gestures used must show variety within the species, and some dependence on learning. Interestingly, bird songs show these characteristics, including regional "dialects." For our purposes, we will focus on language as a symbol system used for communication and thinking.

Behaviourists in looking at language have tried to explain it in terms of complex reinforcers and stimulus-response relationships. In regard to language as a thinking process, they often argue that thought is simply muscle movements reduced to small, unobserved twitches. John B. Watson and Ivan Pavlov both advocated this, and some studies have supported it. (For example, deaf individuals who know sign language will often show activity in hand muscles while problem solving.)

The alternative to this, proposed by cognitive psychologists, is that language represents a symbol system which can mediate thinking processes, and has no direct dependence on "muscle twitches." Further, most cognitive researchers argue that our use of language is based on innate capacities, not simply on reinforced responses.

Language Learning

As noted previously, we all learn to use language, but typically show little concern about how we learn. Yet attempts to learn a second language, particularly as adults, may make us wonder how we found it so easy the *first* time. A brief chronology of early language learning will help illustrate the process.

At about six months of age, a baby will begin babbling, producing a wide variety of speech sounds, only some of which will later be used in their first language. Later, it is difficult to reacquire the sounds which are lost. (For example, English as a second language presents difficulties for French speakers because of the "th" sound. Similarly, English speakers have trouble with "û" in French.) At about one year of age the first words appear. By about a year-and-a-half to two years the child produces two-word "sentences." These phrases were called "telegraphic speech" by earlier researchers, but we now recognize that there is considerable complexity in their production and use. Some such phrases are clear, even out of context. For instance, "that red," for "that is red," or "see mommy" for "I see mommy." In other cases, what seems meaningless out of context is nonetheless understandable in context. For instance, the child, seeing a blue ball rolling off a table, may say "blue fall." Typically, at age two a child will make use of a dozen or so such sentences. From this time on, language skills develop rapidly, so that at age three the average child already knows about 1,000 words. In one case, a two-year-old had fourteen two-word phrases. Seven months later, he knew 2,500 words! As an adult, it has been estimated that the average person has a vocabulary of over 100,000 words, though only a small fraction may be used regularly.

This rapid development of language skills, which does not seem to depend on the specific language being learned or on the cultural setting, raises several problems for a behaviourist approach.

First, acquisition seems to occur too quickly and too consistently to be based on trial and error. Second, there is some indication that we are best prepared to learn a language at the time children normally do. If this "critical period" is passed, it may be difficult or impossible to learn normal language skills later. (Incidents of children raised in isolation support this view.) Third, although the evidence is not conclusive, it seems that we have less difficulty learning a second language as children than as adults. All of these factors suggest that language learning is based on some innate capacities which are tied to early development, and that there are internal rules which govern our acquisition and use of language. Roger Brown, a cognitive psychologist at Harvard who is interested in both language and child development, is among those who favour this view. After reviewing studies of twelve different languages, he feels the viewpoint is compelling. (Studies exist on over thirty languages, but many are rather informal.)

The view that language might be based on innate capacities is hardly disturbing to a cognitive psychologist. After all, such capacities would represent a mediating process for learning, and hence are perfectly consistent with Tolman and Kohler. The Gestalt psychologists, in particular, would find this view comfortable, for many of the organizing rules they describe are thought to be innate. At the same time, it might be a little too glib to say language capacity is innate. For one thing it minimizes the need to explain the process. Also, it makes it very easy to separate our own use of language from any apparent usage by other species, since it can simply be called an innate difference.

Recently, studies of chimpanzees and other higher primates have challenged the view that our language capacity is unique. Earlier in this century, several teams of researchers attempted to teach chimps to speak, often by rearing them as if they were human children. At best, the chimps learned two or three word-like utterances. Then, in the mid-1960s, a husband and wife team of psychologists, Allen and Beatrice Gardner, tried a new approach. Reasoning that it might be an inability to speak, not an inability to use language, that led to previous failures with chimps, the Gardners decided to try sign language. Using a modified form of ASL (a sign language used by many of the deaf in the United States), they began training a young female chimp named Washoe. To their surprise as well as joy, Washoe began using sign language proficiently, albeit with a limited vocabulary. The first published reports about Washoe set off an earthquake in both psychology and linguistics. A rash of studies have followed, some using the methods of the Gardners, some using other methods (including having chimps interacting with a computer console).

The impact on theoretical views has been enormous. Some theorists say use of ASL proves chimps have the same language capacity we do, but this may be premature. Others, notably certain linguists, have argued that ASL has a very loose structure, and is not really a "language" in the sense that English is. This view seems too rigid, considering both the human users of ASL and some of the data with chimps. For instance, Roger Foutts, once a student of the Gardners, had the following "conversation" with a chimp named Lucy:

Roger: "Lucy tickle Roger."

Lucy: "Roger tickle Lucy." (showing some signs of confusion at not being the one to be tickled.)

Roger: "No. Lucy tickle Roger."

Lucy, suddenly understanding, jumped up to tickle Roger.[4]

As yet, no chimp has produced the equivalent of Shakespeare, but then, the studies are still very new. Currently, studies are being done with colonies, where chimps have the opportunity to teach and learn signing among themselves. Such innovative approaches may bring the study of the chimps closer to normal social communication.

---

[4] Reported in Linden, E., *Apes, Men and Language*. New York: Pelican, 1976.

Whatever the outcome, future generations may look at these studies with the same regard as we look on Darwin's work. They may well change our view of ourselves and our place in the order of things.

THE COGNITIVE VIEWPOINT IN OTHER AREAS

As has been seen, cognitive psychologists have been actively involved in studying all aspects of thinking processes. But in focussing on these topics, one should not lose sight of the basic outlook of the cognitive approach: it is not that thinking processes, such as memory, are the most significant aspect of behaviour, but that mediational processes of *some* kind must underlie *all* behaviour. As noted in the introduction, this view can be used to understand many other aspects of behaviour. For example, many of the early Gestalt psychologists were more interested in perception than in learning. Today one can see cognitive influences in computer simulations of thinking processes (e.g., chess-playing computers), development (as in the work of Jean Piaget), and even applied behaviourism (where psychologists like Meichenbaum are advocating "cognitive behaviour modification").

Despite all this, it is difficult to talk about "cognitive *influences* on other areas" because such influences may be unconscious or even coincidental. For this reason, it seems more sensible to look at areas where the views expressed are *consistent with* the cognitive approach, rather than attempting to trace the origins of the views.

Attitudes and Cognitive Dissonance

One area heavily influenced by the cognitive approach is social psychology. (In this case, the influence is probably direct, owing to the work of Kurt Lewin, an early Gestalt psychologist.) A major topic that has concerned social psychologists is attitude formation and attitude change.

One of the best known theories of attitude change is the *theory of cognitive dissonance* developed by Leon Festinger in 1957. According to Festinger, we all like to behave in a self-consistent manner. Our actions should fit our words, and our attitudes. However, sometimes situations arise in which conflicts are created. For example, suppose you hate New York City but have good friends living in Manhattan whom you want to see. This creates conflict between your attitude towards New York and your attitude towards your friends. The negative feelings accompanying this type of conflict are called cognitive dissonance, and Festinger's theory deals with the nature of these conflicts, and how we resolve them.

In the example given, you could decide New York isn't so bad, and go, or you could decide you really don't care that much about seeing your friends, and not go; in either case, your attitudes would be consistent with your actions. Or, you might persuade your friends to visit you. In this case, your attitudes remain firm, but the conflict is resolved by introducing a new factor. This is analogous to a smoker who says, "Sure, I know smoking can cause cancer. But I'd be miserable *without* smoking!" Dissonance theory states that conflict (dissonance) can lead to changes in attitudes; usually the weakest belief is the one to be changed.

Dissonance reduction is a common occurrence. Consider the following case: have you ever waited outside in the winter for a movie, perhaps for an hour or more? What was your reaction to the movie thereafter? According to dissonance theory, you very likely thought you enjoyed the movie, since it would be conflict-arousing to think you suffered outside for a terrible film. In a laboratory analogy of this situation, Festinger found that participants in a purposely dull experiment were more positive about it if they were unpaid than if they had been given $10!

Dissonance theory has probably generated more research than any other theory in social psychology. Partly this has been because the issues it raises are interesting, and partly it is because of seeming weaknesses in theory. For one thing, the theory does not predict precisely what will happen in a given situation. For example, a smoker confronted by evidence which links smoking to cancer may react in several ways: he may quit smoking; he may reject the evidence as being only coincidental; or he may justify the discrepancy in some other way, as in the earlier example. Festinger himself initially suggested that we tend to ignore information which creates conflict, but this phenomenon (called "selective exposure") seems to be less widespread than Festinger believed.

A second issue concerns how widespread dissonance reactions are in daily life. The evidence suggests that not all conflicts produce dissonance. For instance, a person *forced* to do something inconsistent with their beliefs will usually not experience dissonance. (This may explain why the people paid $10 for the boring experiment felt no dissonance about taking part—the money could be seen as the factor "forcing" them to take part.) Generally, dissonance is most likely to occur when someone *voluntarily* does something which is inconsistent with how they like to view themself. (Thus, the people who did the boring experiment without pay experienced dissonance.)

Whatever the outcome of these issues, Festinger's theory shows the influence of the cognitive approach both in name and in substance. As a theory of social behaviour, it clearly states that mediating processes are important in understanding people's actions. The stimulus situation alone is insufficient; rather, one must consider internal processes represented by "attitudes" and "dissonance reduction." In many ways, these terms are parallel to "mental maps" and "insight" in the area of learning. The cognitive approach plays an important role in understanding social behaviour.

Emotions and Attribution Theory

Another area where the cognitive viewpoint has had impact is the study of emotions. At first glance this may seem contradictory, because we tend to think of "cognitive" as meaning "logical," and emotions as being "irrational." However this paradox is only superficial. The study of emotions has revealed that emotions are not purely physical, but in fact involve a significant cognitive component. The basis of this lies in what is called *attribution theory*.

Attribution theory, in general, deals with how we account for our behaviour, especially in terms of internal (e.g., physiological) vs. external (e.g., social) factors. The cognitive processes involved provide the basis for how people understand any experience. This viewpoint originated with Fritz Heider, an early Gestalt psychologist who was particularly interested in social behaviour. Today, attribution theory is used in understanding emotional behaviour, as well as in social psychology.

We are all aware of the varied nature of our emotions. Fear, anger, depression, joy, and excitement are part of everyone's experience. Yet understanding where emotions come from, and how we label them, is a more difficult matter. In part, we know that emotions are based on physiological conditions, such as changes in heart rate, breathing, and blood pressure. These changes, which are referred to as changes in physiological *arousal*, are easy to recognize subjectively, at least in extremes. But it is not clear that changes in arousal can account for the *variety* of emotions we experience. For example, try listing some of the physiological changes you experience when you're very angry and when you're very happy. If you think carefully, you'll probably find a great deal of overlap in the two cases. It is this problem that has led to examining the role of cognitive factors in emotional response.

Strong evidence for a cognitive influence comes from a study by Stanley Schachter and Jerome Singer in 1962. Schachter and Singer used injections of adrenaline to create physiological arousal in their volunteers, who thought the experiment concerned the effects of vitamin C on vision. (Adrenaline production is part of our normal response to stress or emergencies.) Some people were correctly told what to expect (e.g., increased heart rate), some were given no information, and others were misinformed (told to expect numbness, itching, and headaches). Each person, after being given the injection, was asked to wait in another room, with a fellow "volunteer." The other person was actually a confederate of the experimenter.

The results of this procedure were enlightening. Those volunteers given correct information about the injection did experience arousal, but attributed it to the drug, and felt no emotion. Thus, arousal alone did not produce emotion. (A control group given saline injections felt no arousal, and also no emotion. This indicates arousal is necessary, but not sufficient, to feel emotion.) Those who had been given either no information or false information *also* felt aroused by the drug, but did not suspect the drug was the cause. As a result, they tended to look at their situation for clues to their state. Depending on the behaviour of the confederate in the room, who sometimes acted happy and sometimes angry, they experienced either euphoria or anger. Thus, the drug created the arousal, but the subject's *interpretation of the situation* determined the type of emotion they felt. According to Schachter and Singer, when we lack an appropriate internal explanation of our arousal, we will attribute it to an external cause, which we label as emotion-provoking.

In everyday terms, this attribution theory of emotion has numerous applications. For example, a driver who has a near accident may experience a strong degree of arousal. In coping with the emergency, the physical changes are ignored. Later, the person may feel tense and irritable. Not recalling the previous crisis, he attributes these feelings to something in the immediate situation, such as, "Gee, my job's really getting to me today."

In a different approach pioneered by Stuart Valins, male subjects were shown pictures of nude girls taken from *Playboy*, while listening to what was supposedly their own heart beat. Actually, the heart beats were a tape recording, prearranged so that for half the pictures heart beats were faster than for the other half. The volunteers consistently rated more positively those pictures associated with a faster heart beat. Confronted with evidence of seemingly greater arousal, they interpreted it as meaning they liked those pictures more. Interestingly, this cognitive factor was so strong that the men persisted in their ratings even after it was explained that the heart beats were fake! More speculatively, Elaine Walster and Ellen Berscheid have

suggested that *any* type of arousal, positive or negative, can be interpreted as love. This would explain, they say, why hostages sometimes fall in love with their captors, or people in distress with their
rescuers. As they put it, "Adrenaline makes the heart grow fonder."

Attribution theory suggests that cognitive factors play an important role in our emotions. There is considerable evidence to support
this view. However, attribution alone cannot account for *all* of
emotional behaviour. By itself, it cannot account for the occurrence of
arousal, or the relation between degree of arousal and the intensity of
our feelings. But, through attribution theory the cognitive approach
has had an impact even in such an "illogical" area as the emotions.

SUMMARY

The cognitive approach emphasizes the role of mediational processes
in human behaviour. These internal processes affect behaviour at
several levels, including (a) learning and storing facts (b) solving
problems and communicating with others, and (c) maintaining self-
consistency and defining one's feelings.

The central assumption—that behaviour can best be understood
by looking at the processes that come between stimulus and
response—can be seen in all of these areas. Mediating processes
apply to both the integrating of new experiences, and the changing of
one's behaviour to fit. The cognitive approach also offers practical
insights, as in how to make remembering and problem solving more
effective.

No other approach to psychology considers thinking processes in
quite the same way as the cognitive approach. Some psychologists,
like the behaviourists, ignore thinking processes, while others accept
the existence of thought without examining its nature. One example
is psychoanalysis. Freud's theory, despite emphasizing basic drives,
would be empty were it not for the significance he gave to verbal
behaviour ("Freudian slips"), and to the symbolic meanings of all
actions. Yet, while he acknowledged the existence of thinking and
symbols, he never focussed on the processes involved in our *capacity*
to use such symbols.

At the same time, unsolved problems exist for cognitive
researchers. For one, there is still a great deal of integration to do.
While it is conceded that problem solving, cognitive dissonance and
emotion all involve mediational processes, the descriptions used tend
to vary in each area. They are all "cognitive theories," but as yet there
is no *single* cognitive theory which links all these areas in a coherent,
yet specific, manner. One can talk about "operant conditioning" and

the terms used remain the same, no matter what the topic, but this is currently not true of the cognitive approach. As noted at the beginning of the chapter, this may be due, in part, to the lack of a single important theorist.

A second problem concerns the use of the information-processing metaphor, particularly in memory and problem solving. This metaphor is borrowed from computer science, with terms like input, storage, and retrieval of information being used. With respect to these tasks, computers are infallible: errors are always the result of either human mistakes in programming, or equipment failures. Yet humans *do* make mistakes, even within these terms. People forget; computers don't. People sometimes ignore available information; computers cannot ignore information provided to them. People may rationalize to reduce dissonance; computers are always coldly logical. It is clear, then, that people are not identical to computers in their functioning, and the information-processing metaphor, however useful in some ways, is very limited in others.

Further, although we have considered a cognitive approach to emotions, there is not, as yet, an emotional approach to cognition. That is, the *motivation* for decisions and actions has usually been ignored. Although Kohler recognized that perception and learning can be influenced by a motivational state (for instance, being highly motivated can increase functional fixedness), this aspect has not been well-developed. By contrast, although Freud tended to minimize the details of cognitive processes, he *was* vividly aware that we are influenced by our emotional state.

It remains for the future to solve some of these issues, particularly in terms of creating a general theory of behaviour. In this sense, the cognitive approach is no more perfect as a means of understanding human behaviour than is any other approach. Over time, we try to increase our understanding. At one time, Descartes described human behaviour as being like that of hydraulically operated marionettes. Today, we speak in the language of computers, but look beyond it. It seems the metaphors change, the questions remain. It is characteristic of human behaviour that we seek to understand the world, including our own actions. And it is characteristic of the cognitive approach that we will continue to ask *how* it is that we understand.

Further Readings

The background of the cognitive approach can be seen first hand in Kohler's *Gestalt Psychology,* available as a Mentor paperback.

For some insights into memory, Donald Norman's *Memory and Attention* is a readable book which makes extensive use of excerpts from original sources.

Luria's *The Mind of a Mnemonist* presents the story of a man with one of the most unusual memories ever recorded—not only did he have perfect recall, but also synesthesia (cross-wiring of the senses).

For a look at memory through the eyes of a professional mnemonist, see Lorayne and Lucas, *The Memory Book.*

Linden's *Apes, Men, and Language* is a Pelican paperback which gives both a highly readable account of studies of language learning by chimps, but also deals with the philosophical issues these studies raise.

Walster and Berscheid's "Adrenalin makes the heart grow fonder" presents an interesting account of how cognitive theory is applied in studying emotions like love.

6

THE PSYCHOANALYTIC APPROACH
Gordon R. Emslie

Editor's Preface

Of all the psychological approaches, the psychoanalytic theories pioneered by Sigmund Freud have had the greatest impact on the lay mind. When television networks defend violent programs by suggesting that watching dramatized aggression makes it less likely people will aggress in real life, we are hearing a direct Freudian postulate. When novelists present us with five unpunctuated pages, representing the thoughts running through the head of a major character, we are witnessing a variation of Freud's free-association technique. When your neighbour accuses you of forgetting to return his borrowed screwdriver because you harbour unconscious hostile feelings towards him, he is using a Freudian analysis. When we speak about acting "unconsciously," "repressing our feelings," or having a "fixation" about something, we are using psychoanalytical terminology. The fact that we often use Freudian terms and concepts without being aware of it is perfectly appropriate, for if one were to single out the major contribution of Freud, it would be his discovery of unconscious motivations.

It is ironical that Freudian thought should have made such a profound impression on the lay world, for psychoanalysis has come in for more harsh criticism and outright rejection from psychologists than any of the other approaches presented in this book. The reason is that many aspects of the theory are difficult to test. Some Freudian postulates that are testable, such as the notion that viewing dramatized violence reduces one's own tendencies towards aggression, have failed the experimental acid bath. Nevertheless, even the most rabid anti-Freudian psychologists sometimes find themselves using concepts that are curiously similar to psychoanalytical notions—perhaps they are unconsciously using Freud. And when it comes to explaining man's irrational actions, nobody has developed a more comprehensive scheme than the psychoanalysts. The cognitive theorists might have cornered the market in explaining man's more rational behaviours and thought processes; when it comes to man's irrationality, Freud is still pre-eminent.

THE PSYCHOANALYTIC APPROACH

Let us journey back to the 1880s and imagine the task of a psychiatrist in the Victorian age. Science had been making huge advances, and people felt a breakthrough was imminent which would solve the puzzle of human behaviour. Sigmund Freud, a young physician trained in the prestigious medical schools of Vienna, shared this belief. But the best medical training seemed no match for the phobias (excessive fears), obsessions (recurring thoughts), compulsions (involuntary repetitious actions) and conversion hysterias (physical complaints that have psychological causes) that made life miserable for psychiatric patients. Whereas science was rational and systematic, neurotic behaviour seemed senseless and self-defeating. The laws of the physical world, it appeared, were not applicable to mental life. Nor was the new discipline of psychology much help.[1] Taking chemistry as a model, psychologists of the day attempted to reduce experience to its fundamental elements. But a chemical analysis of the body—50 per cent carbon, 20 per cent oxygen, 10 per cent hydrogen—does not tell one much about human beings. In the same way, the early analyses of the mind had little meaning for the practitioner who needed to know, not so much what the mind contained, but how it worked.

Freud was thrown upon his own resources. He began a careful analysis of his personal experiences, and of the case histories of his patients. The more he examined his evidence, the more it appeared to him that orderliness and logic in human behaviour were only thin veneers, covering something more basic and more primitive. The *real* key to human behaviour, Freud concluded, did not lie in conscious experiences. The key lay in a portion of the mind inaccessible to direct experience—the unconscious. Here, seething and irrational passions reign supreme. The newborn infant is completely at the mercy of unconscious passions. As he or she grows to adulthood, forces in the environment, particularly the parents and the institutions of society, "civilize the savage." Reason, sense and concern for others are grafted over the primitive, animal-like core.

INSTINCTS

To describe the passions inherent in this core, Freud used the term "Triebe," a German word usually equated with the English term "instincts." We should be careful in using this translation, however,

---

[1] Wilhelm Wundt, generally recognized as the "father of psychology," established the first psychology laboratory at Leipzig in 1879.

for when we think of an instinct, we usually imagine a very inflexible pattern of behaviour. Freud's "Triebe" are not so rigid (if instinctual behaviour could not be changed, society could hardly exert its civilizing influence). To make the point clear, Freud distinguishes four aspects of an instinct—its *source*, its *aim*, its *impetus*, and its *object*.

Source: Where do the instincts come from? In the first place, Freud assumes an inherited mechanism—the human nervous system is simply built that way. This provides the capacity for instinctual behaviour. But what translates this potential into action? We are familiar with the idea that food provides physical energy. Freud extends the notion to insist that *all* activity—mental as well as physical—is a product of body metabolism and, therefore, ultimately dependent upon our food intake. Specifically, the source of an instinct is body metabolism; the instinct itself is the mental representation of this activity.

Born in Moravia (now Czechoslovakia) in 1856, Sigmund Freud spent most of his life in Vienna. Upon graduation from the medical school there in 1881, he specialized in neurology and became a leading European authority on paralysis. In the 1890s Freud's attention turned increasingly to "psychoanalysis"—a term he first used in 1896. He attracted a group of very able colleagues, many of whom eventually broke with Freud to develop their own theories. Carl Jung (who contributed such notions as "the racial unconscious" and "middle-age crisis") and Alfred Adler (who discussed the "inferiority complex") are well-known examples. Freud's emphasis on sexuality so outraged Victorian society that he was subjected to much personal abuse. Even the medical and academic communities were slow in their acceptance. Despite his brilliance, it was not until 1919 that Freud was given the title "professor." Nevertheless, internationally, Freud's fame continued to grow and reached a peak in the 1920s and '30s. Just at this time, however, two other enemies—illness and antisemitism—became increasingly menacing. In 1923, Freud underwent the first of his thirty-three operations for cancer of the jaw. Pain and fear were to be constant companions for the rest of his life. As a Jew, the Nazis declared Freud an "enemy of the state." His books were publicly burned in the 1933 Berlin bonfire. When Germany invaded Austria in 1938, Freud was persuaded to leave for London. He died there a year later at the age of eighty-three.

Aim: If we must eat to stay alive, and if eating is the power source of the instincts, then it follows that we can never escape our instincts. Inevitably instinctual energy builds up within us, creating tension. When the tension becomes uncomfortable, the person is motivated to reduce it—an instinct, in fact, exists only to destroy itself! This may become clearer if you consider not an instinct, but another universal human experience, hunger. When you feel hungry, you become active. You raid the fridge, munch your favourite sandwich and feel better! Hunger makes you do something (eat) to eliminate your hunger. Later, when you feel thirsty, you drink. Thirst leads to activity which destroys thirst. Anger makes you blow off steam, until you're no longer angry. Tiredness leads to sleep, and you wake up refreshed. Life is the process of attending to this or that source of discomfort in an effort to return to an earlier, tension-free state of existence. Tension leads to action; action brings relief. Relief is temporary, however, because the body's metabolism continues to build up pressure and the cycle repeats. Unless we can break out from this cycle, the only way to be really free of instinctual pressure is to die. As Freud put it, "The goal of life is death." A less drastic "solution" might be to return to the kind of existence we enjoyed at the very beginnings of life, even before birth. There were few demands on us then, and needs that did arise were generally looked after by our mothers. According to Freud, this explains why much of our behaviour is characterized by a nostalgic regressive tendency— "back to the womb."[2] In all cases, the underlying motive, the aim of an instinct, is tension reduction.

The source and the aim of an instinct do not change. Flexibility in instinctual expression is provided by variations in impetus and object.

Impetus: By impetus, Freud means the strength or intensity of an instinct. Although he is not very specific, he would probably agree that individual differences in the strength of instincts may be inherited. More importantly, the motivational force of an instinct may vary from time to time in a given individual. If we did not notice any difference before and after expressing an instinct, the principle of tension reduction could not operate.

Object: The object of an instinct is the thing which will satisfy the person, that is, bring about tension reduction. Food is the object of

---

[2] Have you ever wondered, for example, why you curl up in bed (= fetal position?) or why floating in water (= amniotic fluid?) is pleasurable?

hunger. However, in psychoanalytic theory, the term "object" is used in a wider sense to mean all of the activity intervening between the arousal of the instinct and its satisfaction. The acts of getting up, going to the store, buying a hamburger and eating it, would all qualify as objects of the hunger drive. Since each of these steps can be performed in numerous ways, it is clear that the "object" may vary considerably from person to person.

Having examined the concept of instinct in general, we must now turn to a more specific discussion of the role of instincts in human behaviour.

Human Instincts

Freud proposes that every human is born with two fundamental instincts:
(a) a set of life-maintaining forces to which he applies the name *Eros*.[3]
    These include physiological needs such as those for food, water, air, etc. (necessary for survival of the individual) and the sex drive (necessary for survival of the species). The energy associated with the life instincts is termed *libido*.
(b) a set of opposing forces pushing towards aggression, destruction, and ultimately death. The term *Thanatos*[4] summarizes these.

It is important to note two points about this description of human nature: it makes no mention of social interest, of cooperation, of creativity, of morality or even of consciousness; and it specifically includes aggression. Taken together, these points suggest a basically self-interested animal, ill-equipped for living with other people.

If instinctual expression is inevitable, and if the instincts themselves are somewhat anti-social, how is it possible to avoid chaos? The answer lies in the fact that the *object* of an instinct can change. The engineer cannot eliminate a flooding river, but he may be able to protect society by digging drainage ditches. Similarly, society cannot put an end to human instincts, but it can offer suitable outlets so that neither the individual nor others are harmed.

To take an example: Eros and Thanatos build up tension within us. While we are alive, Eros (life instinct) is stronger than Thanatos (death instinct). But if outlets for aggression are consistently denied, there comes a point when destructive forces may take over and precipitate suicide. Rather than placing taboos on violence, therefore, society should provide "harmless" outlets. Let people blow off steam

---

[3] From the Greek god of love.
[4] Ancient Greek personification of death.

in socially approved orgies of aggression! Wars, fox hunting, parliamentary debates, and violent sports might all serve. Once basic control of instinctual expression is achieved, society can rechannel human nature in ever more desirable directions, to enhance rather than merely maintain life. For the individual in society, however, life is a compromise between our own self-interest and the self-interests of those around us. Since we all begin from a position of weakness (infancy) and are always outnumbered, we are forced on to the defensive. Instincts and society are both hard masters to serve, and conflict is inevitable. The story of life is the attempt to cope with the frustrations brought about by this conflict.

PERSONALITY STRUCTURE

We begin life, according to Freud, blissfully unaware of conflict. The newborn infant has no conception at all of the outside world or external reality. Its "personality" consists only of an *id*[5]—the name Freud gave to that part of personality structure[6] which houses instinctual urges. The id (and hence the infant) is illogical, amoral, and unconscious. It is unable to tolerate tension and is governed by the *pleasure principle;* as soon as instinctual energy builds up, the id functions in such a way as to relieve the tension. The goal of life at this point is self-indulgence, with immediate, maximal expression of the instincts.

The id has no contact with external realities, so it is not constrained in its search for gratification. However, because the id has no contact with reality, it is extremely limited in what it can do to relieve tension. In fact, the id has only two means of tension reduction: reflex activity and primary process thinking.

The first of these, *reflex activity*, is the simplest. Our physiology provides us with automatic reactions, rather like prewired circuits, which take care of minor irritations. Thus we blink to remove foreign matter from the eyes, sneeze to clear the nose and cough to clear the throat and lungs.

Primary process thinking is a more flexible mechanism for reducing tension. It consists of conjuring up an image of the object that will relieve the tension. A hungry infant, for example, might visualize its mother's breast.

---

[5] A Latin word, meaning "it."

[6] Personality structure is an abstract concept. There is no physical structure within the brain corresponding to personality structure. For example, the id is not a place or physical part of the brain.

Primary process is an unorganized, emotional form of imagination such as might be experienced in drowsiness or in hallucinations. It is the kind of wishful thinking you might engage in if you had just broken up with your boy or girl friend, husband or wife. In your daydreams you fantasize a reconciliation and "see" yourself living happily ever after; through primary process thinking you have regained the desired object. Whereas your sense of reality will bring you quickly back to earth, the newborn infant has no means of distinguishing between the image and the external object. If the tension is really to be reduced, therefore, some external agent, usually a parent, must intervene.

With repeated contact, the infant gradually becomes aware of the outside world. Some of the energy used by primary process thinking or by reflex action is devoted, instead, to the process of attending to external stimuli. A simple analogy will clarify this. Just as there are no images or representations of the world recorded in a fresh film in a camera, so the infant has no sense of reality. When the camera's shutter is opened, a representation of the world is recorded on the film. Similarly, as the infant makes contact with reality, a representation of the outside world is incorporated into its personality, constituting a second structure called the *ego*.[7]

As long as the personality consists only of an id, the infant is limited to a recurring series of instinctual urges, and has only the most elementary means of coping with them.

The emergence of the ego, or self-concept, allows the child to distinguish between internal and external stimuli. Not only can he tell the difference between fantasy and reality, but he can match the mental image with the real-life object and, eventually, with the means of achieving it. Since the basic motivation is pleasure, and since real-life objects do a better job of providing pleasure than mental images, more and more psychic energy is devoted to the external world. The principle by which the child lives is now maximal expression of the instincts without punishment; that is, expression in accord with the demands of reality or the *reality principle*. Since the process of ego development is a gradual one which continues throughout life, it is difficult and somewhat misleading to relate it to chronological age. As a working rule, however, ego differentiation is said to occur roughly between the fifteenth and thirtieth month of life. By the age of three, the child is aware that instinctual impulses may sometimes be frustrated. The desired object may not be readily available, parents are not always ready to drop everything to attend

---

[7] From the Latin word for "I."

to a child's needs, and instinctual expression is occasionally punished. The child, therefore, modifies his behaviour according to these external demands. But there is still no sense of morality at this point: no internal, self-imposed restraint, no guilt or shame.

These moral functions are properties of a third personality "structure" which emerges in the fourth year of life, the *superego*. Part of the reality attended to by the ego is the existence of the child's parents—who they are, what they do, and so on. But a significant portion of this reality consists of their telling the child what to do and what not to do. "Wash your hands," "Stay off the street," "Don't fight," "Be polite," etc. In doing this, they convey to the child their conception of society's set of values. The code of approved behaviours is incorporated as the *ego ideal*—what the ideal "you" should be like. Things you must not do, the "no-no's," are internalized as the *conscience*. Both ego ideal and conscience are sub-components of the superego.

The recently developed ego is still a fairly primitive thinker and the child is in no position to sift through and evaluate all these propositions. If a camera was an appropriate analogy for the ego, a tape-recorder is an analogy for the superego. The superego records messages and plays them back faithfully. The child takes what he or she is given and carries that "little voice of conscience" through life. In adulthood the mature ego might edit the tape, or add new tracks, but the basic message is beyond conscious control. With the emergence of the superego, the goal of life becomes maximal expression of the instincts, not only without punishment, but also without guilt. What the superego has added, then, is the *moral principle*.

Before leaving this section, the following points should be noted:

1. Terminology tends to become confusing: despite its name, the ego ideal is part of the superego and not of the ego; conscience is not predominantly conscious.

2. Although we are aware of the voice of conscience, the guidance of the superego falls below the threshold of consciousness. We are largely unaware of the origins of our ethical code; we may not know why untidiness upsets us, only that it does. Our intellect may tell us that divorce is a sensible solution to marital strife, yet our emotions may condemn it. Homosexuality between consenting adults may fit well with our respect for individual freedom, but still leave us feeling, "It's just not right."

3. Rational and moral standards often conflict because the ego, being conscious, continues to mature, while anything relegated to the

unconscious is cut off from further development. The ego reflects current social reality, while the superego tends to consist of a childish interpretation of the moral code of the previous generation.

4. It is convenient to speak of the conscious and the unconscious as though they are totally separate entities. In practice there is no sharp dividing line; there are many levels of consciousness, forming a continuum. Three levels are often distinguished:

Unconscious—contains material that is not accessible to present awareness. The material cannot be recalled by an exercise of will;

Preconscious—contains material that is not presently in awareness, but which can easily be made available or recalled at will;

Conscious—the level of present awareness.

PERSONALITY DYNAMICS

By the age of five, the typical child has acquired the three basic personality structures of Freudian theory. We shall now examine their interactions.

The dominant member is the id, the storehouse of the instincts. It is here that all energy originates. The ego and the superego "borrow" energy from the id in order to deal with the reality of the physical and social environment. The word "borrow" is used advisedly, since the major task of these junior personality components is to serve the needs of the id.

In practice, this means that the ego must balance the id's incessant demands for direct instinctual expression against the puritanical self-restraint of the superego. To do this, the ego uses up some of its borrowed energy. Other energies are used to extend the network of instinctual outlets to provide socially approved alternatives to blatant sexuality or aggression. The remainder of the ego's resources is employed to extend secondary process thinking.

Secondary process thinking involves realistic and logical trains of thought, embracing what in everyday language would be referred to simply as "thinking." Psychoanalysts broaden the definition to cover perceiving, remembering, abstracting, judging, and generalizing.

Despite all these higher mental abilities, Freudians paint a rather pessimistic picture of our capacity for self-understanding. The id is totally unconscious, and much of the superego is also beyond voluntary control. What we know of ourselves and what we mistakenly take to be our total personality is, in fact, a very small portion—the ego. Freud compared the situation to an iceberg which has 80 per cent of its mass below the surface. The ship's pilot who attends only to the tip of the iceberg is heading for trouble. A society which refuses to recognize humanity's irrational instincts is likewise in peril. For the individual, the goal of therapy is to extend the person's knowledge of his or her own personality; to make conscious what was once unconscious.

PSYCHOSEXUAL DEVELOPMENT

Having seen in overview how the ego and the superego become differentiated, we must return to infancy and examine the process of instinctual discharge in some detail.

The id, you will remember, houses the two instincts, Eros and Thanatos. Although these are actually conglomerations of desires, their major components are sex and aggression, respectively. If personality is dominated by the id, if sex and aggression are major constituents, if tension must be vented, then it follows that behaviour must reflect these basic tendencies. This is true even in the case of an infant, indeed, especially in the case of an infant, for the id is the sole personality structure at this stage in life.

Now if an infant is to express sexuality, it is obvious that it isn't going to do so in genital intercourse. Although sexual motivation is present throughout life, its experience and expression range over several body parts (erogenous zones) and various "love objects." According to Freudians, the individual progresses through five stages of *psychosexual development.* At each stage a different part of the body becomes the centre of attention and a different object the centre of attraction.

Oral stage

In the first stage, from birth to fifteen months (approximately), sexual feeling is located in the mouth and upper digestive tract. These areas are said to be "libidinized" (invested with sexual energy), in that the baby derives pleasure from taste, touch and movement in these areas. When a body part is sensitized in this way, the potential for tension is created. The object most directly capable of soothing oral arousal is the mother's nipple. Such an object, associated with instinctual attraction, is described as being "cathected." Feeding becomes much more than the simple fuelling of the body. It is the first means of sexual and aggressive expression; the child has a need for oral stimulation.

If this need is met by constant and immediate gratification, the child may come to the conclusion that life is easy, that he or she is the centre of the universe, and that everything in the world is there for the taking. This, according to Freudians, sets the stage for the selfish, optimistic and gullible personality in adulthood. If, on the other hand, oral needs are frequently unmet or unduly delayed, the child may get the idea that life outside the womb is painful. Such a child develops nostalgic, pessimistic character traits. In addition, he or she may resort to substitute activities, such as thumb-sucking or nail-biting.

If oral needs are neither over-indulged nor unduly frustrated (and Freudians offer little practical advice as to how this might be achieved), in about fifteen months the infant will progress to stage 2.

Anal stage

The second year of life sees the emergence of the ego, and the toddler begins to exert voluntary control over his actions. Recognizing this, the parents place increasing demands on the child. One of the most important of these is likely to be toilet training. These two forces, maturation of the nervous system and parental attention, bring about a shift in anatomical location of sexual feeling from the mouth to the anus and lower digestive tract.

Consider the position of the child. He experiences pleasure in having his bowels full and yet his parents urge him to destroy this sensation by using the toilet. When he does eliminate, he sees his very own creations, some of his first accomplishments, flushed away! Many a parent has found a child happily smearing faeces as if they were paints or playdough. Revulsion to body waste is learned later in life, and the two-year-old genuinely treasures his byproduct. From the child's point of view the parents' efforts to toilet train are likely to be seen as contempt for his creativity. The toddler has two options. He can either play Mom and Dad's game or resist. If the choice is to go along, the child accepts that faeces are dirty and incompatible with orderly living, learns that regularity is important, and that there is a time and a place for all things. Cleanliness takes on value. If unduly stressed, this learning lays the foundation for compulsive tidiness and excessive preoccupation with punctuality.

If the child chooses to resist, future development depends upon the reaction of the parents. Stern punishment will probably bring the rebel into line and propel him on to stage 3. The cost, however, may be bitter resentment. If the child could express his feelings they might be verbalized as, "Well, I'm beaten this time but I'm darned if it's going to happen again." He grows into an adult always looking over his shoulder for an authority figure who is about to steal from him. He becomes suspicious, quarrelsome and miserly.

Parents who give in to their child's reluctance to become toilet trained run a double risk. Firstly, they fail to convey the social value of tidiness and may see their child grow into an out-and-out slob. Secondly, by reducing external demands on the child, they may delay ego development and general psychological maturation. Once again, therefore, the trick is to achieve that elusive "happy medium."

Phallic Stage

With or without major battle scars, the child moves on. About the age of four, sexual sensitivity switches from the anus to the genital area and the single most crucial stage of psychosexual development begins. Although the term is strictly applicable only to males, this stage has become known as the phallic stage for both sexes. It should be carefully distinguished from the genital stage which is considered below.

To this point it has not been necessary to differentiate between male and female psychosexual development. In the phallic stage, however, the object toward which sexual desire is directed is the parent of the opposite sex, necessitating separate analyses for boys (Oedipal conflict) and girls (Electra conflict).

Oedipal Conflict[8]

With the new-found sensitivity of his genital region, the young boy is likely to manipulate these parts in much the same way as he played with his fingers at an earlier age. Even today parents are often dismayed to find their sons masturbating; in Victorian times, when Freud was writing, dismay was frequently accompanied by threats or physical punishment. The boy becomes aware that sexual arousal might be dangerous.

At the same time, Freud suggests, the boy feels primitive sexual attraction for his mother. This need not imply that the four-year-old has any concept of sexual intercourse, only that he desires close

---

[8] The term comes from a Greek legend in which Oedipus marries the widow of a man he had killed. Oedipus didn't know it at the time, but his victim and his bride were his own parents.

contact. The trouble is that Mom already has a steady boy friend, his father! In the boy's eyes, Dad monopolizes mother's attention, setting up an intense rivalry. At first, the child attempts to break up the cozy relationship by hanging on Mom's apron strings or even by squeezing into his parents' bed. Eventually, however, he becomes dimly aware that Dad is just too powerful a rival, and that victory in this love match is an impossible dream.

The positive feelings we may presume the child had for his father are now clouded by jealousy. "If only Dad were out of the way," he fantasizes. "But wait a minute. Dad would be furious if he knew about these thoughts of mine. He'd punish me for sure!" In the child's primitive logic, what is father likely to do? The child himself locates his sexual stirrings in the genital area. If Dad were to seek revenge, therefore, might he not direct his attack on the boy's penis? At this point the child is consumed by strong and conflicting passions: love for his father, who buys him toys and takes him fishing; hate for his father, who is a rival for mother's affections; respect for the father, who protects him from bullies; fear of the father, who might punish him; pleasure from genital stimulation; anxiety over the possibility (in the child's mind) of castration; mixed feelings toward his mother whom he adores, but who rejects him; aroused by sexual desire, yet frustrated in all his attempts to express it.

All this emotion but no realistic solution! What to do? Actually, there is nothing to do, for, according to Freud, the solution is achieved without the conscious participation of the child. All sources of tension are relegated to the unconscious by the mechanism of *repression*. Although the ego is largely conscious, there is a part of it— called the censor in earlier psychoanalytic writings—which functions to protect sanity, either by removing conflicts from awareness (repression proper) or by preventing their entering consciousness in the first place (primal repression). This is a sort of early warning system which is discussed in more detail in the section on defence mechanisms. At this point, we need note only the effects of repression:

—The child's resentful feeling toward his father are eliminated from consciousness. Ambivalence is removed, leaving the child with essentially positive attitudes toward the parent of the same sex.

—The child identifies with this idealized image and begins to copy his father's mannerisms and behaviour. In short, he adopts a masculine sex role. He also accepts his father's attitudes and moral standards, thereby strengthening superego development. Part of this fusion of roles is based on the concept of *identification with the aggressor:* "Dad isn't going to harm himself. If I am Dad, I have nothing to fear." (If you can't beat 'em, join 'em!")

—By identifying with the father, the child obtains indirect access to mother: "Dad is Mom's lover. I am Dad. Therefore I am Mom's lover."

—The act of repression merely moves material from a conscious to an unconscious plane. Repression does not eliminate the tension but it does separate it from its sexual object. The freed energy persists in the unconscious and is potentially available for rechanneling into alternative outlets. At the same time, repression is an active process, so every act of repression uses energy which might otherwise have been applied to ego or superego development. Overuse of repression, therefore, can weaken the person's contact with the external world.

—Repressed impulses involve instinctual desires which are not easily held in check. Just as a cork's buoyancy will force it back to the surface, so do repressed desires struggle to return to consciousness. It takes effort—a further drain on ego resources—to prevent this.

Before going on to discuss the plight of a female child in the phallic stage, we should note that the above sketch concerns the typical two-parent nuclear family. The absence of a parent, or some other anomaly in the family, requires reformulations beyond the scope of this chapter. In essence, the assumption is that a father or mother substitute will be found. A single mother's employer may be seen as a rival. If the mother is the missing parent, Oedipal attachment may be transferred to a teacher, aunt, grandmother, or other female figure.

Electra conflict[9]

For children of both sexes, the earliest emotional attachment is to the mother (the traditional soother of bodily needs). Around the age of four, the girl's genitals become sensitized and she finds pleasure in handling them. Her parents' disapproval of this behaviour convinces her that she is "bad." She then assumes that her lack of a penis is a direct consequence of her sinfulness. Whereas the boy merely fears castration, for the girl the dastardly deed has already been done! Now who would do such a thing? Mother, of course, since she must have

---

[9] In Greek mythology, Electra talked her brother into killing their mother.

found out about the little girl's lust for her father. Mom's own disfigured genitals show that she, too, has sinned and is capable of further wicked deeds. Clearly, Mother is no longer worthy of the girl's affection and she turns to Dad, half hoping that he can magically provide a new penis. This, of course, is out of the question. Since the girl's ego is unable to cope, repression steps in, banishing her feelings to the unconscious.

According to Freud, however, the emotional turmoil is so severe that even repression is unequal to the task. Enough of the passions are repressed to allow the girl to identify with her mother and adopt a feminine sex role, but some incestuous wishes linger on. The girl remains emotionally attached to her father, unconsciously motivated by "penis envy." This means that less of her sexual energy is freed for redirection. Less energy is devoted to personality development, and less is available for contributions to society. She becomes a second-class citizen. Understandably, this aspect of Freudian theory has been widely attacked. Why should the girl assume her penis has been cut off, instead of the boy imagining that his genitals are abnormal, swollen by a cancerous growth? Why is it necessary to argue for biological inferiority, when there is strong evidence that the second-class status of women rests on social exploitation through many generations? These and other related points are argued cogently in *Sexual Politics* (Millett, 1970).

Latency

Now on diverging paths, both the boy and the girl of five or six years enter a period of relative tranquility known as latency. Because of repression in the phallic stage, no body part is sensitized, and the child is not strongly attracted to any (conscious) love object. Eros and Thanatos continue to exist, however, and the need for periodic expression remains. The task during latency is to provide the personality with indirect and, preferably, socially approved methods of tension reduction. Many defence mechanisms are used at this stage, so discussion will be provided under that heading. In essence, latency is a saw-off between the repressive forces and the energy of banished impulses struggling to regain consciousness. This balance is maintained for six or seven years, until upset by the arrival of puberty.

Genital Stage

Two aspects of puberty combine to jolt the adolescent out of sexual dormancy. First, there is the release of hormones and the physiological upheaval of pubescence. This increases bodily metabolism, and strengthens instinctual impulses to the point where it is increasingly difficult to keep them in check. Secondly, there is mounting social pressure for recognition of one's sexuality. Some of the adolescent's peer group may have matured faster and already be exhibiting obvious secondary sex characteristics. The child's parents may begin to make sly remarks in her or his presence, "My she's quite the young woman!" or "Won't be long before Peter begins dating."

Upon the re-emergence of the sex drive, sensitivity is located where it was before the ravages of the phallic stage forced it underground, i.e., in the genital zone. However, as a result of the Oedipal and Electra situations, the mother or father is no longer the specific love object. The target now is the opposite sex in general. According to Freud, boys go off to seek a female companion, with the objective being mature genital sex. Girls resume their forlorn search for the lost penis. While most girls avoid incest, Freud contends that they will gravitate towards a father figure, and will approach true happiness only when they have mothered a male infant, thereby manufacturing a new penis for themselves.

FIXATION AND REGRESSION

This, then, is the normal progression for psychosexual development. While the rate of progress through the stages may vary from individual to individual, the sequence is fixed: the child must proceed in the order of oral, anal, phallic, latency, genital. It is not possible to skip a stage. It can happen, however, that the environment is not entirely suited to a child's needs. In fact, given the inherent conflict between self-interested innate desires and society's demands, some degree of frustration is inevitable. If the clash is serious, development may be sidetracked through fixation or regression.

Fixation

Fixation occurs when psychosexual development is arrested at some stage. If the child is deprived of oral gratification, for example, he may be inclined to prolong this stage in order to make up for lost opportunities. If the child is over-indulged, on the other hand, he may find oral stimulation so pleasant, that he again becomes reluctant to move ahead. Similarly, if the child has permissive parents, fantasies and primitive sexual behaviours will be given full rein. This may bring about a fixation at the phallic stage. With puberty, sexual desire reawakens and the familiar round of dating and sexual experimentation begins. Should any of these experiences prove frustrating, the adolescent is likely to revert to earlier, trouble-free sources of gratification. There may be, for example, regression to the oral stage, with overeating, or regression to the phallic stage, and masturbation. Since none of us is blessed with perfect parents and ideal environments, the path of our development is strewn with frustrations. These are reflected in our adult behaviour as partial fixations or partial regressions. Why is it so difficult to stop smoking?[10] And when we do, why do we often overeat or chew gum? Freudians point out that smoking is a sucking activity. In childhood we did not receive the oral gratification we needed. Smoking provides the means whereby we remedy this childhood deprivation. If we deny ourselves this activity, substitute oral stimulation will be sought: chewing, drinking, nail biting, or even excessive use of the vocal cords. The slick-talking salesman, the college lecturer, the politician or the broadcaster might well ask him/herself what prompted that particular choice of profession!

Partial anal fixations are presumed to result in miserly, tight-fisted personalities. A Scotsman (such as the author is by birth) needs no reminding of the anal stereotype! Another legacy of this stage is an unconscious wish to smear and manipulate the faeces. Fulfillment might be achieved by occupational choices in which mixing or moulding is prominent: chemist, cook, artist, and sculptor are obvious examples.

The phallic stage is characterized by preoccupation with one's own body and craving for the parent of the opposite sex. As in other stages, deprivation or over-indulgence may intensify these feelings so that the phallic personality tends to be excessively self-centred. Since Oedipal or Electra conflicts are incompletely resolved, sex-role identity is often insecure. This may lead either to homosexuality, or to excessive shows of masculinity or femininity. Sexuality is exaggerated, but in a shallow way: the person fixated at the phallic stage exploits people and avoids deep inter-personal relationships. Phallic occupational choices range from authorship of erotic literature (which gives access to sexuality without having to cope with people), to surgery. The latter provides a socially approved and valuable outlet for unconscious aggression toward the parent. In Freud's view, the male surgeon symbolically castrates his father while benefiting his patient. Through her control of the patient's body, the female surgeon gains symbolic access to the penis (if the patient is male). If the patient is female, the cutting movements may provide unconscious revenge against the surgeon's mother.

---

[10] Despite suffering from cancer of the mouth, Freud smoked twenty cigars a day.

Latency is usually considered as a resting phase between stages. If fixations and regressions to this level occur, they would involve non-sexual aggressive expressions of the instincts. Thus, the scientist might direct energy away from sexual conquests and into intellectual struggles. The philanthropist fights for a charitable cause, rather than fighting a physical battle.

The examples in this discussion of partial fixations and regressions have been chosen to illustrate three basic tenets of the psychoanalytic position:

—That behaviour is not random; many of our adult habits (including occupational choice) have a meaning that can be traced back to childhood;

—That conscious experience is not always a reliable guide to underlying motivation; the surgeon genuinely desires to alleviate suffering and is completely unaware of any aggressive intent;

—That even the best in human behaviour is rooted in the worst; high cultural achievements are derivatives of selfish instincts.

The last point should make it clear that there is nothing necessarily wrong about having partial fixations or regressions—we all have them, and in some cases they may lead to highly socially desirable behaviours.

DEFENCE MECHANISMS

The Concept of Defence

We have seen how instinctual energy is redistributed to provide for ego and superego development and for growth through the psycho-sexual stages. We have seen, too, how frustration and conflict are inevitable consequences of the personality/society relationship. In this section, we shall consider the personality's resources in coping with stress.

In the late 1940s and '50s, a series of experiments tested perception by projecting words very briefly (for fractions of a second) on a screen. The duration of the exposure was gradually increased from trial to trial until the subject was able to identify the word correctly. One study in this series used a group of socially taboo words (such as "whore," "bitch," "penis") and a group of neutral, acceptable words (like "apple," "river," "glass"). (McGinnies, 1949) While observing the presentations, subjects were connected to a psychogalvanometer, a machine which measures the electrical conductivity of the skin and records changes. The assumption is that when a person is emotionally aroused, he perspires. The perspiration decreases the resistance between two electrodes placed on his skin and causes a marked fluctuation in the record. For all of the subjects, taboo words required longer exposure than neutral words for correct identification. The interesting feature of the study, however, was the finding that the emotional reaction to the critical words (as shown by the psychogalvanometer record) occurred *before* the conscious reaction (as shown by the subject's verbal report). The taboo words, it seemed, aroused anxiety in the subject and this anxiety in turn brought about a delay in conscious recognition of the stimulus. Subsequent studies have investigated the possibility that factors such as the relative unfamiliarity of the taboo words (as compared to the neutral words) or the reluctance of the subjects to utter obscenities may have accounted for the results. Although there are those who disagree, the general conclusion is that these refinements have not substantially altered the picture. It is a long way from this type of laboratory demonstration to the complex defence mechanisms of psychoanalytic theory. Nevertheless, evidence such as this makes the concept of unconscious defences at least tenable.

Sources of Anxiety

But what is being defended? What is being defended against? Why? What is doing the defending?

Defence mechanisms exist to protect the person's sanity, his rational, conscious being. What is being defended, therefore, is the ego. The ego provides the personality's contact with an environment that is not always friendly. When a threat to well-being is perceived, the resulting anxiety acts as a warning system to trigger defences. If the threat is a real, external danger, this response is defined as *reality anxiety*.

In other cases, the threat may come from an internal source. Whereas the id constantly urges immediate instinctual discharge, the puritanical superego preaches restraint. If both "messages" were allowed to penetrate consciousness, the clash of irresistible force and immovable object would be tumultuous!

Were the id to win, the person might be catapulted into irresponsible actions which would be severely punished by society. Tension caused by fear that the instincts will get out of control is defined as *neurotic anxiety*.

If the superego should emerge victorious, behaviour might grind to a halt since, to the infantile conscience, practically all instinctual expression is disgraceful. Guilt which occurs when a person does something, or even thinks of doing something offensive to the superego, is defined as *moral anxiety*.

The ego enlists the aid of defence mechanisms to fend off one or other of these onslaughts. Occasionally, one force might be denied outright and the other allowed free expression. More typically, a compromise is reached providing indirect instinctual release; id impulses slip through in disguise, as it were. It should be apparent from the foregoing that the defender is none other than the ego itself. But since the main purpose of the subterfuge is to preserve one's self-image of rationality, it would hardly do for the conscious mind to become aware of these manoeuvres. The defence mechanisms are a property of the unconscious ego component referred to previously as the censor.

In summary, a successful defence has the following characteristics:

1. It is unconscious so that the person is not aware of what is taking place;
2. It allows indirect instinctual discharge;
3. By providing this outlet, it reduces the anxiety which comes with instinctual expression;
4. Since indirect expression is disguised expression, the defence avoids offending the superego; guilt is reduced and self-esteem maintained or increased.

Specific Defence Mechanisms

Nearly twenty defence mechanisms, not all clearly distinguishable from each other, have been identified. Because of overlap, classification is of limited value and a simple alphabetical listing is given below. Nevertheless, a few important distinctions may be noted:

1. Some defences, such as *repression*, offer an outright block to instinctual expression, while others, such as *compensation*, provide for distorted or substitute discharge;
2. Some defences, e.g., *fantasy*, allow only for imaginary expression, while others, e.g., *rationalization*, permit the impulse to be acted out in reality, though the motivation is disguised;
3. Some defences may be distinguished in terms of their social value. *Displacement*, for example, merely diverts the impulse, whereas *sublimation* diverts it in socially beneficial directions;
4. Defences may also be classified in terms of their psychological maturity. *Denial*, for example, is considered to be learned

during the oral psychosexual stage, and it is a more primitive mechanism than *atonement*, which is an anal defence.

Whatever scheme is adopted, it is important to avoid thinking of defences as inevitably bad. They are detrimental in the sense that they deny or distort reality. But they are also necessary and of benefit to the individual and to society if used in moderation. This happens because indirect release through the defences is also incomplete release. If you are sexually frustrated, an hour or so with *Playboy* or *Playgirl* magazine may douse the fires somewhat, but it's hardly likely to be as fulfilling as the real thing. The use of defences always leaves a little surplus tension in the system. In optimal circumstances, this surplus is used to promote personality development in the individual and cultural growth in society.

Atonement: reduction of guilt arising from a previous act, by performing a good or socially approved deed, e.g., an unfaithful husband buys his wife a dozen roses.

In atonement (sometimes called *undoing*), some positive action is taken which is the opposite of a prior misdemeanor. Since defences are unconscious, they are not always logical. The original wrongdoing may be imaginary, and the remedy may be corrective only in a heavily symbolic or magical way. Many neurotic compulsions involve this process of two opposing actions. A woman might be compelled to utter obscenities (the "crime"), for example, and then clasp her hand over her mouth as if to force back the words (the "remedy").

Compensation: anxiety about one area of behaviour is balanced by achievement in another, e.g., Napoleon seeks political power to compensate for inferiority feelings resulting from his small physical stature.

Alfred Adler, one of Freud's early disciples, concluded that physical shortcomings and dependency on adults leave every child with a sense of inferiority. Often this simply makes the child try harder. But if there is very little chance of succeeding, no matter how hard he tries, the child may switch his attention to another field in which he can excel. Bernard Shaw put it neatly if somewhat facetiously, "Those who can, do; those who can't teach!"

Less adaptive compensations are found in the delusions of grandeur of some paranoid patients. If you don't like being who you are, then make up for it by "being" Julius Caesar, or Joan of Arc, or Mick Jagger, or whoever can compensate for your weaknesses (see *identification* below).

Denial: protecting oneself from painful reality by an unconscious refusal to recognize anxiety-provoking elements, e.g., a possessive husband believes his adulterous wife has always been faithful.

Denial is one of the first defences to be erected. The developing ego soon learns that the outside world is not entirely friendly. When a goal is blocked, the pleasure principle is frustrated. The id resorts to primary process thinking, wishful thinking, in an attempt to blot out the unpleasant experience. As the ego matures and the reality principle strengthens, wholesale falsification becomes less manageable. However, the tendency to deny persists into later life. A man may deny that his early morning cough has anything to do with his smoking habits. A mother, refusing to admit that her son is dead, keeps his room tidy "for the day Johnny comes home." A soldier laughs and jokes before going into battle, denying his fear.

In stressful situations, denial is a common reaction, but since it requires blatant distortion of reality, habitual use of this mechanism is generally considered maladaptive. An extreme form is seen in cases of amnesia, or loss of memory. When a person has so many troubles that life is unbearable, one solution is simply to deny one's identity. If I am no longer Charlie Brown, born loser, then I no longer have to cope with his problems.

In hysterical disorders, denial may apply to parts of the body. Control of the senses or of the muscle groups may be lost even though no physical injury has been suffered. A mother might develop hysterical blindness as a defence against seeing her daughter's illegitimate pregnancy. A student might avoid an examination failure by developing writer's cramp. In either case, the person is as handicapped as if neurological damage were actually present.

Another instance of emotional shock producing physical consequences is fainting, where loss of consciousness provides an escape from an intolerable experience.

Displacement: transferring feelings or actions from their original target to another object that arouses less anxiety, e.g., a potential murderer takes his aggression out on small animals.

In displacement, id impulses are redirected from their original target to substitute persons, objects or activities. The switch is made because the preferred outlet is either inaccessible or threatening.

An example of an unattainable goal leading to displacement is the childless woman who copes with her desire for a baby by transferring her affections to a lap dog.

Scapegoating, or picking on an innocent person, is a familiar example of displacement in the face of threat. Consider the worker who is unjustly criticized by his employer. Since he cannot trade insults with his boss and still keep his job, he apologizes and meekly withdraws. Inwardly he is seething, and he takes it out on his assistant. The assistant, in turn, goes home to scold his daughter. The daughter beats up her brother, the brother kicks the cat, and some poor mouse meets an early death! Each individual in the chain has displaced anger from the target to a substitute object.

In clinical psychology, the displacement mechanism is often used to explain phobias. Repressed Oedipal fear of the father, for example, might be displaced on to penis-like or castration-symbolic objects. Freud reported the case of "Little Hans," in which he interpreted a phobia about being bitten by horses as expressing Hans's displaced fear that his father might castrate him. The boy couldn't bring himself to recognize aggression in his father, and saw it instead in the innocent horse.

The common phobia of snakes is interpreted by many analysts as representing a boy's displaced fear of his father's penis. For girls, the phobia is seen as a cover-up for actual attraction: if the snake is the penis, what better disguise for penis (snake) envy than apparent revulsion? In the girl's case, not only is the object of the impulse displaced, but the impulse itself is transformed. This additional element is the basis of another defence, *reaction formation*, considered below.

Fantasy: imaginary expression of an impulse, e.g., a frustrated bachelor daydreams of sexual conquests.

You will remember that the id responds to instinctual urging by conjuring up an image of the desired object. If the ego cannot provide real-life gratification, the personality may revert to this primitive form of wish fulfillment. Starving people fantasize about sumptuous feasts; the lonely child invents an imaginary companion; the employee, who was humiliated by his boss, daydreams about what he might have said.

Like denial, fantasy is a common and harmless initial reaction to frustration. But time spent in fantasy is time out from the real world, and can be overdone.

Fixation: arrestment of libido in a pre-genital phase of development, e.g., a twenty-five-year-old man craves his mother's attention, and is not interested in other women.

Fixation allows a person to conceal his or her sexual impulses by substituting behaviours that provide sexual satisfaction in pre-genital stages for the heterosexual intercourse of the mature, genital stage. Thumb-sucking is a common sexual outlet for the infant in the oral psychosexual stage. A fixated adult may continue to suck his thumb, as a means of achieving sexual satisfaction in a manner that is not obviously sexual.

An *absolute fixation* implies a level of immaturity beyond which the person has never progressed. Certain types of "perversion" may meet this criterion: for example, a transvestite may prolong his Oedipal attachment to his mother by dressing in women's clothing.

Partial fixations are more common. They involve occasional returns to pre-genital-stage behaviours, and were discussed in the section on psychosexual development.

Identification: equating one's ego with that of an admired or feared model, e.g., World War II concentration camp inmates sometimes copied the behaviours of their Nazi guards.

Identification with respected persons increases self-esteem because their admired traits become part of one's own personality (see *introjection* below). Movie stars and sports heroes are frequent targets for this process.

Identification with feared persons was discussed earlier with respect to the Oedipal and Electra situations. In this case, the identifier reduces his anxiety by "borrowing" his opponent's strength.

According to Freud, we all seek to aggress and indulge our sexuality, but are frequently frustrated. Fictional heroes, on the other hand, are not subject to the constraints of reality. Every time James Bond meets a beautiful woman, we meet that woman (or are that woman, as the case may be). When he slugs a hit-man, we are right up there punching away with him. By identifying with such figures, we act out, indirectly, and reduce the tension of instinctual desires.

Examples of exaggerated identification occur in some paranoid disorders when the patient incorporates not part, but all of the model's personality. His delusions of grandeur lead him to believe that he really is Christ, Napoleon, the Prime Minister or the President.

Intellectualization: masking anxiety-arousing feelings by discussing them in a detached, intellectual manner, e.g., a patient in psychoanalysis insists on discussing Freudian theory rather than its application to his personal emotions.

The person threatened by his inner feelings might, nevertheless, wish to explore them. One way to do this is to engage in academic study. Thus, a practitioner in one of the mental health professions might be motivated by an unconscious desire for personal understanding, as well as a wish to help others. Since the goals are not necessarily conflicting, this need not cause concern unless the camouflage breaks down. Unsuccessful operation of the intellectualization defence is suggested by the relatively high suicide rate among psychiatrists, as compared to other physicians. Of course, it is difficult to know whether the specialty attracted suicide-prone individuals in the first place (as intellectualization would require), or whether the emotional demands of the work made them suicidal.

In psychology, much recent work has investigated racial differences in intelligence. Critics of the genetic approach have argued that researchers in this field intellectualize their racial prejudice under the guise of scientific objectivity.

Introjection: adoption of the beliefs, attitudes and/or behaviour patterns of others, e.g., a teenager adopts her parents' attitudes toward pre-marital sex.

Introjection is part and parcel of identification. In using identification, the person not only imitates the model but also incorporates, or introjects, aspects of the model's personality into his own. The formation of the superego discussed earlier is a good example of this process. Introjections may appear as recurring depressive thoughts. For example, a child who has been told over and over again by her parents that she's "no good" may end up believing the message. The parental, "You're no good" is translated into, "I'm no good."

Isolation: separation of the cognitive and emotional components of an impulse so that thoughts and behaviour can be viewed in a detached manner, e.g., a scientist develops poisonous gases without allowing herself to consider what use might be made of her discoveries.

In isolation, the person loses track of the emotional significance of his actions. Threatening aspects of personality may also be isolated so that they appear to exist somewhere else outside the personality, e.g., a person's aggressive tendencies might appear as hallucinatory voices urging him to murder.

If the ego is unable to reconcile the conflicting demands of id and superego, it may isolate the two, splitting, to create two or more separate personalities. Hyde gives expression to the id instincts, while Jekyll reflects the socially approved modes of behaviour demanded by the superego. Documented case histories of multiple personality, however, are very rare.

Projection: attributing one's own undesirable traits to other people or agencies, e.g., an aggressive man accuses other people of being hostile.

Whereas elements from other personalities and external sources may be *intro*jected, negative aspects of oneself are frequently *pro*jected, that is, transferred from the ego to an outside target. This protects the ego by removing from consciousness any wishes, feelings or impulses that might result in punishment. At the same time, (mis)perceiving all these undesirable qualities in other people allows the person to boost self-esteem in a "holier than thou" attitude.

The defence is said to develop from early learning. During the oral stage the ego differentiates between edible and non-edible substances: the former are swallowed, the latter rejected. By analogy, the projective defence "spits out" threatening experiences and externalizes them as part of the environment.

The tendency to perceive internal impulses as external dangers is seen most clearly in paranoid delusions of persecution. The paranoid, who is seething with aggressive impulses, believes other people are trying to harm him. Instead of admitting that he hates his wife, a husband projects and believes she hates him. Not only does this free him from the guilt of having "terrible thoughts," but it also gives him an excuse for counterattack, that is, for expression of the very impulse defended against. "I killed her, Your Honour, because she was trying to poison me—I loved her dearly!"

Rationalization: devising apparently rational, socially approved reasons for one's behaviour (but not the real reasons), e.g., a violent man justifies a vicious attack on his child saying, "Punishment is good for children—they need to be taught discipline."

When we say, "I'll quit smoking as soon as I get that essay written," or "Just one more drink to steady the nerves," we indulge in a form of rationalization. To qualify as a genuine defence mechanism, of course, the self-deception would have to be unconscious.

In motivational terms, rationalization often takes the form of "sour grapes." The person wants something but, when he can't get it, he decides that he really didn't want it after all. The rejected lover protects his self-esteem by putting down the other person: "She's a tramp," "Plenty more fish in the sea," "Got along without her before I met her, going to get along without her now." The student who flunks an examination places the blame on an incompetent teacher.

> Psychiatrist: "Why is it that all your responses to the Rorschach ink blots involve sex?"
> Patient: "Don't blame me—it's you that keeps showing me these dirty pictures!"

Rationalization is involved in some cases of overly zealous behaviour. The person who is forever campaigning against pornography rationalizes that he must know what he's talking about. He

The tendency to project is so common that it forms the theoretical base for a number of *projective personality tests*. The subject is presented with ambiguous material and asked to describe what he sees. Since there is little or no structure in the stimulus, any details he does report must come from him. These projections are presumed to originate in the unconscious, and hence reveal hidden personality dynamics.

Two of the most widely known projective techniques are the *Rorschach Ink Blot Test* (Rorschach, 1942) and the *Thematic Apperception Test,* often called the TAT (Murray, 1938).

You can approximate the Rorschach cards by pouring a few drops of ink on a blank piece of paper and folding the page in half. The result will be a symmetrical pattern of ink (see Figure 1). If you scrutinize the blots you will begin to see faces, animals, objects, etc. The process is similar to seeing shapes in cloud formations.

In actual practice, a standard set of ink blots is used. The subject's responses are interpreted by comparing them with the responses of various groups, such as schizophrenics, criminals, or mature adults.

Figure 1
What Do You See?

People see all kinds of things in ink blot pictures. Look at the one above and tell me what it might be, what it could signify for you. There are no right or wrong answers, no other rules or regulations: everyone has his or her own ideas. (Task and instructions modelled on the Rorschach Ink Blot Test.)

The TAT consists of a set of cards portraying vague social situations[11], about which the person is asked to tell stories. What is happening in the picture? What led up to this situation? What are the people in the picture thinking? What are they feeling? What will the outcome be? Fantasy and identification, as well as projection, lead the subject to his own unique compsition.

The picture in Figure 2 is rather too structured to qualify as genuine projective material, but by showing it to your friends and asking for analysis you will obtain some evidence of individual differences. You may also encounter rationalization and denial when you explain that the "real" interpretation is two people walking across a football field with the moon coming up between the goal posts!

A modified version of the TAT has been found valuable in the business world. The person likely to succeed in business tends to tell stories emphasizing problem solving or achievement. For example, shown a picture of a man at a desk, he or she may say, "He's calculating the stress load on the bridge his company is building, and he's trying to decide which materials to use." To the same picture, another person may report that, "He's thinking about the party he's going to that evening." By projecting a social theme, the latter has shown that for him or her, affiliation (being with others) is a more important need than achievement.

Figure 2
What's Going on?
Make up a story about the situation shown in the picture above. What is happening? What led up to this situation? What are the people thinking? What are they feeling? What will the outcome be? (Task and instructions modelled on the Thematic Apperception Test.)

---

[11] One of the "pictures" is actually a blank card.

is free, therefore, to browse through the bluest and most erotic literature he can find—and all in the name of decency!

Reaction formation: disguising unconscious motivation by behaving in the opposite way, e.g., excessive protestations of love may indicate underlying hatred.

If nothing succeeds like success, then nothing hides like reaction formation. Hides, that is, from the user of the defence. Onlookers are less likely to be fooled, for reactive behaviour tends to be too animated, too exaggerated and too inflexible to be entirely believable. As Shakespeare put it, "The lady doth protest too much, methinks." The pornography crusader is an example. On a conscious level he genuinely detests the materials he encounters. The unconscious motivation, nevertheless, is attraction. Similarly, excessive politeness may cover up arrogance, bravado may hide fear, and abstinence conceal secret temptation.

Clinically, reaction formation is most clearly demonstrated in obsessive-compulsive disorders, where repetitive rituals prevent the release of opposing motives. The compulsive desk-tidier and lint-picker cannot be smearing (the unconscious anal impulse) as long as his entire waking hours are spent cleansing the environment. The hostile parent can hardly be accused of aggression while smothering the child in "love."

Regression: reversion, in the face of stress, to an earlier stage of development, e.g., an adult throws a temper tantrum when he doesn't get his own way.

Whenever a person meets frustration, there is a tendency to resort to earlier, tried and trusted methods of gratification. The troubled student may quit college to return home; the familiar is a defence against uncertainties. Threatened by a new arrival in the family, an older child might revert to bed-wetting in an attempt to regain the parental attention he feels has been stolen by the baby. Other illustrations of partial regressions were given in the discussion of psychosexual stages.

Only rarely are behaviours observed which might be described as complete regressions. One example is a form of schizophrenia known as catatonia. An adult may assume the fetal position, lose control of his bladder and bowels, and sit for hours thumb-sucking in the corner of the psychiatric ward.

Since the psychosexual stages form a hierarchy from least to most mature, the depth of pathology is usually gauged by the level of regression. Oral symptoms are more ominous than anal, anal more severe than phallic, and so on. Elements of fixation and regression are considered to be present in all forms of mental abnormality.

Repression: unconscious exclusion of memories, feelings, etc. from awareness, in order to prevent anxiety or guilt, e.g., a girl "forgets" she is no longer a virgin.

There are occasions when it is appropriate to hide one's true feelings, for example, when the person you are attracted to is happily married to someone else. If the decision to block an impulse is a conscious, deliberate one, you are using *suppression*. The defence mechanism, *repression*, on the other hand, is not under voluntary control. It has close ties with denial. Denial, however, involves unconscious exclusion of present events or future uncertainties, whereas repression is concerned mainly with inhibition of memories of past events.

Since repressed material continues to exist in the unconscious and constantly strives for expression, repression is not a once-and-for-all event. It requires ongoing expenditure of energy. If repression is the habitual response to stress, the person's emotional batteries may run down.

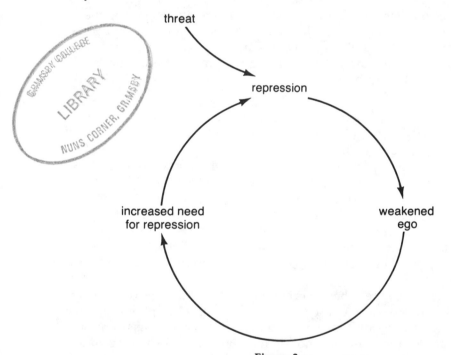

Figure 3
The Vicious Circle of Repression
Repression is an unconscious defence against threat. Like other defences, repression denies or distorts reality. This means that the ego's conception of the external world is inaccurate, and it is unable to cope with the demands of reality. The threatened personality is then forced to defend itself with additional rounds of repression, and the cycle repeats.

   Excessive repression drains the ego of its resources. Unable to cope with reality, the weakened ego enlists the support of additional defences. But these defences use up even more energy, and a vicious circle is begun which may culminate in the neurotic disorder known as neurasthenia, a condition characterized by complaints of chronic weakness, easy tiring and quick exhaustion.

Sublimation: acceptance of socially approved or useful substitute goals in place of those originally sought, e.g., an aggressive man becomes a boxing champion.

   In the general sense, sublimation may be taken to mean any defence which is socially tolerated and/or useful. Since the genital stage of psychosexual development represents ultimate maturity, the term sublimation should be reserved for rechanneling of pregenital impulses. Several examples have been given already in the occupational choices presented in the section on psychosexual development.

   Since, by definition, sublimation is adaptive, neurotic exaggerations do not occur. Freudians credit sublimation for our artistic, intellectual and social creations. Leonard da Vinci's painting of madonnas, for example, was interpreted by Freud as a sublimated expression of longing for reunion with his mother, from whom he was separated at an early age.

ADDITIONAL MECHANISMS OF TENSION RELEASE

While defences provide emotional safety valves, instinctual release through these mechanisms is incomplete. Surplus energy may appear in such behaviours as "Freudian" slips, dreams, and psychiatric symptoms. Each of these outlets involves the assumption of *psychic determinism,* the idea that mental events do not occur by chance. However random they may appear, thoughts and behaviour are meaningfully related to hidden, unconscious processes. Forgetting and dreaming are purposeful, not merely haphazard activities of the nervous system; there is a reason why a person develops one particular symptom of maladjustment rather than another.

Freudian slips

Repression involves an ongoing inhibition of material. The ego's censor acts as a kind of prison guard, whose job it is to keep undesirable citizens (instinctual impulses) away from the civilized community (consciousness). Since it is impossible for the guard to be constantly alert, he is fooled sometimes by prisoners who slip through in disguise. In the same way, periodic lapses in repression allow instinctual desires to escape in symbolic form. These appear as misperceptions, memory losses, mispronunciations, slips of the pen, and other apparent accidents. Engrossed in a detective novel, for example, you may betray your aggressive desires by reading "trying to rape" when, in fact, the print is "tying a rope." A defeated politician writes to "con*rat*ulate" his opponent. A child "forgets" to bring home a disappointing report card. Freudians maintain such events are "caused" and have meaning in the context of the individual's personality. Like the defences, they are adaptive in the sense that they provide a release of tension.

Dreams

In Freud's view, dreams provide innocent gratification of urges. As repression is relaxed during sleep, impulses slip through to emerge in fantasy. So that these are not recognized for the primitive wish-fulfillments that they are, a second line of defence, *dreamwork*, is invoked. Major dreamwork mechanisms include dramatization, displacement, condensation, and symbolization. Rationalization (secondary elaboration) and repression are also involved at a later stage.

Dramatization:

In this defence, internal conflicts are externalized in physical activity. Thus, the wish to overcome frustrations might result in a dream of flying under one's own power. The person who is troubled by feelings of guilt may dream of an assault on a besieged castle, rather than of "an attack of conscience."

Displacement:

In displacement, either the target or the motivation is altered. A boy may dream of a visit to the barber's as a dramatization of castration anxiety. The target is displaced from his penis to his hair. Similarly the motivation is displaced from an intention to castrate someone to clipping hair, an apparently friendly act.

Another form is displacement of emphasis, in which the real meaning of a dream is invested in some apparently obscure detail. A long, involved dream sequence concerning a South Seas frolic, for example, may contain a fleeting image of a policeman who turns out to represent the dreamer's father and associated Oedipal fantasies.

Condensation:

This mechanism is responsible for the fragmentary nature of dreams. Overlaps, gaps and bizarre transitions confuse the plot, as though the sentences in a story had been jumbled or randomly cut. A single dream symbol may stand for two or more ideas, persons or events. Conversely, a single idea may be represented by two or more symbols in the dream.

Symbolization:

All of the dreamwork mechanisms involve symbolism. Every image or action is symbolic of something else. Since, for Freud, dreams are "the royal road to the unconscious," the something else is Eros and Thanatos, sex and aggression. Both personal and universal symbols are used. As the name implies, personal symbols are related to an individual's unique life-circumstances. A favourite song may be particularly meaningful, for example, because it evokes memories of one's childhood or a first love. A girl whose father is a baseball fan might wonder why she dreams constantly about earthenware. (Earthenware——→jugs——→pitchers ——→baseball——→father.) Universal symbols are those recognized by a given culture, and shared by many people. The dove symbolizes peace, the crucifix symbolizes Christianity. For psychoanalysts, anything long and pointed is symbolic of the penis, or of a weapon; hollow objects and receptacles stand for the vagina, or a victim; any rhythmic or penetrative activity represents sexual intercourse or physical assault.

With a moment's thought, it will be appreciated that it is exceedingly difficult to avoid such symbols in your dreams. To take a vacation, you must pack your bags (fill the vagina); visualizing the Toronto skyline, you must gaze upon the CN Tower (the world's biggest penis); to visit a museum, you must first enter the building (have intercourse).

To Freud, of course, the fact that dreams have such a high frequency of sexual-aggressive imagery proves his point. The skeptic, on the other hand, argues that Freudians see what they want to see.

Dreams consist primarily of infantile wish fulfillments (primary process thinking). The purpose of dreamwork is to hide impulses from the conscious ego. Should dreamwork fail in its task, the dream would lay bare the raw emotions of the dreamer. Since this would provoke extreme anxiety, the personality protects itself by halting the dream in progress—we wake up in a cold sweat to discover that we have been having a nightmare. The anxiety we experience is a brief glimpse of the terror that would have confronted us had the dream been allowed to continue.

If a dream *is* followed to its conclusion and its disguise is found to be incomplete, the ego applies repression to remove the memory from consciousness. The person who claims to have no dreams is

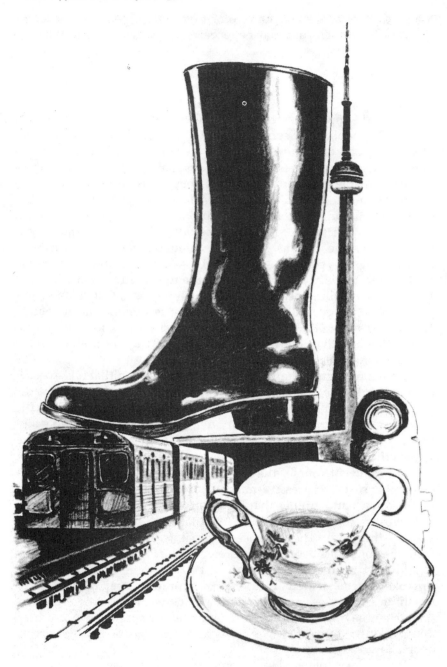

Figure 4
Some Sexy Pictures
You don't believe it? Then see the text!

mistaken; dreaming does occur but is forgotten (repressed). The dream cannot be made available for inspection for fear that the dreamer might see through his own disguise and come face to face with his innermost desires.[12]

In many cases a dream is remembered, but not without further distortion, caused by secondary elaboration.

Secondary elaboration:

The dream as actually experienced is a confused tangle of images. When recalled, however, it is usually more coherent. When the dreamer awakes, the ego uses secondary elaboration to rationalize the dream. Without the dreamer knowing it, sequences are re-arranged and elements added or omitted so that the dream "makes sense." It might well make sense to the conscious mind, but it's the wrong sense!

The Memory Lingers On . . . or Does It?
Try this simple test. Keep a pencil and writing pad by your bed and, as soon as you wake up, write down the details of your last dream. A few days later, without consulting your notebook in the meantime, jot down your recollection of the dream. Compare the two accounts. Which is more detailed? Which is more "rational?" Which parts were forgotten between the first and second recalls? Why did you forget those parts in particular?

Latent and manifest content:

By the time a dream is reported to an analyst the original message—referred to as the hidden or *latent* content of the dream—is thoroughly distorted. The interpreter's task is to sift through this symbolic morass—the apparent or *manifest* content—in an attempt to arrive at the true meaning. He does this by asking the person to freely associate to each element in the dream. No matter how stupid the associations may seem, the person is to say whatever comes into his head. Taking a fragment from a previous example, the person might

---

[12] Experimental evidence suggests that everyone does, indeed, dream every night. Whether forgetting is explained by repression in the Freudian sense, however, is a matter of controversy.

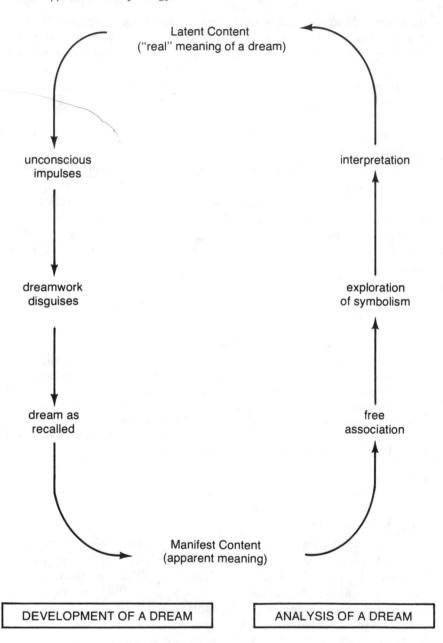

Latent Content
("real" meaning of a dream)

unconscious
impulses

interpretation

dreamwork
disguises

exploration
of symbolism

dream as
recalled

free
association

Manifest Content
(apparent meaning)

DEVELOPMENT OF A DREAM

ANALYSIS OF A DREAM

Figure 5
Freudian Theory of Dreams
See text for explanation.

be given the stimulus element, "policeman." An abbreviated and over-simplified train of thought might proceed as follows: policeman →pounding→ beat →heart beat→ heart throb →throb→rob →Robert Smith →Dad. If other association chains also converged upon the father, the analyst would feel justified in concluding that the dream has Oedipal overtones.

Free association, therefore, is not really "free" at all; it is constrained by the workings of the unconscious mind, by psychic determinism

Psychiatric Symptoms

In psychotherapy, the symbolism surrounding a patient's symptoms is explored. Stress or some recent misfortune may explain why a person has suffered a "nervous breakdown," but why is he depressed instead of violent, or hysterically deaf rather than blind? Why these specific symptoms, the analyst asks, and why at this particular time in this particular individual?

Neurosis, however unpleasant, always benefits the patient in some way (*secondary gain*). In general, symptoms demonstrate our helplessness and may force others to pay attention to us. With their help, our problems may be solved.

As exaggerated defences, symptoms also provide indirect expression for instinctual tensions. These outlets are maladaptive, but survive because temporary gain obscures long-term disadvantages. In elevator phobias, for example, the person may be inconvenienced, embarrassed in company, and fatigued by stair-climbing. But the behaviour is "sensible" to the extent that it keeps the individual out of contact with the feared object. The situation is crystalized in the story of the compulsive finger-snapper. Asked why he does this, he replies, "Because it keeps the tigers away." "But there are no tigers in Canada," exclaims the interviewer. "See—it works!" he retorts triumphantly.

According to Freud, symptoms are also meaningful in that they symbolize unconscious anxieties. For the phobic, elevators may represent menacing female genitals. For the compulsive, tigers may symbolize an aggressive mother. Other examples have been included in the discussion on defence mechanisms.

As in dreams, the important symbols are personal ones, and one should beware of a cookbook approach in which symbols are unequivocally related to interpretations. A tiger may mean one thing for one person (e.g., a football fan) and quite another for someone else (e.g., a zoologist). It is important, too, to appreciate that symbolization and motivation are unconscious. The neurotic is not "faking it," not knowingly attention-seeking and not aware that his behaviour may be "meaningful." The psychiatrist's job is to explore the symbolism so that the meaning of the neurosis can be interpreted to the sufferer. Once the patient has insight into the nature of his unconscious desires, there is less need for him to be on the defensive. Energy is restored to the ego and the person is once again equipped to deal rationally with the external world.[13]

SUMMARY

The purpose of this chapter has been to provide insight into the psychoanalytic perspective on behaviour. Presentation of the general approach has taken priority over discussion of details, revisions or elaborations. Emphasis has been placed on description, rather than analysis of psychoanalytic concepts. Evaluation is itself a complicated topic, which can be raised but scarcely probed.

To begin with, we should note that any personality theory sets out from philosophical assumptions about human nature. One could argue that our failure to end war proves humanity's inherent aggressiveness. But, since at any given time more countries are at peace than at war, it could also be argued that cooperation is the rule and aggression the exception. For the present, at least, such fundamental propositions are untestable. The theorist must simply state his convictions and explore their implications for human behaviour. The fact that a theorist might start from a different premise from our own should not be allowed to cloud our judgment. The test is how faithfully the relevant deductions have been made.

In a general sense, Freud meets this requirement. The assumption of powerful instincts leads logically to the search for evidence of these forces in everyday life. Freud replies with sexual-aggressive analyses of child behaviour, dreams, neurotic symptoms, accidents, and so on. Self-interest conflicts with public interest and demands defensive behaviour on the part of the individual. Psychoanalysts properly offer their lists of discrete mechanisms.

In more specific terms, however, Freud can be criticized on the grounds that his deductions are often too general. If your toilet training was harsh, a Freudian might predict that, as an adult, you will be compulsively tidy. But he would also say that you might indulge in a

---

[13] See Chapter 8 for a fuller discussion of psychotherapy.

reaction formation against cleanliness, and hence become an extremely messy individual. Several other examples could be given whereby Freudian theory can be made to predict widely divergent consequences from the "same" experiences. The theory does not specify clearly the conditions under which each outcome might arise. This means that it is much better at accounting for observed behaviour than it is at predicting events in advance. Freud, it has been said, explains everything while explaining nothing! The remedy lies, obviously, in more carefully stated reformulations and extensions of psychoanalytic principles.

Another criticism is that the theory is built upon the recollections of nineteenth-century, neurotic, Viennese women. As Freud himself was at pains to point out, memories are not always a faithful representation of what actually took place. In addition, data provided by mentally troubled patients might yield valuable insights into abnormal behaviour, yet have little bearing on healthy development; the psychology of women may not apply to the psychology of men; personality dynamics of nineteenth-century Europe may not be generalizable to twentieth-century America, Africa or Asia.

Finally, very little is known about the details of psychoanalytic sessions. We are given Freud's interpretations of the data, but no independent record of the patient's actual behaviour. The case study method is a relatively poorly controlled and subjective approach. To a large extent, acceptance of its findings is a matter of faith rather than proof. Believers argue that the richness of clinical insight is self-apparent; skeptics demand hard evidence, and controversy rages.

These limitations point to the need for further research and updating. In and of themselves they do not destroy the value of the theory, for while it might be desirable for hypotheses to be "right," it is by no means essential. One of the major contributions of a theory is to act as a stimulus for future research. By this token, psychoanalysis must be counted as a resounding success. Before Freud, recognition and systematic study of the unconscious was minimal; early development was of little interest since it was assumed that psychological processes were the same in children as in adults; sexual motivation was something to endure, but not to investigate. Many psychologists who would not call themselves Freudians have responded to the challenge, sometimes supporting psychoanalysis, sometimes refuting it, but always contributing to our knowledge. Much of this work would not have been undertaken had Freud not provided the impetus. Some of it arose in direct rivalry to psychoanalytic propositions. Freud's is a pessimistic view of the human situation. It emphasizes the unconscious, the irrational and the self-destructive. There is evidence aplenty for all of these characteristics in our behaviour. But is that all there is to us? Is there no cause for optimism? Many psychologists, especially those of the humanist persuasion (discussed in the following chapter), say, "Yes":

> "This point of view in no way denies the usual Freudian picture. But it does add to it and supplement it. To oversimplify the matter somewhat, it is as if Freud supplied to us the sick half of psychology and we must now fill it out with the healthy half. Perhaps this health psychology will give us more possibility for controlling and improving our lives and for making ourselves better people." (Maslow, 1968, p. 5)

Further Readings

Freud's major biography is *The Life and Work of Sigmund Freud* by his long-time colleague, Ernest Jones. Among more recent works dealing with Freud and his followers are Roazen's *Freud and his Followers,* and McGuire's *The Freud/Jung Letters: The Correspondence between Sigmund Freud and C. G. Jung. Passions of the Mind* by Irving Stone is a novel based on Freud's life.

For those interested in reading Freud's own works, J. Strachey's editing of *The Standard Edition of the Complete Psychological Works* is recommended.

Hall and Lindzey's text *Theories of Personality* gives standard text coverage, while Maddi's *Personality Theories: A Comparative Analysis* is particularly valuable in comparing and contrasting the various approaches. To extract full benefit, be sure to read Maddi's introduction for an explanation of the book's organization.

Paperback summaries of the psychoanalytic approach are available in Hall's *A Primer of Freudian Psychology* and Brown's *Freud and the Post-Freudians.* Nye's *Three Views of Man* briefly compares psychoanalysis with the humanistic and behavioural approaches.

More detailed discussions of psychoanalysis are given in Anna Freud's *The Ego and the Mechanisms of Defence* and Fenichel's *The Psychoanalytic Theory of Neurosis.* Freud's discussion of Little Hans and a re-analysis of the case from a behavioural perspective are reprinted in Southwell and Merbaum's *Personality: Readings in Theory and Research.*

Among the many applications of Freudian psychology have been Spector's *The Aesthetics of Freud: A Study in Psychoanalysis and Art,* Kaplan and Kloss's *The Unspoken Motive: A Guide to Psychoanalytic Literary Criticism* and Fromm's *Psychoanalysis and Religion.* Also of interest are the treatment of feminism by Mitchell in *Psychoanalysis and Feminism,* and politics in Johnston's *Freud and Political Thought.*

Psychoanalytic interpretations of several historical personalities are available including Erikson's *Young Man Luther* and *Ghandi's Truth.* Langer has written *The Mind of Adolf Hitler: The Secret Wartime Report.*

Recent attempts to examine psychoanalytic theory in the light of experimental evidence are found in *The Experimental Study of Freudian Theories* by Eysenck and Wilson and *The Scientific Credibility of Freud's Theories and Therapy* by Fisher and Greenberg.

7

THE HUMANISTIC APPROACH
John Medcof

Editor's Preface

Like psychoanalysis, humanistic psychology has often been panned by hard-nosed, experimentally oriented psychologists who accuse it of being fuzzy, literary and unscientific. This is not altogether a fair appraisal. The therapeutic techniques of Carl Rogers have been subjected to more experimental testing than most psychotherapeutic procedures; in fact some commentators have suggested that Rogerian therapy may be the only one of the "talkie" therapies (as distinct from therapeutic techniques that rely on drugs or contingent reward systems) that has a demonstrable, scientific basis. The resistance to the humanistic approach often centres on a reluctance amongst some psychologists to accept the humanistic concept of man's basically "good" nature. Very often the same psychologists who attack Freud for his pessimistic view of man's primitive, animal-like nature, are the ones who have the most difficulty accepting the diametrically opposed, optimistic, humanistic viewpoint.

This is not really surprising, for the hard-nosed behaviourist, psychobiologist or experimentally inclined cognitive theorist has difficulty with any theory that appears to be based on a notion about an innate, intrinsic nature of man. He is much more inclined to see behaviour as being the result of learning, inner states, or cognitive-processing strategems imposed on a plastic human being.

Humanistic psychology has had its greatest impact in the field of therapy. There it has exerted a profound influence in removing much of the mystery and the god-like aura of psychotherapists. It has humanized the attitudes and the approach of an entire generation of therapists.

THE HUMANISTIC APPROACH

For many years North American psychology was dominated by two major schools of thought. The psychoanalysts, with their view of instinctive, irrational man doomed to conflict, and the behaviourists, who saw man as a puppet, controlled by the strings of his environment. They vied with each other in their attempts to understand and explain human actions, emotions and thoughts. These great schools, with their sub-schools and splinter groups, were the two great forces of psychology. Then a third force appeared. It gathered strength in the fifties; it flowered in the sixties; it consolidated in the seventies: humanistic psychology. This viewpoint sees man not as a puppet, nor as driven by instincts, but as a growing, generous, healthy being in control of his own destiny.

Why had the humanistic movement taken so long in coming to psychology, and why did it finally have its impact when it did? The twentieth century saw a dramatic increase of material well-being in many parts of the world brought about by a succession of scientific advances. Science had become venerated. Behaviourism was an attempt to apply scientific methods to the study of humans. Success seemed inevitable; it was just a matter of time. It never occurred to many people that anything important about humans could be found by methods other than those of science. Humankind would advance by controlling and suppressing emotions and feeling, and by the pursuit of the scientific and rational. This was the spirit of the first half of the twentieth century. People in general, and psychologists as well, suscribed to it.

Then came the great recentering. Humanistic psychology contributed to and was sustained by the social turbulence of the sixties. It was a period that stressed anti-materialism, anti-war, anti-science and freedom for the individual. The philosophy of the third force was in harmony with the spirit of the decade. The humanistic movement grew dramatically and gained mass acceptance; its time had come.

In the seventies this evolving, experimenting movement began to consolidate and take stock of itself. What was valuable was retained; worthless fads were abandoned. Many psychologists adopted portions of the new thought.

There are two men who have been associated with humanistic psychology from the first. They were guiding lights in the early years, major influences during the explosive growth of the sixties, and remain patriarchs of the field today. In North America they have been prime movers. If you wish to capture the essence of humanistic psychology, it is essential to examine their ideas. They demonstrate both the strengths and weaknesses of the approach. These men are Carl Rogers and Abraham Maslow.

Carl Rogers has shown a deep concern for individuals and their feelings about themselves. He has a belief in the basic goodness of humans. He has faith in their capacity to develop themselves and to overcome their problems. He has also grappled with the immensely difficult task of making more objective the concepts and theories of humanistic psychology.

Abraham Maslow (who died in 1970) was primarily concerned with how people can fulfill themselves and become self-actualized. Humans are more than animals; they can be healthy and growing. He has delineated the characteristics of the psychologically healthy persons we can all become.

These two men and their movement are the subject of this chapter.

THE PSYCHOLOGY OF CARL ROGERS

Like any important theory, Carl Rogers' is built around a few basic concepts which can be described initially in a clearcut, simple manner. As the theory is further developed, however, it becomes clear that these basics are neither simple nor clearcut. At the beginning, though, it is instructive to treat them as if they were. In the case of Rogers, the "would-should dilemma" as a source of incongruence is a good place to start. It is at the crux of much of his theory. Luckily (or unluckily) the dilemma is found everywhere, so examples of it are not hard to find.

The Would-Should Dilemma

The conflicting demands of work and family can produce a would-should dilemma. Some people find it very difficult to while away their evenings playing with their children, gardening or socializing with friends. While they are pursuing these comfortable pastimes, they remember that things are behind at the office. They feel uneasy about "wasting" their time. They *would* like to play with their children but *should* really be getting some work done. There is a direct conflict between what they would really like to do (for reasons that are not entirely clear) and what they feel they should do (for reasons that are equally unclear). Incidentally, some people have a problem that is a mirror image of the one described above. They *would* like to get some work done at the office but feel they *should* spend some time with the family.

In our society sex is at the base of a good many would-should dilemmas; a woman with a strict upbringing might feel strongly that she should not have sex too often, because it is not proper. But going without it makes her irritable and edgy. Sex affords some satisfaction, but this satisfaction is often followed by discomfort and depression. There is a vague feeling of guilt. Here again, what the person would do is directly opposed by what she feels she should do.

Since Rogers is a clinical psychologist, many people come to him with psychological problems. Often they feel that their problems must be rooted in some grotesque psychological abnormality. Rogers has observed, though, that in many cases the real problem is a would-should dilemma. There is a conflict between what people believe they should do and what they feel is best for them. The discomfort caused by this dilemma arouses anxiety. After seeing a great many cases that seemed to fit this pattern, Rogers developed a way of looking at people which gives some insight into these kinds of problems. Rogers suggests that within each of us is an *organismic valuing process* which is our true, deep-down, basic set of values. For example, most of us feel in a very profound way that killing another person is wrong. If we were required to kill someone it would be very difficult to do so. This is our organismic valuing process. Of course it contains values concerning a wide range of activities, including our likes and dislikes of many things. The organismic valuing process is an important part of our natures, so that to go against its values makes us upset, edgy or may even cause us to do totally irrational things.

Another aspect of us, according to Rogers, is a *need for positive regard*. This is the need to have other people respect us in various ways and to look upon us as worthy beings. We feel good when other people compliment us, or look on in admiration when we do something well. This need for positive regard is a deep need, and we will go to considerable lengths to satisfy it. We will sometimes go against our own organismic valuing process to earn the positive regard of others. We may do things we don't like in order to get on someone's good side or to have them respect us. Some teenagers have just such a problem when they get behind the wheel of a car. They seek to impress their friends by a reckless display of their driving skills. If a suitably impressive demonstration is given, there may be talk of it for several days. The driver beams with pride, although deep inside he knows he has done something stupid. His need for positive regard is pushing him to drive wildly. His organismic valuing process is pushing him to stop the foolishness. It's a terrible dilemma to be in, but such dilemmas confront us all our lives.

These concepts of the organismic valuing process and the need for positive regard may be applied to the would-should dilemma of the woman with the unsatisfactory sex life, mentioned earlier. To use Rogers' terms, the woman's (let's call her Nancy) organismic valuing process has a need for sex in its loving positive sense. She needs not only to receive, but also to give love in this way. But a puritanical upbringing has stifled this tendency. Her parents made it clear to her that sex was dirty. No woman with any self-respect could get any enjoyment from it. If a person found sex fulfilling, that person was obviously dirty and sinful. To get positive regard from her parents, Nancy had to abide by their beliefs. The pressure to conform was so great that she eventually came to accept these anti-sex values. Of course, they did not become a part of her innermost organismic valuing process, but they did become a part of her value system. Rogers' term for taking in values and ideas, without regard to how they suit the organismic valuing process, is *introjection*. The girl introjected her parents' negative ideas about sex, uncritically. She did it to get her parents positive regard, without careful consideration of the implications. The introjection of unsuitable values led to her unsettled mental condition, marred by edginess and depression. This unpleasant state of affairs Rogers calls *incongruence*. Nancy was suffering incongruence because of the conflict between her organismic valuing process (her own true values) and the values she had introjected in order to get her parents' positive regard.

The key to Nancy's would-should dilemma, and the motivation to adopt her parents' standards, was her need to gain positive regard. The positive regard of the parents was only given when Nancy conformed. This is an example of *conditional positive regard*, or positive regard that is withheld unless a person meets certain conditions. Nancy's parents made it clear that as far as they were concerned, sex was bad. If Nancy found anything good about sex, she was bad, too. In fact, if she showed any positive attitudes towards sex at all, they would withdraw their positive regard from her. Their positive regard was given only if Nancy met certain conditions specified by them. They were saying, in essence, "We consider you a worthy person only if you behave as we think you should behave." In Rogers' terms they were laying down *conditions of worth*. It was a result of this conditional positive regard that Nancy introjected her parents' values about sex. She came to believe that to be worthy, she could not be interested in sex. If she wanted to have a positive self-concept, interest in sex must not be a part of her. She came to believe, in a sense, that she was not interested in sex. This, of course, leads to incongruence, because her organismic valuing process values sex positively.

The Phenomenal Field

To clearly understand the nature and origin of incongruence, it is necessary to know something about the nature of human awareness.

What are our perceptions of ourselves, others and the world in general? Rogers' concept of the phenomenal field is important in this context.

A person's *phenomenal field* is that individual's unique perception of the world. Each of us looks upon the world in our own way and interprets it slightly differently. The ability to be consciously aware of one's own phenomenal field, and to appreciate that of others, is important. Many bitter disagreements arise, even between people acting in good faith, because the protagonists are not aware of the differences in their phenomenal fields. Consequently, they cannot understand why they disagree; the only explanation is that the other party is dishonest. If both parties come to feel this way, complete communication breakdown can occur. Often disagreements between supervisors and subordinates can take this disastrous turn. The disagreements come about because supervisors are, generally speaking, different from those who carry out the basic functions of the job.

Generally, supervisors are more task-oriented than line workers and see the world differently. At the work place they are more concerned with the job, less concerned with social relationships than the average employee. Another common difference is that the person performing the task often enjoys the actual doing of the task more than does the supervisor. The salesperson enjoys selling and gets real satisfaction from mulling over, planning and executing a sales plan. Innovation is often the most thrilling part of the process. The standard tactic may bring in a reliable income, but many salespeople are constantly trying variations.

Sometimes they lose sales because of this creativity. Although in the long run they may improve and be better off, in the short term they often take losses. Supervisors tend to be less excited about the actual process, and are more concerned (as they must be if they are to do their jobs properly) with monthly quotas. For example, a salesperson may be behind because it is Christmas, and more time is being spent with the family. In addition, several new prospects of a completely new kind have been tried, just to see what would happen. A supervisor might be less than delighted. If the sales patterns of the unit do not conform to the general plans of the company, economic disaster can occur.

In a case such as this there are good reasons for both parties to feel as they do. A reasonable compromise must be sought. But it is hardly likely to happen if supervisor and salesperson do not see each other's points of view. If the supervisor insists that a prospect is merely a potential sale outlet, there can be no real solution. The salesperson does not see a prospect simply as a potential sale, but also as an individual with whom an interesting interaction can take place. The interaction is an important part of the joy of selling. Remove the personal aspect and selling becomes a job, not a vocation.

It is easy to see how a supervisor, who has not actually sold for some time, may come to see a prospect in a way quite different from a salesperson. The prospect occupies a different place in the phenomenal field of the supervisor than he does in the phenomenal field of the salesperson. Unless both understand that they mean different things by the word "prospect," much unproductive disagreement can occur. Each individual has a unique phenomenal field.

It is important to remember also that the phenomenal field, a person's view of reality, may not correspond very well with physical reality. For example, a person with a "chip on his shoulder" may perceive an accidental brush with a stranger as a threat. He may over-react because of his misperception of what has occurred.

Another characteristic of the phenomenal field is that it can come to be divided into parts. For example, one part of our field of awareness is the concept of self. The concept of *self* is the person's view of himself acquired through his various life experiences. This self-concept is a very important part of a person's world view. Another part of the phenomenal field is one's perception of the ideal self. The *ideal self* is one's perception of how one should be, which is based upon past learning. Most people know that their awareness of who they actually are is different from their awareness of the kind of person they would like to be.

To summarize, it is assumed that there is a real world which has a certain nature. Each individual has a more or less accurate awareness of the world, which is called his or her phenomenal field. Two components of the phenomenal field are the self and the ideal self.

A precondition for psychological health is that the real world, phenomenal field, self and ideal self must all be compatible with one another. If there are serious incompatibilities between any of the parts, the individual will experience incongruence.

The Actualizing Tendency

The organismic valuing process is one aspect of what Rogers calls the actualizing tendency. The *actualizing tendency* is a single, far-reaching motive which Rogers says all people are born with. It motivates us to grow and develop into mature healthy adults. It motivates the baby to walk. It makes us curious, so that we will learn. It motivates our interest in beauty. It fuels our sex drives. Generally speaking, it arouses us to do healthy, generous, loving things. Nancy's state of incongruence can now be described as follows. Her actualizing tendency has a healthy interest in sex. It motivates her to be curious about it. This curiosity is positively valued by the organismic valuing process. But Nancy also has a self-concept which, because of introjected values, says that interest in sex is not a part of her. Nancy, who considers herself above interest in sex, at times experiences curiosity about it. There is a discrepancy between who she believes she is and what she experiences herself doing. Her incongruence therefore involves an inconsistency between her self-concept and her experience (phenomenal field). It might seem to Nancy that some part of her is out of control—a disconcerting experience.

Incongruence has further ramifications. Nancy may become aware that somewhere in herself there is an interest in sex. It is starting to become part of her self-concept. She realizes she would like to date men, but her ideal self is still a repository of her anti-sex bias. To fulfill her ideal self-concept she should not like to date men. Here we see a would-should dilemma, which is a discrepancy between the self and the ideal self. If this discrepancy is large enough, strong feelings of guilt and inadequacy can occur. These, in turn, lead to inappropriate actions and feelings associated with further complications of incongruence. Nancy is already wrestling with discrepancies between self and ideal self, and between self-concept and phenomenal field. The emotional turmoil that results can lead to misperceptions of the world around her. She may fail to see things that are present; she may see things that are present but distort them; or she may see things which are not actually present. For example, because of her deep-seated interest in men, she may dress more provocatively. To help support her ideal self-concept, though, she may perceive her clothing as less provocative than it actually is. To admit to herself that she is dressing provocatively would force her to be more aware of the discrepancy between self and ideal self, which would make her feel uncomfortable. Furthermore, her manner of dress would tend to lead men to make more than the usual number of sexual advances towards her. She would perceive men to be preoccupied with sex. To be consistent with her ideal self, there would be a tendency to withdraw from them more and more. If she does, her actualizing tendency would suffer greater frustration and her problem would be further complicated. These misperceptions of her clothing and of men's intentions are a distortion of reality and involve a discrepancy between her phenomenal field and the real world. This example shows that incongruence can involve any one of, or a combination of, three discrepancies; between self-concept and the rest of the phenomenal field, between self and ideal self; and between the phenomenal field and the real world. These aspects of experience are so intimately interwoven that the dynamics of one or two affect the dynamics of the whole. The would-should dilemma at the beginning of this chapter, which appeared to be relatively simple, involves a complex interaction of several factors. Rogers gives such importance to this interaction that it should be further explained.

Rogers takes a holistic view of the human organism. By *holistic* he means that all parts of the human personality interact and affect each other so that the function of one cannot be understood by looking at it in isolation. A bowl of jelly is holistic. No matter where you poke it, the whole thing jiggles. The exact place of the poke affects the pattern of the jiggle. Because people are holistic, incongruence, self, ideal self, the phenomenal field, and reality cannot be fully understood without understanding what is occuring in all the others, and what the relationship is with all the others.

It is time now to turn from Rogers' concept of dysfunction to his concept of the optimally functioning, healthy human being—to what he calls the fully functioning person.

The Fully Functioning Person

Rogers' concept of mental health is essentially a description of the kind of environment a person must experience if he is to overcome his problems and develop his full potential. This description is based upon years of clinical experience.

Rogers noted that many people who have difficulties do not have sufficient confidence in themselves. For example, Nancy cannot say to herself and others, "Deep down I like and need sex. Therefore I will have sex, regardless of what people say. This anti-sex value is not good for me." Rogers would say that she lacks confidence in her own ability to evaluate. He feels self-confidence is essential for the full development of the individual. The conditional positive regard offered by others can stifle this confidence, particularly if those others are important to the individual. Self-confidence can be developed only if we receive from others something called unconditional positive regard. *Unconditional positive regard* is the attitude that a person is prized and loved, no matter what that person does. If Nancy's parents had had unconditional positive regard for her, they might have indicated to her that, although they personally disapproved of sex, they would love her even if she indulged.

Unconditional positive regard is important for the proper development of the individual, but it is difficult to handle. Some parents carry it too far. You can hear them saying, "Isn't little Georgie cute, look how he's gouging your little girl's eyes. He's all boy. Look how athletic he is, jumping all over your furniture. Oops! He broke your lamp. Well, live and learn. Come here Georgie, I'll give you a big hug." Obviously, children reared with this degree of unconditional positive regard will be a problem. What Rogers suggests is that the child must be guided, without recourse to ego-damaging techniques.

"Georgie, you idiot! It's an amazement to me that a son of mine could knock over that lamp. Where are your brains? Do you have any? When are you going to grow up? You do stupid things all the time." Such outbursts may be effective in intimidating Georgie, and preventing eye gouging and lamp breaking, but they also leave him with the impression that anything he might do or think is bad and unacceptable. Few parents are as extreme as the examples given here, but it remains a fact that it is very difficult to effectively operate in the middle ground. It is not easy to make it clear that, although Georgie does bad things for which he is punished, Georgie *himself* is loved and valued.

Most children perform more acceptable actions than unacceptable ones so, on balance, they can grow with a positive self-concept. Parents must be careful to point out to children their good and bad actions and choose their words carefully when disapproving. If children are not severely frustrated in some aspects of life, they will tend to choose positive actions. There must be guidance without coercion.

Another area in which unconditional positive regard is apparent is the relationships of married couples. Newlyweds and young lovers tend to see each other as perfect. Undesirable traits are not perceived. In longer relationships a new kind of unconditional positive regard appears. Spouses are loved in spite of their "defects," or maybe even because of them. "Mary really let me have it last night. One of her classic tongue lashings. I hadn't done a thing, but something was on her mind that had to be let out. It's good she got it off her chest. Every time she does it though, she really calls me a lot of names, even when what's bothering her has nothing to do with me. But she's a good wife. I wouldn't give her up for the world." In this case the bad trait is a blemish on a person who is essentially a positively valued individual. And the blemish ceases to be a blemish in a sense; it is one more part of the loved one.

Some situations do not work out so nicely, and something has to be done. The course Rogers suggests is an honest discussion of the problem. Does one of the partners have a trait which seriously threatens the organismic valuing process of the other? Can the individual change himself, alter that trait, without getting himself into a condition of incongruence? How strong are the conditions of worth? How much do one or both partners have to change in order to maintain the relationship? How damaging will the continuance of the problem be? Perhaps the adjustments are too great to make it worthwhile to continue the relationship. Open discussion is an important element in the proper development of the person.

Unconditional positive regard, then, is essential for the individual to grow. A person who does grow, who does develop his potential and live harmoniously, is called by Rogers a *fully functioning person*. Such people are also called congruent, to contrast them to people who are incongruent.

But Rogers suggests that unconditional positive regard alone is not sufficient to permit a person to become fully functioning. To develop into, and to remain a fully functioning person, one also needs *empathic understanding*—a genuine appreciation, by another person, of how one feels. The inability of parents to bridge the generation gap often results from the fact that they forget how it is to be young. Or a husband may not know what it is like to be a woman, and so makes married life difficult. If you are receiving advice from someone who totally lacks empathic understanding, who cannot see your point of view, the advice will probably not be very good. To grow, you need empathic understanding from someone.

Congruence is also important in this context. *Congruence* is another term for the state of being fully functioning. Unlike the latter term, though, it suggests a particular thing about that condition: it highlights honesty and openess with oneself and others. One says what one believes in a clear and open way, without aggression. There is no blatant assertiveness that might hurt someone unnecessarily.

To become fully functioning one must work at becoming congruent. One must practise thinking and acting in a congruent way. Maturity involves full congruence. But an important part of becoming congruent is to be in contact with someone who is congruent with you. Discussions with such a person allow a healthy exchange of feelings and observations.

Unconditional positive regard, empathic understanding and congruence have beneficial effects in the following way. They allow the person to explore the self honestly, without the distortions and restrictions imposed by conditional positive regard. The person can determine the nature of his own actualizing tendency and organismic valuing process. This allows an honest and realistic evaluation of the self. This self will be openly expressed, because the person will have confidence in the self. Although there may be conflicts with the environment, there will not be distortions. Discrepancies between reality, phenomenal field, self and ideal self will all be reduced.

Work and Rogers' Theory

Before leaving Rogers, it is worthwhile to look at another example to illustrate the basic concepts and to show the nature of the interactions. Rogers' theory can be used to explain many work situations, particularly those which involve people with self doubts. A change of jobs is a good example.

People who move to new jobs often show personality change for the worse, at least initially. Considered in terms of Rogers' theory, this is not surprising. Consider that the former job was probably held for some time. The person could handle the job and feel confident while doing it. Such feelings are very important for sustaining positive self-regard. In addition, co-workers in the old job were aware of that competence. If the person made an error, everyone knew it was just a slip and they would probably laugh it off. Here is a kind of unconditional positive regard. Co-workers respected the worker even when he made mistakes. They had empathic understanding, since they made mistakes themselves. Congruence was probably also present. Through long familiarity people become aware of each others weaknesses. They trust each other, and are honest with one another about their views. The kind of situation described here is not uncommon. A long-held job can be very good for one from a psychological point of view. It can fulfill all the requirements which Rogers suggests are necessary for psychological health and growth. It is not surprising that many people are reluctant to leave such jobs, even when more pay is offered elsewhere.

Contrast this with the conditions which prevail at the new job. The novice is unfamiliar with the work and makes mistakes. This lack of competence damages self-esteem. Feelings of self-doubt naturally arise. The people at the new workplace are, at the same time, evaluating the neophyte. There is no unconditional positive regard here. The new person will not be accepted until competence is shown and social compatibility is demonstrated. There is no congruence, either. People do not open themselves readily to strangers. The newcomer and the established workers may be a bit afraid of each other. Some time will have to pass before openess can develop.

The new job situation provides almost none of the things Rogers considers essential for good psychological health. That is why people new at a job may do very inappropriate things. They may be very touchy; they may be quieter than usual; or perhaps they may be too talkative, loudly boasting of past accomplishments. In fact, new co-workers can be obnoxious. Only later, when more positive regard, congruence and empathic understanding are shown, do people really become themselves. It is obvious that workers already used to the environment can help by not being too harsh.

The job changer will probably find problems at home as well as at the office, according to Rogers. This belief stems from his holistic view of people. What happens to the business self will affect the home self. The person upset by the new job may take some of that upset home with her. She may snap at the children, argue with the husband, or perhaps be very sensitive to criticism of any kind. Rogers says this is the way a normal person will often act in unfavourable circumstances.

Home life in turn, affects the office. If the home life is good, providing positive regard, congruence and empathic understanding, it will help the person handle a new job. It can happen that at the time when people are most unpleasant to their families they most need them, because they are the only source of positive feedback they have. Pity people on new jobs, who are not supported by families or old friends.

Some people, when they become aware that it is normal to act in unusual ways while under stress, take the attitide that they have no responsibility to curb this behaviour. It's normal and it is expected, so why do anything about it? The problem with this is that the behaviour does nothing to improve the situation. Many people do not understand the problem, and do not react in an understanding way. Others may understand at first, but may lose patience. In addition, Rogers advises that each of us is responsible for our own actions. If we do not attempt to conduct ourselves in a responsible way, we relinquish a very important part of being fully human. Mentally healthy people have a drive to transcend their environments and to be in full control of the self, despite the situation.

Conclusion

The major value of Rogers' theory for the average person is in the guidance it can provide in trying to clarify oneself to oneself. Would-should dilemmas are rife, and must be dealt with if one wants to control one's own life. Incongruence is the negative consequence of not honestly facing such situations. But clarifying oneself to oneself, and determining to carry on in a way that eliminates incongruence, require self-confidence and the belief that one knows what is best for oneself. Unconditional positive regard, congruence and empathic understanding are necessary precursors to such confidence. Without both environmental factors and personal determination, a fully functioning person is unlikely to emerge.

THE PSYCHOLOGY OF ABRAHAM MASLOW

The discussion of Carl Rogers, just completed, shows the importance of coming to terms with oneself. To get the most out of life, honesty about oneself and others is necessary. Abraham Maslow would agree with this idea. But unlike Rogers, who was greatly concerned with the effects of others opinions on our own self-concepts, Maslow is primarily concerned with the motives that drive people.

A clear understanding of the motives of oneself and others is critical for an intelligent consideration of life options. Often one can get so caught up in the motives of the moment, that a clear view of what is really happening in the situation is not present. Maslow's theory provides a system in terms of which motives can be examined, weighed and selected.

A good example of the ways in which our motives can hinder our views on what options are actually available to us, is welfare. Most of us accept the value systems we are presently involved in, and struggle, work, falter and scramble accordingly. We often don't really think about alternate ways. It seems, in some cases, that we are afraid to think of other possibilities. But if it really is such a rat race, why don't we just quit? Which of us could not, in the next week or two, scrounge up $1,000 in cash? Borrow from friends, lie a little at a bank, sell the car? With the $1,000 a fine new colour television can be purchased. The next step is to rent a very cheap room, move in the TV set, and settle into a life of television watching and perhaps beer and pizza snacking. Regular welfare cheques can easily support this modest, but comfortable, life. Why don't we just do it?

The reasons that most people give for not doing this can be easily dealt with. What of my job? Forget the job. It only creates problems and unnecessary work; ample food is available on welfare. What of my family? No problem. They will be on welfare too, or at least living with relatives. You can visit them occasionally, if you wish. It won't be the standard of living they're used to, but it will be adequate. What of my responsibilities, my mortgage? Forget them. They can't collect if you aren't working; there is no garnishee on welfare payments. What's the worst they can do to you, send you to jail? It's very unlikely, but if they do, no problem. There are colour televisions in jail as well, plus a wide range of other recreational facilities.

It is difficult for most of us to see this as a life option, but it is there. Any of us can walk out the door any time we want. If we can convince ourselves that this is so, it can cast a whole new light on the way we see our present situations. What are we doing here anyway? What motivates us to stick it out here, when there are plenty of other options readily available to those who will take them?

The reason we do not walk out is, of course, that our present situations provide many rewards, and fulfill many needs. It's true that welfare will provide the basics of food, clothing, shelter and some entertainment, but there is much more to life than these. We cannot live by bread alone. The most surprising thing is how seldom we take stock of these other needs in ourselves and others, and try to clearly analyze situations in terms of them.

An expanded view of the needs of individuals can give useful insights in many cases. A friend of my parents was in the hospital once, with some ailment I cannot now remember. Getting out of hospital required bed rest and medication. But he would have none of it. He was always up and around the ward. The nurses were constantly sending him back to bed. He also refused medication, and resorted to rather childish tricks to avoid taking it. My opinion of the man and his behaviour was low (at the time I was in my teens). Here was a man who needed to get better, but he was refusing to do all the things necessary in order to get better.

Fortunately his wife had more insight than I. She realized that he needed to get better, but he also had a powerful need to feel competent and in charge of the situation. Being required to lie in bed and take medicine left those needs unfulfilled. The direct commands, by nurses, doctors and friends, to behave were of no avail for they completely missed the real reason for the behaviours. Finally his wife arranged to have some of his office work brought to his hospital bed. His need to feel competent and effective was satisfied by two or three hours' work a day. The rest of the time he rested in bed and took his medicine.

Because a hospital is primarily concerned with the physical well-being of people, it is often forgotten that patients have a lot of other needs as well, not easily satisfied in the hospital setting. Lack of fulfillment of these needs can lead many hospitalized people to act in counter-productive ways. Taking into account a wider view of motivation than is suggested by the immediate circumstances can alleviate unpleasant situations.

This concern for "unobvious" motives is one of the hallmarks of Maslow's theory. What are these needs that cause people to do strange things for no obvious reason? How can these needs be fulfilled in a more useful way? All psychologists are interested in these problems. But Maslow's theory deals with them in a direct and provocative way.

Growth and Deficiency Motivation

Given Maslow's proposition that we have a wide range of motives, and that many of them are not very obvious, it becomes appropriate to consider what these motives are and how they operate. Not surprisingly, they do not all operate in the same way. One important difference is captured by the terms *growth motivation* and *deficiency motivation*.

Deficiency motives operate on the principle that one will act to rectify or remove a deficiency or discomfort one is experiencing. Action removes the discomfort, and as a result the motive disappears. This way of thinking about motivation derives from the study of a variety of motives found in humans and animals. The need for food operates on this principle. Immediately after eating, one seldom engages in activities related to getting or eating food. Several hours later, though, the body is beginning to run low on the materials necessary to sustain itself. The hunger motive is aroused. One engages in activities that lead to the ingestion of materials that the body needs. After ingestion, the hunger motive disappears, at least until several hours later when the deficiency returns.

The deficiency-motivation concept is sometimes called "the tension reduction model" of motivation. Most states of deficiency involve a feeling of tension of the type the reader has experienced when cold, hungry, tired or thirsty. When such a state of tension exists, we try to reduce the tension by putting on a sweater, eating, sleeping or drinking. The reduction in tension "satisfies" the motive; we feel comfortable, and the motive disappears.

The deficiency-motivation idea has widespread acceptance in Western society. It appears in several scientific theories as well as in the everyday thinking of most lay people. This acceptance is well deserved, since it provides a clear and workable explanation for a wide variety of phenomena. The strengths of this idea should not, however, be allowed to obscure the fact that some kinds of motives are better understood if other concepts are used.

Consider the motivation for hobbies, for instance. Why do people collect stamps, garden, play sports, or engage in any one of a number of "useless" activities? They do not bring in any money;

usually they lose money. What deficiencies do they correct? Is someone who does not collect stamps really lacking in anything? The deficiency model of motivation does not explain very well situations in
which people do things "for the fun of it." Sometimes the deficiency
idea can give an explanation, but usually a more satisfying explanation is given by the idea of growth motivation.

Growth motives operate on the principle that even when no deficiencies remain, people may be motivated to develop beyond their
present condition, to do something over and above the maintenance
of the status quo. Why, for instance, do mountain climbers climb
mountains? There are as many reasons as there are mountaineers, but
central to many is the "feeling of accomplishment" they get from it. It
cannot be said that people who do not climb mountains suffer from
some deficiency. Yet there is, without a doubt, some powerful motive
in the mind of the mountaineer. This motive has to do with growth
and development, rather than with correcting inadequacies.

A gardening analogy is appropriate here. Seeds, like humans,
have a sort of growth motivation. A maple seed, for instance, lacks
nothing. It is a complete entity in and of itself. You do not have to
feed, water, or allow it to sleep in order to keep it "alive." Give it
warmth and moisture, though, and it will grow. The right environment allows it to develop into something much more than a seed; it
becomes a maple tree. But becoming a tree did not correct any deficiency in the seed. The seed simply has a "will" to grow. Similarly,
humans have a will to grow beyond their present condition.

Human growth is like that of the seed. It requires the right kind
of environment if it is to take place. A human in the wrong circumstances will only be concerned with correcting some of his or her deficiencies, rather than with growing beyond the present state.

The Study of Healthy People

Maslow's interest in growth motivation was closely related to his
interest in the study of psychologically healthy people. Maslow
became concerned that in the past psychologists had dealt almost
exclusively with emotionally troubled people. The great psychoanalysts, for instance, were mainly preoccupied with what could go
wrong with people. This is not surprising, since most of their professional lives were spent dealing with, and helping, the troubled. This
focus, though, led to a very one-sided view of humans. Stress in
psychological theories has tended to be on people's weaknesses,
losses and failures.

Maslow determined to provide a fuller, more complete, view of humans. He decided to do a study of psychologically healthy people. By looking at strong, independent and capable people he wanted to show what we could all hope to become. We would have something to grow towards. There could be more to people than the escape from deficiencies.

Maslow had a very optimistic view of human nature. This optimism presumably arose, at least in part, from the study of shining examples of humanity. What Maslow discovered through his study of such people will be discussed in detail later. For now, we can keep in mind the kind of people with whom Maslow concerned himself.

Hierarchy of Needs

One of the things that becomes obvious if you study healthy people, or any people for that matter, is that different people are driven by different motives. In addition, any single individual will have many motives, often for doing a single, particular thing.

An everyday event such as buying insurance is a good example of multiple motives. Some people buy it because they want to be sure that their basic needs and those of their families will be taken care of. They may be interested in the cheapest way to provide the basics. Others may be less concerned with the monetary return on the policy and more preoccupied with it as a demonstration of affection for the spouse and family. Although the drive for basic needs is involved, to this person the policy is primarily a vehicle for expression of love and, perhaps, an attempt to get love in return. Someone else may be interested in insurance as a vehicle to enhance personal prestige. Having $1,000,000 worth of life insurance may be a way to impress one's friends with one's importance. Incidentally, it may enhance one's self-esteem as well. Another person may be interested in insurance as a sort of hobby. Financial management might be a preoccupation with this person, so the intricacies of how the insurance fits into the overall plan and the options available are a source of fascination. There may not be much real interest in the benefits of the insurance. These are only a few of the many, many reasons that could be involved. Most people will be motivated by more than one reason.

As Maslow studied motives in a broad range of situations, he noticed that they tended to fall into a certain pattern. He concluded that motives could be categorized, and that the categories could be arranged in an hierarchy. This "Hierarchy of Needs" has become almost synonymous with Maslow's name. The needs in the hierarchy are inborn, so we all have them, at least to begin with. These needs, in order, are as follows:

1. Physiological needs   These are concerned with maintaining the body as a physical, biological entity. The needs for warmth, food, water and oxygen are good examples. Lack of these needs ensures death. Fulfillment of these needs, though, guarantees only physical life. Psychological humanity may or may not also be present.

2. Safety needs   These are, in the most basic sense, concerned with safety from physical danger. In our society most people do not have to carry guns for self-protection. For us, this kind of safety need is fulfilled. But psychological safety, or security, is also involved, here. A child in an environment with no clear rules, in which punishment is meted out according to no recognizable system, will be deficient in this need. Adults may find themselves in equally insecure environments.

3. Belongingness and love needs   These are concerned with giving and receiving acceptance, trust and affection. Sex, by the way, is a physiological need which can play an important part in the development of love. Maslow's concept of love here is very idealistic, but he makes the important point that something of this sort is needed by almost everyone.

4. Esteem needs   These are concerned with self-respect and a feeling of personal competence, as well as the good opinion of other people. All people need to be respected for something. Lack of such respect inhibits the desire to actively participate in the world. Self-esteem and esteem from others are intimately interrelated. Love needs and esteem needs, since they so often go together in our society, are very often confused. You may avoid this confusion if you keep in mind the classic concept of the army sergeant; the men may respect him but at the same time do not love him, or his discipline.

5. Self-actualization needs   These are not defined in as direct a way by Maslow, so it is more difficult to make a clear statement about them. People have a drive to become what they are capable of becoming. A person who recognizes herself as possessed of musical talent may have a need to pursue music for its own sake. As a component of self-fulfillment, music may be pursued instead of more profitable ends. Without music a gap is left in her life. What is suggested here, is a drive to fulfill one's potential. Of the five needs in Maslow's hierarchy, only the self-actualization needs are growth motives; the others are deficiency motives.

This is the basic hierarchy of five needs suggested by Maslow. He also discussed other needs, such as the need to know and understand, and the aesthetic needs. These, however, were not placed quite so clearly in the system. In this writing it will be sufficient to discuss only the five needs in the basic hierarchy.

Maslow used the word hierarchy because he felt that these needs formed a hierarchy of prepotency. All these needs are not equally strong. The physiological needs are strongest and if they are unfulfilled interest in the other needs disappears. A hungry person will risk life and limb (safety need) in order to get food. Maslow's contention is supported by an experiment done during World War II. A number of enlisted personnel agreed to systematically starve themselves for a period so that scientists could study the psychological and physical effects of severe food deprivation. The starved people showed less and less interest in the world as they got hungrier and hungrier. At the close of study they sat about listlessly, thinking constantly of food. Even their dreams were filled with food. Their motivation to do anything but eat disappeared.

Once the physiological needs are satisfied, the next most powerful needs come into play, safety needs. Concern for safety will predominate until security is obtained. Only with security will the person move to the next level in the hierarchy, belongingness and love. This will, in turn, predominate until satisfied, and the person can move along to esteem.

Self-actualization will not be perceived as a need by people until all the others are fulfilled. It is the highest need, but it is also the weakest.

Maslow considered that very few people become self-actualized—less than one per cent of the population. This is mainly because most of us never get to the point of satisfying all our lower needs, and even if we do, the weakness of the self-actualization need causes it to lie fallow. This is unfortunate, for all of us are born with the capacity for self-actualization.

These five basic needs operate in all our lives. Going back to the insurance example discussed before, it can be seen that every level of the hierarchy is involved. The value of the hierarchy is that it can provide a guide for a more complete analysis of a situation. Insurance is like hospitals, it is usually thought of only in terms of its most obvious function, fulfilling the physiological and safety needs. But as we have seen, there is a great deal more. Knowledge of these other factors is important in fully understanding and dealing with the situation. Maslow's theory cannot give a list of motives for every situation, but it can help imaginative people, with insight and initiative, to formulate their own understanding of many situations.

It should be stressed that the hierarchy describes the usual state of affairs you find in most people. However, in some cases you see inversions of the order. The political revolutionary may risk his life (safety need) in order to further his ideals (self-actualization need). A parent may contravene the safety need to save a child. The hierarchy is a useful guide, but should not be used rigidly and without thought.

Deprivation of Needs

It is clear that each of us has a host of needs, and that all can be categorized somewhere in Maslow's hierarchy. It is also safe to say that we spend a great portion of our lives striving to fulfill these needs. Unfortunately, complete fulfillment is seldom achieved. It is important, then, to consider what happens when there is deprivation of needs.

What happens when the physiological needs are chronically unsatisfied is obvious. First physical sickness will result, and finally, death. During this period there will be little interest in things other than the physiological needs. This is an important psychological side effect. People who perceive their physiological needs to be in danger of being unmet, or who are actually experiencing a lack, will resort to almost any measure to correct the deficiency. Criminal behaviour is commonly a result of this kind of condition.

Unsatisfied safety needs lead to sickness and/or death as well. Psychological insecurity can be very damaging too, although not always in terms of physical sickness. People who experience extreme insecurity often engage in what is called neurotic behaviour. They may be over-concerned with controlling their worlds. Attempts to bring order might include excessive tidiness, constant direction-giving to relatives, and relentless worrying about unimportant things. Close associates of such people often fail to see the unfulfilled need for security which is the basis of such behaviours.

Deprivation of the love need can also be very damaging. The "sickness" here is not always obviously physical, although in extreme cases there have been people known to have died of "broken hearts." The listlessness and withdrawal (recall the hunger studies mentioned above) resulting from the loss of love in these cases led to death. In this connection, Maslow also noted that chronic deprivation of the love need can lead to what is known, clinically, as the anti-social personality. Such people, because they have never known love, lose the ability to receive and give it. The result is a total lack of feeling for fellow humans. The ability to kill, without feeling any remorse or guilt, could be a symptom. A more common occurrence is for someone who lacks love to be chronically involved in a struggle to get it.

Deprivation of the esteem need also leads to characteristic symptoms, whose severity depends on the severity of the deprivation. One symptom is a single-minded seeking of prestigious positions, whatever the cost. Excessive bragging or the continual belittlement of others is another symptom. We usually respond to such behaviours with putdowns. But this can only make the condition worse, particularly if we are really good at it. The real solution to the problem is to trace the source of lack of esteem. In many cases the best way to eliminate bragging is with compliments. However, in such cases these are very difficult to give.

Deprivation of the self-actualization need does not lead to the obvious difficulties that occur when the lower needs are unfulfilled. Recall that the four lower needs are deficiency needs, aroused when something is lacking. If that lack continues, sickness and/or death may result. Self-actualization, by contrast, is a growth need. Lack of fulfillment here leads to more subtle difficulties. In fact, some people may not consider them to be real problems at all. People who do not collect stamps do not usually suffer from stamp-collecting deficiency.

But to be fully human, we must self-actualize. People who "have everything" sometimes report uneasiness or vague restlessness. This is the urge to self-actualize. Unless it is dealt with, feelings of alienation and aimlessness can result. It is at this point that the concepts of Carl Rogers have an important role to play. His ideas about self-honesty and self-awareness may be very useful in exploring what can be done to achieve self-actualization.

It sometimes happens, though, that someone who should be well-adjusted and happy, is not. A woman I know is just such a case. She is intelligent and active. She and her husband have no children. Her husband is a successful businessman who must entertain often. The woman arranges such affairs and maintains their apartment in a suitable style. She does these things quite well, but does not derive a great deal of pleasure from doing them. In addition, she cannot hold a job suited to her abilities because of the time demands of the entertainment schedule. As a result, her job (she wants to work) is rather boring for her. Although there are no great demands on her time, and she has all the money she could want, she is constantly irritable and anxious.

An objective observer of this situation might ask what her problem is. She seems to have everything anyone could want. It is true that all her basic needs are taken care of. But what of her need for self-actualization? This is where the problem lies. Her situation is such that her basic needs are taken care of, but in such a way that her time is so full that she cannot fulfill her highest need. What we have here is a basically healthy person, whose environment is causing frustrations. The frustrations lead to behaviours which hide the basic health. It looks as if she has some sort of semi-neurotic difficulty, if you do not fully know her position.

This idea that some environments are such that they cause healthy people to react in obnoxious ways, is a very important one. Only a very stifled and incomplete individual can exist in such an environment without exhibiting the symptoms of irritation, shortness of temper, and the like. Often we become fed up with such people and reject them socially. This is a tragedy for that individual. They become further enmeshed in their trap.

Unfortunately, it is often very difficult to spot the antagonistic components in such situations. Did the woman find no real joy in entertaining? Was the job boring because of the job itself, or because of the other people involved? How does her husband treat her? What kind of activities would allow her to self-actualize? A thousand questions like these have to be worked through and explored before a solution can be found, and every case is different. Maslow does not have "pat" answers, but he does have ideas about the kinds of things that should be considered in cases like these.

Once it is established that a basically healthy person is having difficulty with a stultifying environment, it is necessary to define a course of action for that individual. How can the environment be changed? If it cannot be changed, how can the person get out of it? The onus is on the individual to find or create his own solution to the problem.

One danger in looking for the problem in the environment, rather than in the individual, is that it could lead to inaction on the part of the individual. If the cause of the problem is ascribed to the environment, the attitude that one cannot do anything about it and must continue in the present state ("after all, its not my fault") is a tempting stance to take. Maslow stresses that this is abdication of one's responsibility to oneself. We must all strive for personal fulfillment, regardless of the obstacles. On this point, Rogers and Maslow are entirely in agreement.

We have been discussing the difficulty of working through complex problems, such as that of the woman in the above example. One of the most difficult things to deal with in such situations is the pinpointing of specific higher needs and deriving ways of fulfilling them. This has been mentioned before, but a few more words about it are in order.

One of the chief blocks to effective perception of higher-need deprivation is the cultural conditioning we all receive. Western civilization is remarkable in history for its spectacular success in fulfilling the two most basic needs, physiological and safety. (How long this success will last is another question.) Technology has been extremely effective in satisfying these human wants. Our culture puts very great importance on such satisfactions. In addition, it is a common feature in Western man's thinking to be concerned about the next two needs as well, love and esteem. People regard them highly, and there is some concern that the systems and technology, that so admirably fulfill the physiological and safety needs, prevent the proper satisfaction of love and esteem needs. These points are well taken, but they seldom extend to the need for self-actualization.

A person with the first four needs fulfilled is usually considered to have everything. Members of our culture find it difficult to conceive of there being much more. But, as Maslow points out, there is. Industrial unrest makes a good case in point. When a union goes on strike for higher wages, the usual reaction of the public is, "Not again! They are already making a pile." And they probably are. The workers may have all their basic needs taken care of. The cry for more money is the cry for some mechanism for self-actualization. In addition to buying esteem, it pays for hobbies. It gives the person a chance to find personal satisfaction at home that is not found in many industrial jobs.

Some experts suggest that jobs should be made more interesting and demanding. Others say that this will make people psychological slaves to their jobs, and not just financial slaves as they are now. They say more leisure time is the answer. No matter what the solution, it is agreed that the lack is in self-actulization. It is only in parts of the industrialized world, where the lower needs are so well filled, that this highest one is really a problem.

Characteristics of Self-Actualized People

We have seen that Maslow was concerned with the motives of people. He also was interested in studying people who were very healthy, psychologically. By doing this he sought to show what we can become, rather than what we should avoid. One of the most noted aspects of his work, then, is the study of self-actualized people.

Maslow studied not only some very healthy people with whom

he was personally acquainted, but also some of the great personalities of history. Through the biographies of such people as Lincoln, Schweitzer, Eleanor Roosevelt and Huxley, Maslow crystallized an idea of what the very healthy human is like. On the basis of these studies, he concluded that such people have most, if not all, of the following characteristics.

1. Good perception of reality As Chapter 1 of this book pointed out, most of us perceive a world distorted by our own wants and desires. Self-actualized people are not so hindered. They tend to be objective and unbiased in how they perceive people and situations. They perceive independently of themselves.

2. Acceptance of self, others, and the world in general They have a clear idea of the strengths and weaknesses in themselves and others. But they accept them as natural. There is no emotional attempt to gloss over faults and ignore them. They are there, and getting emotional will not change most of them.

3. Spontaneity They express themselves honestly, except when someone else will be unnecessarily hurt by it. They are not afraid to express their independent judgments, without flaunting them.

4. Focussing on problems rather than on self Instead of being worried about their own status, they are concerned about the things that need to be done in the outside world. The difficulty of bringing about justice, truth, goodness and self-sufficiency in the world around them is a prime concern.

5. Need for privacy and independence Being more autonomous, they experience less need for other people. They also require more time by themselves than do ordinary people.

6. Freshness of appreciation Most of us lose the ability to appreciate simple experiences of everyday events. Self-actualizers appreciate fully, again and again, sunsets, flowers, children.

7. Have peak experiences Self-actualizers have episodes of religious-like ecstasy, in which they report feelings of great power and transcendence of the self (some more often than others).

8. Social interest A strong feeling of commonness with other people, despite their weaknesses and failures. This feeling fuels a genuine concern for all people.

9. Interpersonal relations are restricted Self-actualizers have few friendships, but those they have are strong and deep, and usually with other self-actualizers. Ordinarily, some admirers are present too, but these tend to be one-sided relationships.

10. Creativeness They are creative in ways that transcend the conventional artistic ways. All their activities show originality and freshness. They are not afraid to make mistakes in their new approaches.

11. Democratic character They are very open and spontaneous with other people. There is no feeling of condescension with others, no matter who they are.

12. Resistance to "enculturation" Because of their individuality they are resistant to the pressures that cause most of us to conform to our cultural values. Although they do not flaunt their independence, they certainly have it.

This list is somewhat overwhelming. How could anyone be so perfect? It is not surprising that less than 1 per cent of the population is estimated to be self-actualized.

Conclusion

The path to self-actualization is the indirect route. It cannot be achieved by consciously trying to do the twelve things listed above. The way is to come to terms with oneself. Honestly consider options and motives. Choose, with some trial and error, the way most harmonious for oneself. When this course is truly found, the twelve characteristics will begin to appear naturally.

It's unlikely that most of us will ever become totally self-actualized. But it is possible to live more effective lives by keeping Maslow's ideas in mind. The "great plan" may not be fulfilled, but many day-to-day situations may improve if we use the tools provided.

SUMMARY

Comparing the theories of Rogers and Maslow, it becomes clear that although they differ in many ways, they also have much in common. Humanistic psychology, in general, encompasses a variety of approaches and ideas, but certain themes are common to all of them. The themes common to Rogers and Maslow are a good representation of the themes shared by all the humanistic psychologists.

Rogers, Maslow, and humanistic psychologists in general have great faith in the fundamental strength and goodness of human nature. People are born with a desire to grow, to create, to love. They have the power to direct their own lives. Given a proper environment, all people are capable of fulfilling this promise.

Humanistic psychologists also believe, however, that the environment can have a tremendous impact on the growth of the individual. If the environment is oppressive in some way, if it strangles the individual with rules, opposes natural healthy growth or attempts to direct growth into inappropriate channels, the natural destiny will not be fulfilled. The person becomes aggressive and defensive under such circumstances. If the environment is favourable to growth, if rules are based on real needs, growth in natural channels is encouraged, and honesty and openess prevail. The individual will fulfill his genetic potential, and become strong and self-directing.

This positive assumption about human nature has been found to be a workable one in many situations. For instance, Rogers and other humanistic psychologists deal with people who come to them for psychological help. They insist that the clients find their own strengths and their own goals. They must find their own "cures." The psychologist can help, but he cannot lead the clients to health. Many people respond to this therapy and show marked improvement. A parallel approach can be used in business. If employees are treated as irresponsible, lazy, and as if motivated only by money, they will come to behave in accordance with those expectations, which is a self-fulfilling prophecy. Maslow has suggested that employees should be expected to be active and to be motivated by creativity and beauty, as well as by money. If they are treated in this fashion, they will become healthy mentally and more effective in the work place. Many managers have found this to be an effective approach. All the ills of the world will not be solved by making positive assumptions about humans, but many will be.

Humanistic psychologists also assume that subjective experience is the most important aspect of being human. Although a person's subjective, private experience may not be an accurate reflection of the "real world," that person can act only in terms of his private experience. Human behaviour is best understood by examining what people believe and feel, not by knowing what is actually going on in the environment around them.

Humanistic psychologists assign to science a rather limited role in the study of human psychology. They contend that science, by its nature, is designed to study things which can be made available for public observation and verification. Science, therefore, cannot study subjective experience, which, by definition, is not publicly observable. In the future, science may design techniques capable of dealing with subjective experience, but at present it does so very clumsily and in an unsatisfactory way. We must go beyond science and hope that someday it will catch up. The alternative is to discontinue the study of subjective experience, and that is unthinkable to humanistic psychologists. Humanistic psychology gives primary importance to human goodness and human experience. All else is secondary.

Further Readings

Another secondary treatment of Carl Rogers can be found in Nye's *Three Views of Man* which also compares Rogers to Freud and Skinner. Rogers' own telling can be found in his book, *On Becoming a Person: A Therapist's View of Psychotherapy*.

Maslow is sympathetically explained in Goble's *The Third Force*. This book is easy to read and attempts to describe applications of Maslow's work. Maslow himself is well known for his *Motivation and Personality* and *Towards a Psychology of Being*.

8

APPLICATIONS IN PSYCHOTHERAPY
Judith Kelly Waalen

Editor's Preface

Abnormal behaviour has brought fear and tragedy to human societies since the dawn of recorded history. The treatment of the mentally ill has ranged from superstitious awe and fear to harshness and brutality. One of the greatest triumphs of psychology has been the contribution it has made to the humanization of our treatment of these unfortunate individuals.

Two of the five approaches that have been discussed, psychoanalysis and humanistic psychology, have their roots in the clinical field. Psychoanalysis, especially, has concentrated on the explanation and treatment of abnormal behaviours. However, psychobiologists, behaviourists and cognitive theorists have also been active in the field. Each of the five approaches has something specific and unique to say about the definition of abnormal behaviour, its origin and its treatment. In each case the view of abnormal behaviour is inseparable from the assumptions and concepts of the broader theoretical perspective.

In this chapter the author demonstrates how each approach has been applied to therapeutic situations. In each case the sections start with a consideration of healthy vs. unhealthy behaviours, then move to basic assumptions and concepts. It is these foundation stones that provide the rationale for the actual therapeutic techniques. The individual therapies that emerge from the approaches are a logical, even inevitable, extension of the theoretical positions that underlie them.

APPLICATIONS IN PSYCHOTHERAPY

All human beings at one time or another experience feelings of anger, depression, guilt, isolation and lethargy. We speak of feeling "unreal," "hyper," "down," "anxious," and "crisis-ridden." Individuals use these terms to justify their irritable, supersensitive, or outrageous behaviour. Do these feelings signal the presence of pathology in our mental functioning?

Be wary of answering this question too quickly. Many qualifications are necessary, not the least of these being the definition of the concepts of normality and abnormality. Further, it is not possible to answer the question "What constitutes abnormal behaviour?" without considering one's perspective. The five approaches—psychoanalytic, behavioural, cognitive, humanistic and biological—deal with the same events, but view them from different angles. Each approach has distinctive opinions about the normal/abnormal continuum and the remedies to treat disorders.

This proliferation of competing approaches extends far beyond the realm of abnormal behaviour, and is typical of a developing science. Nowhere, however, is the competition as keen as in the realm of mental illness. We have selected the five approaches that are currently influential in the area or show strong promise of becoming so.

MODELS, VARIETIES AND THERAPIES: THE FORMAT

In examining each of the five approaches to abnormal behaviour, the following format will be used: for each perspective, the reader will be introduced to the conception of healthy and non-healthy behaviour. Next, it will be shown how that approach is applied to a set of events and behaviours, and how the events on which it focusses become the basis for defining the varieties of mental illness. Finally, we will examine some of the therapeutic techniques that have emerged from that approach.

THE PSYCHOANALYTIC APPROACH

The influence of Sigmund Freud in the arena of mental illness is notable due to his "discovery" of the unconscious. It is in this part of the personality that conflicts develop. Anxieties developed in childhood remain dormant and unresolved, seeking release in later life. The result is dramatic and bizarre symptoms. A series of unconscious defensive tactics are developed to handle the unresolved traumas of childhood. All of this activity operates below the level of awareness, sapping our reserves of psychic energy. As the system becomes over-taxed, the elusive material becomes conscious in slips of the tongue, feelings of anxiety, or frightening fantasies. These "messages" from the unconscious seek recognition, and our overt adult behaviour is affected. Childhood traumas are played out in adult lives—but in the manner of the child. Freud's definition of mental illness, then, is a failure of the ego to reconcile the opposing forces of the id and the superego, both of which seek recognition on a conscious level. Thus the thrust of the psychoanalytic position is that we are controlled by forces about which we have little or no knowledge. To understand these forces, it is necessary to travel back in time to the stage at which they developed.

Anxiety and defensive strategies are part of everyday life, so the question becomes "When is the behaviour abnormal in psychoanalytic terms?" To Freud, behaviour is pathological when it is no longer controllable by the individual. Everyday living ceases to be possible. Mental illness is a matter of degree, not kind. The stuff of which neurotic behaviour is made is simply exaggerated "normal" behaviour. This is an important concept because it implies that the seeds of pathological behaviour are present in all of us.

Freud was a biological determinist in his approach to human behaviour. However, he went to great lengths to dissociate himself from the idea that abnormal behaviour has biological origins. This departure from the medical or biological approach to human behaviour is a distinguishing feature of psychoanalytic theory. Conflicts do exist within the individual, and the causes of the conflicts are psychological in nature.

The Varieties of Abnormal Behaviour

The psychoanalytic perspective deals most frequently with neurotic behaviour, that is, behaviour which is distorted by the ego-defence system attempting to control anxiety. Neurotic disorders are considered to be of psychological origin, although bodily processes are involved, such as an elevated pulse rate, rapid breathing, profuse sweating, and heart palpitations. However, the causal agent is psychogenic anxiety.

How does one become neurotic? All neurotic reactions reflect an inability of the ego-defence system to handle anxiety. When viewed in this way, it becomes obvious that almost all individuals have the potential to become neurotic. There are five basic steps to the development of a full-fledged neurosis. By using an example, we can trace those steps.

> John B. is a twenty-year-old college student who is being supported by his parents. He did not want to go to college, but at his parents' insistence he enrolled, and has performed marginally for his first two years of college. Lately, he has found that two or three days prior to an exam he feels nauseated, and suffers from headaches and feelings of impending doom. Occasionally, he goes to the examination room, but leaves in a very few minutes complaining of the "flu." Over the semester, he has missed five exams and will probably fail his courses. This fear of failing makes him even more tense, so that even the most routine of school assignments is not completed. He finds that he is sleeping twelve to sixteen hours per day and is convinced that he is suffering from anemia (at the very least). He can't possibly drop out of school, as he would have to work for his father. He resents this dependency relationship with his parents, which has become increasingly onerous in the past few months.

The psychoanalytic position maintains that abnormal behaviour is the result of unresolved childhood experiences and ineffective ego-defence mechanisms. For John, this combination established a neurotic self-perpetuating cycle the first time he became "sick" prior to an exam. Stage one, then, involves the activation of a prior, unresolved experience. In John's case, this means the ambivalence he feels about his dependence on his parents. In the second stage he began to evaluate common life experiences as dangerous and threatening. As we all know, exams are a part of life in a student's world. Because this evaluation is based on a faulty perception, the normal defence system was not activated to protect John. Without the restraint of an active and functional defence system, anxiety erupted, producing psychological feelings of impending doom and apprehension. Accompanying these feelings were the physical correlates of sweating and rapid, shallow breathing (stage three). Anxiety is incredibly debilitating, and in order to channel it away, a self-defeating neurotic manoeuver developed. John slept several hours more than normal, developed headaches, and felt nauseated (stage four). This, of course, enabled John to miss more exams, getting farther and farther behind in his courses. A vicious circle (stage five) was entrenched in a very few months. John will get his wish. He will no longer have to go to college, but failure is the price of his escape.

The characteristic feature of neurotic behaviour is its self-defeating nature. It sets up a cycle of failure that confirms the original fear of failure. Neurotics are successful in the short run, but their strategy is hopeless in the long term.

Symptoms of Neurosis

Involvement in the neurotic experience is not difficult. Some symptoms are experienced by all of us. We will consider three of the most frequently occurring ones before we move on to some specific varieties of psychoneurotic behaviour.

Anxiety The defensive manoeuvres developed by the ego become ineffectual. Normally submerged or unconscious anxiety surfaces at the conscious level. Neurotic anxiety, according to the psychoanalysts, comes in three varieties: free-floating anxiety attacks, and panic—each more serious than the preceding one. Free-floating anxiety is diffuse and low-level apprehension. Anxiety attacks, on the other hand, are specific irrational fears, accompanied by physiological manifestations, such as anxiety, sweating, and elevated pulse rate. Panic, the third variety, is an overwhelming response to the demands of the id. Conscious control of impulses is lost. All three forms of anxiety exact a physical toll as well as a psychological one, often resulting in the emergence of full-fledged neurotic symptoms.

Lack of Insight Neurotic individuals are incapable of understanding the dynamics of their self-defeating manoeuvers. A self-centred preoccupation precludes understanding, because insight means coming to terms with the underlying reason for the neurosis. Lack of insight is a highly adaptive symptom, having both positive and negative consequences. Knowing why we behave neurotically involves a painful recognition of psychic weakness, so avoiding the knowledge spares us discomfort. But not knowing the reasons for the pathological behaviour means that we will continue to behave pathologically.

Fatigue Repression hides dangerous and threatening impulses from consciousness. However, if the impulse is strong, then the energy required to defend against it is great. The result is fatigue, emotional vulnerability and non-specific aches and pains. When repression begins to fail, new defensive manoeuvers are required to keep anxiety at bay. Fatigue symptoms reduce anxiety because they camouflage the problem, reducing the need for the energy-draining manoeuver called repression.

Some Varieties of Neurotic Behaviour

Neuroses reflect a compromise made by the ego to eliminate, or at least reduce, the debilitating effects of anxiety. Some of the more common varieties of neurosis are: dissociative reactions, obsessive-compulsive reactions, phobic reactions and depressive reactions. We will examine these four neuroses to get a better understanding of their psychoanalytic basis.

Dissociative Reactions

Dissociative neuroses are dramatic attempts to escape from the debilitating effects of anxiety by splitting off some portion of the personality from the rest. The portion that remains intact is normally unaware of the existence of the dissociated portion. This compromise not only involves the psyche, but the central nervous system as well. Literally, one part of the brain does not receive the information that the other part does. There are several forms dissociative neuroses can take. Among them are somnambulism (sleepwalking), amnesia and multiple personality.

Sleepwalking is the most common form of dissociation. In psychoanalytic terms, this neurosis reflects a symbolic attempt to escape from an anxiety-producing situation, albeit in a brief and incomplete way. The sleepwalking discharges anxiety temporarily. Sleepwalking is often seen in adolescents and young adults who unconsciously desire to sever the emotional and financial ties to their parents, but are unable to do so in reality. Leaving the house in the middle of the night is one way of temporarily severing those ties.

Amnesia serves the ego in much the same way as sleepwalking by providing escape from an intolerable situation or unresolved conflict. If a person cannot recall who he is or where he lives, then the troubles disappear, sometimes for a few days, and, in rare cases, permanently. This is running away, with none of the responsibilities or consequences connected with it. As such, this reaction is a highly adaptive one, though destructive in the long run. Psychic surgery subtracts behaviour from an already inadequate repertoire, but to the neurotic individual this radical surgery is absolutely essential.

The rarest form of dissociative neurosis is multiple personality. It is often confused with schizophrenia, but bears no relationship to that psychosis. The neurosis involves the development of two or more personality systems, each with distinct characteristics. Usually, the individual's normal self is the dominant one, and has no information about the existence of the other autonomously functioning personalities. This makes "neurotic" sense if we remember that neurosis shields the owner from forbidden and threatening impulses. What better way to do this than to have a co-existing personality acting out the impulses? The dominant personality remains free of anxiety.

Obsessive-Compulsive Reactions

Obsessive-compulsive neuroses function in the same way other neuroses do. They assuage anxiety. The distinguishing feature of this pattern is that the neurotic is driven to organize, tidy, time, sanitize, and manage his world. This frenetic activity spells safety and security. Control of impulses and the anxiety that surrounds their emergence are contained.

In the psychoanalytic approach, the neurotic manoeuver is seen as a protection for the individual from knowledge of his anxieties, his insecurity, and his guilt. Repetitive acts and/or thoughts serve to discharge the pent-up tension. Keeping busy is as essential to an obsessive-compulsive neurotic as the maintenance of life itself. Vacations are terrifying if they are not organized down to the last detail. Homes are so clean that the washed walls never have an opportunity to dry. Decisions are carefully weighed and measured, but then come to a grinding halt. What if it is the wrong decision? The process starts again. Obsessive-compulsive neurotics are very common, and a great deal of television advertising about cleanliness appeals to them. However, this pattern of behaviour is a self-defeating one, particularly because of its effect on interpersonal relations. Going back into the house five times to make sure the water taps are shut off is hardly the way to endear oneself to impatient companions. Insisting on changing the sheets and showering before and after sexual relations will cool the ardour of even the most patient of suitors. Procrastinating about each and every decision until the other person in the relationship takes charge is bound to annoy even the most authoritarian of spouses. Eventually those closest to obsessive-compulsive people give way to hostility and resentment. This threatens the fragile neurotic defence system still further. Even with therapy, obsessive-compulsive neurotics rarely lose their rigidity, although it can be reduced to some manageable level.

Phobic Reactions

In psychoanalytic terms, phobias are the simplest neuroses. They involve the use of three defence mechanisms: repression, regression and displacement. Repression blocks from consciousness the reason for feeling anxious. Regression (age-inappropriate behaviour) exempts the phobic from participating in events and situations about which he is irrationally fearful. And displacing the source and presence of anxiety on to an object or situation that can usually be avoided prevents the individual from experiencing anxiety. This tripartite process is a modest attempt at self-cure. However, like all neuroses, the "cure" is a costly one, for two reasons: one avoids those life experiences that are feared, thus restricting possible growth-enriching events. Secondly, phobias tend to generalize. An uncomplicated phobia about open places may gradually expand from open-air theatres or panoramic vistas to large rooms, such as gymnasiums or concert halls, to one's living room. Many seriously disabled phobics stay in their homes for years at a time. Even stepping into the yard is enough to activate that anxiety that formerly was displaced on to open-air theatres and vistas.

What can we be phobic about? To put it succinctly, anything and everything. Dirt, snakes, death, fire, growing old, the dark, heights, to name a few, are the most common phobias. Some people hide their phobias, climbing mountains to mask acrophobia (fear of heights). Most, however, use phobias to gain attention or to solicit protection, albeit on an unconscious level. Phobic reactions have functional consequences (sympathy, support, avoidance of responsibility), but the trade-off is a narrow, restrictive life governed by fears over which one has minimal control, even under the best of circumstances.

Depressive Reactions

The most serious and complicated neurosis is the depression reaction. The victim has an aura of dejection, joylessness, inconsolability, and lethargy. Living is a hopeless task. In contrast to other neuroses, this reaction is more sensitive to external threats, although internal dynamics are still a vital part of the process.

Neurotic depressives act out their lives with an agenda from the past, and, as with any outmoded technique, it simply doesn't work. The normal human psyche is in constant preparation for present and future events, constantly revamping its script of earlier years. The neurotic depressive drops the script revisions and substitutes instead a broken record theme—playing it over and over again. The theme is one of self-disparagement ("I'm so useless, I can never do anything right."), self-pity ("How can you possibly care for me. I am such a failure."), and lowered self-esteem ("No one loves me."). The unfortunate aspect of this defensive strategy is that eventually the projections are fulfilled. After years of intimidating manoeuvers to gain attention from loved ones and never believing their reassurances, the loved ones end up shaking their heads, wringing their hands, and walking away. Of course, this confirms the neurotic depressive's belief that they never really loved him—as he suspected all along. Such a vicious circle of ineffective repression, followed by chronic complaining, supplemented by loved ones' assurances, buries the neurotic depressive deeper in self-condemnation. Each time the cycle repeats itself, the "justification" for feeling worthless is greater. A few depressed persons do commit suicide. However, most find less final forms of self-punishment. The depressive neurosis is often sufficient punishment in itself.

There are other forms of neurotic behaviour which are similarly characterized·by the need to repress dangerous id impulses because of the anxiety that accompanies their expression. Ego defence manoeuvers, exhausting and ineffectual, are gradually replaced by neurotic strategies. These strategies prevent the immediate emergence of anxiety, but they are self-defeating in the long run.

THE PSYCHOANALYTIC APPROACH TO THERAPY

The emphasis on neurosis in this section on the psychoanalytic approach underscores some basic ideas held in common by psychoanalytic therapists. First, talking with a therapist is an essential condition of psychoanalytic therapy. Many non-neurotic disorders, however, do not lend themselves to this therapeutic style. Second, psychoanalysts maintain the underlying unconscious processes of neurosis must be explored in order to understand the dynamics of a neurotic sequence. Change only occurs when the underlying factors are brought to consciousness to be analyzed. Third, a neurotic sequence cannot be altered successfully unless drastic reconstruction of the personality takes place. This is done by probing the traumatic events of childhood, reliving them, resolving them, and returning them, devoid of their anxiety and its consequences, to the unconscious. On the face of it, this psychoanalytic process sounds quite straightforward. Quite the contrary. Psychoanalysis is a painful, time-consuming, often unsuccessful process, requiring a sincere desire to alter the personality structure. And, as psychoanalysts stress, the neurotic is fighting all the way to hang on to a set of marginally adaptive strategies that have gained him a great deal of attention. Becoming "normal" is sometimes an insufficient reward to someone who has spent years actively avoiding harsh and threatening thoughts and impulses. In more ways than one "It's what you don't know that hurts you."

Classical Psychoanalysis

Psychoanalysis is not for everyone. Even Freud felt it was best suited to reasonably educated and reliable patients. Later psychoanalysts are often more specific. The most suitable candidate for therapy is between seventeen and fifty years of age, at least average in intelligence, articulate and imaginative in verbal expression, revealing in his shortcomings, prepared to approach therapy as a joint effort, and highly motivated to change. Many psychoanalytically oriented therapists, however, settle for considerably less.

The treatment technique is based on the hypothesis that neurosis is nurtured by repression of vital aspects of the personality and its experiences. Therapy consists of restoring to consciousness that which was removed by repression. The relationship with the therapist provides the ego bolstering necessary to cope with the anxiety produced by the return of the repressed material. To minimize distortion of this material, the technical procedures of free association, the couch position, passivity of the therapist, dream analysis, and the encouragement of transference are used.

In actual practice, Freud observed that if the patient lay in a relaxed position and was encouraged to report his or her thoughts, no matter how shocking or trivial (free association), the repressed memories tended to come back of themselves. In addition to free association, Freud utilized dream analysis, believing that repressed material is revealed in the dream structure. In fact, Freud called dreams "the royal road to the unconscious." The encouragement of transference is also essential to successful psychoanalysis. The patient literally transfers feelings about his parents to the analyst. The emotional turmoil of a neurotic's life history is re-enacted in the therapeutic situation. The analyst "becomes" the parent(s). Interpretation of this transference process by the analyst is carried out in order to expose its nature. This is one of the few places in the psychoanalytic process where the therapist plays an active role. It is used to bring the patient to an awareness of his repressed context, and the historical origin of his conflicts. Resolution of transferences is held to be the most powerful vehicle for producing structural personality changes.

Summary

Freud's views on therapeutic intervention were derived logically from his views on personality development: the power of the unconscious, the importance of early childhood events, the precarious mediation process of the ego, and the possible consequences of ineffectual mediation and compromise. Reactivation of childhood traumas to lessen the tendency to use massive repression and its neurotic correlates is the aim of psychoanalysis. Insight develops, allowing the ego to develop more adaptive patterns of behaviour.

THE BEHAVIOURAL APPROACH

Behaviourists maintain that "mental illness" is either a complex of learned, inappropriate behaviours, or the absence of appropriate behaviour sequences. In the first instance, behaviour is termed "maladaptive"; in the second, the phenomenon is termed "deficit learning." Most forms of "abnormality" are of the acquired maladaptive variety. Society defines such behaviours as pathological. Further, the rules of acquisition of maladaptive behaviour are no different than the rules of acquisition of adaptive sequences. This means that pathological behaviour differs from the non-pathological sort only in its social adaptiveness. As for deficit learning, the person simply has not been reinforced for learning effective social skills; hence, those skills have not developed.

Behaviourists have offered provocative and challenging explanations of abnormal behaviour. Their primary emphasis is on *how* a particular maladaptive sequence is acquired, not why. Knowing the specific conditions that maintain the behaviour are the key to its removal—there are no underlying organic factors to abnormal behaviour. For example, neuroses are simply learned habits. The labels *neurosis, psychosis,* and *personality disorder* merely describe behaviours. The symptom is the disorder. No underlying, unconscious causes are involved. This assumption enables the behaviourist to treat symptoms directly, without delving into past traumas. Obviously there is a wide gap between the behavioural perspective and the psychoanalytic one.

Another major difference between the two approaches concerns the issue of "symptom substitution." The psychoanalytic approach emphasizes that the elimination of symptoms, without getting at their cause, will leave a vacuum in the personality structure which will immediately be filled by a new symptom—possibly more defeating and counterproductive than the first one. Behaviourists, on the other hand, argue that the removal of a maladaptive symptom (through reinforcement withdrawal) enables the individual to develop more productive behaviour simply because he has more time to do so. If another maladaptive behaviour does emerge, it is not evidence that symptom substitution has taken place. Rather, it indicates that, since the first behaviour has been extinguished, a less prominent, but well-established, behaviour has the opportunity to appear more often. Several behaviourists have gone to great lengths to demonstrate that symptom substitution does not exist. It is in their interest to do so. After all, their position on abnormal behaviour is that symptoms are simply learned habits bound by the principles of classical and/or operant conditioning, not signs of some deep underlying conflict or biological defect.

As we have said, behaviourists define abnormal behaviour as socially maladaptive or deficient behaviour. The varieties of such behaviour are infinite. Consequently, the behaviourists spend little time devising a classification system to cover pathological behaviours. When similarities are found between individuals, they are attributed to similarities in social patterns of conditioning.

This position by behaviourists, that there is probably no workable operational definition for mental illness, has led to some interesting questions. Why, for example, do many people who are classified as mentally ill display similar symptoms? The behaviourists maintain that role learning of "sick" behaviours is one way of gaining sympathy, attention and psychological treatment. Acquiring characteristics that mental health professionals have defined as symptoms of mental illness, makes it more likely that treatment will be provided. Over the years, people have become quite sophisticated in their knowledge of psychiatric symptoms. Acquiring a particular set serves two functions: it provides structure and meaning to otherwise diffuse and chaotic experiences that the individual is having; and it gives the professional a cluster of symptoms that he can diagnose and treat. Sounds callous, doesn't it? However, keep in mind that from a behavioural perspective, humans behave in ways that will maximize reinforcement and minimize punishment.

Behaviourists view institutionalization as a further continuation of the learning process. For anyone who has read Kesey's *One Flew Over the Cuckoo's Nest*, it should be obvious that institutionalized settings exert strong pressure to assume the qualities that fit the diagnosis. If one is diagnosed as a simple schizophrenic, the expectation is that the individual will be passive, withdrawn, slow to comprehend, and pliable. Those behaviours will be reinforced; others will not. This is not intentional on the part of the mental hospital personnel, but mental hospitals can drive patients crazy if they are reinforced for their "crazy" behaviours, instead of their sane ones. This indictment of the biological or medical model (to be considered later in this chapter) is a noteworthy one and should not be discounted.

Behaviourists have been quite successful in their treatment of maladaptive behaviours. They may accept a diagnosis that has been applied to an individual, but they are more concerned with the circumstances that maintain (reinforce) the behaviours on which the diagnosis is based. Once an understanding of the environmental circumstances surrounding maladaptive behaviours are discovered, a program of extinction can be developed. Behaviour modification therapists have treated sexual inadequacy, hysterical blindness, phobias, stuttering, hyperactivity, alcoholism, mutism, self-mutilation, hypochondria, and anorexia nervosa (psychological loss of appetite).

BEHAVIOUR THERAPY

The treatment of maladaptive behaviour can proceed in a number of ways. Two approaches are most frequently used. The first approach involves translating the language and techniques of non-behavioural approaches into the terms of positive and negative social reinforcements, and applied reinforcement principles. This approach is a theoretical one, and emphasizes that regardless of what a clinician thinks he is doing, he is in fact employing behaviour therapy.

The second approach is a more pragmatic and applied one, involving the development and use of specific behaviour modification procedures. The resulting techniques will be the basis of our discussion of behaviour therapy. The techniques include behaviour elimination methods (desensitization and aversive learning), and behaviour formation methods (selective positive reinforcement and token economy).

All these treatment techniques have certain elements in common. The therapist must be aware of the maladaptive behaviours in very specific terms. Reporting "nervousness" as a general problem must be narrowed to the circumstances and frequency of that nervousness, as well as the behavioural form that it takes. Once identified, the therapist can establish a program of procedures to eliminate the maladaptive responses and establish new, more adaptive ones.

Behaviour Elimination Methods:
Desensitization and Aversive Learning

When a persistent maladaptive habit, such as fear of sex in a married woman, is brought to the attention of a behaviour modification therapist, the following sequence occurs: by questioning the woman, the therapist pinpoints those specific instances and conditions that trigger her symptoms of anxiety, revulsion and disgust. Once those events are isolated, the therapist trains the patient in deep muscle relaxation. After a few sessions when she is able to relax at will, the therapist asks her to imagine the least anxiety-producing aspect of sexual relations. As tension increases, she is to'd to relax. Once relaxation is achieved with the lowest-level fear, the therapist gradually moves up the hierarchy of sexual fears. Relaxation must be achieved at each level before another sexual experience is introduced. Since fear and relaxation are incompatible responses, relaxation when a sexual thought or act occurs inhibits fear or disgust. Gradually, a program of physical contact with the husband is attempted by the woman, using the same principles. Eventually, the fear of sex is desensitized and replaced by more adaptive responses that previously were blocked. Notice that no attempt is made to explore the "deep underlying cause" for this fear of sex. Such explorations are unwarranted, and unnecessary, maintain the behaviourists.

Desensitization is also used where anxiety is less obvious than in the previous example. Psychophysiological disorders are of particular interest, because they are so common and represent a very real threat to the biological functioning of an individual. Ulcers, high blood pressure, asthma and migraines represent a few of these emotionally based disorders. Usually people with psychophysiological disorders have learned to inhibit emotional responses for fear of rejection. This inhibition results in the channeling of neural responses to vulnerable organ systems (respiratory, cardiovascular, gastro-intestinal, and so forth). The treatment of such disorders involves identifying the events which lead to inhibited emotions, in order to desensitize the patient and reduce the anxiety. Training an ulcer-prone individual to communicate his fears is essential to breaking the neural connection to the stomach, where excess acid secretion causes a peptic ulcer.

A second behaviour elimination method is called *aversive learning*. In contrast to desensitization, aversive learning attempts to *eliminate* maladaptive responses that are interfering with a person's functioning. The acquired maladaptive response usually has been paired with pleasant experiences. Consequently, the therapist seeks to sever the connection between the two, and teach the individual to associate the maladaptive response with unpleasantness. The most widely used application of aversive learning is in the treatment of alcoholism, drug and cigarette addiction, homosexuality and pedophilia (child molestation).

Typically, the maladaptive behaviour is paired with a noxious stimulus (such as a painful electric shock) so that the individual learns to inhibit the response. In the case of pedophilia, the adult male is shown pictures of young children that are similar in gender and appearance to the child he has molested. Emotional responsiveness to the photographs is recorded electro-mechanically, and when an erectile response occurs, an electric shock is administered automatically. The shock is terminated when the emotional response subsides. The rationale behind this technique is that the pedophile comes to associate feelings of pain with sexual arousal surrounding young children. In much the same way, drinking becomes associated with discomfort through the use of a drug that induces nausea and vomiting after liquor has been ingested. In both desensitization and aversive learning, an attempt is made to weaken and extinguish existing maladaptive responses. In the following techniques, the goal is to foster adaptive responses through behaviour formation methods.

Behaviour Formation Techniques:
Selective Positive Reinforcement and Token Economies

An important departure from traditional psychotherapeutic practices has been the development of behaviour formation techniques. In other approaches, the emphasis is on eliminating undesirable or counterproductive behaviours, thus freeing the patient to develop new, constructive patterns on his own. In behaviour formation approaches, this acquisition of constructive behaviour is directed by a carefully designed program called *selective positive reinforcement*. Essentially, the program provides rewards for desirable behaviour, and withholds them for undesirable behaviour. In theory, and in a controlled environmental situation, the procedure works quite nicely.

The use of selective positive reinforcement has an infinite variety of applications. It is simply a technique that makes reward contingent on adequate performance. One application of this technique is with the condition labelled *anorexia nervosa*. People with this acquired condition have difficulty in swallowing and retaining food. In some cases, this psychological loss of appetite is so severe that the person must be fed intravenously in order to be kept alive.

The goals in *anorexia nervosa* are to re-establish eating behaviour, and to make eating behaviour a positively reinforcing event. Normally no attempt is made to obtain a detailed psychiatric history, although unsolicited reports are often provided by the patient. An illustrative example is provided by Bachrach, Erwin and Mohr in *Case Studies in Behaviour Modification* (Ullman and Krasner, 1965). Some details of the case follow:

> The patient was a thirty-seven-year-old female whose chief complaint was "a block about food." Her weight of 118 pounds had remained stable from age eleven to eighteen. Over a period of about nineteen years, her weight loss was gradual but continuous, and by the time she reached her thirty-seventh birthday she weighed forty-seven pounds. Her appearance was described as a "poorly preserved mummy."

Her in-patient care consisted of denying her any pleasures unless she ate. Her hospital room was barren, no visitors were allowed, and contact with the nursing staff was kept to a minimum. Only at mealtimes was there anyone present to communicate with her. Even then, verbal interaction was contingent upon attempts at eating. Gradually, reinforcement (a radio brought in, talking with the researcher, and so forth) was withheld until food was consumed. Caloric intake was adjusted upward. All additional social reinforcers were postponed until after meal time. Later, the patient was allowed to eat with other patients in more pleasant surroundings. In approximately two months, she gained fourteen pounds. The prognosis for her complete recovery was good.

There are two interesting aspects to this particular case: the reluctance of the nursing staff to participate in such an "inhuman" experiment and the powerful effect of reinforcement. Clearly, this case required immediate attention because death was a very real possibility. The behaviour therapists felt that this concern necessitated a radical alteration of the patient's environment. The decision to remove all pleasures from the patient, in an attempt to prevent her demise, seemed warranted, especially since other forms of therapy had been attempted. The use of the reinforcement properties of social interaction, provided only at mealtime, turned out to be a happy choice. It also became obvious to the behaviourists that this pairing of positive reinforcement with eating had to continue in some form once the patient was released from the hospital. Her family was instructed in the rudiments of behaviour modification and given a list of instructions to follow. As you might suspect, the list was a continuation of the same principles that had restored eating behaviour in the hospital: never allow the patient to eat alone; dine under enjoyable conditions; don't make an issue of eating, and so forth. Previous to her hospitalization, none of the conditions were present. Mealtimes were erratic, unpleasant, and ultimately, non-reinforcing.

The use of selective positive reinforcement has many applications. The requirements for its use usually involve a controlled environment (at least initially), an understanding of the reinforcement properties of the maladaptive sequence under consideration, and a program which allows for more adaptive behaviours to emerge so that reinforcement can be provided.

In a similar way, *token economies* have been developed in psychiatric institutions to develop and strengthen constructive and useful behaviour of patients by applying operant conditioning techniques. As in selective positive reinforcement, token economies do not attempt to eliminate maladaptive behaviour (although that is often a by-product). Rather, the aim is to establish functional behaviours by means of reinforcement in the form of tokens or chips. Specifically, tokens are earned for engaging in constructive behaviour (making one's bed, going to meals, attending to personal hygiene, participating in group activities, etc.). These tokens may be exchanged for a wide variety of desired activities and goods, such as choosing a group with whom to sit in the dining room, a weekend pass, reading and writing materials, choosing television programs, or a private visit with the doctor.

The aim of a token economy system in a mental institution is to break the dependency relationship that tends to develop between patient and caretaker. Usually this means that all patients, regardless of their ability to function, receive almost identical benefits in non-token economy settings. One need not function in order to obtain rewards. Because unconditional reward is rarely encountered in a non-institutional setting, it becomes less and less likely that a patient will be able to function outside of an institution, the longer he resides in one. Since the goal of psychiatric institutions is rehabilitative, behaviour which is functional and productive should be rewarded, and behaviour which is neither, should not. Most psychiatric institutions do not have token economies throughout. However, many have established such systems on a ward basis. The principles of a token economy system are only different from most reinforcement systems in the real world (e.g., a paycheque for doing a job) in one respect: rewards are more stringently controlled. All behaviour is carefully monitored and tabulated, so that the appropriate number of tokens is given to each patient. An interesting by-product of this type of system is that it makes the appearance of disruptive or bizarre behaviour less likely to occur, simply because maladaptive behaviours cannot coexist with functional ones.

To some, the token economy system smacks of crass bribery. Even Skinner would prefer other reinforcers to the rewards that tokens currently bring. However, to him and many other behaviourists, one uses what works. And in our present society, rewards in the forms of gifts, praise, and affection are highly valued. So that is what is used.

Summary

The behaviourists' approach to the treatment of maladaptive behaviour flows logically from their research on human and animal learning. They disdain "deep underlying causes" of behaviour, for, to them, the symptom is the disorder. Consequently, their treatment techniques focus on present behaviour and the conditions that activate and maintain it. The application of behaviour modification techniques includes treatment of a wide range of behavioural symptoms with a moderate degree of success. However, generalization to real-life situations is often unsuccessful in the absence of reinforcement control.

THE COGNITIVE APPROACH

Cognitive theorists, as a whole, are not noted for their work in the conceptualization and classification of abnormal behaviour. For the most part, when they do become involved in the area, it is usually in the treatment process. As such, they have no fixed philosophy about the origins and manifestations of psychopathological behaviour.

One theorist, George Kelly, stands out as an exception. His view of psychological disorders is conceptualized in terms of cognitive theory. The goal is to develop a scientific study of abnormal behaviour and its treatment. The result is a cognitive, and intellectually stimulating theory of human behaviour.

Essentially, abnormal behaviour is seen as an inability to understand and anticipate reality. It occurs because the individual does not make suitable judgments, focussing on key aspects of the world and consigning them to poles of dimensions, such as *safe-dangerous*, or *cruel-kind*. He does not have the appropriate *constructs* by which to judge events accurately.[1] The acquisition of new constructs is seen as the only possible alternative to this anxious, guilt-ridden, threatening and hostile way of relating to the world. This approach stands in sharp contrast to the psychoanalytic approach which stresses the unconscious surge of energy victimizing the individual. Like the humanistic approach, there is an emphasis on conscious processes, not unconscious ones.

A psychological disorder, then, is the failure of an individual's construct system. Or as Kelly (1955) has stated it, an emotional disturbance is "any personal construction which is used repeatedly in spite of consistent invalidation." When predictions are repeatedly shown to be incorrect, anxiety, tension, guilt or hostility result. Rather than alter his constructs of reality, the individual redoubles his efforts to gain attention or confirmation. This effort is self-defeating, generating more and more invalidation. One type of personality that emerges from this series of events is a narrow, rigid, and closed one. With a limited set of constructs, prediction of events in the world becomes impossible. Another response might be to select new constructs, but this frantic search, too, is often ineffectual. In both cases, the psychologically disturbed individual is able to anticipate events with only limited accuracy. Mental illness, therefore, is a failure to learn, or cope adequately with the world.

Human beings choose either destructive alternatives or constructive ones, or a combination of both. The choice, once made, sets the

---

[1] Kelly views a *construct* as a sort of pattern which the individual uses, testing the world against it. It is similar to the schemata discussed in Chapter 1. By applying his patterns, or constructs, the individual decides whether events, people and objects fall at one end of the construct or the other—that is, they are categorized into groups.

For example, I find the construct *sincere-insincere* a useful one in categorizing people. By assigning the people I meet to one pole or the other, I have a basis for acting towards people. However, if I habitually use a construct such as *light-dark* to construe people, I would probably be less able to understand them and predict their behaviour. *Light-dark* is a less appropriate construct for people.

stage for further development. Consequently, difficulties of psychological adjustment are, to a large extent, of our own making. Destructive constructs of the world, especially in the area of interpersonal relations, mean that individuals using them are consistently incorrect in their predictions. No wonder they are in psychological difficulty. Violating social norms exacts a heavy price—that of being regarded as mentally ill.

Psychological Disorders

Kelly's approach to mental illness involves recasting already familiar symptoms into terms relevant to cognitive theory. Of particular importance is the research done with schizophrenic patients. Schizophrenia is a broad term used to describe the behaviour of about half of the mentally ill hospital population in North America. There is general agreement that this syndrome involves disturbances in thought, concept formation, affect (mood), and emotional responsiveness. If, as Kelly maintains, a psychological disturbance involves a personal construction of reality that is consistently invalid, the treatment of schizophrenic disorders would be of particular interest. Research by Bannister and Fransella (1966) suggests that schizophrenics are less consistent in their construing of people than normals. Damaged interpersonal constructs over a long period of time are consolidated into a cognitive style labelled "schizophrenia."

Other psychological disturbances are similarly viewed as resulting from the choice of destructive alternatives. In depressive reactions, for example, construct systems are too narrow and rigid. In manic reactions there is a construct overload, leading to frenetic, grandiose, and feverish excitement. Paranoia is seen as a sophisticated persecution construct, where all reality is perceived as threatening.

Other less severe syndromes can also be viewed in cognitive terms. Anxiety is seen by Kelly as an awareness that one's constructs are no longer applicable or relevant. The anxiety-ridden individual has run out of viable constructs. Without constructs with which to judge reality, one cannot anticipate events or deal with problems. This view of an anxiety reaction is in sharp contrast to the Freudian view. Recall from our earlier discussion that the psychoanalytic position is an intrapsychic one. Anxiety is caused by unconscious forces, seeking recognition in non-adaptive ways. Kelly's cognitive theory is essentially a social psychological one. External events, not internal ones, are the stimulators of anxiety.

To a lesser degree, one can observe construct failure in everyday life. A college student construes himself as competent and mature. Yet, when he returns home for vacations, his parents may still use their old constructs of immaturity and incompetence. Hostility often results.

Therapeutic Change: Fixed-Role Therapy

Kelly's work raises the issue of experience and its relationship to personality. Some people reconstruct their lives on a regular and thoughtful basis; others rarely do—and only under intense interpersonal pressure. As you might suspect, Kelly endorses the development of non-rigid constructs, so that even the concept of change becomes an integral part of one's personality. Building suitable construct systems is the aim of Kelly's psychotherapy.

Kelly's approach to psychotherapy bears a strong relationship to two scientists working in a laboratory on an exciting, new scientific experiment: the development of broader, more flexible constructs. Both client and therapist are active in the process of discovery. New constructs are developed by the patient-scientist, tested, and then accepted or discarded depending on their usefulness. The therapist guides, encourages, offers suggestions, and responds to the new constructions.

Kelly called his own form of psychotherapy *fixed-role therapy*. This treatment alternative is based on the premise that human beings are what they construe themselves to be. Their behaviour is a function of those constructions. A character sketch written in the third person by the patient provides the initial data from which habitual constructions are deduced. From a careful analysis of the patient's sketch, a team of clinical psychologists prepares a fixed-role sketch, designed to be a beneficial and objective role model for the patient. The sketch is shown to the patient to determine if the portrait represents who the patient would like to be. Upon acceptance of the sketch (or a revised version, if necessary), the patient is asked to act like the person described in the sketch. In other words, the patient is to suspend his old identity for fourteen days, and substitute an active portrayal of the sketch. The experiment begins with frequent meetings with the therapist. During these meetings, the therapist responds to the patient as if he were the person in the fixed-role sketch.

A distinguishing feature of fixed-role therapy is that attention to psychodynamic forces is minimal. Dwelling upon past performances is eliminated, and little personal threat or defensiveness is activated due to the impersonality of the sketch, and the scientific nature of the endeavour. This is a radical alternative to the emotionally charged nature of classical psychoanalysis.

Not all people who engage in fixed-role therapy successfully alter their constructs. But for those who do there is a new zest and productivity to their lives. Change is no longer feared, but is actively pursued for the purpose of development; the past is no longer dwelled upon, the future is anticipated; the individual is no longer swamped with invalidated constructions, he freely determines his own behaviour.

In summary, Kelly views human beings as scientists. We generate hypotheses about life and test them against real events. These empirical tests become the basis for theories about reality. As more and more hypotheses are subjected to empirical scrutiny, some theories or propositions are accepted; others are rejected. This is Kelly's view of normal behaviour. Those individuals who maintain theories, even though they are repeatedly disconfirmed, are mentally ill. Hostility, depression, anxiety and other unpleasant experiences result from their faulty interaction with others. For Kelly, behaviour is determined by one's constructs, and since constructs are alterable, better constructs can be found, leading to more adaptive behaviour. Fixed-role therapy encourages the development of new constructs in a direct and unorthodox way. Why it sometimes fails is better answered by the humanistic approach which follows.

THE HUMANISTIC APPROACH

The most radical view of abnormal behaviour is held by the humanists. Unlike the other approaches we have been considering, the humanists see a psychological disturbance as a potentially liberating experience—a stepping stone to personal growth and development.

The humanist movement maintains that we live in a non-humanistic world which stresses crass materialism and conformity to a set of social criteria, not of our own making. Conforming to the values of others is the first step on the road to mental illness, because it implies that the individual does not trust his own ability to appraise and evaluate experience. He lets others do it for him. Using society's criteria is unnatural and may result in the splitting off of intense and personal human feeling from the "plastic personality" constructed by and for others. This is mental illness—conforming to a world made by others, at the expense of our own innate potential. Conversely, mental health is creating and acting in a world designed by us—not by someone else. Liberation comes when an individual faces the harsh and painful truth that he is trapped in an empty existence, and, more importantly, that he never resisted while the trap was being set. This restriction of one's inner potential manifests itself in narrow life experiences fraught with cynicism, despair, loneliness and hostility. To protest is the beginning of liberation. To change is difficult but necessary if mental health is to be achieved. It is a matter of choice.

Not all persons who develop false personalities experience anxiety, bitterness, and estrangement from themselves and others, at least initially. Defensive strategies are often employed to deceive us into believing we are healthy and adjusted. Carl Rogers talks about two such strategies: distortion and denial. *Distortion* is a technique whereby contradictions between self and social evaluations are falsified so that they do not appear to be contradictions. *Denial* is simply ignoring contradictions. The failure of these strategies produces the same feelings of loneliness and despair that other individuals have who never resorted to using them. They are simply stop-gap measures with no real value. Abraham Maslow writes in much the same vein. Being trapped at lower levels of the need hierarchy prevents individuals from developing their potentials. Alienation, cynicism and a sense of emptiness are common feelings.

Why is it necessary to experience pain and emotional turmoil in order to grow and fulfill oneself? The humanists point out that resisting the cultural pressures to conform is difficult. It involves constant vigilance on the part of each individual. Mental health is a personal achievement which requires daily effort to maintain. Positive disintegration of the person's self-structure, if that structure has been created by others, is the only way to achieve psychic growth. Since most of our family and friends live in a state of "non-being", becoming fulfilled is often lonely and done at the cost of close relationships.

Varieties of Psychological Maladjustment

Humanists do not label people. They consider that diagnostic labels tend to confuse rather than clarify the understanding of individuals. It is a de-personalization tactic which is fundamentally alienating. The only distinctions about mental states that are made tend to be broad and general ones. Either there is congruence between the self and experience, or there is not. Congruence indiciates adjustment; incongruence indicates maladjustment. Mental health is loosely defined as the presence of a constellation of feelings, attitudes and behaviours—by the absence of abnormal symptoms, as the biological approach defines it. Rogers' characterization of the fully functioning person (1961), and Maslow's qualities of the self-actualizing person (1970) demonstrate the humanistic position on psychological adjustment. An abbreviated list of these qualities follows:

1. Openness to experience in a natural and spontaneous way. An adjusted person responds to life without gimmicks or trinkets. Their unconventionality is a reflection of inner strength—and often, unfortunately, the object of envy. Social conventions are not violated intentionally, and are often subscribed to if they do not impinge on the individual's sense of morality. But an adjusted person can and will stand apart from them easily. "But what will the neighbours think if we don't mow the lawn?" is not the kind of statement made by a spontaneously reactive person.

2. A philosophical sense of humour transcending class, ethnic, or educational barriers. Adjusted individuals laugh at the human condition, never at individual human failings. Their humour is purposeful, never deprecating. Some of Mark Twain's writing serves as a good literary example. Occasionally M*A*S*H television scripts attempt it. Jokes that hurt, denigrate, or thinly disguise hostility are reliable indicators of maladjustment.

3. Organismic trusting of self and an unburdened acceptance of others. The actualizing person senses when a decision is a good one. That sense of trust is also generalized to others' capabilities. Strengths and weaknesses are balanced, relationships attempted, assessments made, and friendships are solidified or terminated, graciously, guiltlessly and without shame. The adjusted person does not maintain a hopeless relationship simply for the "sake of the children." Nor does he or she interact with many people on a superficial level. Self-actualizing friendships are emotionally involving and time-consuming, and far more enjoyable than superficial chit-chat about bar-b-que utensils or "Let me tell you how much I drank last week at a really great party. . . ."

4, A sense of detachment and a need for some private solitude. In a society such as ours, it is difficult for many individuals to conceptualize "being alone." For the healthy ones, however, time to retreat into one's inner resources is highly valued. It is also indicative of an even more profound quality: experiential freedom. The fully functioning person feels fully responsible for his or her destiny. Privacy and solitude is required to make choices about personal goals, free of contaminating external influences. To the non-adjusted, being alone and being lonely are synonymous.

5. Creativity and constructiveness. Psychological maturity yields imaginative goals, novel ideas and ingenious solutions. The creative characteristic cuts across all facets of adjustive functioning, and indicates a freshness of appreciation for life. Stale people produce sterile, non-innovative solutions to crises and are loathe to change. "But we've always done it that way" is the frequently heard, plaintive cry of the bureaucrat.

The humanist maintains that discovery of everyday realities is a pleasant and fulfilling experience. However, it does mean that one is often at odds with society's mainstream. Psychological maturity is hard work and the developing and refining of the required qualities does not come easily. An egalitarian character structure is essential, and the ability to resist the silly, mundane, trivial and outrageous demands of others requires great psychic strength. Launching oneself into the stream of life is not for the faint-hearted.

Humanistic Psychotherapy

In the humanistic view, most of us would benefit from some form of therapy. However, comparatively few of us seek it. A seeker of humanistic psychotherapy has already taken a major step, because seeking is an indicator of psychological maturity. Some seekers, however, are at a temporary loss as to how to proceed once they have recognized their own personal sense of incongruence. There are numerous alternatives ranging from encounter groups to non-directive therapy. However, there is general agreement on the goal of therapy. Essentially, the goal is to provide a therapeutic environment which allows the innate actualization process to start up again. Many forms of humanistic therapy involve groups. This is an important distinction, for the other forms of therapy we have been considering take place on a one-to-one basis. Some humanistic therapists do hold individual sessions, but generally as a prelude to group involvement. Another distinction concerns the collective agreement of humanists that conscious feelings and attitudes are the primary sources of data—not behaviour. In this regard, humanists are similar to the cognitive theorists in emphasizing psychological processes. There is also a link to the behaviourists, in that both deplore "depth exploration." An individual's present feelings are not related to his past traumas in any direct way. There may be a common thread, but it is the present that is of primary concern to both approaches, albeit for different reasons.

The Rogerian Therapeutic Process

The well-defined procedures of psychoanalysis, behaviour modification and fixed-role therapy make for an objective discussion. However, Rogers' *client-centred therapy* has no prescribed vocabulary, nor a set of preconceived goals. Consequently, it is not easy to describe in the abstract. The technique is consistent with Rogers' view that the individual is the centre of a constantly changing body of experience, and all experience has unique meaning for each individual. No two people experience life in the same way. Communicating one's unique perception of reality provides a framework that is personally designed by the patient. Two examples are used here to illustrate the need for the establishment of parameters, not by the therapist, but by the client.

Jonathan M., a thirty-five-year-old family man slid into middle adulthood with ease. He is locked into a government job which is boring but without risk. He is anxious for a promotion, but has begun to feel that his rigid conformity to the rules is getting in his way. He talks about "everything falling apart," but is still searching for a scapegoat. He mumbles about Women's Lib giving his wife fancy ideas about a college education, and his kids no longer looking up to him with the blind respect he has grown used to. Jonathan also mentions feelings of depression hitherto unknown to him. Making money and going to football games have lost their appeal. More and more frequently he asks himself, "Where am I going?" This question is replacing the "I should . . ." behaviour which contributed to his present crisis.

Laura J., a twenty-six-year-old woman, feels she is suffering from "role strain." She has been running wildly about for the last five years balancing a demanding job, an ambitious husband, and her young child. She says the formula for happiness that she followed has been a dismal failure for her, and she blames herself for it. She feels guilty about not being home with her child. Her husband seems to be subtly sabotaging her efforts to manage all three spheres of her life. She now is seriously considering quitting her job. Her primary feeling is, "I never have time for myself."

Both of these people will be preoccupied with their focal problems in the beginning of the therapeutic process. Both will tend to feel that workable solutions are impossible. Gradually, as the therapeutic process of exploration continues, both may appear to be in worse psychological shape than when they entered therapy. There is greater depth of feeling. Sadness and happiness are felt with greater intensity, now that the barriers to free expression are loosened. This "barrier dropping," so that the tidal wave of unexpressed emotion can surface, is a necessary step in Rogerian therapy. Learning that feelings and tension don't control you but are controlled by you, is the first step in self-mastery.

Rogers and other humanists often use a group setting for therapy because freedom of expression has to be tried out in order to prove its worth. Group responses can also provide valuable insights about how an individual is perceived by others. Honesty is encouraged and fostered by all group members. Self-pity is discouraged. Insight and emotional expression receive high praise.

The successful graduate of Rogerian therapy no longer fits in with those he interacted with previously. The people he left behind (in a figurative sense) may find him "overly emotional," "impatient with trivia," "less reliable," and so forth. Most people are not prepared to accept the massive personality changes in their self-actualizing friends who have successfully negotiated Rogerian analysis. Changes of this magnitude are threatening to the non-actualizer.

The result may be a major upheaval in life-style. Jonathan, for example, may dump his stifling job for the college education he has always wanted. Living in reduced economic circumstances, however, may be unacceptable to his traditional wife. The relationship may take a serious turn. Significant personality changes do not take place in a vacuum. Similarily, Laura may terminate her career temporarily in order to have time for herself. In so doing, the new awareness and feelings about herself and others will have profound effects on her marriage and her mothering. Successful therapy means change.

Summary

The humanistic approach sees mental illness as lapsed growth. Each individual has an innate tendency to actualize. When growth is stopped, the obstacles to it must be removed, even if it means a profound alteration of the human psyche. Congruence between self and experience must be restored so that we can resume living "in the stream of life." Onerous and restrictive cultural pressures do exist, and will continue to do so. Resistance to them is essential to the development of an integrated, fully functioning self. Humanistic psychotherapy provides the milieu for getting in touch with the vital, dynamic, and emotional self that has been temporarily thwarted.

THE BIOLOGICAL APPROACH

This view is the most traditional and widely accepted approach to mental illness. Its most obvious appeal is in the concept of "illness." Illnesses are impersonal; they happen to us, but have nothing to do with us personally; they are imposed on us; we do not choose to become ill. By the same token, mental illness, like physical illness, is best treated by health-care professionals. The responsibility for cure is not in the patient's hands but the therapist's.

These connotations of mental illness stem from the view that factors under biological control are the primary determinants of such disorders. Heredity, neurophysiology and biochemistry, particularily, are singled out as explanations. On the less sophisticated level, one hears biological referents used to explain a variety of "mental" symptoms. One widely used example is, "I have bad nerves." Think about this statement for a moment. "Bad nerves" has become the cause *and* explanation for bizarre or unusual psychopathological behaviour. No personal responsibility is taken for its occurrence.

Disease—or medically oriented explanations of mental illness—is well-established. Attempts to classify the wide range of symptoms date back 150 years, culminating in an elaborate classification system which is widely used today. It is important to keep in mind that this classificatory scheme is a product of a biological or medical view of mental illness. Other approaches use the terminology to expedite understanding, but are uncomfortable with it, particularly the humanists (who deplore labelling), the behaviourists (who deny the importance of unconscious dynamics and biological factors), and the cognitive theorists (who are more active in the treatment process than in diagnosis).

The current international diagnostic system has seven major categories and numerous subcategories, including three which are used in the United States only. All of the major categories are noted below, but only a representative sample of subcategories is included. If the reader is interested in the full list of clinical categories, he should refer to the *Diagnostic and Statistical Manual*, published by the American Psychiatric Association.

List of Clinical Categories

1. Mental Retardation

Within this general category, various syndromes are specified, all relating to below-normal intellectual functioning in the areas of learning, social adjustment and maturation. The impairment may be attributed to one of several factors, such as infection, brain disease, chromosomal abnormality or environmental deprivation.

2. Organic Brain Syndromes

Within this general category, various syndromes are specifically related to brain dysfunction that is attributed to tissue or structure lesions. Some of the subcategories include senile dementia, alcoholic psychosis, and syphilis of the central nervous system. Many human attributes, such as intelligence, memory, and emotional states, are affected by these brain dysfunctions.

3. Psychoses Not Attributed to Physical Conditions

There are four subcategories within this general condition: schizophrenia, affective disorders, paranoid states and psychotic depression. These are all severely disabling disturbances, usually requiring institutionalization.

4. Neuroses

Within this major category, several distinctions are made. Among them are the syndromes labelled anxiety neurosis, conversion reaction, phobias, obsessive-compulsive reactions and neurotic depression. The principal characteristic of neurosis is conscious or unconscious anxiety, without gross distortion of reality.

5. Personality Disorders and Other Non-psychotic Mental Disorders

This collection of syndromes includes a variety of disorders which are unrelated to one another. They include personality disorders, sexual deviations, alcoholism and drug dependence. These deviations have in common conduct that is censured and punished by the controlling members of society.

6. Psychophysiological Disorders

This category includes reactions involving actual changes in the biological functioning of the body, brought about by an inability to manage personal and interpersonal relations. The subcategories are based on the organ system affected, as in cardiovascular, skin, gastrointestinal and respiratory disorders. These reactions are common, and are often misdiagnosed as physical problems, rather than psychophysiological ones.

7. Special Symptoms

This category includes diverse symptoms that are not due to organic illness. Included are head pain, speech disturbances, sleep disorders, enuresis (bed wetting) and tics.

8. Transient Situational Disturbances (Used in United States only)

This category includes adjustment reactions to various stages in the life cycle: infancy, childhood, adolescence, adult life, and late life.

9. Behaviour Disorders of Childhood and Adolescence (Used in United States only)

The various subcategories include the hyperkinetic reaction, the runaway reaction, the unsocialized aggressive reaction, and the group delinquent reaction.

10. Conditions Without Manifest Psychiatric Disorder and Non-Specific Conditions (Used in United States only)

This category involves social maladjustment (such as marital or occupational) with obvious psychiatric symptoms.

Implicit in this elaborate classificatory scheme is the premise that diagnosis of a patient's psychological system serves a purpose. While there is great debate about this premise, it is usually maintained that careful diagnostic procedures insure that correct techniques will be used to treat the patient's symptoms. The rationale for this position is that there are many similarities in patients belonging to a particular diagnostic category. Assigning a patient to a specific category has profound treatment implications. A person diagnosed as psychotically depressed is likely to receive electroconvulsive therapy (shock treatments); if he is diagnosed as a schizophrenic, powerful tranquilizing drugs will be administered. An additional function of diagnostic precision is that it enables the therapist to predict the probable outcome of the illness based on other patients' progress. This search for similarity in symptoms is in obvious opposition to the humanistic position, which stresses individual uniqueness.

The Biological Approach to Therapy

Once an extensive study has been completed, including a detailed physical examination, a psychological evaluation by means of personality tests and a personal interview, a diagnosis is made in accordance with the accepted diagnostic categories considered in the preceding section. On the basis of the diagnosis, treatment options are considered. Finally, a recommendation for a specific course of treatment is made. Collaboration of non-psychological medical personnel may be required.

The Medical Therapies

Each of the therapies we will discuss affects the physiological condition of the patient. That is, the action takes place on the biological level of functioning, which, in turn, affects the psychological level or behaviours. It is important to remember that not all abnormal behaviour has a biological basis. However, altering the biophysical condition of the patient may enable him to function normally, or at least participate in psychotherapy that would otherwise be impossible. We will consider two biophysical therapies currently in use, namely chemotherapy and electroconvulsive therapy.

Chemotherapy —Drug therapy was in limited use until 1952. At that time, two tranquilizers, resperpine and chlorpromazine, were found to produce calming effects on agitated hyperactive patients. Since that time, many new drugs have been developed for use in the treatment of mental illness. Hospital admissions have declined, and lengths of stay have been reduced.

Tranquilizers are undoubtedly the most familiar psychiatric medicine. They are used in the treatment of anxiety and hyperactivity, which occur in many syndromes. Tranquilizers tend to operate primarily on emotional and motor functions. Intellectual functioning is normally not grossly impaired. Two major drugs in the tranquilizer group will be discussed with an illustrative application for each.

Chlorpromazine and its derivatives are the most widely used drugs for schizophrenia. As we discussed in the cognitive approach, schizophrenia is identified by the presence of some or all of the following symptoms:

1. autism or a detachment from reality
2. confused and/or bizarre communication patterns
3. disturbance of affect—limited emotional responsiveness
4. delusions (false beliefs), hallucinations (perception of non-existent phenomena), and/or stuporous behaviour (psychomotor retardation)
5. distortion of perception of self and others

There are several types of schizophrenia, and transition from one form to another is quite common, at least in the early stages of the psychosis. Prior to chemotherapy the prognosis (possibility of recovery) was poor. Currently, 50 per cent of institutionalized schizophrenics will be discharged without re-admission. However, the longer the disorder has been present, the more resistant it is to treatment.

Chlorpromazine is used to reduce a schizophrenic person's activity level, to dampen his hostility and to allow him to sleep. In severe cases 50 mg. dosages are administered every thirty to sixty minutes until the person is quieted. In less severe cases, reduced doses are administered with the aim of making the patient more amenable to some form of psychotherapy. In this situation, chemotherapy is only one phase of the therapeutic process.

Another tranquilizer, a naturally occurring chemical called lithium carbonate, has been successfully used in the treatment of affective disorders—psychoses affecting the basal level of emotionality. Typically, the disorders in this category are marked by alternating periods of manic excitement and depression. However, some patients experience only repeated elation or repeated depression. Periodic recurrences are the norm. Lithium has proven to be effective in reducing the intensity of the manic phase of this psychotic disorder.

The typical symptoms of a manic individual include elation, hyperactivity, a flight of ideas, insomnia, impaired judgment, and aggressiveness. One individual, diagnosed as manic, was arrested by police for excessive speeding. He explained he was trying to get up escape velocity for Venus. Most people with affective symptoms require institutionalization, since their impaired judgment and/or deep depression presents a great risk to the patient and his family. Grandiose schemes are liable to bankrupt the family, and depressions may lead to suicide.

Lithium carbonate can produce results in seven to twenty-one days. However, its specific biochemical action is unknown. Administration of lithium requires close medical supervision and the drug may have adverse side effects. For this reason, institutionalization is the preferred alternative, since careful monitoring of the patient is possible.

At present, there are about seventy-five kinds of tranquilizers, twenty-five kinds of anti-depressants, fifty kinds of sedatives, sixty-five kinds of stimulants, fifteen kinds of anti-convulsants, and numerous hallucinogens used in the treatment of mental illness. Obviously, chemotherapy has made significant advances since 1952. Most research studies lend support to the use of drugs for psychiatric purposes. However, there exists widespread concern for the "efficacy versus toxicity" dilemma: how does a clinician balance the positive effects of drugs against possible biological complications? Further, factors that seem to effect the reaction to a chemical substance include psychosocial factors, such as the belief the patient has in the ability of a particular drug to help him, and the emotional responsiveness of the physician who administers the drug. Viewed with these considerations in mind, chemotherapy becomes a complex matter.

Electroconvulsive therapy (ECT) —The use of electricity to induce therapeutic *grand mal* convulsions in patients with depressive disorders has declined sharply with the advent of chemotherapy. However, its use is still the treatment of choice for many therapists because of its record of results. Briefly, the process involves attaching electrodes to the patient's head and administering a 70- to 130-volt current for a fraction of a second. The convulsion that follows is a severe one; rigid flexion of the body, followed by rapid jerking movements, and finally, unconsciousness. When the patient awakes he is temporarily confused, often complains of muscle pains, and has no memory of the convulsion. Normally, a patient is administered ECT three times per week for two to six weeks.

Severely depressed patients often respond to ECT. Apparently the convulsion interrupts the depressive process. One such syndrome merits our discussion: *involutional melancholia*. People diagnosed as involutional melancholics are usually in the climacteric phase of life (females—late forties, males—late fifties). They are anxious, agitated, preoccupied with dying, obsessively concerned with bodily functions, frustrated, pessimistic, irritable, unable to sleep, and depressed. Hallucinations and delusions are common. They often lose weight, become dehydrated, and convince themselves that their bodies are decaying as punishment by God for being sinful. The danger of suicide is great. Because of this risk, involutional psychotics are usually institutionalized. Customarily, ECT is administered until the depression and its accompanying symptoms have been interrupted. Euphoria and temporary amnesia are often reported by patients during the course of ECT.

Electroconvulsive therapy is used on involutional melancholics for two reasons. First, a non-threatening technique needs to be applied quickly, since physical deterioration proceeds so rapidly and suicide is a distinct possibility. Second, the personality characteristics of most involutional melancholics preclude the use of less drastic measures, such as psychotherapy. They lack insight, possess a rigid moral code, are over-conscientious, insecure, and meticulous. Their advancing age is also a significant factor, because radical personality changes are rarely desired by patients whose dreams and ambitions have been largely unfulfilled and are unlikely to be fulfilled.

Research evidence suggests that the efficacy of ECT is confined to depressed persons. Using this technique on other types of patients produces either minimal or negative results. Most patients experience memory loss after ECT treatments. It is temporary, but it can be upsetting to patients who are trying desperately to be alert to their environment. There is no pain experience during the electricity transmission, but patients often regain consciousness with headaches and generalized body pains, and a feeling of humiliation. ECT, in its attempts to restore patient functioning, often robs those very patients of their sense of dignity. Having a *grand mal* convulsion is tinged with sociocultural prejudice, and most patients are aware of the process, although they have no personal memory of their own experience.

Many other types of mental illness are treated with biophysical agents. Vitamin therapy has successfully restored some patients, enabling them to live productive and fulfilling lives. Nutritional deficiencies having behavioural correlates, such as irritability and acute sensitivity, respond well to alterations in diet. Industrial medicine is doing major research on the effects of pesticides and herbicides and other industrial hazards on the psychological stability of workers who are inadvertently exposed to these chemicals. The intimate connection between body processes and psychological functioning implies that the biological approach has a significant contribution to make in the treatment of mental illness.

Summary

The biological approach views abnormal behaviour as a disease. It relies heavily on the fields of medicine, biochemistry, and genetics. Like physical medicine, the biological or illness perspective tends to categorize symptoms for the purpose of prescribing treatment and predicting outcomes. There is the presumption that biological factors play either a determining role or a compensatory role in the acquisition of mental illnesses. This assumption of organic etiology is logically applied in the treatment process, where drugs, electroshock, and even surgery are used to modify, reduce, or enhance elements of psychological functioning.

The Five Approaches to Abnormal Behaviour

The five approaches we have explored differ in their conception of what constitute abnormal behaviour. Table 8.1 summarizes those differences. We have also seen that the initial conception of abnormal behaviour affects the categorization of such behaviour. Treatment alternatives flow logically from each of their respective theoretical positions. These five approaches—psychoanalytic, behavioural, cognitive, humanistic and biological—have made significant contributions to our understanding and will continue to do so, as will others. However, survival of any approach depends to some extent on the prevailing beliefs about human nature that both social scientists and laymen hold. These beliefs and their ramifications will be explored in Chapter 9.

Table 8.1
A Comparison of Five Approaches to Abnormal Behaviour

	Psychoanalytic	Behavioural	Cognitive	Humanistic	Biological
Basic Model	Intrapsychic conflict	Maladaptive learning	Invalidation of constructs	Incongruence between self and experience	Illness or medical
Important Concepts	Id, ego, defence, anxiety	Operant conditioning, reinforcement properties	Constructs, invalidation	Thwarted actualization needs, self-concept.	Symptoms, classification, prognosis
View of Abnormal Behaviour	Internal problem of unconscious forces seeking resolution	External problem related to personal reinforcement history	A consequence of freely determining one's own behaviour in a rigid way	Estrangement from self due to inability to withstand societal pressure	Clinical symptomatology having organic, genetic or biochemical correlates
Therapeutic Intervention	Psychoanalysis	Behaviour modification	Fixed—role therapy	Non-directive therapy	Biophysical treatment; drugs, ECT, surgery
Major Theorists	Freud	Skinner	Kelly	Rogers, Maslow	Kraepelin, and several others

Further Readings

Freud's *The Psychopathology of Everyday Life* is a wordy but valuable exposure to Freud's psychoanalytic reasoning. The emphasis is on the significance of slips of the tongue.

Nick Heather's *Radical Perspectives in Psychology* is a rare and thoughtful critique of "mainstream" psychology and psychiatry. The section on psychology and the oppressed is particularly relevant to students of abnormal and clinical psychology.

In the two volumes of his *The Psychology of Personal Constructs*, George Kelly details both his theoretical and empirical investigations from the cognitive perspective of constructive alternativism.

Abraham Maslow's *Toward a Psychology of Being* is a readable presentation of the principles of humanism. The emphasis is on the discovery of people's natural tendencies and the fulfillment that is possible (though not inevitable) once this discovery is made.

Abnormal Behaviour and Personality by Theodore and Renee Millon is encyclopedic in scope, but not in form. They present a coherent theoretical approach to the categorization of symptomatology. It is a giant leap beyond the traditional abnormal psychology text.

B. F. Skinner's *Beyond Freedom and Dignity* presents the philosophy of behaviourism. The ramifications of human engineering on a grand scale are explored.

9

A COMPARISON
OF THE APPROACHES
Judith Kelly Waalen

Editor's Preface

In earlier chapters the biological, behaviourist, humanist, cognitive and psychoanalytic approaches were examined in detail. Not only does each of these approaches focus on a different aspect of human behaviour, but each involves some very basic assumptions about important facets of human nature. By examining and comparing the different assumptions embodied in the approaches, one obtains a deeper understanding of the approaches themselves and an insight into why the approaches sometimes lead to very different analyses and conclusions about human behaviour. This is not merely an academic question. The way we mould our society through legislation and socializing practices is determined, in part, by our understanding of the determinants of human behaviour. Consider, for example, our attempts to reduce aggressive actions. The conclusions that our legislators arrive at about the best means to contain aggression are dictated by the approach they follow, and echoes of the approaches discussed in this book will often be observed in their thinking and actions.

Legislators, and the voters they represent, often are not aware of the assumptions built into their understanding of social issues, and into the psychological approaches that underlie that understanding. When you have read this chapter you will be in a position to recognize the approaches that often guide legislation, and be able to pinpoint the assumptions about human nature that are involved.

Chapter 9 first contrasts the five major approaches by considering their stances on major philosophical issues dealing with the nature of man and the factors that control his behaviour. Then two important current problems, aggressive behaviour and the acquisition of sexual identity, are examined from the five different points of view. The different insights each approach leads to, and the implications for society of leaning exclusively on one or the other approach, are made explicit.

A COMPARISON OF THE APPROACHES

What is a model? How does one develop a specific approach to understanding behaviour? How do we apply a perspective that has already been developed to ongoing social life? This chapter attempts to answer such questions by interesting the reader in the creative observation of human behaviour. We propose to do this by presenting a scheme by which alternative approaches are used to explain our actions. In doing so, we will explore the dominant viewpoints in psychology that have been presented so far: the behavioural, the cognitive, the psychoanalytic, the humanistic and the biological. Each of the models is a set of interrelated assumptions and observations about human functioning. But a model is always simpler than the phenomena it is supposed to explain. This necessary simplification has led to the development of alternative conceptions of human behaviour, sometimes opposing, sometimes complementing, sometimes supplementing each other, but never complete. Human behaviour is so complex that no one approach alone explains all of it.

As we have discussed in the earlier part of the book, we all construct maps in order to comprehend, explain, and appreciate the world. But because we do not always label our activities as mapping or modelling, we sometimes fail to realize the extent to which we are all theorists of human behaviour. The work of psychologists is not mysterious. Building maps of reality is part of human behaviour, a part of our everyday lives. Some of us are simply more disciplined at it, and, perhaps, more preoccupied with it. As we will see, all the approaches in psychology show evidence of specific assumptions about the nature of human nature. All the approaches in psychology are built on sets of assumptions. The nature of the assumptions guides research and affects theory construction.

FREEDOM vs. DETERMINISM

One of the major assumptions made about human nature involves the extent to which our behaviour is determined by factors over which we have no control. This is called the *Freedom—Determinism* assumption. In a simple sense, human beings are either free to construct their lives, or their behaviour is determined and they have no choice about the course their lives will take. Psychological approaches assume various degrees of freedom or determinism. One approach may stress determinism, but place the source of control outside of the person (environmental determinism); another approach may stress internal determinism by stressing the role of unconscious motives (biological determinism); and another may stress freedom to choose as a basic human quality. The position that a psychologist takes on this issue will profoundly affect the conception of human nature that he or she holds. The position of each psychological model on the Freedom-Determinism dimension will now be considered.

The Psychoanalytic Approach

As we have seen, Sigmund Freud viewed man's basic nature as consisting of strong inherent instincts: Eros and Thanatos. What this means is that our lives are controlled by internal, unconscious forces of which we are largely unaware. This radical departure from the earlier historical view of man as rational and controlled gradually gained acceptance. By the 1950s this conception of man as biologically determined had become respectable. Maintaining this position rules out such concepts as free will, choice, and self-determination. We may have the illusion of freedom, but, Freud insisted, we are incapable of actually "choosing" between alternative courses of action. We don't consciously generate our own behaviour. This position is labelled *Biological Determinism*.

The Behavioural Approach

In most respects, behaviourists assume that behaviour is shaped by the environment. Specifically, our behaviour is a product of prior reinforcements; we do what we have been reinforced to do. If our environmental histories and present social conditions emphasize the development of specific behaviours (competitive, loving, aggressive, sympathetic), those are the behaviours we acquire. External conditions determine our behaviour.

Many of us accept conditioning principles. This being the case, one wonders why we often control others (or are controlled by others) in an irregular, contradictory or capricious fashion. Skinner feels that we have been conditioned to believe that the concepts of freedom and dignity somehow operate outside the cause-effect principles of conditioning. We believe we are controlled and free at the same time. But we can't have it both ways, say the behaviourists. Either we assume that social forces determine behaviour, or we assume we are free agents totally in charge of our own behaviour.

Both alternatives require that we take our responsibilities seriously, but the source of control is different. Behaviourism contends that society controls the behaviour of its members, and is responsible for that behaviour. When a parent admits "My child is out of control," he is actually saying "I'm a lousy controller." When an employee says, "I wish I would be recognized as being valuable to the company," he is really saying, "My behaviour is controlled by external factors, especially positive ones." For behaviourists, human behaviour is always determined by environmental factors. Their position is an extreme one. We have no personal freedom; rather, our behaviour is determined exclusively by the agents of socialization which currently mould our environment and, ultimately, our behaviour. This position is labelled *Environmental Determinism*.

The Cognitive Approach

The emergence of the cognitive approach in psychology is relatively recent when compared to the psychoanalytic or behaviourist approaches. It is not a unified perspective, but most cognitive theorists reject both biological and environmental determinism. The principle of "silent organization" that they espouse stresses that humans have a wide range of internal cognitive constructs. This ability to organize the world enables human beings to *freely determine* their behaviour. Freedom-Determinism is not an either-or proposition for cognitive psychology. When individuals face new events, they exercise both freedom of decision and limitation of action. They select events out of the environment to respond to, and thereby exercise freedom of choice. They also interpret events around them, but those interpretations are bounded by the schemata they use. Both freedom and determinism are woven into the cloth of cognitive theory.

The Humanistic Approach

According to the humanists, no one is a pawn in life at the mercy of external forces—unless he or she chooses to be. Human beings are free to guide their destinies. This position is best articulated by Carl Rogers (1974). He has written that, in his experience with people in therapy, it is impossible to overlook the reality and significance of human choice. For all humanistic psychologists, humans struggle to grow, making difficult decisions (although not necessarily good ones) that profoundly affect their lives. The decisions that are made create the unique individuals that result. Each person is his own architect.

This commitment to freedom is one of the distinguishing features of humanism. Its opposition to the behavioural and psychoanalytic approaches is basic and obvious.

The Biological Approach

Some attention is paid to the biological limitations of the human species in the preceding four approaches. This attention, however, pales when compared to the emphasis of the biological psychologists. Their position is that genetic, biochemical and constitutional factors set the boundaries within which environmental factors operate. Choice of heredity and choice of environment are not available to any species, any group of people, or to any child. As a result, we are left to conclude that biological psychologists stress both biological determinism and environmental determinism. To them, these factors are sides of the same coin, because it is impossible to conceive of an organism without an environment; they are inextricably interwoven with each other. This approach rarely disagrees with the assumption of the behaviourist or psychoanalytic theorists, because both accept a biological basis for behaviour. Their disagreement, such as it is, revolves around the behaviourists' minimization of biological factors, as affecting human behaviour.

In summary, the positions held by the five approaches on the freedom-determinism assumption about human nature are:

1. In the psychoanalytic approach, man is depicted as biologically determined by the instinctual forces of sex and aggression.

2. In behaviourism, man is depicted as completely determined by his conditioning history.

3. In cognitive psychology, man is depicted as freely determining his own behaviour.

4. In humanistic psychology, man is depicted as fundamentally free and responsible for his behaviour.

5. In biological psychology, man is depicted as doubly determined; biologically and environmentally.

NATURE vs. NURTURE

One of the oldest and most vocal debates in psychology has raged around the Nature-Nurture controversy. Is our behaviour controlled by inherited, genetic factors (nature), or is behaviour shaped by our experiences and our environment (nurture)? There is no simple answer to the question, and many modern psychologists reject the either-or tone of the question. Both nature and nurture are given a role in shaping behaviour. The two may also interact. Through the process of evolution, the environment may modify the nature of a species; the nature of a species, in turn, may modify the environment.

The different psychological approaches do, however, tend to stress different ends of the nature-nurture dimension. The stress may have significant repercussions. For instance, if aggression is seen to be inherited, there is presumably little we can do to modify aggressive behaviour, since environmental factors are viewed as insignificant. On the other hand, if an approach stresses nurture, or the influence of the environment as a prime shaper of behaviour, then it becomes important to specify how behaviour is learned, so that behaviour may be modified.

The Psychoanalytic Approach

Freud's theorizing shows his reliance on human anatomy and physiology, and stresses the biological nature of human beings. His theory of infantile sexuality proposes a series of psychosexual stages, through which all people pass in a fixed and invariate sequence. Each stage involves a different area of the body as the source of pleasure and a different love object. These tend to be the same for all people, irrespective of different environments. Freud agrees that individuals may have different experiences as they pass through the oral, anal, phallic, latency and genital stages, and there may be different resolutions of conflicts which will result in adults with individual personalities. However, throughout his discussion the importance of the environmental factors that may bring about different outcomes is always secondary to the all-powerful, biologically based id. In the final analysis, the psychoanalytical approach takes a strong position at the nature end of the nature-nurture dimension. It is nature, not nurture, that dominates behaviour.

The Behavioural Approach

As one might suspect, behaviourists place little weight on the influence of nature in determining behaviour. Two people differ from one another because of the different environments to which they have been exposed, not because of differences they have inherited. If their environments had been interchanged at birth, their personalities ten years later would also have been interchanged. This emphasis on nurture (environmental influence) explains why Skinner has spent most of his professional life determining the effects of environmental factors. The procedures used by educators, advertisers, parents, and employers are of special interest, because these people are directly responsible for much of the behaviour that we acquire. Educators determine the content to be learned, and reward students who learn it with high grades; parents use contingent reward training on their children—positive reinforcement (love, praise, candy) is dispensed when approved behaviours appear; employers use a variety of techniques to increase productivity—bonuses, profit-sharing, and quotas. These techniques, and their effects on behaviour, are the data base of behaviourism. Their commitment to the nurture extreme of the nature-nurture dimension is total.

The Cognitive Approach

Cognitive theorists stress that behaviour is organized through the brain, and cognition is the principle by which organizing takes place. When life begins, the two elements of history from which it is drawn, the hereditary and the social, merge in the new whole and cease to exist as separable forces. In other words, heredity and environment are abstractions; the reality is the interaction of nature and nurture. Most cognitive theorists consider discussions about the ultimate or relative importance of heredity or environment to be futile. Both are simply aspects of the same phenomenon, for neither can exist without the other.

The Humanistic Approach

We might suspect that since the humanists maintain that human beings are largely free to shape themselves and determine their own destinies, the nature-nurture issue would be irrelevant. Quite the contrary. Before any self-direction can take place, each individual must discover the universal inner nature of the human species. According to Maslow, this inner nature is a biological reality, and once discovered will guide us toward healthy, fruitful, and happy development. Further, movement toward healthy development is a natural tendency in humans. If a person is provided with unconditional positive regard, he is free to experience reality without distortion and respond to life in a meaningful way. The acceptance of reality makes it likely that the person will accept himself, and therefore others, without qualifications.

To humanistic psychologists, life's master motive—the tendency to actualize—is a biological reality. This emphasizes the nature pole of the nature-nurture assumption. However, humanists also accept that we are significantly influenced by environmental variables. The statement, "If conditions are favourable, we will be able to realize our potential," is such an understatement that one often glosses over the ramifications of it. How many individuals enjoy those favourable conditions that Maslow talks about? How many persons have experienced unconditional acceptance from others? If social conditions are unfavourable and a person has been exposed to periodic unemployment, appalling educational facilities, hazardous living conditions, and conditional acceptance, his attitudes and behaviours will certainly be different from the person who has been exposed to optimum conditions. Humanists, therefore, do accept that our environment influences us. If conditions exist that are conducive to growth, humans will realize their potential. If conditions are unfavourable, they will not. A chronically hungry man will never found a brave new world.

To the humanistic psychologist, both nature and nurture play roles in determining behaviour. Nature and nurture set the boundaries, within which we are free to develop.

The Biological Approach

It should not be surprising that biological psychologists emphasize the continuing interaction between behaviour and its biological base. By looking at some of the physical characteristics man has developed, we begin to see the relationship between nature and nurture. The development of two critical behaviours—the use of tools and walking upright—separated man from his predecessors. Bipedal locomotion freed the hands for tool-making, which, in turn, put new selective pressures on the brain. Brain tissue devoted to higher mental processes increased. As a result, technology became more sophisticated and the division of labour followed as tasks became more complicated. Skull capacity increased, requiring relatively short gestation periods, so that the head of a child could pass through the birth canal. Because the infant was minimally developed at birth, a long period of nurturing was required in order to insure its survival. Specialization of sex roles began. The survival of all members of the species was aided by the evolving of the family as a social institution. As a consequence of this interaction between nature and nurture, cultures began to evolve. Medicine, agriculture, and industry have shaped new environments for us to live in. The pattern of natural selection has been modified by the creature it created.

While the interaction with society (nurture) has affected man as a species, the unique genetic potential and the experiences of his early life shape his individual qualities. Throughout the skeletal, muscular, endocrine, and nervous system of human bodies, there is incredible variation. Society's stimulation of that biological uniqueness will affect its unfolding. Thus, the biological approach emphasizes the complex interaction of nature and nurture, and the subsequent result of that interaction on the biological organism called Homo sapiens.

In summary, the positions held by the five approaches, on the nature-nurture assumption about human nature, are:

1. In the psychoanalytic approach, nature is always primary, and nurture is always secondary in the determination of human nature.
2. In the behavioural approach, the role of nurture is of paramount importance.
3. In the cognitive approach, nature and nurture are mirror images of the same process—interaction. They cannot be separated.
4. In the humanistic approach, nature and nurture are boundaries, within which human nature is free to develop.
5. In the biological approach, there is continuing interaction between behaviour (nurture) and its biological base (nature).

MOTIVATION

A third assumption which allows for meaningful comparisons between the five approaches concerns the issue of motivation. Motivation involves two aspects of behaviour: (1) why our activity takes one direction rather than another, and (2) why we are active at all. Do humans engage in activities primarily to reduce tension, as Freud would have us believe? Or is motivation directed toward growth and fulfillment, as the humanists maintain? Or are humans internally motivated at all? Diametrically opposed positions on this dimension produce different explanations of human behaviour. One cannot simultaneously hold all views.

The Psychoanalytic Approach

The psychoanalytic position is that man is motivated by unconscious forces that are rarely known to him. These unconscious forces create tensions which demand release. Once satisfaction occurs, the tension is reduced—temporarily. This view of motivation is often called a tension-reduction model. Needs arise, satisfaction is achieved, needs reduce. However, this simple equilibrium model of unhampered self-indulgence is complicated by external factors (parents, educators, employers) that oblige us to rechannel our needs into acceptable social and cultural endeavours. When this happens, defence mechanisms such as sublimation and displacement, discussed in Chapter 6, provide indirect routes for tension reduction. Whether satisfaction is

gained directly or indirectly, however, the Freudian view of motivation is basically a simple and straightforward one: internal needs
create a tension, which is reduced. Behaviour is motivated primarily
by a need to reduce tension.

The Behavioural Approach

Motivation does not have a place in Skinner's behaviourism.
However, it is worth noting why this is the case. Because of the stress
on the importance of external conditions, behaviourists believe that
statements like "It's human nature to be greedy," and, "They achieve
because they have high motivation," are simply unacceptable as
explanations of human behaviour. Statements which attribute the
causes of behaviour to internal mechanisms are considered actually to
delay the development of a scientific study of behaviour. According
to Skinner, adequate explanations of behaviour can be formed simply
by attending to the stimulus conditions surrounding the behaviour.

How does a behaviourist account for what appears to be motivated behaviour? Where does one locate the "engine" that drives
organisms towards goals? To answer these questions, one might
examine the relationship between bar-pressing behaviour and food
deprivation in laboratory animals. If an animal has been deprived of
food for several hours, it will eat more rapidly when given food—and
prefer food to water. Non-behaviourists would be likely to attribute
this behaviour to the "hunger motive." To Skinner, the term
"hunger" is simply a way of describing the relationship between
external stimuli (food) and observed responses (eating). On the
human level, Skinner maintains that it is a very good thing that the
species finds food reinforcing; humans would not have survived as a
species if they did not. In other words, "motives," "drives," and
"attitudes" are simply convenient ways to describe stimulus-
response relationships. They are not viewed as autonomous internal
mechanisms that mediate the stimulus-response connection, as the
cognitive theorists maintain.

The Cognitive Approach

Cognitive theorists (not all of whom stress motivation) reject both the
psychoanalytic and behaviourist versions of motivation. Humans are
active and struggling organisms simply because they are alive, cognitive theorists suggest. Human beings select and interpret stimuli, and
the responses that occur are responses to the selected stimuli and
their interpretations, not to the stimuli themselves. Their dynamic

model of human behaviour can be represented in the following way:

SELECTION→STIMULUS→INTERPRETATION→RESPONSE

This model starts with human activity as a given. And the human organism is involved in all stages of the sequence. This involvement on the part of the individual is the essential difference between cognitive and behaviourist approaches. Behaviourists assume an arsenal of responses within the individual; cognitive theorists do not. We play it by ear, so to speak, selecting, evaluating, and interpreting life events as they are encountered. Each individual responds to life in an unique way—depending on cognitive factors of selection and interpretation. For example, one person may choose to respond to the educational experience because it is important for his career aspirations. He interprets the experience as a useful one, and consequently finds it rewarding. Another individual may not involve himself in the educational enterprise because he perceives the experience as boring. These elements of selection and interpretation are present at birth, and direct and organize our behaviour at all times. Being alive implies motivated activity. For the cognitive approach, it is not necessary to assume a position on motivation.

The Humanistic Approach

The humanists maintain that people are naturally motivated toward growth and fulfillment, rather than being pushed or pulled by outside forces. If social conditions are favourable, this inborn drive will flourish, and foster positive development. The vital actualizing tendency is inherent, and primary in all human beings. The humanist concept of motivation emphasizes tension activation, not tension reduction. Humans do not seek equilibrium (as emphasized in the psychoanalytic approach), but fulfilling activity.

The Biological Approach

In contrast to the behavioural position, biological psychologists see each individual as unique because of the complex interplay of the physical characteristics that are received from parents, and the ways in which the environment touches his life. Environmental factors include a wide variety of influences—the physical environment in the mother's uterus before birth; the nutrition and stimulation the child receives, and the rules of the social system in which the individual lives. But without the hereditary factors contributed by way of the egg and sperm, an individual cannot even begin to develop.

From the biological point of view, human behaviour is the end result of a very large number of constitutional characteristics interacting with an infinite number of situational factors. The complexity of this view precludes any generalizations about the motivation that might be reflected by a piece of behaviour. Biologically oriented psychologists do not find the concept of motivation a particularly useful one, and make little use of it.

In summary, the positions held by the five approaches on the concept of motivation are:

1. The psychoanalytic approach maintains that man is motivated by pleasure-oriented instinctual forces which seek tension reduction.

2. The behavioural approach maintains that motivation is simply a convenient concept to describe the relationship between a stimulus and its response.

3. The cognitive approach maintains that motivation is a term synonymous with being alive.

4. The humanistic approach maintains that motivation is a positive internal force, that generates fulfilling goal-seeking behaviour.

5. The biological approach makes no generalizations about motivation, due to the complexity of the human organism.

MAN APART vs. MAN A PART

Another significant assumption made by psychologists concerns the position they take regarding the Man Apart/Man a Part polarity. Are humans a species distinctly different from all other species on this earth? Or are they an integral part of a complex physical world, sharing a rich evolutionary heritage with other species? Some psychologists see human nature as distinct (Man Apart). Others subscribe to the position that man and other species function according to the same behavioural laws (Man a Part). The five approaches we have been considering have distinct positions, although the overlap is greater on this assumption than on any of the others.

The Psychoanalytic Approach

Freud insisted that human beings obey the same laws of nature as any other species. While he did not dwell on the need for comparative psychological research between animals and humans, this position led him to conclude that all behaviour is ultimately understandable through scientific means. For all practical purposes, however, this assumption plays a minor role in the psychoanalytic approach.

The Behavioural Approach

Behaviourists agree that different kinds of animals engage in different kinds of behaviour, but it is their position that underneath the differences are a set of common laws. For example, horses can learn to jump better than people can, people can learn to talk better than dogs can, and dogs can learn to follow a scent better than humans can, but the rules by which learning takes place are the same for all. The processes of operant and classical conditioning occur in all species, humans and animals alike.

The logical extension of this is that all human behaviour may be seen as learned performances (tricks) in response to signals which are present in the environment. The complex behaviour of humans is simply a more refined version of the spectacular ballet performances of porpoises, or the complex behaviour of seeing-eye dogs. The principles for learning behaviour sequences are the same for all species. The "trainer" must have something the organism wants; the place of training must be suitable (to avoid distraction); reinforcement must be given at the proper time, and so forth. Under such conditions, behaviour can be moulded, and eventually becomes routine and predictable, regardless of the species. Evidence for this generalization across species is seen in the use of the Skinner box for training rats, giving way to teaching machines (for training children to read) and token economy systems (for training mental patients to lead productive lives).

The Cognitive Approach

Cognitive theorists see human beings as active, forever engaging in experiencing the world around them, attempting to learn, to understand, and to find meaning. In this respect, all human beings are scientists in the broad sense. This position on human behaviour separates man from other species. As a result, animal research tends to be seen as irrelevant for understanding human behaviour. The Man Apart assumption implies that human beings must be understood by studying human beings; no other species will do.

The Humanistic Approach

Humanists set man apart, as the cognitive theorists do. They assert that whereas objects and animals are bound by the principle of cause-

and-effect, humans are not. Events that happen to us as children are not the cause of our adult behaviour. In the same vein, the phrase "You made me do it" is absurd to a humanist. No adjusted person is a pawn in life, manipulated by another person to behave in a certain way. For humanists, when individuals use cause-effect statements they are attempting to transfer the burden of freedom and responsibility from themselves to others. The humanist position is that humans are different from all other species on the earth, and as a consequence we should act differently. Humanists are totally committed to the Man Apart position.

The Biological Approach

The biological approach maintains that man is an integral part of the natural world, an animal, and a product of evolutionary processes that are the same for all living things. Darwin's *The Origin of Species* paved the way for acceptance of the view that we have much in common with other animals, including an evolutionary history. Modern man, like all other life forms on earth, is the product of evolution, and a part of the animal Kingdom.

The positions held by the five approaches on the Man Apart/Man a Part dichotomous assumption about human nature are:

1. The psychoanalytic, behavioural and biological approaches see man as a part of nature, subject to the same laws as any other species.
2. The cognitive and humanistic approaches set man apart from the physical world.

CONCLUSION

Although the full implications of holding specific assumptions about human nature can hardly be grasped from the abbreviated descriptions given above, the reader can appreciate that these approaches differ from one another in a number of ways. First, they each have quite distinct orientations to the individual. For example, in humanism man is seen as free to shape his destiny, on the one hand, and in behaviourism, is a product of his conditioning history, on the other. The other three approaches are less extreme in their respective positions on this assumption, but each is different in its emphasis. Second, the impact of the environment on the individual varies from one approach to the next. In the behavioural viewpoint, it would be difficult to over-estimate the impact, whereas in the biological approach the role of environment is a modifying, and often minimal, one. Third, each approach handles the concept of motivation in quite distinct ways: the psychoanalysts see man as a tension-reducer, the cognitive theorists treat motivation holistically (as a broad goal-directed principle), and the behaviourists would like this "fiction" expunged from our vocabulary. Fourth, each approach sees man's relationship to nature in a specific way. Humanism and the cognitive approach see man as a being apart from nature, while the psychoanalytic, behavioural, and biological approaches see man as an integral part of nature, albeit for different reasons. Because of the wide range of assumptions made by each of these approaches, the reader may begin to suspect that each approach would arrive at a unique description and analysis of the same event. He would be absolutely correct in his suspicion.

TWO SOCIAL ISSUES

Our world is called a violent, sick and insane one by many contemporary writers. People argue about the causes of violence, racism, and sexual discrimination. As a student of psychology, you may wonder what psychologists have to say about these distressing and controversial matters. As you might suspect, there are differing causal explanations and differing prescriptions for change. These differences in theory and research are tied to the basic assumptions about the nature of human nature that have just been discussed. This section will consider two human social issues, destructive social aggression, and the acquisition of gender identity, from the five points of view that have been covered in this textbook.

DESTRUCTIVE SOCIAL AGGRESSION: FIVE APPROACHES

The puzzle of human violence is a complicated one. Some pieces are to be found in the home (battered spouses, abused children), in the schools (vandalism, sadistic teasing, assaults), in the business world (union busting, industrial sabotage), in our movie theatres (bloody and violent films), in our sports arenas (hockey, football), and on our streets (rapes, homicides). Aside from being momentarily appalled or excited by it, our understanding of destructive social aggression between individuals, between groups, and between nations is limited. The solutions available for the reduction or elimination of destructive behaviour are few, and the causes put forth by the various approaches are many. We will consider the respective positions of the five approaches we have been comparing. For our immediate purposes, aggression is defined as the expression of anger or hostility. More specific discussions of aggression will be included as each approach is considered.

The Psychoanalytic Approach

Given the psychoanalytic view of human nature, one might suspect (and be correct) that there is an instinct for aggression present at birth. Freud's formulation of a death instinct (Thanatos), from which aggressive impulses stem, is assigned a central role as an energy source, along with a life instinct (Eros). In general, aggressive impulses are condemned by society, and inhibitions against their expression are instituted very early in a child's life, primarily by establishing emotional family ties and by strengthening the controlling functions of the superego. When we strip away these ties, we have chaos. Peter Brook (1964), the director of the film, "Lord of the Flies," comments:

> "My experience showed me that the only falsification in Golding's fable is the length of time the descent to savagery takes. His action takes about three months. I believe that if the cork of continued adult presence were removed from the bottle, the complete catastrophe would occur within a long weekend."

In Brook's view, and Freud's as well, aggression is so vital a part of our biological inheritance that all we can hope to do is control it through the ever-continuing presence of rules and regulations that monitor behaviour, and through the skilled use of ego defence mechanisms. As we have seen in the psychoanalytic chapter, much of the work of the ego's defensive system is to protect us from acting out our aggressive impulses and desires directly. Ready-made fantasies (such as pornographic films, or violent television shows) allow people to dissipate their aggressive feelings in a substitute manner by watching rather than doing. The psychoanalytic position maintains that this viewing has cathartic effects in reducing (but not eliminating) those socially unacceptable feelings to do the same things. Some "enjoyment" is possible, but in a socially harmless way. Sometimes aggression takes covert or disguised forms: "forgetting" an important meeting with a friend or "constructively criticizing" a fellow student. Both may signal the presence of unacknowledged aggressive feelings prompted by jealousy or envy. Often individuals deny the presence of aggressive impulses by demanding law and order in society. What they are actually asking for is protection FOR others, not FROM others, although they do not realize it. What must be painfully apparent by now is that human beings, in psychoanalytic terms, are never what they appear to be. The ego's defence mechanisms protect very well—almost too well. Humans are saddled with a destiny of destruction, hostility, violence and aggression which takes many varied and misleading forms . . . and is always present. However, this basic quality of human behaviour is rarely acknowledged in its brute form—and among many, it is vigourously denied.

The Behavioural Approach

The depressing view of human aggression put forth by the psychoanalytic approach is offset by the behavioural point of view, which maintains that all behaviour is learned—including the aggressive variety. To be more specific, aside from striking out when physically attacked, aggressive behaviour in humans emerges and continues to strengthen when it is rewarded. As with other behaviours, the analysis of aggression focusses on the consequences of behaviour. If aggressive behaviour is rewarded, it becomes part of the behavioural repertoire (the behaviourists' term for "personality"). If aggressive behaviour goes unrewarded, it fails to emerge, or, if already acquired, it is extinguished over time. Research with children indicates that their assaultive actions pay off most of the time: that is, they get what they want. For the behaviourist, ideas about inner forces that promote aggressive behaviour are unnecessary. Any behaviour that is rewarded is bound to occur again.

This viewpoint suggests that effective control of aggressive behaviour requires a change in the pattern of rewards that aggression brings. However, ignoring aggressive behaviour and withholding the rewards that maintain it are only part of the answer. The person's aggressive behaviour (hitting, verbal sarcasm, teasing) may signal a lack of skills necessary to obtain attention through alternative behaviours. Once the missing skills are acquired, the attention a person seeks can be obtained by non-aggressive means. Aggression loses its functional value.

Rewarding aggressive behaviour is done in many ways in our society, say the behaviourists. For example, a father teaches his son to play punchball by punching the ball and then eliciting a similar response from his child. He praises the boy's punching behaviour. The son punches harder, and is again positively reinforced. Once the strong punching response has been established in the son, it can generalize to situations other than a punchball game. Little girls may become the "punchball" or, in adulthood, business competitors or one's spouse.

Parents are not the only teachers and reinforcers of aggressive behaviour. The values of our society are translated into television shows and films and have become the topic of a most heated debate. In one of the most influential studies of TV violence and its impact on human behaviour, the U.S. networks were given the right to veto any researcher on the project. Only two networks exercised this option. They chose to remove all the behaviourists, with the result that only those researchers whose views would endorse violence (or at least be neutral about it) carried out the research. What is interesting is that their assumptions about human nature became the basis for acceptance or rejection of the researchers. The scientists with a behaviour-ist viewpoint were excluded; the psychoanalytically biased researchers were not.

The Cognitive Approach

Both of the previous views of aggression, Freud's position that aggression is a relatively automatic response to life events, and Skin-ner's position that aggression is a product of environmental condi-tioning, are largely deterministic. Recently, however, cognitive theorists have shifted the emphasis toward the role of cognitions in behaviour. With respect to destructive social aggression, a person's interpretation of life events is important in determining whether or not aggressive behaviour occurs. In the cognitive approach, aggres-sive behaviour is more likely to occur if the action of another person is interpreted as a deliberate attempt to inflict abuse, be it physical or verbal. The interesting dilemma here is that one's individual percep-tions may be incorrect. Potentially abusive events may be experienced in different ways by different people at different times. For aggressive behaviour to result, the vital consideration is how each person inter-prets the circumstances. One person may perceive an experience as threatening, as capable of doing at least psychological violence to the self; another may experience hostility and wish to behave vindic-tively or inflict harm; another may experience anxiety because he thinks that his ability to respond to this perceived abusive act is limited.

The position, then, of the cognitive approach is that the aggres-sive response arises from learned social experiences which define the dimensions and situational constraints of the expression of aggres-sion. Individuals, whose life experiences have made them cognitively sensitive to aggression, will interpret life events as potentially abusive more frequently and more readily than will others. If people are rarely exposed to violent acts, they are less likely to interpret situa-tions as cause for aggression.

It is important to keep in mind that cognitive theorists do not stress this type of analysis of emotional behaviour. Their interest in this area is primarily in determining how people establish interper-sonal networks; how individuals maintain cognitive consistency; and how they reduce dissonance. The previous explanation of aggressive behaviour is equally applicable to other forms of emotional behaviour, and more "rational" varieties as well. This approach does not favour the mechanistic approach of Skinner, but rather maintains that it is through our cognitive constructions that we come to know the world. And we understand and experience to the extent that we re-create it by our own perspective and cognitive actions. For cognitive psychologists, knowledge is not a copy of reality.

The Humanistic Approach

Humanists are more explicit about destructive social aggression than are the cognitive theorists. Their position is that aggression is most likely to be demonstrated by persons who aren't fully functioning human beings. These would include people who have not received unconditional positive regard, or who have been the victims of discrimination, poverty, war. Since all human beings want harmonious interpersonal relations, destructive aggression occurs only when the actualizing tendency is thwarted. In other words, individuals who have not progressed up the "hierarchy of needs" ladder are the most likely to engage in aggressive acts. And, in some situations, these acts should be considered appropriate and justifiable. Maslow (1962) writes in *Toward a Psychology of Being*:

> "Clearly what will be called personality problems depends on who is doing the calling: the slave owner? the dictator? the patriarchal father? the husband who wants his wife to remain a child? It seems clear the personality problems may sometimes be loud protests against the crushing of one's psychological bones, of one's true inner nature. What is sick, then, is not to protest while this crime is being committed." (p. 7)

This idea of Maslow's is shocking to some, especially in the light of numerous skyjackings and terrorist attacks carried out to protest the crushing of psychological and physical bones. Revolutionary tactics are defined by the other approaches we have been considering as socially destructive; the fabric of the social order is being torn apart. However, these acts, when viewed from the point of view of the poor, the downtrodden, the oppressed, may be acts of self-fulfillment and liberation, and for a better world.

Theoretically, fully functioning persons are able to recognize feelings of anger and hostility, and because they do not need to deny them, they are in a position to manage these feelings in a constructive and mature way. People who are not fully functioning are defensive about their feelings of anger and hostility, and often vent these feelings in a destructive manner. The key to a humanistic world free of hate, prejudice and destruction is to enable all people to become fully functioning by providing the essential preconditions for actualization: food, shelter, love, liberty, justice and freedom. In fact, humanists tend to see some cases of extreme aggressiveness in our society as the pursuit of these essential preconditions, in order to build a non-aggressive world. This position is in direct opposition to the other approaches we are considering in this section. It offers us a socio-political justification for human aggression rarely found in psychological theories.

The Biological Approach

In this approach, the search for causes of human aggressiveness begins with our ancestry, because the emotional patterns which underlie aggression evolved thousands of years ago. Prehistoric humans were hunters. Their survival depended on developing behaviours that supported this function. Aggressive dominance has had survival value for the human species in the past, but today that very quality constitutes our greatest behavioural problem. Noted writers have pointed out that we are the most ruthless species that has ever lived on earth, that we are the only species who engages in systematic warfare and that we are the only species in which our aggression threatens our survival. "The issue, however, is not whether we are aggressive, but why." (Wiggins, *et al*, 1976)

Some biological psychologists state that there is no evidence that aggression is an instinctive force possessing internal energy and requiring periodic release, as the psychoanalysts would have us believe. Essentially, the position is that there are internal mechanisms which, when stimulated, do lead to aggressive behaviour. But the stimulation of those mechanisms is environmental and hence under social control. Other biological theorists, however, are not in agreement with this position. They tend to postulate an explanation for aggression that is similar to the psychoanalytic one.

THE IMPLICATIONS

It is now time to draw together some of the threads of this section on destructive social aggression and reiterate the positions of each approach in a few simple points. It should now be clear that these diverse opinions on the issue call for somewhat different remedies. However, it also becomes obvious that each of these approaches calls for some reasonable social control (although the extent and direction of that control is a contentious issue).

In taking the psychoanalytic position on aggression to its logical conclusion, the harnessing of instinctual energy is essential to the advancement of human civilization. That man's best is rooted in his worst (the energy of the id), implies that the primary role of society is to teach us to constructively channel that energy through the use of sublimation, and to inhibit the energy that cannot be sublimated.

It is no wonder that Freud placed so much emphasis on child-rearing practices during the first five years of life. It is also no wonder that children tend to blame parents when they transgress for, if parents had done their jobs adequately, there would be few transgressions. When we transgress (temper tantrums, fighting, sexual exploitation), it is because our "lessons" were inadequate. At the peak of Freudian influence, thousands of parents carried the burden of guilt for their children's failures. Early weaning, punitive toilet training, and faulty sex education were particularly singled out as causes. Human nature is a product of internal physical forces, but control of these forces is society's job, which may be done, partially, by providing cathartic experiences that allow us to "blow off steam." This approach suggests that the world would be a less violent place if we took the time to scream, to rage, and to engage in vicarious aggression by attending violent films and sports events. The time spent in releasing deep-seated hostility would prevent the wholesale violence prevalent today. Our repressive society, Freudians maintain, frowns on this tactic of emotional release.

For very different reasons, behaviourists advocate consistent and thoughtful social control. If we are "empty boxes" at birth, then what goes into the boxes is society's decision (initially parents, then educators, then a host of socialization agents in the larger world). With this technology of behaviour, based on behaviouristic principles, the objectives are limitless. Since destructive social aggression served no purpose in Skinner's democratic society, it would receive no reinforcement. As we know from previous discussion on learning principles, behaviours that are never reinforced cease. In a properly designed culture we would change as our lives became progressively more reinforcing. After all, as Skinner says, happiness is positive reinforcement.

The cognitive approach stresses that children imitate adult models. The major difference, however, between the cognitive and the behaviourist approach is that cognitive theorists maintain that the child is intrinsically motivated to imitate. Behaviourists never posit intrinsic motivation to do anything. For cognitive theorists, the child's need for approval from his parents and other important figures is a product of imitation, not its cause. Rewards and punishments provide important cues which enable children to cognitively assess the competance of their responses, and foster their sense of morality. Moral development is dependent on moral models. If one applies this to the learning of destructive social aggression, it is quite an indictment of the models in our present society.

Again, as in the psychoanalytic and behaviourist approaches, the onus is on the socializing agents in our society to provide challenging examples to imitate.

Society's role in the first three approaches is paramount. From what we know of the principles of humanism, we might conclude that society's influence is minimal in encouraging and maintaining destructive social aggression. Actually, this is not the case at all. If significant others in a child's life provide unconditional positive regard, the self-concept that emerges will be a product of the child's own individual development. As an adult, he will engage only in those behaviours which have positive consequences for others. On the other hand, if the building of the self is not encouraged by others, or the criteria for the design of the self are imposed by someone else, the results are disastrous. The limited and static development of the self makes for petty, closed-minded, empty and cruel individuals— an obvious distortion of innate potential. By this analysis, human beings who engage in destructive aggression are casualties in a process over which they have had little control. However, the casualties are not doomed forever by their childhood experiences, since it is possible to transcend one's limitations.

Humanists are consistent in their belief that if one is exposed to heavy pressures of conformity and adaptation, the self that emerges is exactly what others deem it should be—caricature of what might have been. These are the people who are most likely to engage in socially reprehensible acts. They have nothing to lose. To reduce destructive social aggression, then, requires changing society at its root. The status quo has got to go.

Unlike the humanists who view us as innately good, but potentially corruptible, the psychologists who propose a biological tendency to aggress have a relatively easy time explaining destructive social aggression: the trigger has been pulled, releasing the aggressive tendency. Unfortunately, biological psychologists offer no prescriptions for an ailing world. Subscribing to the principle of ethical neutrality, they simply present the results of their research. However, the public has not been content with this lack of applicability, and has sought (with the aid of such popular books as *The Naked Ape*) to make use of psychobiologists findings in most ingenious ways. One such example serves to illustrate this phenomenon. As we said earlier, Darwin's theory of evolution underlies much of the work in biological psychology. However, they are not the only group to be influenced by his work. Over one hundred years ago, a prominent view of social life emerged which is still prevalent today. This position holds that human social life operates the same way as biological/environmental evolution does. Specifically, individuals struggle to secure power, money, prestige, and status. How well these individuals succeed depends on such factors as initiative, competence and individualism. Social stratification is a measure of fitness in the social struggle; those who are fit rise to the top, those who are not move to the bottom. Everyone is free to compete with his talents against everyone else, and only the fittest survive. Economic competition serves the evolutionary process of improving society. Little did Darwin realize that his work on biological evolution would be transformed into a working model of British and North American social and economic life. The irony is that, although Darwin was very careful to support his ideas with evidence, he did not find even one single instance of intra-species aggression. The blame for this drastic view of human life does not rest with those psychologists who subscribe to a biological basis of human behaviour. Rather, this example only serves to illustrate the relationship between science and society. Given different historical conditions, one might be applying a humanistic approach to explaining the workings of our world. The psychoanalytic approach had its heyday in the early part of this century. Behaviourism gained prominence in the mid-quarter, particularily in America and the Soviet Union. None of them have been sufficiently appealing, however, to supplant this "survival of the fittest" model. As for the cognitive approach, its time has yet to come in this century.

THE DEVELOPMENT OF SEX ROLES

We are all females for the first few weeks after conception. However, shortly thereafter, sexual differentiation begins when the growth of the ovaries is either suppressed (male) or not (female). This genetic differentiation also allows for hormonal production: estrogen and testosterone are produced in differing amounts, once sexual differentiation has taken place. As the fetus develops, sexual identity becomes an integral part of the biological organism.

At birth our sexual identity is noted by all concerned and society's psychological pressures and cultural practices begin to be applied. Appropriate colours are chosen in which to clothe the child. Toys are purchased with the child's sexual identity in mind. A process of encouraging identification with the same sex parent begins. The acquisition of sex-based social skills is advocated. Males are encouraged to acquire a list of skills which includes achievement, self-reliance and competition. For females, the list is quite different. Girls are taught to develop nurturance, sentimentality and obedience. This education in sex-role identity begins early, as male children are taught to masculinize their environment and female children are encouraged to feminize theirs.

The five approaches we have been considering tackle this issue of sex-role development in quite different ways. Each will be considered in turn. No approach satisfactorily answers all questions about sex-role development, but each makes a significant contribution to our understanding of this complex and contentious issue.

The Psychoanalytic Approach

The psychoanalytic approach is the most traditional one. For Freud, the stages of phychosexual development are fundamental in the acquisition of the sexual self (be it male or female). Most important for our discussion on sex-role development is the phallic stage, and its accompanying Oedipal conflict. If you will recall (from Chapter 6), the Oedipal conflict is responsible for the identification of male children with their fathers, and female children with their mothers. The previous two psychosexual stages, the oral and the anal, occur in much the same fashion for boys and girls. However, the emergence and resolution of the Oedipal conflict differs, depending on the sex of the young child. In fact, the distinction between the sexes was noted when the name Electra conflict was substituted for the female's Oedipal conflict. Consequently, we will treat the conflicts for each sex separately. For both sexes, however, the crucial time is the phallic stage, and consequently the erotogenic zone of the body is the genital area. This is an important aspect of Freud's theory to keep in mind as we discuss his views on sex-role development.

The male child's first love is his mother. She has taken care of his needs for several years. The intense feeling he has for her manifests itself in a desire to possess her. This desire for possession is complicated by the strong sexual feelings of the phallic stage. Consequently, his desire takes on sexual overtones. His chief rival for sexual possession is, of course, his father whom he perceives as a rival for mother's affection. The father will not tolerate this rivalry and the male child perceives this. Because of the genital sensitivity in this stage of psychosexual development, the male child translates this fear of father's power as a sexual threat. The boy may fervently believe that if he does not cease this competition, his father will castrate him. An adequate resolution of this conflict occurs when the child ceases to desire sexual possession of his mother. In other words, if he concedes the battle, he wins psychological security. As these feelings pass, the psychoanalytic approach suggests the boy will transfer his strong identification with his mother to his father. This process of identification, occurring around six years of age, provides the male child with the attitudes and sex-related behaviours of his father, who presumably knows what it means to be masculine in our society. By becoming like his father, he is able to maintain his mother's interest, although on non-sexual terms. When he grows up, he tends to marry a girl just like the girl that married his father.

The female has a harder time of it than does her male counterpart. Like the boy child, the girl's first love is her mother, who nurtured her for the first three or four years of her life. However, as she moves into the phallic stage, she discovers that she and her mother are anatomically incomplete. Both lack a penis. This shocking observation causes her to reconsider her choice of love object. Devaluing her feminity, the girl turns to her father. Rivalry with her mother for his attention begins. However, since there is obviously no threat of castration that makes any biological sense, the girl is not as greatly pressured as her male counterpart to cease this strong sexual identification with her father. Usually, a re-identification with her mother is done grudgingly, if at all. To be female means to be passive, receptive, and penis-less. Retribution for her incenstuous desires is not feared as intensely as by her male counterpart, for she has already lost what he fears to lose.

The psychoanalytic approach maintains that the cornerstone of adult sexuality is laid by the time a child (regardless of sex) reaches six or seven years of age. Attitudes toward others as sexual persons are formed, conceptions of one's gender are developed, and identifications with the same sex parent (later generalized to others) are solidified. A time of consolidation and integration takes place during the latency period—a sexually quiescent time which ends abruptly at puberty. With the onset of puberty, a second sexual awakening begins. Initially, this outburst of sexuality is directed toward a member of the same sex. However, for most adolescents, this brief interlude is followed by sexual interest in members of the opposite sex, steady dating of one person, and probably marriage.

Essentially, the psychoanalytic view of sex-role development involves a delicate combination of the child's libidinal impulses and parent-child interactions. Sex roles are learned from parents during the phallic stage of psychosexual development. "Being masculine" or "being feminine" are social definitions of behaviour. The undefined sexuality of a young child is moulded in one direction or the other, depending upon his or her gender designation.

Not all attempts at resolution of the Oedipal (Electra) conflict are successful ones. Many adult males and females are fixated at the phallic stage of development for a variety of reasons. We will consider only a few of them. If, for example, a boy's father is a passive nonentity, Freud believed that there would be little reason for the boy to identify with the father. A possible consequence of this environmental circumstance is that the male child (and later, male adult) would prefer the company of women to men. Interaction with other males would be an uncomfortable experience, and thus avoided. Another phallic type may constantly have to assert his masculinity. Sexual relations with women are vigorously pursued and viewed as conquests. Often this type of male is simply identifying with his same-sex parent, who acts much the same way. However, in other cases, a domineering mother and an ineffectual father set the stage for non-resolution of the Oedipal trauma. As an adult, the male fears that women will castrate him (if only symbolically) and, consequently, develops an aversion to them on an emotional level, although usually not on a sexual level.

A female fixated at the phallic stage of development presents quite a different picture, particularly when her father treats her like a boy, expecting her to be a tough, insensitive, aggressive achiever. The turmoil when the female is growing up turns the home into an armed camp—mother against daughter, daughter against mother—both seeking attention from the father. In adulthood, the young female may end up dissociating herself from women altogether and become bitter and lonely as a result. Another casualty of the Electra trauma occurs when the mother places great emphasis on "trapping" men, and the father plays a negligible role in the daughter's upbringing. A curious blend of characteristics develops. The young woman is both flirtatious and sexually naive, desperately needing the attention of males, but unprepared for the sexual and emotional complications of such attention.

Freud was not hopeful that women or men would resolve their respective conflicts with ease. And, since the resolution is so shaky, so is our later interaction with members of the opposite sex. The psychoanalytic approach maintains that the anatomical distinction between the sexes does leave its mark on mental functioning. Failure of parents to provide the proper milieu at the proper time for their sexually energized youngsters is seen as the cause of inadequate sex-role development.

The Behavioural Approach

Behaviourists are no less emphatic in their stress on early environmental experiences. The main differences are that Skinner posits no definable stages of development, nor is there an instinctive basis for sex-role development as in the Freudian view. This implies that our attitudes toward sexuality and the development of sex roles results from our individual reinforcement histories. The dispensers of reinforcement are thus the objects of scrutiny.

Recall that Skinner maintains that operant conditioning shapes behaviour. Shaping is carried out in successive stages until the appropriate response is acquired. Initially, parents will accept partial or incomplete behaviour sequences, but gradually more is required of the child before reinforcement is dispensed. In looking at sex-role development, it is important to keep in mind that there are no innate sexual differences between males and females. Sexual differences that do emerge are the result of shaping-reinforcement practices of parents. In the behaviourist's view, because sex-typed behaviours yield differential consequences when displayed by males and by females, they rapidly become valued and practised differently by each sex. Positive reinforcement is impossible to resist. Appropriate sex-typed behaviour (as defined by our society) is learned by trial and success. When a male child is praised for a display of "masculine" behaviour, he is bound to repeat it. If he is scolded or ignored when he cries, he will learn to gain attention in other ways that yield praise. Similarly, when a female child is doted on for "playing house" she aquires house-playing behaviours rapidly. When she is punished for fighting or climbing trees, the behaviour is eventually extinguished. Gradually, visible sexual identity emerges which tends to correspond with society's definitions of appropriate masculine behaviour and appropriate feminine behaviour.

"Appropriate" sex-typed behaviour is learned by trial and success. What is rewarded by others will be repeated; what isn't, extinguishes. The learning of all forms of sexual expression, appropriate and inappropriate, occur in much the same way. For example, a child who is taught "beware of sex" may begin to associate sex with any number of events, resulting in bizarre conceptions of adult sexuality. Another example demonstrates that homosexuality may be an accidental by-product of the typical attitudes conveyed by parents toward their children. A child is punished for his sexual curiosity and play with members of the opposite sex. No mention is made that similar activities with members of the same sex are forbidden. The child learns to avoid heterosexual contacts. Comparable homosexual interests have no such prohibition attached to them. And, in another sequence of events, either by direct observation or by exposure to TV, a child comes to associate violence and brutality with sexuality. This pairing of violence and sex is very powerful, and, as an adult, he expects them to occur together in the real sexual act. These few examples could be extended ad infinitum to illustrate that the stress in the behavioural approach is on the particular events and their particular consequences that shape sex-typed and sexual behaviour. Unlike the psychoanalysts who use the concepts of castration and penis envy to "explain" the acquisition of sexual attitudes, the behaviourists prefer to treat this acquisition as a learned phenomenon without any unconscious or cognitive correlates.

The Cognitive Approach

Before concluding that sex-typing and attitudes toward sexuality are solely products of learning, we should take note of the cognitive approach to these matters. Some cognitive psychologists maintain that the most important factor in the learning process is the female's realization that she is a female, and the male's realization that he is a male. That is, children start out with a sex-typed identity, not the other way round, as the behaviourists maintain. And because of this categorization of themselves as females or males, the mother is modelled by the girl and the father by the boy.

Children identify themselves by gender, and gender categories develop between the ages of three and seven. Genital differences are noted and sexual stereotypes are formed. According to this approach, parents do play a role, but this role is one of facilitation rather than one of determinism. Gender identity is a given. Many cognitive researchers tend to de-emphasize the developmental aspects of sex-typed gender identity, and concentrate instead on the intellectual-cognitive functions of males and females. Their research endeavours have covered a broad spectrum of variables from cognitive style to verbal ability. Some of their findings follow.

The conceptualization of human sexuality researched by Masters and Johnson (1970) suggests that the primary cause of orgasmic dysfunction in females reflects women's cognitions concerning acceptable sexual feelings and practices. Masters and Johnson consider that the teachings of society often result in women adapting by inhibiting or distorting their natural sexual capacity. The role is fulfilled at the cost of natural sexual functioning. Their view maintains that sexual pleasure is to be found in the head; that is, cognitive factors play a major role in sexuality. Other types of research stress sex differences in the areas of intelligence and cognitive functions without regard for the causal factors that produced those differences in the first place. To name two differences, girls perform better than boys in verbal ability, beginning at about eleven years of age, and boys are superior in problem solving. However, within each of these areas there is variability by sex, and differences tend to be small. We are left to conclude that one's sex is only a minor factor in determining cognitive-intellectual functions. Other factors which are at least as important are sex role stereotypes, sex-role identity, child-rearing practices, and socio-cultural structure.

In sum, the cognitive approach stresses the striving for cognitive consistency as the primary determinant of sexual roles and sexual attitudes. Accordingly, once we make the cognitive self-categorization of "girl" or "boy," then the positive valuation of behaviours, attitudes, abilities and objects consistent with our gender identity follows. Further, we see evidence of dramatic differences in sex-typed behaviours after puberty, lending credence to the position that sex-based behaviour is not fixed in childhood, as Freud maintained, nor simply a product of stimulus-response connections, as the behaviourists maintain. Interaction with a variety of people, books, and films, and a person's perceptions and interpretations of those interactions develop sexual identity and attitudes toward sexuality.

The Humanistic Approach

The range of research in the cognitive approach concerning sex-role development is varied and topical. We may contrast their many areas of exploration with the singular interest of the humanists. Each individual's reality is what he or she experiences. Consequently, each and every individual is unique. The categorization of people is eschewed by the humanists, whether it be by race, creed, colour, class or sex. In fact, to attempt to coerce individuals into behaving in masculine or feminine ways is seen as an attempt to interfere in the development of the self.

As a result of their commitment to individual development, humanists say little about sex-role development per se. They simply pronounce that openness to experience is responsible for healthy sexual functioning and well-developed sexual identities. Sex roles, as we know them, should be dropped so that individuals can actualize their potential, not spend their time behaving in predetermined ways as "a girl should . . ." or "a boy should. . . ."

The now familiar theme of humanism permeates all facets of human behaviour. Sex-role development precludes, to a large extent, the development of a vital and unique self. As such, sex-casting is not seen as vital or necessary, but rather as detrimental to the actualization of one's potential. This approach is in sharp contrast to the four others we are considering in this chapter.

The Biological Approach

Our final comparison—the biological approach—is far less contentious than the humanistic point of view. Essentially, it is the familiar one of interaction. As Wiggins (1976) points out,

> "Sexual reactivity and gender identity rest on a genetic background that has an evolutionary history; but they are profoundly altered by prenatal stimuli and early social experience."*

As in the cognitive approach, the research endeavours of contemporary biological psychologists are varied. Many of their findings, as one would suspect, have biological bases to them. The result of this research is that sex differences do exist—and that is a biological fact that accepts no meaningful denial. The male is physically stronger, but less resilient than the female. The female is more nurturant, affiliative, and consistent than is her male counterpart. In addition, many sex differences are under genetic control, and not of recent origin, having both a phylogenetic and ontogenetic history. For example, certain behaviours are more adaptive than others in the reproductive roles that females and males fulfill; the infant needs a reliable and consistent nurturer during its protracted dependency. That women bear children and lactate defines the scope of the roles that have been played in order to facilitate species survival. As a result of this continuing interaction between biology and environment, male roles and female roles have biological bases to them. In other words, these roles are explained in terms of the physical bodies that each sex possesses. The relationship between biology and behaviour is assumed to be an intimate one.

The biological approach to sex-role development has the most impressive research evidence of all the approaches we are considering. Sexual identity is demonstrated by the presence (female) or absence (male) of Barr bodies and the karyotype. This genetic material sets the stage for the acquisition of behaviour most appropriate to it. The resulting sexual differences flow naturally from their biological roots.

THE IMPLICATIONS

As with the previous section on aggression, it is a useful exercise to apply these five approaches to contemporary North American life. The implications of each approach for healthy sexual functioning are

---

* Wiggins, Renner, Clore, Rose, *Principles of Personality*, © 1976, Addison-Wesley, Reading, Massachusetts, p. 273. Reprinted with permission.

sometimes complementary to others, but often openly contradictory. We will briefly look at some of the similarities and differences.

The psychoanalytic approach has received the greatest criticism in the last decade for one very simple reason. To resolve the Electra conflict, as Freud envisioned, it means that women must continue to behave as their mothers did, by becoming passive and subordinate. Many women today resist this identification process, because adopting the feminine role of a housewife (as most mothers are) is not sufficient to attract career-conscious young women. Freud would view this tactic as psychologically unhealthy—with correspondingly dire consequences. Given that many women today actively resist identification with their mothers, it is obvious that fathers have an especially important role if this resistance process is to be a successful one. Fathers who encourage their daughters to excel and to achieve, without rejecting their femininity, appear to be the greatest facilitators of healthy psychological adjustment in their daughters in this post-Victorian world. Many women, successful in academia and the world of commerce, report father-daughter relationships of this kind. In other homes, of course, fathers do not encourage their daughters to achieve simply because they are females. These men appear to be following the principles of Freud. As a consequence, their daughters dutifully and simply resolve the Electra conflict, incorporating the attitudes of femininity defined in the early twentieth century by Freud. As one can readily observe, Freud was a conservative theorist quite anxious to preserve the prevailing socio-economic division of labour prevalent in his time. Where better does it show but in the area of female psychology?

Young boys, one might assume, have a better time of it. To emulate one's father is not fraught with the same ambivalence that accompanies a young girl's journey into adulthood, simply because men have a more valued place in our society's hierarchy. However, the North American male may also be disadvantaged. He may be discouraged from developing such desirable traits as sensitivity and tenderness, on the grounds that those qualities are not masculine. After all, the model that he identifies with (usually his father) doesn't possess those qualities. His mother does. As a result, many boys leave the phallic stage of development with a bizarre conception of women—a dualistic fantasy. A woman is either a seductress (a whore) or she is like his mother (a madonna figure). Imagine the dilemma as the male matures if no reasonable resolution is made concerning this dualism. In some instances, he marries his "mother" (or a reasonable facsimile) and has numerous affairs with the other type of woman on a quite abusive basis, often resorting to rape. In other instances, he relates to women in an impersonal way (sex included) and has his most meaningful relationship with "the boys" (sex excluded).

Ironically, the challenge of the phallic stage has done more to separate the sexes than to bring them together in a meaningful way. Considering the fact that most people marry members of the opposite sex at least once, one wonders why nature has played such a dirty trick. Or is it simply one theorist's view of human sexuality that is responsible for the battle of the sexes? Given the wealth of literature and research in the last decade attacking Freudian theorists, one suspects that Freud's patriarchal ideology is responsible. In a broader context, if the double standard of morality and the organization of sex roles has maintained the reproductive family function in more or less the same form as a century ago, then Freud's theory has had far more impact than is usually assumed. That his influence is waning may also be prophetic for the future.

A less conservative approach to sex-role development is held by the behaviourists. Skinner has proposed that sex roles should be altered radically. His specific focus in *Walden II* regarding sex roles was to emancipate women from their traditional family roles, enabling them to have more dignified and respected lives. Altering the social order is no small feat. However, the principles for large-scale social engineering are no different than the principles for small-scale laboratory studies. A suitable environment is created, shaping successive approximations of non-sexist behaviour is carried out, and reinforcement is appropriately dispensed. Unfortunately, many behaviours are well-established and highly resistant to extinction. Male roles as we have defined them are far more reinforcing than female ones. In the housework arena, most women know that anyone (regardless of sex) can wash dishes, scrub floors, and make beds. There is no difference in the outcome of these tasks if men do them. However, some men may find these tasks mundane and unrewarding and resist changing the current division of labour. Behaviourists would be the first to admit that sex roles are not biologically based, but their home lives might speak louder than their academic research. Skinner further points out that the radical restructuring of role functions would be distressing to some women as well. However, once the transition is made, the transitory insecurity will extinguish.

In our present social circumstances, the inequitable portrait of male and female roles has a tremendous impact on children. In the behaviourists' view, male and female roles, when practised by the appropriate sex, receive praise and encouragement, so it is difficult to resist. The essential point here is that children learn by observing and imitating the behaviour of others. This learning is not categorized by sex, at least in the early years of learning. Sex-typing is a product of parental shaping and reinforcement, and children are quick to observe who gets the toy dishes and who gets the toy soldiers. It is as simple as that.

The cognitive explanation of sex-role learning, as we discussed earlier, goes beyond the stimulus-response explanation of the behaviourists. Each child develops rules from observations. These rules or generalizations are then applied to broad classes of behaviour (Kohlberg, 1966). As the child grows up, the rules become more accurate and sophisticated. Exceptions can be incorporated.

The formation of sexual identity rests on two interrelated elements: the exposure of a child to a variety of persons in his own category, as well as to persons in the other category, and the sex-role structure of the society of which he or she is a part. A broad exposure to a variety of persons permits the development of a broad definition of one's sex role. And the more flexible the societal definitions of femininity and masculinity, the more flexible the child's definitions will be. A rigid society does not tolerate broad sexual roles or sexual anomalies, but an open one is more likely to do so. From these social experiences, whatever their limits, a male child develops rules about the state of being male in his world. Similarly, a female child shapes her world. One runs the risk in the cognitive approach of assuming that present sex-role behaviour accounts for the next generation's conception. Consequently, sex roles and sexual identity are inflexible and culture bound. This, perhaps, represents a failure of the cognitive approach to address itself to the changing nature of sex roles. The emphasis on internal psychological development, to the exclusion of broader social changes, yields a static explanation of how individuals learn sex roles.

The humanists offer a dynamic alternative to the previous three approaches, all of which emphasize the positive and necessary role of parental forces in the emergence of a sexual identity. Humanists indict our society because of its harsh and unrelenting stress on the inhibition of openness to experience. Their liberal position maintains that openness to experience leads to healthy sexual functioning and well-developed social identities. Conversely, closed persons will have unhealthy attitudes and restrictive sexual identities. Our society's stereotypes of what is masculine and what is feminine actively discourage the development of healthy individuals. For example, to be masculine means to actively suppress sympathy, tenderness, kindness, and intuition, simply because these characteristics have been labelled as feminine. The humanists advise men to resist this cultural practice. It is only for non-actualizers.

Another oppressor of sexuality, and, consequently a block to self-actualization, is an off-shoot of "closedness": romantic love. The silly, dependent, childish girl-seductress spends all her energy trying to be attractive enough to grab a strong, virile, and independent man so that she can spend the rest of her life trying to gratify his desires. Sex becomes bait, a manipulative weapon. Such notions about romantic love make sex a marketable item. If the woman indulges too freely, the "commodity" loses its marketing value. Sexual expression becomes a contrived set of responses to special events—those which yield the greatest economic and social benefit. Romantic love stories are published daily and voraciously read by people attempting to reduce distance between those they desire and themselves, or those who have given up all hope of doing so and want to participate in these endeavours vicariously. To the humanists, this is a futile, self-defeating, oppressive manoeuver. And only the non-actualizers will fall for this oppressive illusion and be constrained by it. It is no wonder that women and men seeking to actualize their biological potential have found it necessary to decline society's help. Seeking to learn to express themselves sexually, they have found that it is neces-sary to resist the enforced conformism of our society. They pay a heavy price. In the face of such onerous sexual stereotyping, it is very difficult to become a healthy, sexually adjusted adult. Those people who do are capable of active and enjoyable sexual expression. Those who don't (and, the humanists maintain, that is most of us) are fear-ful of expressing their sexual feelings, they are defensive about their own bodies, they display false but socially acceptable attitudes and feelings about what it means to be a woman or a man, and engage in stereotypical sex-typed behaviour themselves.

The humanists place some of the blame for our sexual oppression on Freudian psychology, but most of it is reserved for the social system of which we are a part. The actualization of our biological potential cannot exist within an economic structure which rests so heavily on the traditional nuclear family, the breeding ground for sexual stagnation and sexist behaviour. Maintaining a double stan-dard in sexual matters is vitally important because the "unfaithful-ness" of a wife, for example, threatens the family structure on which our society depends. Ironically, the approach that is so fundamen-tally North American—humanism—is very critical of the social order from which it emerged. The emphasis is on resistance to cultural pressures, not acceptance of them. To be a fully functioning human being means to develop all of our potential, not just half of it. There are no Ideal Men nor Ideal Women in humanism. Sex-role dissolution, not sex-role imitation is the humanistic prescription for healthy sexual development.

Our final perspective—the biological approach—offers no prescriptions for an ailing world. The psychobiological view, as we have seen, tends to be developed inductively. This slow amassing of research information, still in its childhood, has yet to produce a broad theoretical position on sex-role development. Many treasured points of view on the evolution of humans and their subsequent division of labour now are being seriously challenged. However, we do know that women bear children and lactate. These two biological functions have defined the scope of both male and female roles. What is less clear is that, if the female role defines the scope of the male role, why do women receive fewer social rewards than men?

A further research finding suggests that sexual responsiveness is not primarily controlled by hormones. The shift from biological control to social convention has broad implications. Now that the cortex controls sexuality, instead of our sexual glands, social learning is necessary for the acquisition of human sexuality. Sex education now is as vital to human interaction as the learning of language. Our sex-role behaviour is no longer contingent upon biological cues, as it is in other species. Sexuality is one of the most distinctive characteristics of human beings. Our bodies supply the equipment; but our culture supplies the technique. The interplay of physiological factors, behavioural experiences, cognitive perceptions and psychodynamic forces all serve to mould our individual conceptions of what it means to be a female or a male in our society. The impact of social forces can never be underestimated, regardless of the approach we endorse.

SUMMARY

In this chapter the assumptions of the biological, cognitive, behavioural, psychoanalytic and humanist approaches were examined and compared. These basic assumptions are a key aspect of the schemata the adherents of the different approaches use, but the assumptions often are not stated explicitly. Often, really basic assumptions appear to be so self-evident to the proponents of a particular point of view that they are glossed over. But it is these assumptions, as we have seen, that structure one's view of reality, define what is acceptable and pertinent data, and govern the choice of key concepts.

The implications of different assumptions about human nature and human behaviour become apparent when we examine their consequences. Crucial social issues, such as destructive human aggression and the learning and development of sexual identity, are dealt with in quite different ways by psychobiologists, cognitive theorists, behaviourists, psychoanalysts and humanists. A narrow acceptance of any one particular point of view, ignoring the insights offered by other approaches, could have disastrous results for the future shape of our societies.

Further Readings

Personality: Theories, Basic Assumptions, Research and Applications by Hjelle and Ziegler is a thoughtful, coherent and sensitive treatment of prominent personality theorists. Their position is in keeping with the theme of this chapter—that all attempts to understand and codify human behaviour rest on assumptions about human nature. Their choice of examining a few theorists in depth, rather than a superficial view of many, is successful.

John Shotter's *Images of Man in Psychological Research* explores the implications for psychologists of maintaining a view of man as an object bandied about by external forces. He explores alternative frameworks in a readable and informative way.

Wiggins, Renner, Clore and Rose in *Principles of Personality* provide a broad coverage of the dominant perspectives in psychology. Highly recommended for students pursuing the field of personality psychology.

On Human Nature by Edward Wilson was published too late to be included in the biological section of this chapter. He maintains that in the matter of sex roles we have a clear example of hypertrophy—the growth of habits and customs through the interplay of genetics and culture. Young children imitated sex stereotypes. Over the centuries, cultural sanctions maintained and heightened role differences. The male-dominated society is the result. Wilson's socio-biological emphasis is gaining prominence, particularly among traditionalists.

BIBLIOGRAPHY

Allport, G. W., *Pattern and Growth in Personality*. New York: Holt, Rinehart and Winston, 1961.

American Psychiatric Association, *Diagnostic and Statistical Manual: Mental Disorders (DSM-111)*. Washington: American Psychiatric Association, 1973.

Anonymous, *Stress*. Chicago: Blue Cross Association, 1974.

Atkinson, R. C., and Shiffrin, R. M., Human memory: a proposed system and its control processes. In Spence, K. W., and Spence, J. T., (Eds.), *The Psychology of Learning and Motivation*, Vol. 2. N.Y.: Academic Press, 1968.

Bachrach, A. J., *Psychological Research: An Introduction*. New York: Random House, 1965.

Bandura, A., *Aggression: A Social Learning Analysis*, Englewood Cliffs, N.J.: Prentice-Hall, 1973.

Bannister, D., and Fransella, F., A Grid Test of Schizophrenic Thought Disorder, *British Journal of Social and Clinical Psychology*, 1966, 5, pp. 95-102.

Barchas, J. D., Berger, P. A., Ciaranello, R. D., and Elliott, G. R. (Eds.), *Psychopharmacology*. N.Y.: Oxford University Press, 1977.

Beadle, G., and Beadle, M., *The Language of Life*. N.Y.: Doubleday, 1966.

Bem, S., and Bem, D., Homogenizing the American Woman: The power of an unconscious ideology. Unpublished Manuscript, Stanford University, 1972., Jim Mischel, W., *Introduction to Personality*. New York: Holt Rinehart and Winston, 1976.

Berger, D., Wenger, M., The Ideology of Virginity, *Journal of Marriage and the Family*, Nov. 1973, pp. 666-676.

Berscheid, Ellen and Walster, Elaine, Physical Attractiveness. In Berkowitz, L. (Ed.), *Advances in Experimental Social Psychology*. Vol. 7. New York: Academic Press, 1974.

Blakemore, C., *Mechanisms of the Mind*. Cambridge, Eng.: Cambridge University Press, 1977.

Boring, E. G., *A History of Experimental Psychology*. (2nd. ed.). N.Y.: Appleton-Century-Crofts, 1950.

Brook, P., Filming a Masterpiece, *Observer Weekend Review*, July 26, 1964.

Brown, J. A. C., *Freud and the Post-Freudians*. Harmondsworth, England: Penguin, 1961.

Brown, R., Development of the first language in the human species, *American Psychologist*, 1973, 28, 97-106.

Bruner, J., Goodnow, J., and Austin G., *A Study of Thinking*. N.Y.: Wiley, 1956.

Bry, Adelaide (ed.), *Inside Psychotherapy*. New York: Basic Books, 1972.

Buckhout, Robert. Eyewitness Testimony. *Scientific American*, December, 1974.

Cline, V. B. and Richards, J. M., Accuracy in interpersonal perception—a general trait? *Journal of Abnormal and Social Psychology*, 1960, *60*, 1-7.

Cooley, Charles H., *Human Nature and the Social Order*. New York: Schocken Books, 1964.

Darwin, C., *The Origin of the Species*, (6th ed.). London: Oxford University Press, 1963.

DeBono, E., *The Mechanism of the Mind*. Harmondsworth, England: Pelican Books, 1971.

DeBono, E., *Think Tank*. Toronto, Canada: Think Tank Corp., 1973.

DeBono, E., *The Use of Lateral Thinking*. Harmondsworth, England: Pelican Books, 1971.

DeBono, E., *Practical Thinking*. Middlesex, Eng.: Penguin, 1976.

Dermer, M. and Thiel, D. L., When beauty may fail, *Journal of Personality and Social Psychology*, 1975, *31(6)*, 1168-1176.

Doob, A. N. and Gross, A. E., Status of frustrator as an inhibitor of horn-honking responses, *Journal of Social Psychology*, 1968, 76, 213-18.

Dye, T., *Power and Society; An Introduction to the Social Sciences*. Belmont, Calif: Wadsworth, 1975.

Erikson, E., *Young Man Luther*. New York: Norton, 1958.

Erikson, E., *Ghandi's Truth*. New York: Norton, 1969.

Eysenck, H. J., *Uses and Abuses of Psychology*. Harmondsworth, England: Penguin Books, 1953.

Eysenck, H., Rachman, S., *The Causes and Cures of Neurosis*. London: Routledge and Kegan Paul, 1965.

Eysenck, H. J. and Wilson, G. D., *The Experimental Study of Freudian Theories*. New York: Barnes and Noble, 1974.

Fenichel, O., *The Psychoanytic Theory of Neurosis*. New York: Norton, 1945.

Festinger, L., *A Theory of Cognitive Dissonance*. New York: Harper and Row, 1957.

Fishbach, S., The function of aggression and the regulation of aggressive drive, *Psychological Review*, 1964, *71*, 257-272.

Fisher, S., and Greenberg, R. P., *The Scientific Credibility of Freud's Theories and Therapy*. New York: Basic Books, 1977.

Freud, A., *The Ego and the Mechanisms of Defence*. New York: International Universities Press, 1946.

Freud, S., *New Introductory Lectures on Psychoanalysis*. New York: 1933.

Freud, S., *The Standard Edition of the Complete Psychological Works*. J. Strachey (Ed.). London: Hogarth Press, 1953-1974.

Freud, S., *The Origins of Psychoanalysis*. New York: Basic Books, 1954.

Freud, S., *The Psychopathology of Everyday Life*. (Standard Edition, Volume 6). London: Hogarth Press, 1960.

Fromm, E., *Psychoanalysis and Religion*. New Haven: Yale University Press, 1956.

Garcia, J., Hankins, W. G., and Rusniak, K., Behavioural regulation of the milieu interne in man and rat, *Science*, 1974, *185*, 824-831.

Gardner, A. and Gardner, B., Teaching sign language to a chimpanzee, *Science*, 1969, *165*, 664-677.

Gantt, W. H., Reflexology, schizokinesis, and autokinesis, *Conditional Reflex*, 1966, *1*, 57-68.

Glass, D. C., and Singer, J. E., *Urban Stress*. N.Y.: Academic Press, 1972.

Goble, F. G., *The Third Force*. New York: Pocket Books, 1975.

Hall, C. S., *A Primer of Freudian Psychology*. Cleveland: World Publishing Company, 1954.

Hall, C. S. and Lindzey, G., *Theories of Personality* (2nd ed.). New York: Wiley, 1970.

Hall, C. S. and Lindzey, G., *Theories of Personality* (3rd ed.). Toronto: Wiley, 1978.

Hastorf, A. H., Schneider, D. J. and Polefka, J., *Person Perception*. Reading, Mass: Addison-Wesley, 1970.

Heather, Nick, *Radical Perspectives in Psychology*. London, Methuen, 1976.

Heider, F., *The Psychology of Interpersonal Relations*. N.Y.: Wiley, 1958.

Heine, Ralph, W., *Psychotherapy*. Englewood Cliffs, N.J.: Prentice-Hall, 1971.

Hirsch, J., Behaviour genetics and individuality understood, *Science*, 1963, *142*, 1436-42.

Hjelle, L. A., and Ziegler, D. J., *Personality: Theories, Basic Assumptions, Research, and Applications*. New York: McGraw-Hill, 1976.

Holmes, T. H., and Rahe, R. H., The social readjustment rating scale, *Journal of Psychosomatic Research*, 1967, *11*, 213-18.

Holway, David N. (ed.) *The Merck Manual of Diagnosis and Therapy* (12th edition). Rathway, N.J.: Merck Sharp and Dohme Research Laboratories, 1972.

Jacklin, C. and Mischel, H., As the Twig Is Bent: Sex Role Stereotyping in Early Readers, *The School Psychology Digest*, Summer, 1973.

James, W., *The Principles of Psychology*. N.Y.: Henry Holt & Co., 1890.

Jarvik, M., The psychopharmacological revolution, *Psychology Today*, 1967, May, 51-59.

Johnston, T., *Freud and Political Thought*. New York: Citadel, 1965.

Jones, E., *The Life and Work of Sigmund Freud*. New York: Basic Books. Vol. 1, 1953; Vol. 2, 1955; Vol. 3, 1957.

Jonas, G., *Visceral Learning*. N.Y.: Viking Press. 1973.

Kaplan, A., *The Conduct of Inquiry, Methodology for Behavioural Science*. New York: Thoman Y. Crowell, 1963.

Kaplan, M. and Kloss, R., *The Unspoken Motive: A Guide to Psychoanalytic Literary Criticism*. New York: Free Press, 1973.

Karlins, M., Coffman, D. L. and Walters, G., On the fading of social stereotypes: studies in three generations of college students, *Journal of Personality and Social Psychology*, 1969, *13(1)*, 1-16.

Kelly, G., *The Psychology of Personal Constructs*, (Volumes 1, 2). W. W. Norton, 1955.

Kelly, G., Man's Construction of his alternatives. In G. Lindzey (Ed.), *Assessment of Human Motives*. New York: Holt, Rinehart and Winston, 1958.

Kimble, G., Psychology as a Science, *Scientific Monthly*, 1953, *77*, 156-160.

Kohlberg, L., Stage and Sequence: the Cognitive-Developmental Approach to Socialization. In D. A. Goslin (Ed.), *Socialization Theory and Research*. Chicago: Rand McNally, 1969.

Kohler, W., *The Mentality of Apes*. N.Y.: Harcourt, Brace, & World, 1925.

Kohler, W., *Gestalt Psychology*. N.Y.: Liveright, 1947.

Kuhn, T. S., *The Structure of Scientific Revolutions*. Chicago: University of Chicago Press, 1962.

Langer, W. C., *The Mind of Adolf Hitler: The Secret Wartime Report*. New York: Basic Books, 1972.

Levine, M., Hypothesis theory and nonlearning despite ideal S-R-reinforcement contingencies, *Psychological Review*, 1971, *78*, 130-141.

Lewis, H. R., and Papadimitriou, C. H., The efficiency of algorithms, *Scientific American*, 1978, Jan., 96-109.

Linden, E., *Apes, Men, and Language*. N.Y.: Pelican, 1976.

Lorayne, H., and Lucas, J., *The Memory Book*. N.Y.: Stein & Day, 1974.

Love, Charles A., and March, James G., *An Introduction to Models in the Social Sciences*. New York: Harper and Row, 1975.

Luchins, A. S., Mechanization in problem solving: the effect of einstellung, *Psychological Monographs*, 1942, *54*, No. 248.

Luria, A. R., *The Mind of a Mnemonist*. N.Y.: Basic Books, 1968.

Maccoby, E. and Jacklin, C., What we know and don't know about sex differences, *Psychology Today*, Dec. 1974, 109-112.

Maddi, S. R., *Personality Theories: A Comparative Analysis*. (Revised ed.). Georgetown, Ontario: Irwin-Dorsey, 1972.

Manis, M., *Cognitive Processes*. Belmont, Calif.: Brooks-Cole, 1966.

Maslow, Abraham, H., *Toward a Psychology of Being*. Princeton, N.J.: Van Nostrand, 1962.

Maslow, A., *Toward a Psychology of Being*. (2nd ed.). Toronto: Van Nostrand Reinhold, 1968.

Maslow, A., *Motivation and Personality*. (2nd ed.). New York: Harper and Row, 1970

Masters, W. and Johnson, V., *Human Sexual Inadequacy*. Boston: Little, Brown, 1970.

McGinnies, E., Emotionality and perceptual defense, *Psychological Review*, 1949, *56*, 244-251.

McGuire, W., *The Freud/Jung Letters: The Correspondence between Sigmund Freud and C. G. Jung*. Princeton: Princeton University Press, 1974.

McNeil, Elton, B., *Neuroses and Personality Disorders*. Englewood Cliffs, Prentice-Hall: 1970.

Millett, K., *Sexual Politics*. New York: Doubleday, 1970.

Millon, T. and Millon, R., *Abnormal Behaviour and Personality*. Toronto: W. B. Saunders, 1974.

Mischel, W., *Introduction to Personality*, (2nd ed.). New York: Holt, Rinehart and Winston, 1976.

Mitchell, J., *Psychoanalysis and Feminism: Freud, Reich, Laing, and Women*. New York: Pantheon, 1974.

Murray, H. A., *et al.*, *Explorations in Personality*. New York: Oxford University Press, 1938.

Norman, D., *Memory and Attention*. N.Y.: Wiley, 1969.

Nye, R. D., *Three Views of Man: Perspectives from Sigmund Freud, B. F. Skinner and Carl Rogers*. Monterey, California: Brooks/Cole, 1975.

Ornstein, R., *The Psychology of Consciousness*. N.Y.: Harcourt, Brace, Jovanovich, 1977.

Ornstein, R., The split and the whole brain, *Human Nature*, 1978, May, 76-83.

Palermo, D. S., Language acquisition. In Reese, H. W., and Lipsitt, P. P. (Eds.), *Experimental Child Psychology*. N.Y.: Academic Press, 1970.

Penfield, W., *The Mystery of the Mind*. Princeton, N. J.: Princeton Univ. Press, 1975.

Penfield, W., and Rasmussen, T., *The Cerebral Cortex of Man*. N.Y.: Macmillan, 1957.

Physician's Desk Reference, (32nd ed.). Oradell, N. J.: Medical Economics Co., 1978.

Postman, L., Bruner, J. S. and McGinnies, E., Personal values as selective factors in perception, *Journal of Abnormal and Social Psychology*, 1948, 43, 142-154.

Price, Richard, *Abnormal Behaviour, Perspectives in Conflict*. New York: Holt, Rinehart and Winston, 1972.

Roazen, P., *Freud and his Followers*. Toronto: Random House, 1975.

Rogers, C., *On Becoming a Person: A Therapist's View of Psychotherapy*. Boston: Houghton Mifflin, 1961.

Rogers, C., In retrospect: forty-six years, *American Psychologist*, 1974, 29, 115-123.

Rorschach, H., *Psychodiagnostics*. P. Lemkau and B. Kronenberg, trans. (2nd ed.). Berne: Huber, 1942.

Rosenthal, R. and Jacobson, L., *Pygmalion in the Classroom*. Toronto: Holt, Rinehart and Winston, 1968.

Sagan, C., *The Dragons of Eden*. N.Y.: Random House, 1977.

Sahaktan, W., *Systematic Social Psychology*. New York: Chandler Pub. Co., 1974.

Schachter, S., *The Psychology of Affiliation*. Stanford, Calif.: Stanford University Press, 1959.

Schachter, S., and Singer, J. E., Cognitive, social, and physiological determinants of emotional state, *Psychological Review*, 1962, 69, 379-99.

Seligman, M. E. P., On the generality of the laws of learning, *Psychological Review*, 1970, 77, 406-18.

Selye, H., *The Stress of Life*. N.Y.: McGraw-Hill, 1976.

Selye, H., They all looked sick to me, *Human Nature*, 1978, Feb., 58-63.

Sheerer, M., Problem solving, *Scientific American*, 1963, April.

Shotter, John, *Images of Man in Psychological Research*, London: Methuen, 1975.

Skinner, B. F., *Walden Two*. New York: Macmillan, 1948.

Skinner, B. F., *Beyond Freedom and Dignity*. New York: Alfred Knopf, 1971.

Southwell, E. A. and Merbaum, M., (Eds.) *Personality: Readings in Theory and Research*. Belmont, California: Brooks/Cole, 1978.

Spector, J. J., *The Aesthetics of Freud: A Study in Psychoanalysis and Art*. Toronto: McGraw-Hill, 1972.

Sperry, R., Hemispheric deconnection and unity in conscious awareness, *American Psychologist*, 1968, 23, 723-33.

Sperry, R., A modified concept of consciousness, *Psychological Review*, 1969, 76, 532-36.

Sterman, M. B., Biofeedback and epilepsy, *Human Nature*, 1978, May, 50-57.

Stone, I., *The Passions of the Mind*. New York: Signet, 1972.

Suinn, Richard, *Fundamentals of Behaviour Pathology*. Toronto: Wiley, 1970.

Tolman, E. C., *Purposive Behaviour in Animals and Men*. N.Y.: Appleton-Century-Crofts, 1932.

Tulving, E., Episodic and semantic memory. In Tulving, E. and Donaldson, W. (Eds.). *Organization of Memory*. N.Y.: Academic Press, 1972, 381-403.

Ullman, L. P., and Krasner, L., *Case Studies in Behaviour Modification*. New York: Holt, Rinehart and Winston, 1965.

Valins, S., Cognitive effects of false heart-rate feedback, *Journal of Personality and Social Psychology*, 1966, 4, 400-408.

Walster, E., and Berscheid, E., Adrenalin makes the heart grow fonder, *Psychology Today*, 1971, June.

Warr, Peter and Knapper, C., *The Perception of People and Events*. New York: John Wiley and Sons, 1968.

Warshay, L., Unpublished lecture on the Cognitive Model, Detroit: Wayne State University, Feb., 1978.

Watson, J. B., Experimental studies on the growth of emotions. In C. Murchison (Ed.), *Psychologies of 1925*. Worcester, Mass.: Clark University Press, 1926.

Webb, E. J., Campbell, D. T., Schwartz, R. D. and Sechrest, L., *Unobtrusive Measures: Nonreactive Research in the Social Sciences*. Chicago: Rand McNally, 1972.

Wenrich, W. W., *A Primer of Behaviour Modification*. Belmont, Calif.: Brooks/Cole, 1970.

White, R., *The Abnormal Personality*, (3rd ed.). New York: Ronald Press, 1964.

Wiggins, J. S. and Renner, K. E., Clore, G. L., Rose, R. J., *Principles of Personality*. Don Mills, Ontario: Addison-Wesley, 1976.

Wilson, Edward, *On Human Nature*. Cambridge: Harvard University Press, 1978.

Yates, F. A., *The Art of Memory*. Chicago: Univ. of Chicago Press, 1966.

GLOSSARY

ACTUALIZING TENDENCY   In the theory of Carl Rogers, the single motive with which we are born and which motivates us to grow and develop into mature, healthy adult human beings. p232

ANAL STAGE   The second of Freud's psychosexual stages in which the anal region is the source of sensual pleasure. p195

ANXIETY   Feelings of apprehension and dread usually accompanied by physiological symptoms, such as sweating and elevated pulse rate. p258

ATONEMENT   A Freudian defence mechanism in which a person reduces guilt arising from a previous act by performing a good or socially approved deed. p205

ATTRIBUTION THEORY   A theory describing experience in terms of the perceived causes resting either within the person (internal) or within the environment (external). p180

AUTONOMIC NERVOUS SYSTEM   That part of the nervous system serving smooth muscles, cardiac muscles, and glands. Associated with "involuntary" activity, its two parts—the sympathetic and parasympathetic—serve homeostatic and emergency responses, and vegetative functions, respectively. p84

BEHAVIOUR MODIFICATION   Behavioural therapies based on the general principles of learning, focusing on the "symptom" rather than on internal dynamics. p268

BELONGINGNESS NEED   In the theory of Abraham Maslow, the need to give and receive acceptance, trust and affection. p244

BIOFEEDBACK   Techniques used to modify physiological activity by providing a person with information about changes in the ongoing activity, usually by means of electronic equipment. p90

BIOLOGICAL DETERMINISM   The Freudian position that human beings are exclusively determined by internal forces, namely sex and aggression. p291

BRAIN   That portion of the central nervous system lying within the skull casing. p60

CASE STUDY METHOD   Relatively intense study of individual cases which attempts to reconstruct and understand the events leading up to an occurrence (such as a neurotic breakdown). p223

CENTRAL NERVOUS SYSTEM   In humans, that portion of the nervous system found within the spinal cord and brain. Composed of both efferent (sensory) and afferent (motor) pathways, it is the principal site of integration of neural activity. p60

CENSOR   An unconscious component of the ego which operates the defence mechanisms. p197

CHEMOTHERAPY   A form of biological therapy utilizing drugs to ameliorate symptoms of mental illness. p283

CHROMOSOME   A body in the nucleus of a cell which contains the complete genetic record of the individual. Its name, meaning "coloured body," comes from its tendency to appear dark stained in physiological preparations. p96

CLASSICAL EXTINCTION   The weakening of a conditioned response, as a result of the repeated presentation of the conditioned stimulus which elicits it, in the absence of the unconditioned stimulus. p119

CLIENT-CENTRED THERAPY   A therapeutic approach to psychological disturbances developed by Carl Rogers, oriented toward re-establishing congruence between the self and experience. p278

CODING   The way information is represented or stored in memory. p151

COGNITIVE DISSONANCE   The negative feelings which accompany conflicts among one's attitudes, or between one's attitudes and actions. p178

COMPENSATION   A Freudian defence mechanism in which anxiety about one area of behaviour is balanced by achievement in another. p205

COMPLEX   An unconscious set of related ideas, motives, etc., which influence behaviour. p187

CONDENSATION   A dreamwork mechanism that disguises a dream by superimposing one theme on another or by representing several ideas in a single symbol. p216

CONDITIONAL POSITIVE REGARD   In the theory of Carl Rogers, the respect or good opinion of a person which is withheld unless that person fulfills certain conditions or acts in certain acceptable ways. p230

CONDITIONED REINFORCER   Any stimulus which has reliably occurred in the presence of a primary reinforcer and which has gradually assumed its own reinforcing properties. p124

CONDITIONS OF WORTH   In the theory of Carl Rogers, requirements which one person must fulfill in order to receive the positive regard of another. p230

CONGRUENCE   In the theory of Carl Rogers, the state of being honest and open with oneself and others in a generous and considerate way. Only a fully functioning person can be truly in a state of congruence. p236

CONTEXT   The set of relationships by which information is stored in memory; hence, storage and retrieval are often said to be *context-dependent*. p153

CONTEXT-DEPENDENT   In memory, storage or retrieval which is dependent on recreating the conditions present at the time of learning. Hence, one can speak of context-dependent coding (storage) and context-dependent forgetting (failure to retrieve). p153

CORTEX   The outer layer ("bark") of the cerebral hemispheres, noted for its many folds or convolutions, and the site of such higher order functions as vision, voluntary motor control and long-term memory. p61

DEDUCTION   In a scientific investigation, the derivation of a new hypothesis or prediction from a theory. p34

DEFICIENCY MOTIVE   In the theory of Abraham Maslow, a motive which is aroused when there is something one lacks or is deficient in. The person is active only until the deficiency is corrected, after which motivation disappears. p241

DENIAL   A Freudian defence mechanism in which the person protects him or herself from painful reality by unconsciously refusing to recognize anxiety-provoking elements. p206

DEPENDENT VARIABLE   The variable in an experiment which, it is hypothesized, will change as the result of manipulations of the independent variable. p44

DEPRESSANT   Any drug whose effect is to suppress central nervous system activity (includes sedatives, anesthetics and some tranquilizers). p71

DEPRESSIVE REACTION   A neurotic disorder characterized by excessive guilt feelings, insomnia, joylessness and feelings of rejection. p261

DISCRIMINATIVE STIMULUS   Any situation or stimulus which sets the occasion for operant responding. p137

DISPLACEMENT   (A) A Freudian defence mechanism in which feelings or actions are transferred from their original target to another object that arouses less anxiety. p206 (B) A dreamwork mechanism which disguises by altering the motive, the emphasis or the target of a dream. p216

DISSOCIATIVE REACTION   A neurotic disorder in which some portion of the personality is split off from the rest (e.g., somnambulism, amnesia, multiple personality). p259

DISTRIBUTED PRACTICE   Learning in which study time is dispersed across several sessions at different times, as opposed to a single session of massed practice. p161

DRAMATIZATION   A dreamwork mechanism which disguises personal motives by expressing them in impersonal images of physical action. p216

DREAMWORK   Various unconscious defences used to disguise the meaning of a dream so that it is not emotionally threatening. p216

DRUG   Any substance which has an effect on living tissue. *Psychoactive drugs* are those which have an effect on behaviour when introduced into the physiological system. p67

EGO   In Freudian theory, the part of the personality (largely conscious) that deals with reality. p191

EGO IDEAL   The code of approved behaviours incorporated into the superego—the "ideal you." p192

ELECTRA CONFLICT   A conflict occurring during Freud's phallic stage of psychosexual development, when a girl has ambivalent feelings toward her mother and is sexually attracted to her father. p198

ELECTROCONVULSIVE THERAPY (ECT)   A form of biological therapy used primarily in the treatment of depressive reactions. p285

EMPATHIC UNDERSTANDING   In the theory of Carl Rogers, the genuine appreciation by one person of how another feels. p236

EMPIRICAL DATA   Data that is the product of direct experience or observation. p32

ENVIRONMENTAL DETERMINISM   The behavioural position that human beings are exclusively determined by forces operating outside of themselves. p292

EPILEPSY   Any of a group of disorders characterized by bursts of seizure activity within the brain. In *grand mal* epilepsy, the seizures can involve generalized convulsions and loss of consciousness. p75

EROS   In Freudian theory, a set of life-maintaining forces including the sex instinct. p189

ESTEEM NEED   In the theory of Abraham Maslow, the need to feel respected by oneself and others. p244

EVOLUTION   The process whereby a species (e.g., man) acquires the traits characteristic of its members. p59

EXTERNAL VALIDITY   The property of an experiment that permits the experimenter to generalize from a sample to a population. External validity depends on proper sampling procedures. p49

FANTASY   A Freudian defence mechanism in which an impulse is given imaginary expression. p207

FIXATION   A Freudian defence mechanism in which libido is arrested in a pregenital phase of development. p207

FIXEDNESS   An inability to depart from current, inappropriate schemata. p8

FIXED-ROLE THERAPY   A therapeutic approach to psychological disturbances developed by George Kelly, based on the premise that human beings are what they construe themselves to be. p273

FREE ASSOCIATION   A technique used by Freud to study the unconscious. By reporting whatever comes to mind, no matter how stupid, how irrelevant or how distasteful, the person eventually reveals repressed thoughts and feelings. p219, 263

FREUDIAN SLIPS   Misperceptions, memory losses, mispronunciations, slips of the pen and other apparent mistakes which are unconsciously motivated and therefore non-accidental. p215

FULLY FUNCTIONING PERSON   In the theory of Carl Rogers, a person who is developing his or her potential, living with internal harmony and in a realistic relationship with the outside world. p236

FUNCTIONALISM   An early school of psychology that concentrated on mental processes and the role they play in adaptive behaviour. p3

GENE   A chemical structure found within the chromosome which forms the basic unit of heredity. p95

GENERAL ADAPTATION SYNDROME   A pattern of stress response described by Selye as moving through three stages (alarm, resistance and exhaustion) if stress is prolonged. p84

GENETICS   The branch of biology concerned with heredity and evolution. p95

GENITAL STAGE   The fifth and last of Freud's psychosexual stages representing mature, heterosexual interests. p199

GESTALT THEORY   An approach to psychology based on the assumption that behaviour and experience can best be understood as wholes, rather than discrete parts (e.g., insight versus trial and error). p7, 145

GROWTH MOTIVE   In the theory of Abraham Maslow, a motive to grow beyond one's present condition, to develop further, even if there are presently no deficiencies. Discomfort may be accepted as part of this growth process. p242

HALO EFFECT   The tendency to infer that a person who has one positive quality will also have other positive qualities, or that a person with one known negative quality will also have other negative qualities. p20

HEREDITY   The transmission from parents to children of genetically-determined characteristics. p59

HIERARCHY OF NEEDS   In the theory of Abraham Maslow, people's needs are conceived to be in a hierarchy of importance such that a higher need will not be felt until lower ones are fulfilled. p243

HIGHER-ORDER CONDITIONING   Having a well-established conditioned stimulus function as if it were an unconditioned stimulus in bringing the conditioned response under the control of a novel and physically dissimilar stimulus. p118

HOLISTIC   In the theory of Carl Rogers, the idea that all parts of the personality interact and effect each other so that the function of one part cannot be understood by looking at it in isolation. p234

HORMONE   Any of the chemicals secreted into the bloodstream by the endocrine glands. Some, such as adrenaline and cortisone, are also manufactured for medical purposes. p65

ID   According to Freud the most primitive part of personality—the storehouse of the instincts. p190

IDEAL SELF   In the theory of Carl Rogers, an individual's concept of how he or she should be, ideally. It is acquired through life experience. p232

IDENTIFICATION   A Freudian defence mechanism in which one's ego is equated with that of an admired or feared (identification with the aggressor) model. p208

IMPLICIT PERSONALITY THEORY   A schemata reflecting the way laymen believe personalities are structured. p21

INCONGRUENCE   In the theory of Carl Rogers, an uncomfortable mental state arising from the introjection of values which contradict the organismic valuing process. p230

INDEPENDENT VARIABLE   The variable in an experiment which is manipulated by the experimenter. p44

INDUCTION   In scientific investigations, the derivation of abstract, general rules from observations. p34

INSIGHT   In problem solving, learning based upon sudden solution rather than gradual or trial-and-error performance. p145

INSTINCT   According to Freud, an instinct is "an inborn psychological representation of an inner somatic source of excitation" (i.e., an urge growing out of bodily metabolism). p187

INTELLECTUALIZATION   A Freudian defence mechanism in which anxiety-arousing feelings are masked by discussing them in a detached, intellectual manner. p208

INTERFERENCE   Competition among various items of information in memory, often regarded as a primary cause of forgetting. p155

INTERNAL VALIDITY   The ability of an experiment to demonstrate cause-effect relationships. p48

INTROJECTION   (A) A Freudian defence mechanism in which the beliefs, attitudes and/or behaviour patterns of others are adopted as one's own. p209 (B) In the theory of Carl Rogers, the acceptance of values and ideas by a person without consideration of how well they suit that person's organismic valuing process. p230

ISOLATION   A Freudian defence mechanism in which the cognitive and emotional components of an impulse are separated so that thoughts and behaviour can be viewed in a detached manner. p209

LATENCY STAGE   The fourth of Freud's psychosexual stages in which sexual impulses are repressed. p199

LATENT CONTENT   The hidden content which dreamwork prevents from becoming conscious, but which is the true meaning of a dream. p219

LATENT LEARNING   Learning which is not immediately shown in performance. Tolman argued that such learning was evidence for the existence of cognitive maps. p148

LEARNING   A change in the probability of a response as a result of practice (behavioural) and/or the acquisition of information (cognitive). p148

LIBIDO   The energy of the life instincts in Freudian theory. p189

LONG-TERM MEMORY (LTM)   The retention of information over time intervals of relatively long duration, such as hours, weeks or years; the storage system which underlies such retention. p149

LOVE NEED   In the theory of Abraham Maslow, the need to give and receive acceptance, trust and affection. p244

MANIFEST CONTENT   The content of a dream as initially experienced; the symbolic or apparent meaning, but not the true meaning. p219

MASSED PRACTICE   Learning in which study time is restricted to a single, lengthy session, as opposed to distributed practice; "cramming." p160

MEDIATORS   Events or processes within a person which come between an external stimulus and a response. Such processes must usually be inferred from behaviour, since they are not directly observable. p144

MEDICAL MODEL   The conception that mental disorders are due to physical causes and are treatable by the methods used to treat other medical disorders. p68

MEDITATION   Any of a variety of techniques that seek to achieve mental and physical relaxation, a passive, receptive awareness and harmony of mind and nature. p88

MEMORY   The retention and use of prior learning as measured by such methods as recall, recognition or relearning. p148

MENTAL AGE   The age level at which a child performs on an intelligence test. p52

MORAL ANXIETY   Fear of the conscience; guilt. p204

MORAL PRINCIPLE   The guiding principle of the superego which attempts to minimize guilt by restricting instinctual expression. p192

NEED FOR POSITIVE REGARD   In the theory of Carl Rogers, the need to have other people respect us in various ways and to look upon us as worthy beings. p229

NEGATIVE REINFORCER (Sr−)   Any stimulus event, the termination (escape from) or avoidance of which increases the probability of recurrence of an operant response. p133

NEURON   A type of cell specialized to carry information in the form of electrochemical impulses from one part of the body to another; a nerve cell, the basic unit of the nervous system. p61

NEUROSES   A group of disorders often considered to be of psychological origin, characterized by anxiety and defensive maneuvers constructed to counteract their debilitating effects. p256

NEUROTIC ANXIETY   Fear that the instincts will get out of control. p203

OBSESSIVE-COMPULSIVE REACTION   A neurotic disorder in which unwanted thoughts and desires are kept from consciousness by ritualized and repetitive acts. p260

OEDIPUS CONFLICT   A conflict occurring during Freud's phallic stage of psychosexual development when a boy has ambivalent feelings toward his father and is sexually attracted to his mother. p196

OPERANT SHAPING   The reinforcement of successive approximations of the desired behaviour. p126

OPERATIONAL DEFINITION   A definition that is worded in terms of the operations necessary to measure a concept. p36

ORAL STAGE   The first of Freud's psychosexual stages in which the mouth is the source of sensual pleasure. p194

ORGANISMIC VALUING PROCESS   In the theory of Carl Rogers, the inborn basic set of values which all people possess. p229

PENIS ENVY   According to Freud, the unconscious desire of a female to have a penis, "to be complete." p199

PERCEPTUAL-ACCENTUATION   The tendency to be more aware of those things which are relevant to our needs, motives or interests, or to perceive them as larger, more valuable and more attractive. p23

PERCEPTUAL-DEFENCE   The tendency to be less aware of those things which are not relevant to us, or to perceive them as being smaller, less valuable and less attractive. Perceptual-defence may also cause us to overlook or misperceive things which are humiliating or upsetting. p23

PHALLIC STAGE The third of Freud's psychosexual stages in which the genital region is the source of sensual pleasure. p196

PHENOMENAL FIELD In the theory of Carl Rogers, a person's unique perception of the world—that individual's total field of awareness. p230

PHOBIC REACTION A neurotic disorder in which irrational fear is kept out of awareness; the defensive strategy by which this is accomplished is displacement. p260

PHYSIOLOGICAL NEED In the theory of Abraham Maslow, a drive to maintain the body as a physical, biological entity (examples are hunger and thirst). p244

PLEASURE PRINCIPLE The guiding principle of the id which attempts to reduce tension and maximize pleasure by the immediate expression of instinctual desires. p190

PRECONSCIOUS That part of the psyche which contains material not presently in awareness but which can easily be made available or recalled at will. p193

PRIMARY PROCESS THINKING According to Freud, a primitive, unorganized form of wishful thinking whereby the id can conjure up an image of a desired object. p190

PRINCIPLE OF PARSIMONY A classical scientific dictum that says complex explanations for phenomena should not be postulated if simple ones will suffice. p5

PROACTIVE INTERFERENCE Interference based upon prior learning, making it difficult to learn or recall more recent learning. p159

PROJECTION (A) The tendency to perceive a conspicuous trait in ourselves as being possessed by other people. p23 (B) A Freudian defence mechanism in which one's own undesirable traits are attributed to other people or agencies. p209

PSYCHIC DETERMINISM The Freudian idea that mental events do not occur by chance, that thoughts and behaviour are meaningfully related to hidden unconscious processes. p215

PSYCHOANALYSIS (A) Freud's theory of personality. p185 (B) Freud's method of psychotherapy based on the recovery of repressed early childhood experiences. p221, 262

PSYCHOPHYSIOLOGICAL DISORDERS Bodily impairments (e.g., peptic ulcers, asthma) brought about by psychologically-based influences and their accompanying physiological correlates. Formerly known as psychosomatic disorders. p281

PSYCHOSEXUAL DEVELOPMENT According to Freud, sexual motivation is experienced and expressed in different ways as the individual personality matures. In each of five stages a different part of the body is sensitized and a different love object sought. p194

PUNISHMENT   Any stimulus event which immediately follows an operant response and decreases its probability of recurrence. p134

RANDOM SAMPLE   A random sample of a population is a sample drawn in such a way that every member of the population has an equal chance of being included in the sample. p39

RATIONALIZATION   A Freudian defence mechanism in which false, but apparently rational, socially desirable reasons are devised for one's behaviour. p210

REACTANCE   The tendency of people to change their behaviour when they are observed. p2

REACTION FORMATION   A Freudian defence mechanism in which unconscious motivation is disguised by behaving in the opposite manner. p213

REALITY ANXIETY   Fear of real dangers in the external world. p203

REALITY PRINCIPLE   The guiding principle of the ego which attempts to provide the personality with realistic means of achieving pleasure without punishment. p191

RECENTERING   A term employed by Gestalt psychologists to refer to abandoning an established schemata. p10

REGRESSION   A Freudian defence mechanism in which a person reverts to behaviour typical of an earlier stage of psychosexual development. p213

REINFORCER (Sr+)   Any stimulus event which follows an operant response and increases its probability of recurrence. p123

RELIABILITY   The precision of a test. p50

REPRESSION   A Freudian defence mechanism which functions either by removing conflicts from awareness (repression proper) or by preventing their entering consciousness in the first place (primal repression). p197

RESPONSE GENERALIZATION   When a conditioned stimulus elicits a response that is different from (though similar to) the original conditioned response. p115

RETROACTIVE INTERFERENCE   Interference based upon recent learning, making it difficult to recall something learned earlier. p159

SAFETY NEED   In the theory of Abraham Maslow, a need to experience safety from physical or psychological danger. p244

SCHEMATA   The guidelines which we use to select, structure and supplement incoming data to form the perceptions of which we become aware. p5

SCHIZOPHRENIA   A type of psychosis characterized by withdrawal, disturbances of thought and emotions, and occurrence of delusions and hallucinations. Several forms exist which may have different origins. p99

SECONDARY ELABORATION   A dreamwork mechanism that disguises the true meaning by making the memory of the dream more rational and coherent than it actually was. p219

SECONDARY GAIN   Positive side-effects or rewards obtained from a negative or unpleasant event. p221

SECONDARY PROCESS THINKING   According to Freud, realistic and logical trains of thought used by the ego. p193

SELF   In the theory of Carl Rogers, a person's concept of him or herself acquired through various life experiences. p232

SELF-ACTUALIZATION NEED   In the theory of Abraham Maslow, the need to grow and develop in a way that allows expression of one's natural talents, and to be in realistic contact with oneself and others. p244

SELF-FULFILLING PROPHECY   A process in which our beliefs about people shape our behaviour towards them, provoking responses that confirm our beliefs. p13

SHORT-TERM MEMORY   The retention of information over relatively brief time intervals of seconds or, at most, minutes and the storage system which underlies such retention. p149

SPONTANEOUS RECOVERY   The spontaneous re-emergence of the conditioned response after a rest interval, subsequent to its extinction and at the first presentation of the conditioned stimulus. p122

STEREOTYPE   A schemata which associates a set of personality traits with members of a group. p14

STIMULANT   Any drug whose effect on the autonomic nervous system is to produce an increase in activity (e.g., caffeine). p70

STIMULUS   Any internal or external event, situation, object or factor that is measurable and which may affect behaviour. p108

STIMULUS DISCRIMINATION   The tendency to exhibit differential conditioned responding to only those stimuli which are consistently associated with unconditioned stimuli. p116

STIMULUS GENERALIZATION   The ability of stimuli different from (though similar to) the original conditioned stimulus to elicit the same conditioned response. p114

STRESS   The non-specific response of the body to any demand made on it, often associated with the "fight or flight" reactions of the body to emergencies. p82

STRUCTURALISM   An early school of psychology that concentrated on the conscious experiences of the mind. p3

SUBLIMATION   A Freudian defence mechanism in which socially approved or useful outlets are found for instinctual impulses. p215

SUPEREGO   In Freudian theory, the last of three personality structures to develop; the part of personality concerned with morality. p192

SYMBOLIZATION   A dreamwork mechanism that disguises material in a dream so that an element in the dream represents something else in real life. p217

SYMPTOM   A frequently occurring and significant indicator of illness. p258

THANATOS   In Freudian theory, a set of instinctual forces pushing the personality toward aggression, destruction and death. p189

THEORY   A systematic and ordered set of hypotheses explaining observed phenomena. A theory may be used to generate further hypotheses by deduction. p34

TOKEN ECONOMY   A behaviour modification technique which seeks to establish functional behaviours by means of selective positive reinforcement. p268

TRANSFER   The study of the relation between prior experience and new learning, expressed in terms of positive, negative or zero transfer when prior experience aids, disrupts or has no effect on new learning, respectively. p158

TRANSFERENCE   An integral aspect of psychoanalytic therapy in which the patient unconsciously responds to the therapist as he or she would to parents. p263

UNCONDITIONAL POSITIVE REGARD   In the theory of Carl Rogers, the attitude that a person is prized and loved, no matter what that person does. p234

UNCONDITIONED STIMULUS (US)   An environmental event which precedes and reflexively triggers an unconditioned response. p109

UNCONSCIOUS   That part of the psyche which contains repressed material and other content which cannot be recalled by an act of will. p193

UNOBTRUSIVE MEASUREMENT   A form of measurement where behaviour is observed in such a way that the act of observation does not change the behaviour being observed. p41

VALIDITY   The ability of a test to measure the quantity it is supposed to be measuring. p50